THE
PIVOT

THE
PIVOT

The Future of
American Statecraft
in Asia

KURT M. CAMPBELL

TWELVE

NEW YORK BOSTON

Twelve
Hachette Book Group
1290 Avenue of the Americas
New York, NY 10104
twelvebooks.com
twitter.com/twelvebooks

First Edition: June 2016

Twelve is an imprint of Grand Central Publishing.
The Twelve name and logo are trademarks of Hachette Book Group, Inc.

The publisher is not responsible for websites (or their content) that are not owned
by the publisher.

The Hachette Speakers Bureau provides a wide range of authors for speaking
events. To find out more, go to www.hachettespeakersbureau.com or call (866)
376-6591.

Library of Congress Cataloging-in-Publication Data has been applied for.

ISBN 978-1-4555-6895-6 (hardcover), 978-1-4555-6896-3 (ebook)

Printed in the United States of America

RRD-C

10 9 8 7 6 5 4 3 2 1

To Rush Doshi, Ryan Oliver, and Nirav Patel,
three who give me confidence for the future

Contents

Acknowledgments xi

Preface: The Job Interview xv

Introduction 1

**CHAPTER ONE: The Pivot Defined: The Origins,
Successes, and Critiques of an Asian Gambit** 11

    What's in a Name? 12

    The Pivot in Action 13

    Addressing Critiques of the Pivot 17

    Conclusion 32

**CHAPTER TWO: The Stage for the Pivot: The Stakes and
Dimensions of a Rising Asia** 33

    Facts and Figures

    Population and Living Space 36

    Poverty, Health, and Education 40

    Urbanization, Sanitation, and Pollution 43

    Economy 47

    Infrastructure 52

    Energy 56

    Climate Change and Natural Disasters 59

    Sector Deep Dives

    Shipping 62

    Defense Spending 65

    Technology 69

    Film Industry 72

    The Art Market 75

CHAPTER THREE: Patterns Preceding the Pivot: Historical Themes in American Ties to Asia... **82**

The Tyranny of Distance... 84

Myth, Mockery, and Menace...................................... 87

To Sell a Million Shirts... 95

To Save a Billion Souls 102

The Costs of Conflict... 105

Secondary Theater... 116

Short-Staffed 122

Democracy Promotion... 128

Conclusion 132

CHAPTER FOUR: The Pivot's Antecedents: The Recurring Elements of American Strategy in Asia.............................**134**

The Persistent Features of Asia Strategy......................... 135

The Inconsistent Application of Asia Strategy................... 138

Revising Asia Strategy for the Future............................. 146

Conclusion 151

CHAPTER FIVE: The Pivot and the Asian Future: Guiding the Choices of a Changing Region **153**

Hegemony or Balance... 155

Twenty-First Century or Nineteenth 160

Stakeholders, Free Riders, or Spoilers........................... 163

War or Peace.. 169

Democratic Advance or Retreat................................... 188

Prosperity or Protectionism 191

Conclusion: Commitment or Retrenchment.................... 195

CHAPTER SIX: The Plan for the Pivot: Fashioning a Ten-Point American Strategy for Asia **197**

Clarifying the Pivot and Mobilizing the Public 201

Bolstering and Integrating Alliances............................. 203

Setting the Contours of China's Rise 230

Building Partnerships 251

Embracing Economic Statecraft 266

Engaging Regional Institutions 271

Diversifying Military Forces....................................... 277

Promoting Democratic Values 284

Strengthening People-to-People Ties 288

Involving European Partners 290

Conclusion 292

CHAPTER SEVEN: Risks to the Pivot's Promise: Challenges to America's Asia Strategy **294**

Fracturing Foreign Policy Consensus 295

Deadlock and Dysfunction 297

Inadequate Defense Spending 300

Retrenchment in the United States 303

Continuing Challenges in the Middle East 307

Longer-Term Planning 310

Developing Human Capital 312

Mutual Frustrations and Decoupling 314

Conclusion 316

CHAPTER EIGHT: Implementing the Pivot: The Lessons of Modern Diplomacy **318**

Twenty-first Century Diplomacy 318

The Balance of Power versus the Power of Balance 320

The Only Americans We Have 321

Working in the Garden 323

Making Maximum Efforts 324

Showing Up 326

"China Is a Big Country" 327

The Two-level Game Theory 328

Closing the Anecdote Gap 330

Strategic Dialogue 331

Thank You for Your Service 334

Conclusion 337

Notes 351

Index 385

About the Author 401

Acknowledgments

This book in many ways is the culmination of personal encounters and diplomatic experience with Asia over the course of my professional life to date and, because of that, the list of those deserving appreciation is long. Indeed, the tributaries for this manuscript are found decades back. It was while I was wearing a navy uniform during a ship visit to Yokoska outside Tokyo that my interest in Asia was initially piqued. Joe Nye, the distinguished global thinker, afforded me the first opportunity to practice diplomacy toward the region and serve under him at the Pentagon. I will always be grateful for this initial chance to sharpen my bureaucratic skills while learning about the security dimensions of policy in the region. John Hamre at CSIS supported my focus on Asia during our time working together to build the Center. Secretary Clinton took a chance on me by allowing me to serve as assistant secretary for East Asia and the Pacific during her tenure at Foggy Bottom, and I have never had a more empowering, inspirational, and engaged boss. If there is insight to be found in this book, much of it either comes from her or was gained under her watch. Jake Sullivan, the director of policy planning during my time at State, was a full partner in helping to implement the Pivot, and he is for many of us the very model of the decent and devoted public servant. My many colleagues at the State Department, too many to name each personally, served as a constant source of inspiration and motivation. Special appreciation goes to Jim Loi, Rich Verma, Bill Burns, Dave Shear, Jennifer Park Stout, Tom Nides, Derek Chollet, Dan Schwerin, Laura Rosenberger, Mark Tesone, Dan Kritenbrink, Kin Moy, Kurt Tong, Joe Donovan, Atul Keshup, Jim Zumwalt, Sung Kim, Vic Raphael, Harold Koh, Nisha Biswal, Patrick Murphy, Frankie Reed, Bill Todd, Ford Hart, Ray Burghardt, Rust Deming, John Roos, Nick Merrill, Megan Rooney, Philippe Reines, Joe Yun, Edgard Kagan, Scot Marciel, Lona Valmoro, Cheryl Mills, and Huma Abedin for their devotion to diplomatic duty. Jim Steinberg deserves his special due as one of this generation's great strategic thinkers and practitioners. Much of his unique insight and wisdom was gained and applied in Asia, and hopefully just a little of it rubbed off on me during countless hours together fly-fishing or enjoying life out west in Aspen and Sun Valley.

I'm also appreciative of interagency colleagues at the White House and Pentagon who labored with me to help animate and implement our Asia policy. Michèle Flournoy, Jeff Bader, Danny Russel, Evan Medeiros, Ben Rhodes, Chip Gregson, Admirals Gary Roughead and Pat Walsh, among others in the military, helped by putting their oars in the Asia-Pacific waters. A special thanks goes out to my intrepid partner in business and diplomacy, Nirav Patel, an enormous talent defined by loyalty and hard work.

This book owes an enormous debt to Rush Doshi, my chief research assistant, counselor, first drafter, and enthusiast for the project when my spirits dipped. You represent the best of the next generation of Asian expertise and, hopefully, government practitioners. If so, we can be confident about the future. Thank you, Rush, for your remarkable contributions to every dimension of this book. Ryan Oliver, my special assistant at the Asia Group, labored long and hard helping me with various tasks associated with this manuscript, researching, photocopying, and chasing down all my inane requests. David Collier, Ely Ratner, and Shannon Hayden each and all provided essential research and insights at various stages of this project. Mira Rapp-Hooper and Brian Andrews provided detailed comments and revision suggestions on various parts of the draft manuscript. Graham Allison and Nick Burns at Harvard provided that necessary encouragement to finish this manuscript by making me an adjunct fellow at the Belfer Center at Harvard's Kennedy School of Government. The Belfer Center has a wonderful program connecting its senior fellows with young researchers at Harvard, and I am especially grateful that they were able to introduce me to Rush Doshi and to support him in his work with me. Several Asian diplomats over the years, including Ichiro Fujisaki, Kim Beazley, Chan Heng Chee, Cui Tiankai, and Han Duck-soo provided fascinating insights into how Asia thinks and works. These pearls of wisdom are sprinkled throughout the text. I'm also thankful for the camaraderie and friendship of those on the other side of the political aisle who nevertheless have been steadfast and loyal in an increasingly bitter age. Rich Armitage is a role model for strength and fortitude, a diplomat and warrior who has left canoe-size shoe prints for those following in his wake. Mike Green was my original tutor in many aspects of Asia and represents excellence in things ranging from Asian strategy to bagpiping, having done the latter with skill and passion at my wedding. Randy Schriver and Sak Sakoda served with me back in the day and those distant bonds are still tight even to this day.

I am deeply grateful to the team at Twelve Books. My editor, Sean Desmond, sought me out very early in the process of my writing this book and recruited me to the label with patience and sincerity. Libby Burton helped with every dimension of the production of this manuscript.

My dear friends Scott Gould, James Adams, and Tom O'Gara each provided the required reassurance and motivation to get over the finish line, and all offered encouragement or distraction when my energy flagged.

A book like this is a challenging endeavor and it requires quiet time for reflection and research, not easy things to find in my house these days with three wonderful girls—Caelan, Ciara, and Coco—filling our home with laughter, music, and just plain noise. Still, they have been understanding beyond their years about my punishing travel schedule and extended periods dedicated to writing and procrastination. They shine the light on me every single day. And finally, to my wife, Lael, nothing is possible for me in this world without you by my side. Asia and above all you have been my life's two great passions, and I will never pivot away from you.

Preface: The Job Interview

In diplomacy, as in life, it is sometimes difficult to know where the story begins. For me, while I have worked on Asia for the better part of the last twenty years, the story begins with a call from Hillary Clinton's scheduler in early December 2008.

I had been spending the few weeks since the presidential election working on the Pentagon transition team, sequestered away in a windowless steel-reinforced bunker poring over documents concerning the management of the military establishment. I had served in the Pentagon a decade earlier, before 9/11, the war on terror, and the grinding military campaigns in Iraq and Afghanistan. It had been a very different place then, and the institution was only barely recognizable from the period before the attacks on the American homeland, including the Pentagon itself, on 9/11. We were now a nation that had been at war for nearly a decade, and nowhere was that reality clearer than at the Pentagon.

The hijacked airliner that smashed into the building had left a charred, burned-out section in the five-sided geometric military headquarters along the Potomac, and along certain corridors near the site of the crash, it was still possible to catch just a whiff of smoke in the hallway air. Since then the Pentagon had been rebuilt with a myriad of extra security features. The windows facing the outside civilian world on the E-ring were coated with a yellow veneer, which cast an eerie pallor on all the occupants inside. The outside world had an oddly tinted patina, like an old black-and-white movie that had been improperly colorized. Nearly every military man and woman wore one of the new digitized camouflage uniforms, and most had served numerous tours in dangerous circumstances and harm's way. Soldiers and marines bore physical scars from previous combat, and Purple Heart ribbons signifying wounds from conflict were worn with pride on uniform breastplates. In contrast, many civilian policymakers had seen little military service, which was an occasional source of tension between them and their military colleagues.

Sitting in my barren cubicle that day, I picked up the phone to hear the remarkably cheerful voice of Clinton's new personal assistant. Would I possibly have some spare time in the next day or so to meet with the secretary-elect in her transition office at the State Department? Um, yes, of course. I had to restrain myself from asking, "Is right now too soon?"

I had been an early supporter of then senator Hillary Clinton, briefing her on many occasions and raising money for her campaigns. In former defense secretary Donald Rumsfeld's terms, I was a "bitter-ender," staying with her until the very last of a disappointing fight during the Democratic primary, even when it was apparent that her once-hopeful campaign had crumbled under the weight of internal recriminations and divisiveness. Many of my fellow policy wonks had instead carefully rebranded themselves as having been on Team Obama right from the start, leaving the remaining few of us feeling vulnerable. I had watched the jubilant ascendance of President Obama and his team with a mixture of longing and anxiety, the twin sentiments of nearly all Washington players whose candidates are defeated during election season.

Still, after all the acrimony and blood feuding, the Democratic team had pulled together and prevailed in the general election, and there was now a generalized hope about what president-elect Obama would do, not only on the national scene, but on the international stage as well. Despite my excitement about the momentousness of President Obama's election, there are consequences in American politics for being on the losing side, and I had few expectations for a senior job inside the Pentagon. I spent my time during the transition interviewing unrepentant hard-liners from the Cheney-and-Rumsfeld camp in the Pentagon's policy shop who were about to lose their jobs and were deeply wary of president-elect Obama and where he might take the country.

So the call from Secretary Clinton's team was a welcome surprise, and we settled on a meeting later in the week. I was to keep the meeting confidential. President-elect Obama had asked her to be his secretary of state the week before, to the surprise of nearly everyone, especially Senator Clinton. Under enormous pressure from the president-elect, some of his senior advisors, and former president Bill Clinton, Secretary Clinton had relented and accepted the job. She and her small team were ensconced in the small transition office on the ground floor at Foggy Bottom as she studied up on briefing papers and began to assemble her team. Jim Steinberg, my good friend and the designated deputy secretary of state, called me the night before my scheduled meeting: "Be prepared for either Asia or PM [political-military affairs]— either is possible, but it's also possible that you will be watching the whole thing back at your old office at the Center for a New American Security."

It was a beautiful early-winter day in Washington with the leaves nearly off the trees as I went in the main entrance of the State Department. I walked into the vast entry foyer, the Hall of Flags, and was instantly struck by the light. The space was open and immediately appealing, like a multicultural bazaar, with diplomats from across the globe strolling the lobby waiting for their appointments with important counterparts. After the hunkered-down Pentagon, the scene represented a visible contrast between the inherent hope of diplomacy and the darker realities of ever-present war.

As I waited in the appointments line, I reflected on the journey that had brought me to this place. In many ways I had enjoyed the typical Washington policy career, serving in think tanks, in government, and as part of elite retreats like the Aspen Strategy Group. My case of Potomac Fever was fairly severe. In other ways, however, my story was a little unconventional. I'd been a professor at Harvard in the early 1990s and had studied in the former Soviet Union at a conservatory of music. I had also served as a reserve naval officer in the Office of the Chief of Naval Operations and worked on the Joint Staff in the Pentagon as a Council on Foreign Relations fellow. It was on a duty assignment for the navy that I had made my first visit to Asia. I was stationed for a short time at the naval base south of Tokyo in Yokosuka and marveled at the US and Japanese naval forces that served together, with Japanese destroyers and submarines tethered at the pier next to their sleek gray-and-black American counterparts. The mammoth cranes that loomed over the base dated back to a time when the Imperial Japanese Navy was wreaking havoc across the Pacific in the early 1940s. There were still caves in the hills around the base that had been sealed for decades, with whispered stories of lost weapons caches and skeletal remains, a legacy of Asia's darkest days.

I had been awarded a White House fellowship in the early 1990s and come to Washington at the start of the Clinton administration, working first at the Treasury and then at the White House before arriving at the

Department of Defense. I learned of the importance of the economic and commercial dimensions of our Asia policy and saw the intensity of the ongoing deliberations between Japan and the United States over how to remedy trade challenges. I also witnessed firsthand the deliberations between the White House and Congress over whether to grant China most-favored-nation trade status.

At the end of two years, as I prepared to return to teaching at Harvard, I received a call out of the blue that would change my life forever. It was from Joe Nye, the distinguished professor and international relations strategist, who was on academic leave and serving as the assistant secretary for international security affairs at the Pentagon. He asked me if I would be interested in coming over to head up his Asia shop there and to assist on what came to be called the "Nye Initiative," an effort to revitalize the critical security partnership and alliance between the United States and Japan. This was a relationship that was ripe for revival after the end of the Cold War, when both Washington and Tokyo were searching for a larger sense of defining strategic purpose. I said yes and thus started a journey that charted my career course for Asia.

It was during these five years that I developed a strong passion for the region, its diverse people, and its often opaque politics and diplomacy. I had a terrific team, most of whom have remained lifelong friends, and a big old office along the B corridor of the Pentagon where I could sometimes glimpse a hint of the sky through the lone window, barely six inches wide, near the corner of the ceiling. On my first day, a construction worker on a ladder affixed a bar across the tiny opening. I told him I thought it unlikely that anyone would be trying to crawl in to steal secrets. Without missing a beat, he responded, "It's not to keep intruders out, it's for keeping you in." Still, I found the work rewarding and consequential. I labored with others to develop military ties with China, design a strategy to respond to the Taiwan Strait Crisis, deal with the challenge of military basing in Okinawa after the tragedy of the 1995 rape, hold the first-ever trilateral military talks between the United States, Japan, and South Korea, quietly develop contingency planning among allies for possible instability in North Korea, and make the first defense contacts with Vietnam since the end of the Vietnam War.

Joe Nye and then secretary of defense Bill Perry instilled a tremendous spirit of camaraderie in the office of the secretary of defense during those days, and we prioritized steps to reaffirm the historic centrality of our alliances and our forward presence. It was during this period that I first met the first lady, Hillary Rodham Clinton, and I briefed her before her historic visit to China in advance of the Global Women's Summit. I would never have imagined then that I would be one day walking into her office—as I was now—to talk about her upcoming tenure as secretary of state.

I was quietly escorted into the drab corner offices of the transition space on the ground floor of the State Department. There in a small cluster of offices many of the vanquished members of the former Clinton campaign were huddled together. It was as if they had lost the larger battle for the country but had secured a small foothold of territory in a nearby Washington office building. It felt a little like one of those last guerrilla strongholds at the end of a bloody civil war. I sat down and gathered my thoughts. I had a clear preference to serve in the Bureau of East Asian and Pacific Affairs. In many respects it was my dream job, but I'd never thought I would have the chance to serve in such a capacity. The entryway to the Bureau of East Asian and Pacific Affairs on the sixth floor of the State Department was lined on each side with black-and-white photos of the esteemed diplomats who had served as assistant secretary in the bureau during the previous century. It was a veritable who's who of twentieth-century diplomatic distinction, with statesmen such as Dean Rusk, William Bundy, Averell Harriman, and Philip Habib smiling down from their framed places in history. I had pretty serious doubts about whether I belonged in such distinguished company. Still, I tried to keep them to myself.

President Obama's chief Asia strategist from the campaign, and my close friend, the former diplomat Jeff Bader, was just about to be appointed as the senior director at the National Security Council (NSC), and there was no clear front-runner for assistant secretary for East Asian and Pacific Affairs at State. I had formerly been identified as a defense guy with no experience at the State Department and so was thought of as an unlikely candidate for the job. Nevertheless, I reviewed my talking points about how it was time to start to reposition American power and prestige toward the rising East after a period of deep and often unbalanced focus on the dark contours of conflict in the Middle East. The United States would also need to implement a more comprehensive region-wide effort to secure America's position in the region into the twenty-first century.

Just as I was rehearsing the lines in my head, an assistant came out and ushered me into the corner office where Hillary Clinton sat. I am not sure that there has ever been a more unlikely secretary of state, certainly not since President Lincoln appointed his own political rival William Seward to the job in 1861. The room Clinton was working in had been hurriedly prepared and seemed somehow lacking in the basic accouterments of prestige, with drawn blinds to hide both the cracking plaster around the windows and the internal deliberations from passersby at street level. There was an industrial-style executive desk stacked with papers and transition binders, and an aged leather couch surrounded by uncomfortable chairs. At the center of the room was a rug featuring the diplomatic seal of the United States, its eagle with the twin offerings of arrows and olive branches fraying underfoot. The office had a temporary feel and the somewhat shabby surroundings seemed an unlikely place to find secretary-designate Hillary Clinton.

Nevertheless, there she was, buoyantly welcoming me in, showing me to the seat next to the couch and looking none the worse for wear after a brutally punishing two years of nearly nonstop campaigning. Her presence made the dreary room seem regal and welcoming. She plopped down on the couch and put her legs up on an end table. She wore her familiar dark pantsuit and was surrounded on all sides by thick binders and briefing books. With a deep laugh, she exclaimed, "I never thought you and I would find ourselves in this place, but here we are." She then recounted how President Obama had asked her to serve as secretary of state. She had been resting at home in Chappaqua, New York, after the disappointing election, licking her wounds and reflecting on what had gone wrong, and the call had come as something of a surprise. Close aides to the president had warned her that such a call would be coming, but she really did not believe it until she heard Obama's distinctive voice on the other end of the line, extending a very different kind of olive branch and an offer. At first, she explained, she was too tired and angry to even consider such an offer, but over the course of several days, her husband and others wore down her opposition and beat back her concerns. Finally, she explained, a close friend had given her this advice: imagine the tables were turned and it was you reaching out to Obama—how would you feel if he said no to you? That did the trick. It really is the call to service that stirs her.

And so here she was sitting in this out-of-the-way transition office, assembling a team for her next stint on the very high wire of public service.

I had told myself that no matter what, even if an offer came, I would wait, consider it carefully over the course of several days, and consult with my wife and family before responding. In short, I would not lean in but would hold back and dutifully reflect.

After a few minutes of conversation, she homed right in on Asia and put forward a nuanced perspective that demonstrated she had thought about the challenges ahead. As she was speaking, I noticed that across from me on the table in front of her were a number of my recent articles, precisely highlighted with a yellow marker and with neatly scribbled comments in the margins. I can read upside-down writing, a skill perfected in junior high school, but instead tried to focus on her words. It was clear she had prepared for the meeting in a way that I hadn't.

"My biggest concern, Kurt, is that we are overinvested in the wars and machinations of the Middle East," Clinton explained. "We are consequentially engaged there and our role is both required and essential, but we've got to find our bearings and reorient more toward the future. Asia is the future and our diplomacy must reflect this in a much more fundamental way." She went on to describe the region's wondrous innovations, its rising middle classes, its growing purchasing power, and how these powerful trends connected with American jobs and exports. She spoke extensively and knowledgeably about her philosophy for effective engagement in the diverse region. "China is the big story, no doubt. But for us to be successful, we're going to have to work with others more effectively. We've got to embed our China policy in a larger Asia strategy." She spoke of trying to encourage a new leadership in Japan to arrest its national torpor, spoke about a greater focus on Southeast Asia, and opined on the need to more effectively integrate trade and commercial advocacy into a larger framework. This was music to my ears and deeply reassuring. Implementing a region-wide, all-in strategy would be essential to underscoring a narrative of renewed, decisive American diplomacy toward the region.

Then she homed in for the kill.

"Kurt, I've talked to Jim Steinberg about this, and we want you on the team. Richard Danzig indicates that you might be going to the Pentagon but I want you with me here at the State Department. I want people who I respect and who I can trust, and it wasn't lost on me that you stayed on the campaign to the end. That's the kind of resolve and dedication we're going to need in the years ahead. So join me and my team. Let's support President Obama. Come be my assistant secretary of state for East Asian and Pacific affairs."

Without any hesitation or further reflection, I exclaimed, "I'm in! I accept! I'll sign up right now!" So much for careful, judicious reflection. Clinton seemed happy, but I could sense her mind was already shifting to the next challenge, that of building a strong team for the long hours and many challenges just ahead. I was on board and there would be time soon enough for me to get to work. We shook hands and she carefully guided me to the door. "Tell them no at the Pentagon, and start thinking about our game plan for Asia. I want to hit the ground running," Clinton said as I made my way out. She then deftly pivoted and welcomed the next group, a stern-faced crew of intelligence analysts who had been patiently waiting to brief her. She seemed equally pleased to see them, but I was confident that her enthusiasm for me was somehow more sincere and superior. Such is the Hillary Clinton personal touch in close quarters in action.

That meeting set me on a path toward senate confirmation and nearly four years of service as the chief American diplomat for Asia. I would go on to make seventy-nine trips in that capacity, to every country in the region and to many other countries around the globe that were developing their own approaches to the Asian Century. I would travel with Secretary Clinton on nearly twenty occasions. I could not know then, as I walked out of State with a sense of exuberance, about the challenges that would lie ahead. Dealing with the biggest nuclear crises ever to hit Asia, after the earthquake and tsunami in Japan. Developing a comprehensive and sustained strategy for dealing with China's phenomenal and increasingly complex rise to global power. Staring down a dangerous leadership in North Korea bent on provocation. Developing a strategy for dealing with territorial encroachments across the South China Sea. Finding a way for the United States to join the nascent multilateral institutions of Asia. Articulating a public vision for the American Pivot to Asia. Leading the opening of a long-cloistered Burma that was venturing tentatively onto the international stage. Reengaging New Zealand as a friend and security partner after decades of strategic neglect. Revitalizing unofficial political and security relations with Taiwan while seeking to sustain peace and stability across the Taiwan Strait. And trying to find sanctuary for an unpredictable and volatile blind Chinese dissident at a time of high politics between the US and Chinese governments.

This book is informed by my whirlwind, jet-lagged diplomatic adventure at the State Department, a four-year effort to implement a multidimensional strategy toward Asia in the face of Middle East headwinds and domestic constraints. It is partly a story of diplomacy in a time of war. As the assistant secretary of state for East Asia and Pacific affairs in Foggy Bottom, the senior-most government official with daily responsibility for the vast Asia-Pacific region, I was a participant in every major encounter during this entire dynamic period. More important, however, this is a book about the future. It uses the past as prologue to argue for a much more engaged approach for the United States in Asia going forward. It also describes clearly and without ambiguity what the United States needs to do to sustain the Asian gambit in the complex period on the horizon. Part historic account, part travelogue, in parts both intense and humorous, with some elements of backward reflection but more focus on forward-looking analysis, this book is intended to explain the strategic steps and hidden moves behind a remarkable American gambit on the international stage: the Pivot to Asia.

THE
PIVOT

Introduction

There is a quiet drama playing out in American foreign policy, far from the dark contours of upheaval in the Middle East and South Asia and the hovering drone attacks of the war on terror. The United States is in the midst of a substantial and long-term national project, which is proceeding in fits and starts, to reorient its foreign policy to a rising Asia even in the midst of punishing and inescapable challenges in the Middle East. The central tenet of this bold policy shift is that the United States will need to do more with and in the Asia-Pacific to spur domestic revival and renovation as well as to keep the peace in the world's most dynamic region. If the larger Middle East can be described as the "arc of instability," then the region stretching from Japan through China and Southeast Asia to India can be seen as representing an "arc of ascendance," Asia's march on the future. American policy must heed this unrelenting feature of the future: that the lion's share of the history of the twenty-first century will be written in the Asia-Pacific region.

While the Asian Century detoured to the Middle East in the years following the September 11 attacks, this is now beginning to change as the United States devotes greater attention and resources to this dynamic region. With sensibilities deeply informed by twenty-first-century strategic realities, the United States has led a "Pivot" (or "rebalancing," as many prefer) of American diplomacy toward the nuanced yet demanding tasks of engaging a rising Asia. The Pivot is premised on the idea that the Asia-Pacific region not only increasingly defines global power and commerce, but also welcomes US leadership and rewards US engagement with positive returns on political, economic, and military investments. Former Australian ambassador to the United States Kim Beazley may have put it best: "Asia is the sunny uplands for America, and no region appreciates you more." The Pivot employs multiple instruments of statecraft, and although the visibility and tangibility of its military component has led the hard power investments to receive outsize attention, the initiative has been equally defined by diplomatic intensification and economic engagement that is long overdue, considerable, and ultimately consequential.

This book is about a necessary course correction for American diplomacy, commercial engagement, and military innovation during a time of unrelenting and largely unrewarding conflict. While the United States has intensified its focus on the Asia-Pacific under President Obama relative to previous administrations, much more remains to be done. In the Obama administration's second term, the intense demands of Iranian diplomacy, the unfolding Syrian tragedy, and ongoing operations in Afghanistan continue to consume the scarcest of all government resources—top-level time and attention. Debates and discussions over Middle East policy are important and necessary, but their shrillness and sheer volume often drown out reasoned arguments for a more balanced understanding of America's national interests, one not fully consumed with unwinnable wars and ungrateful partners but motivated by the promise of harnessing the dynamism of the world's most vibrant region to the benefit of every American. While the United States is a global power with responsibilities across the planet, its efforts in the Asia-Pacific have often failed to measure up to the region's importance and demand a greater share of the proverbial pie of US strategy and engagement abroad.

That the future of the United States will be intertwined with Asia's may seem unremarkable or even obvious given the portentous rise of the region's great powers, the stunning emergence of its economies, and the worrisome escalation of its nationalist conflicts; but the reality of the opportunities and challenges that await in Asia have yet to be felt—truly acknowledged and felt—in the White House Situation Room, along the State Department's corridors, inside the Pentagon's windowless planning cells, within American boardrooms, and in most of the country's classrooms and lecture halls. Rarely has a great power taken such a remarkable detour away from so vibrant a region, and one with such great consequences for its future.

This book is mostly about that future. It discusses how the United States should construct a strategy that will position it to ride and maneuver upon the Asian surf break now rising on the near horizon. It is sprinkled with personal experience and anecdotes from nearly twenty-five years of military, diplomatic, academic, and think tank experience, but these reflections are meant to inform the path ahead rather than gild the recent record of diplomacy. The overarching intention of this book is to provide a clarion call for cunning and dexterity and ingenuity in the period ahead for American statecraft in the Asia-Pacific region.

Since the end of the Cold War, both Democratic and Republican administrations have undertaken important efforts to update our strategy and footprint in the Asia-Pacific. These efforts have often been motivated by the inescapable fact that the twenty-first century will have an increasing Asian focus. During the Clinton administration, Joe Nye undertook a badly needed effort to revitalize the US-Japan relationship. During the Bush administration, Ambassador Bob Blackwill in New Delhi helped set the foundation for a deeper and more consequential relationship between the United States and India. Richard Armitage helped deepen and intensify each American allied relationship across Asia and modernized interagency contingency planning. Gary Roughead anticipated the coming challenges of maritime presence and patrol in Asia through programmatic innovations as chief of naval operations. Robert Zoellick at the State Department articulated the case for how China should participate more constructively in the international community with his "responsible stakeholder" framework. Mike Green at the National Security Council sought to implement a twin engagement strategy toward Japan and China. After 9/11 the entire US foreign policy apparatus commenced a multi-administration effort to engage Asian states on questions of terrorism and instability in the Middle East and South Asia. Steve Hadley and Condoleezza Rice at the National Security Council made this Asian "out of area" support for military campaigns and civil society building in those regions a priority. Still, these efforts have not, either together or alone, commanded the attention, imagination, or resources required in the most important corridors of power in Washington.

The Pivot is intended to build upon preceding policy innovations in an evolutionary way, but fundamentally represents a marked elevation of Asia's place in US foreign policy. After coming to office, President Barack Obama determined that the United States should play a more central role in the Asian Century. "Our desire to pivot," he stated, "was a response to a decade in which we understandably, as a country, had been focused on issues of terrorism, the situation in Iraq and Afghanistan. And as a consequence, I think we had not had the same kind of presence in a region that is growing faster, developing faster than any place else in the world."[1] This was a vision essentially shared by Hillary Clinton, a onetime political adversary subsequently chosen to become the sixty-seventh secretary of state. Secretary Clinton took it largely upon herself to develop the strategy for revamping American power and prestige in the most dynamic region on the planet. To undertake such an effort required building a team inside government to design and implement a substantial policy shift. To assist in this challenging endeavor, a handful of trusted confidantes and like-minded officials were recruited to the task, including me; Jeff Bader, the Yoda-like fount of Asia wisdom at the White House; Jake Sullivan, the policy wunderkind of the State Department's policy planning shop; Jim Steinberg, one of this generation's finest strategic thinkers; Evan Medeiros, the respected China specialist from the Rand Corporation; and Danny Russel, the cunning career diplomat. Nirav Patel, Jim Loi, and many other loyal diplomats in the East Asian Bureau helped staff the entire endeavor. This policy shift had interagency supporters as well, including the able Pentagon policy chief Michèle Flournoy and the president's own messaging guru Ben Rhodes, as well as Mark Lippert, who would serve with distinction at the White House, Department of Defense, and as American ambassador to the Republic of South Korea. Several senior military officers supported the cause, including the chief of naval operations Gary Roughead, Admirals Harry Harris and Pat Walsh, and my old friend Marine General Chip Gregson. Tom Donilon, the president's national security advisor, provided essential air cover for the entire effort.

As a global power, the United States has responsibilities that reach into every corner of the globe, and these are unlikely to diminish. As we came into office, however, there was a shared conviction among the above that the Asia-Pacific region had not been accorded a policy prominence commensurate with its true importance. A successful American outreach to the region was therefore essential to promote greater levels of engagement and cooperation in Asia on a wide swath of topics ranging from trade and territory to terrorism and climate change. An unsuccessful approach might well lead to a new arms race with China, regional conflict, strategic competition, a breakdown of global governance, and even war.[2] The stakes remain high today and are getting higher with every passing day.

The Asia-Pacific region exerts an undeniable and inescapable gravitational pull, and it also features enormous stakes and opportunities, all of which will help drive the imperative for a greater regional focus. It is home to more than half the world's population, contains the largest democracy in the world (India), the second- and third-largest economies (China and Japan), the most populous Muslim-majority nation (Indonesia), and seven of the ten largest militaries. The Asian Development Bank has predicted that before the middle of this century, the region will account for half of the world's economic output and include four of the world's ten largest economies (China, India, Indonesia, and Japan).[3]

But it is the trajectory of Asia's evolution, not just its dizzying scale, that makes the region so consequential. According to Freedom House, during the last several years, it has been the only region in the world to record steady improvements in political rights and civil liberties. And despite questions about the ability of emerging markets to sustain rapid economic growth, Asian nations still represent some of the most promising opportunities in an otherwise sluggish and uncertain global economy. At the same time, Asia struggles with sources of chronic instability, owing to the highly provocative actions of North Korea, the rise of competing nationalisms armed with perceptions of historical grievance or prophesy, the growth of defense budgets throughout the region, vexing maritime disputes that roil relations in the East and South China Seas, and nontraditional security threats such as natural disasters, human trafficking, and the drug trade.

The United States has an irrefutable interest in Asia and the course it will take in the years and decades ahead. It is the leading destination for US exports, outpacing Europe by more than 50 percent according to the United States Census Bureau. Both US direct investment in Asia and Asian direct investment in the United States have roughly doubled in the past decade, with China, India, Singapore, and South Korea accounting for four of the ten fastest-growing sources of foreign direct investment to our shores.[4] The United States also has five defense treaty allies in the region (Australia, Japan, the Philippines, South Korea, and Thailand), as well as strategically important partnerships with Brunei, India, Indonesia, Malaysia, New Zealand,

Singapore, and Taiwan, and evolving ties with Burma. Major US military bases in Japan and South Korea are central to Washington's ability to project power in Asia and beyond. The region is therefore central to American security, yet has largely been underrepresented in the strategic commentary, especially since the events of 9/11.

Asia is also crucial to success on virtually every one of Washington's policy goals in the twenty-first century. The path to arresting climate change runs through Asia, already the producer of more carbon emissions than any other region. The prevention of nuclear proliferation will require the cooperation of Asian nuclear powers, some of whom have been active proliferators. In the struggle with radical Islam, Asia's moderate and modern Muslim democracies—like Indonesia—offer a powerful reply to those who hark back to medieval Islamic traditions in Iraq and Syria. The isolation of human rights pariahs or states engaged in nuclear pursuits will not be possible unless Asian states cooperate with economic sanctions and diplomatic strictures. The verdict on which economic principles will define the twenty-first century will be reached in Asia, home to three of the world's four largest economies and increasing levels of interdependence. On so many issues central to the world's future, Asia is at the center of the action.

Not to be ignored is the crucial reality that Asia is also a region that supports and often demands a greater American role. According to a 2015 poll conducted by Pew Research Center, 92 percent of Filipinos, 84 percent of South Koreans, 78 percent of Vietnamese, 70 percent of Indians, 68 percent of Japanese, and 62 percent of Indonesians hold favorable opinions of the United States.[5] Even China has increased its favorable view from 34 percent in 2007 to 44 percent in 2014. The region looks to the United States for leadership and welcomes a US presence, offering positive returns on US investments of time, attention, and resources. Unlike other regions that occasionally contemplate or even advocate for a lesser American role, Asia wants more from the United States across virtually every vector of engagement.

Clearly, then, US interests are inextricably linked to Asia's economic, security, and political situation, and it is therefore essential that the United States expand and deepen its commitment to the region.[6] Our vision in the early days of the Obama administration was that a new effort was needed to accomplish this goal and that it would require the orchestration of comprehensive and extensive diplomatic, economic, developmental, people-to-people, and security initiatives toward Asia. The Pivot was intended to capture and safeguard the region's potential while avoiding the pitfalls posed by fraught relationships, changing power dynamics, and historical disputes rooted in memory and nationalism. Only then could the United States affirm its role in preserving the peace and securing the bounty of this dynamic region—to the ultimate benefit of Asians and Americans alike.

This book advances two overarching arguments. First, that Asia should be placed more centrally in the formulation and execution of American foreign policy. Asia has often—if not always—played a secondary role behind more pressing global or regional concerns in Europe during the Cold War and the Middle East during the war on terror. It is time to revisit these global rankings and to finally elevate Asia to a new prominence in the councils of American policymaking. Second, that in elevating its ambitions and attentions, the United States should pursue a comprehensive and flexible strategy in Asia, backed by top-level attention and adequate resources, with the aim of fulfilling its traditional post–World War II role in the region, keeping credible its alliance commitments, and sustaining Asia's "operating system" (the complex legal, security, and practical arrangements that have underscored four decades of prosperity and security). Such a strategy will require that we move away from the kind of "China first" or "G-2" approach that has often dominated US policy toward Asia and will instead involve embedding China strategy in a larger regional framework, one that advances relations with countries across the region, including China. This book will demonstrate that the chief pillars of such an integrative strategy should include bolstering traditional alliances, forging new partnerships, engaging regional institutions, diversifying military forces, defending democratic values, embracing economic statecraft, and developing a truly multifaceted and comprehensive approach to an increasingly assertive and capable China.

This book is divided into a preface, introduction, and eight chapters. The preface tells the story of how I became the assistant secretary for East Asia and the Pacific in the first term of the Obama administration, under Secretary of State Hillary Clinton. This introduction puts forward the organization and major arguments of the book and introduces the case for the Pivot.

The first chapter defines the Pivot and discusses its origins, registers its successes, and then addresses the major criticisms that are often leveled against it. It refutes arguments that the Pivot simply continues past policy; shortchanges commitments in other regions; provokes China; and lacks resources and follow-through. It explores the question of terminology (e.g., you say *Pivot*, I say *rebalance*).

The second chapter describes the stage on which the Pivot is unfolding, by exploring the stakes and dimensions of a rising Asia that spans across Japan's megacities to China's factories and India's technology campuses. It discusses Asia's challenges, such as sanitation and infrastructure, as well as its emergence as the center of gravity for several economic sectors, including shipping, defense, technology, film, and even fine art.

Chapter Three discusses the Pivot's antecedents by tracing the history of US engagement in the region from the earliest days of the colonial era through the opening of Japan by Commodore Perry's "black ships" to the more recent US freedom of navigation challenges in the South China Sea's disputed waters. This treatment calls attention to eight enduring trends in American engagement: the tyranny of distance, the danger of misunderstanding, the pursuit of commerce, the importance of faith, the costs of war, the recurrence of distraction, the dearth of resources, and the pursuit of democracy. It especially notes an American tendency to accord the region a secondary status in the making of global strategy, and a general American trend of failing to grasp complex and nuanced regional dynamics across generations of US involvement with Asia.

Chapter Four focuses on the main features of US Asia strategy over our long history with the region, and explains enduring trends, periods of discontinuity, and recurring tendencies. It demonstrates that a consistent feature of American Asia strategy has been to use diplomatic, economic, and military means to prevent the emergence of a dominating hegemon in Asia, thereby making the region safe for American pursuits like trade promotion, faith advocacy, democracy support, and territorial security. The argument is made that, in addition to preventing hegemony, the United States also needs to strengthen the region's operating system in the period ahead to ensure Asian states adopt twenty-first century rules that sustain prosperity and promote cooperation on transnational challenges. Finally, the chapter situates the current Pivot to Asia within the larger and longer legacy and tradition of American strategic encounters with Asia.

Chapter Five discusses how, after decades of rapid growth and heightening tensions, Asia is now facing a profoundly important period of uncertainty, flux, and transition that will define its future and require resolute American action and presence. Asia is being pulled between hegemony and a regional balance of power. Its operating system is drawn between twenty-first century and nineteenth-century rules of the road. Its established and emerging powers are deciding whether to become stakeholders or spoilers. It militaries are drifting between conflict and peaceful coexistence. Its transitional states are deciding whether to embrace democracy or fall back on authoritarian ways and domestic repression. And its economic structure and trade relations are being pulled between high standards and soft protectionism. Because Asia will in many circumstances end up living somewhere on the spectrum between these two sets of stark choices, a crucial and enduring component of the Pivot will be to bend the arc of the Asian Century more toward the imperatives of Asian peace and prosperity and longstanding American interests.

Chapter Six offers a plan for the Pivot, comprised of several detailed policy prescriptions. It covers a wide range of US policy toward Asia, including ties with allies such as Australia, Japan, and South Korea, relations with new partners like India and Vietnam, and the development of a nuanced China policy that displays resolve and unambiguously invites cooperation. It also argues for the persistent importance of economic statecraft, the necessity of a strong military presence, the critical role of emerging international institutions, the value of consequential diplomacy, and the need to better integrate our European partners into our Asia policy.

Chapter Seven explores the very real challenges that confront the implementation of this multifaceted strategy for Asia. Many of the looming obstacles are domestic, including US partisan politics, diminishing defense budgets, a feeling of public disillusionment and exhaustion after more than a decade of warfare, the difficulty of long-term planning within the government, and a continuing lack of human capital to address Asian issues. To this list it also adds two major international factors—the continuing crises in the Middle East and new threats in Russia and Eastern Europe that could continue to draw the US away from Asia.

Chapter Eight offers some personal observations on modern diplomacy and engagement in Asia, as well as on the implementation of the Pivot—lessons that perhaps might serve to inform a new generation of would-be diplomats about new avenues of diplomacy in the period ahead. This chapter, which draws on my distinct and extensive experiences across Asia, is an effort to distill some essential truths and humble insights about modern diplomacy that come from many years of service, dozens of diplomatic crises, hundreds of trips to Asian capitals, and thousands of diplomatic meetings.

Finally, the conclusion elaborates upon some of the main insights and prescriptions of the preceding chapters, making the case for the Asian imperative in the formulation and execution of American statecraft in the twenty-first century.

CHAPTER ONE

The Pivot Defined

The Origins, Successes, and Critiques of an Asian Gambit

"As the war in Iraq winds down and America begins to withdraw its forces from Afghanistan," began Hillary Clinton's October 2011 article in *Foreign Policy* magazine, "the United States stands at a pivot point."[1] With that simple turn of phrase, the administration's Asia policy gained a name. Later, in her memoir, *Hard Choices*, Secretary Clinton explained that "journalists latched on to [the word *pivot*] as an evocative description of the administration's renewed emphasis on Asia."[2] The word, mentioned but three times in a 5,500-word article, was suddenly and indelibly affixed to US policy.

Few words in the modern foreign policy lexicon trigger as many different reactions as the word *pivot*. While President Obama likes the term and continues to use it from time to time, others are sharply critical of it and prefer to describe the reorientation of US policy more toward Asia as "rebalancing."[3] Gauging reactions to the word *pivot* is like evaluating responses to a Rorschach test. Some see a long-overdue reorientation of national purpose to a rising region after our country's being mired in costly war and turmoil for nearly a generation. Others see the policy as essentially nothing new—merely a continuation of a long-standing high-level American role in the region. A vocal number see it as provocative toward China, and still others see the Pivot as an abrogation of responsibility in Europe and the Middle East. This chapter explores some of the major questions and criticisms surrounding this sometimes confounding and often misunderstood policy initiative. It will explain the Pivot's origins and history, examine its major initiatives, register its policy successes, and then address the prominent critiques. We begin with a simple question.

What's in a Name?

In Secretary Clinton's famous *Foreign Policy* piece she set out to offer a written account of a strategy to reorient American foreign policy toward the rising East. "One of the most important tasks of American statecraft over the next decade," she declared, "will be to lock in a substantially increased investment—diplomatic, economic, strategic, and otherwise—in the Asia-Pacific region."[4] To do so effectively would require bolstering alliances with states like Australia and Japan, working with new partners like India and Vietnam, strengthening our military and economic tools of statecraft, engaging multilateral institutions, and maintaining our democratic values, all while intensively engaging Beijing and seeking to shape the contours of China's rise. This strategy, though well under way, with key players in the White House, including Tom Donilon, advocating for greater balance in American global pursuits, had not yet been named. The memorable article describing it had emerged from intense consultation among the secretary and her core team at the State Department that had been informed by years of quiet conversations with sage counterparts across Asia and astute Asia watchers here in the United States. Throughout the region there was a widespread sense that the United States—once the stalwart and standby in Asia—was falling behind largely because of American preoccupations elsewhere and a failure to diagnose the subtle and not-so-subtle signs of lagging influence. Given Asia's importance to the future, these concerns strengthened our collective faith in the need for a new approach.

When the article bearing these arguments finally emerged, the response was surprising. In most cases when a new twist of policy is introduced to much administration fanfare, it disappears from view soon thereafter, to the disappointment of its bureaucratic designers. It is the rarest of occurrences when a government lays out a policy innovation and the new approach begins to attract enormous attention and serious questions—rarer still when it garners a new label, one that leaves the policy designers scrambling to respond to the label's unspoken implications and unintended consequences. Once the word *pivot* became affixed to US Asia strategy, there were immediate questions about what the word meant for the durability of US commitments in the Middle East and the future of transatlantic ties. These concerns could have been addressed by better situating the initiative into the larger existing framework of global responsibilities. Indeed, much of the debate over the impetus for and implications of the Pivot is owing to the less than ideal policy explication and public rollout after its initial introduction. I would personally plead guilty for these shortcomings in the rollout, but alas, there are few do-overs in diplomacy.

Although some raised questions about terminology, for the most part, the reception to this renewal of focus on Asia was quite positive. Kim Ghattas, reporting for the BBC, wrote that "although it makes few headlines, there seems to be consensus that the Obama administration's Asia policy is smart and has been successful."[5] Similarly, the *Washington Post* editorial board welcomed it for offering "hope" that the United States "will go beyond simple muscle-flexing" and develop a truly "multi-layered approach to match the complexity of China's rise as a modern superpower."[6] Richard Haass, the president of the Council on Foreign Relations, wrote that the Obama administration's "argument for paying more attention to Asia has been widely accepted, and correctly so" and noted in a television interview that with respect to foreign policy, "the Pivot was the best idea of [Obama's] presidency."[7] Even those critical of certain aspects of the policy felt that "the strategy is basically right."[8] Asia had been given short shrift for too long and it was high time that this was addressed through a new strategy. The dedicated implementation of such a strategy, no easy task at a time of unrelenting conflict in the Middle East and South Asia, would nonetheless prove critical for positioning the United States to prosper, thrive, and protect in the coming Asian Century.

The Pivot in Action

The Pivot is the first major step down what remains a long and winding road to significantly reapportion US attention and resources toward Asia. While very substantial work remains, much has already been accomplished. The Pivot has unquestionably had an important and enduring impact on US foreign policy and on the politics of Asia itself. Within Asia the Pivot reassured allies of the US presence and sent a clear signal to Beijing that America would remain engaged there for decades to come. In this regard the Pivot consisted of a mixture of policies and actions—diplomatic, military, and economic— that together made a more credible American commitment to the region. The Pivot also has helped establish a set of metrics of performance to better allow practitioners and observers to judge results.

With respect to diplomacy, the United States in recent years has undertaken a variety of initiatives throughout the region. Every effort has been made to intensify and diversify existing diplomatic channels with allies across the region. It engaged Southeast Asia's multilateral institutions with greater intensity than at any point in US diplomatic history, signing the ASEAN (Association of Southeast Asian Nations) Treaty of Amity and Cooperation, joining the East Asia Summit, and dispatching senior officials to the ASEAN Regional Forum—all while helping elevate these institutions from "talk shops" and Asian culture–themed dance and singing competitions with batik shirts into dynamic forums for discussing regional challenges and disputes. It developed a strong, robust, and generally productive relationship with China that remained faithful to global rules and universal values. It also revitalized unofficial political and security relations with Taiwan while seeking to sustain peace and stability across the Taiwan Strait. After decades of strategic neglect, the United States reengaged New Zealand as a friend and security partner. Importantly, it reopened ties with Burma, engaging the junta and persuading it to adopt political reforms by jettisoning a failed Bush-era policy that had isolated the country and driven it toward Beijing. Overall the United States was guided by a simple goal: to intensify its bilateral relationships with nearly every Asian state from India to Vietnam and from Malaysia to Mongolia, and to embed itself in Asia's growing web of regional institutions. There was also a conscious attempt to embed formal and recurring diplomatic processes and meetings across the region, to mimic in some ways US practices in Europe. It had traditionally been seen as an American advantage not to be encumbered with formal mechanisms, but it was our judgment that the absence of such established channels was a weakness in US strategy, and much of the region perceived that absence as problematic as well.

Some of the key aspects of the Pivot owed less to overarching strategy and more to clear American actions in the wake of unforeseen crises. Nimble and flexible response to Asian crises and disasters has been a hallmark of recent efforts to engage the region. In the midst of deadly North Korean provocations, the United States bolstered South Korea with diplomatic assistance and military signals to the North. After Japan was ravaged by a tsunami and the most devastating civilian nuclear crisis ever to hit Asia, the United States provided extensive humanitarian resources and military support. Finally, in the face of continued Chinese territorial provocations in the East and South

China Seas, the United States has developed a strategy for dealing with territorial encroachments and protecting freedom of navigation through the use of military deployments, coordination with allies, international institutions, and resolute public diplomacy.

A strategic rebalancing of military assets has been an important, though not defining, aspect of the current Pivot. In 2012, Secretary of Defense Leon Panetta declared, "by 2020 the Navy will reposture its forces from today's roughly 50/50 percent split between the Pacific and the Atlantic to about a 60/40 split between those oceans."[9] The Defense Department later announced plans to reposition 60 percent of the air force to the Asia-Pacific by the same date.[10] The United States stationed 2,500 marines in Darwin and dispatched two littoral combat ships near the Straits of Malacca, with two more to follow. America improved security ties with each of its allies and increased exercises and training with a wide range of close partners, including India, Indonesia, New Zealand, and Vietnam. Crucially, it deepened military-to-military ties with China and even invited China's navy to participate in a major naval exercise, RIMPAC (the Rim of the Pacific Exercise). Much attention is often given to these strategic elements of the Pivot, because they are visible in a way that, to the untrained eye, economic negotiations or greater diplomatic interaction are not. This leads to the false perception among some that the Pivot to Asia is primarily a military policy, when in fact intensified, forward-deployed diplomacy is at its core.

Economic ties have been an equally significant component of the Pivot as well. The United States expended serious political capital on negotiating the historic Trans-Pacific Partnership (TPP) that puts US rules and standards at the center of Asian trade. The concluded agreement, which covers 40 percent of the global economy, once fully implemented, will phase out over 18,000 import tariffs, establish uniform rules on intellectual property, and even open the Internet in Communist Vietnam.[11] Negotiations for a bilateral investment treaty with major Asian economies, such as China and India, are well under way as well and will provide a surge in cross-border investment. In addition, the United States has increased its foreign aid to the Asia-Pacific by 7 percent and its exports by more than 8 percent since 2008, and modified and finalized a free trade agreement (FTA) with South Korea, initially negotiated under the Bush administration, that has intensified trade and investment with Seoul.[12]

Within Washington the Pivot pushed US government agencies and military services to focus more attention on Asia, especially in matters of personnel policy. The State Department, for example, created seventy new positions for specialists on East Asia and the Pacific, and evidence suggests a similar internal reprioritization on Asia occurred in other parts of the executive branch.[13] These modest personnel moves are actually critically important. The United States has grown adept at cultivating a class of policy experts and military officers intimately familiar with the villages and valleys of the Middle East and South Asia, but the twenty-first century will require a cadre of policymakers at least as fluent in the languages, history, and politics of the Asia-Pacific. The Pivot began the process of cultivating that talent. To date the department has been run by officers who cut their diplomatic teeth largely in the Europe or Middle East theaters; Asia-trained and -focused diplomats must increasingly assume important positions along Foggy Bottom's corridors of power.

Asian states have largely welcomed these efforts. Singaporean prime minister Lee Hsien Loong generously welcomed the renewed focus on Asia: "We fundamentally think it's good that America is interested in Asia.... Their presence since the Second World War...has generated peace, stability, predictability, and enabled all the countries to prosper, including China." For these reasons, he noted, "We are naturally very happy that President Obama and Hillary Clinton have made the effort and have put Asia quite high on their agenda."[14] In a brief survey of regional reactions to the Pivot, Robert Sutter finds that "most regional powers have been publicly or privately pleased to see the stronger U.S. commitment to the Asia-Pacific region."[15] The existing data supports these views. According to a 2014 survey of Asian strategic elites conducted by the Center for Strategic and International Studies (CSIS), a clear majority of respondents felt that continued US leadership would be in the best interests of their countries, while nearly 80 percent supported the Pivot to Asia.[16] These sentiments are not confined to Asian elites but are also identifiable within the larger Asian public. A 2015 poll by the Pew Research Center found that more than half of the publics of Australia, Japan, India, the Philippines, South Korea, and Vietnam support increased American military resources in the Asia-Pacific.[17] Similarly, a majority of the public in every Asian state involved in the TPP, with the exception of Malaysia, is in favor of the agreement.

The initiatives above are merely an illustrative list clarifying the range of American efforts implemented in Asia under the general banner of the Pivot, and are far from an exhaustive catalog of US policies in the region. They should make clear that the Pivot to Asia was not idle rhetoric but a substantial national project with far-reaching consequences.

Addressing Critiques of the Pivot

The Pivot's early successes, high-profile endorsements, and considerable Asian support have not inoculated the policy from domestic criticism. From its earliest days, the Pivot has garnered critiques that are at times fair and reasoned and at other times exaggerated and inaccurate. In general, criticisms of the Pivot have fallen into five broad categories: (1) the United States never left Asia to begin with, (2) superpowers should not pivot, (3) the Pivot risks provoking China, (4) the Pivot lacks resources and follow-through, and (5) the word *Pivot* should be replaced with the word *rebalance*. Below I briefly address each of these common criticisms.

We Never Left Asia

Some argue that *Pivot* is a misleading term that implicitly criticizes the previous administration for having abandoned or withdrawn from Asia, when in reality the United States had always remained deeply engaged there. As Thomas Christensen, a distinguished Princeton professor and Bush administration appointee involved in Asia policy, argues, in addition to "fitting well with earlier criticism of the Bush administration," the Pivot is also misguided because "the United States had never left Asia and the suggestion that we had left and had suddenly returned would do diplomatic harm."[18] More forcefully, Ralph Cossa and Brad Glosserman of the Pacific Forum CSIS argue that the "only thing new about the U.S. Pivot toward Asia is the word 'Pivot.'"[19] Dan Blumenthal, another Bush-era appointee, argues that the rhetoric of the Pivot to Asia and the notion that the United States is "back in Asia" is a form of "adolescent trash-talking" that denies or reduces the efforts of previous administrations.[20]

This is certainly not the case. Of course Bush administration officials charged with Asia policy worked diligently and intelligently to craft important initiatives that advanced American interests in the region on matters ranging from the Indian nuclear deal to the sensitive diplomacy

surrounding Taiwanese president Chen Shui-bian's pro-independence initiatives. But despite their intrepid diplomacy, the overall policy apparatus
to which they reported was still powerfully and overwhelmingly shaped
by the aftermath of the September 11 attacks and thoroughly consumed
with the Middle East and South Asia, which naturally limited the degree
to which Asia policy could rise to the top of the US foreign policy agenda.
If anything their criticisms are somewhat partisan, resting as they do on the
incorrect assumption that the Obama administration's Asia policy is a simple
continuation of Bush-era policy and essentially bereft of fresh initiatives or
pathbreaking achievements.

In contrast, the view that the Bush administration focused on the Middle East at the expense of Asia—and that the Obama administration has
rebalanced—is not simply partisan. Ashley Tellis, a former Bush administration appointee and respected Asia expert, does not deny the significance
of the Pivot and asks instead, "Why did it take the United States so long to
rebalance?" He answers that "in the first few months of the Bush administration there was actually an effort made to do what would a decade later
be called rebalancing." Unfortunately, he writes, "the tragedy of 9/11 intervened" and "distracted the United States from what was the central geo-
political challenge"—China's rise within Asia.[21] As a result, to a very real
degree, American focus and attention in Asia did not live up to the emerging
challenges gathering on the horizon. Mike Green, another high-level Bush
administration appointee, acknowledges that this had negative implications
for policy in Asia. "The US Navy and Air Force in the Pacific theater," he
wrote in 2008, "have had to sacrifice new systems and capabilities necessary
to maintain the balance of power because of the heavy ground requirement
in Iraq and Afghanistan."[22] These commitments took a toll not only on the
US military but also on regional diplomacy. Secretary of State Condoleezza
Rice notably missed two important meetings of the ASEAN Regional Forum
(ARF), in one case opting to travel instead to the Middle East, prompting
many Asian states to fear for American focus in Asia at a time when China
was conducting a diplomatic offensive by signing ASEAN's Treaty of Amity
and Cooperation, completing a regional FTA, and founding new regional
organizations.[23] In her memoirs Secretary Rice discusses the thought process
that nearly led her to miss yet another ARF meeting: "I felt ridiculous heading to Southeast Asia while trying to negotiate an end to war in the Middle

East," she writes. "But I decided to just accept the contradiction and make quick work of the stop nearly five thousand miles from where I should have been."[24] For many senior officials, Asia was a distraction. Even when the United States was not absent in Asia, it was clearly absentminded, preoccupied with concerns elsewhere. But to be fair, this is a bipartisan tendency that has afflicted senior officials in both parties. Indeed, the Obama administration has suffered its own bouts of preoccupation with the Middle East, with seemingly endless meetings on the most tactical of issues plaguing this conflict-filled region.

Therein lies the central difficulty of the Bush administration's Asia strategy. Top-level attention largely flowed to the urgent exigencies of war in the Middle East rather than to the patient and long-term game of nuanced strategy that awaited in Asia—and Asian leaders knew it. In contrast, Secretary Clinton and President Obama articulated from the outset of their time in office a desire for a renewed focus on Asia—even with all the ongoing drama in the Middle East. This was why, when Secretary Clinton became the first US secretary of state to visit the ASEAN headquarters in Jakarta, ASEAN secretary-general Surin Pitsuwan remarked to her, "Your visit shows the seriousness of the United States to end its diplomatic absenteeism in the region."[25] When the Obama administration discussed a return to Asia, some domestic critics found these public declarations problematic, fearing that the announcement of an American return to Asia would only raise concerns about a future departure. What these criticisms miss is that, rightly or wrongly, after a decade of grinding wars and the shock of a deep financial crisis, Asian states had already had their faith in the American regional presence badly shaken—a powerful and vocal public commitment that the US role there would be enduring was precisely what they needed to hear, and the Pivot was a means of restoring their faith. In this way the Pivot to Asia is not a repudiation of past efforts in Asia, many of which were successful and prudent, but rather an argument against the overall orientation of the previous foreign policy strategy, which focused inordinately on the seemingly endless war on terror, often at the expense of this dynamic and vibrant region.

Of course, many aspects of the Pivot to Asia are built on sensible policies of previous administrations. The Trans-Pacific Partnership, a signature initiative of the Obama administration actively promoted and carefully negotiated during his tenure, was initially joined in the final year of the Bush administration. Other aspects of the Pivot—such as more dutiful attention to Southeast Asian countries, multilateral groupings, and nascent institutions, the engagement of Burma, and the reapportioning of military assets—mark a clear break from past policy. The scale and scope of the Pivot, as well as the high-level support, attention, and focus it has been able to garner within the US government, surpass what has gone before it in recent years.

Superpowers Don't Pivot

Many of the common criticisms of the Pivot are in tension with each other. Some argue, for example, that the Pivot is no departure from previous policy, but in the same breath also argue that it is a difference so great that it constitutes an abrogation of commitments to the Middle East and Europe. In other words, the Pivot both does so little it scarcely matters and so much that it causes serious harm.

In reality the Pivot to Asia is a substantive and consequential realignment of American foreign policy priorities in consonance with the demands of the twenty-first century. There is a good-faith argument to be made that pursuing—or even announcing—such a realignment is not appropriate for a superpower with commitments in all corners of the globe. This policy, however, was conceived as a pivot not from one theater to another *but from one strategy to another.* In this sense critics are far too literal in their interpretation of the term. After a decade of war and relative neglect of Asia, the Pivot was meant to be a movement toward strategic engagement and a better balancing of diplomatic and military resources. Words, however, create perceptions, and incorrect perceptions can obscure the truth. For that reason many critics announced their concerns about US commitments in other regions upon hearing the word *pivot.* In fact, the lexicologists at the State Department had the vision of a basketball player in mind when they initially came up with the term. The idea was to transition smoothly from one place to another and back with a stable foundation underneath. Unfortunately, the visual most commonly conjured by the word is that of the United States turning away from other long-standing roles and commitments.

The most common form of this argument has focused on the Middle East, noting that it would be unwise or unrealistic to shift Washington's focus to Asia given the conflicts in Afghanistan and Syria, the instability in Iraq and Libya, and the long-running confrontation between Iran and the Western powers. As Amitai Etzioni of George Washington University has argued, the challenges of Asia, and those posed by China in particular, "will be decades down the road—while the U.S. is challenged in the Middle East right now."[26] Moreover, at a time of rising Russian revanchism, evident in the war in Ukraine, Russian intervention in Syria, and Putin's menacing threats to the Balkan states, Europe too needs US attention. In light of these constraints, über-strategist Robert Kagan argues that the United States must remain involved in Europe, Asia, and the Middle East. "We can pivot," he writes, "but we can't leave."[27]

Kagan is correct, which is why no one supporting the Pivot to Asia is advocating a withdrawal from any other part of the world. Foreign policy is not a zero-sum game, and the criticism that paying more attention to Asia is either an admission of strategic defeat or a departure from other regions is fundamentally misleading. As Secretary Clinton notes in her recent memoir, "America had the reach and resolve to pivot *to* Asia without pivoting *away* from other obligations and opportunities."[28] The Pivot is not a form of abandonment, abrogation, or withdrawal, but a reprioritization of strategic focus based on the notion that what has for too long been regarded as a "secondary theater" must now be given its just due. It is a pledge to ensure that the share of US time and attention spent on Asia should be commensurate with a region that features the world's largest economies, biggest populations, fastest-growing markets, and greatest carbon emissions, as well as several paths to dangerous great-power conflict. As we will see in chapter four, Asia is a central regional feature and focus of virtually every American goal today—from increasing exports to combating climate change and managing the global economy. The Pivot is not premature, but urgently required to address grim global governance challenges and simmering territorial disputes. In light of these concerns, Henry Kissinger has himself remarked that "a rebalancing of American policy was inevitable."[29] Even former president of the European Council Herman Van Rompuy has been no less blunt: "The twentieth century was an Atlantic century, while the twenty-first is going to be a Pacific one.... We Europeans should...be frank with ourselves."[30] Indeed, the only countries pivoting more rapidly to Asia than the United States are European.

Those who argue that the Pivot is a movement away from other regions miss a crucial reality—our Asia policy is intricately tied to policy outside

Asia because US credibility has transference properties across regions. Actors in the Middle East and Europe, for example, look for signals of American resolve in American policy in the East and South China Seas, just as Asians watch carefully for signs of American credibility in the Middle East. Moreover, the same Asian countries engaged by Pivot are now quietly building a substantial stake in the furtherance of peace and stability across the Middle East and South Asia and very much want the United States to preserve its influence in those regions.[31] One of the remarkable achievements of the Bush administration was to enlist Asian assistance in "out of area" pursuits in the Middle East. Indeed, the United States encouraged many Asian nations to broaden their regional horizons to embrace Middle East and South Asian challenges. These "out of area" activities have not been fully appreciated, but they have included massive outlays from Japan to civil society projects across the Middle East, the deployment of ground forces from Korea to Iraq and of special forces from Australia and New Zealand to several of the region's hot spots, and generous humanitarian support from Indonesia, Malaysia, and Thailand for civic training and many other programs. China has been more active in the behind-the-scenes diplomacy aimed at constraining Iran's nuclear program, conducting Afghan peace talks, and addressing Indian Ocean piracy. Taken together and even alone, these are all substantial refurbishments to American policy toward the Asia-Pacific region. Given Asia's size and interconnectedness with the world, any global problem is now increasingly an Asian problem. Implementing sanctions against wayward regimes in Africa and the Middle East, for example, necessarily involves intense Asian engagement, because it will be impossible for sanctions to truly bite without the cooperation of Asia's rising economies and financial services. A key goal of the Pivot, then, is actually to encourage and accelerate the interconnectedness of Asia policy with other regional and global pursuits.

Provoking China?

A common response to the Pivot has been concern that it might needlessly and dangerously antagonize China. As we will see, these arguments are somewhat misleading. First, the Pivot is primarily about increasing ties to Asia, not containing China. Second, building a constructive and productive relationship with China has been an important part of the Pivot ever since it was first announced. Finally, and most importantly, the Pivot was intended to remind Beijing of US staying power at a time when some Chinese policymakers were dangerously anticipating a US withdrawal from Asia and ready to discount American influence in the region.

Although some see the Pivot as driven by concerns over China, they often forget—as Robert Sutter rightly reminds us—that it "has been driven by a much broader set of strategic, economic, and political considerations" than those related only to China.[32] If anything, the Pivot rejects the "China first" approach to Asian diplomacy that places bilateral ties between Washington and Beijing at the center of the regional agenda; instead it embeds China policy within a much wider and more inclusive regional framework. This is a framework built on the principle that the United States must boost its overall diplomatic, economic, and military ties with many Asian states in order to grow its own economy, solve global challenges, and keep the peace in a region that will define the future. The notion that the Pivot to Asia is primarily China-focused appears even more tenuous when one considers that Asia is home to many countries of profound global significance, including the world's largest democracy (India), the world's third-largest economy (Japan), the world's largest Muslim democracy (Indonesia), and many of the world's most important manufacturers (Korea, Taiwan, Malaysia, Vietnam). In addition to improving ties with these consequential and dynamic states, which is self-evidently important, the Pivot is also about allaying regional concerns about US staying power in Asia after American preoccupation with competing foreign pursuits and a troubling domestic economic slowdown.

That said, US China policy is an important component of the Pivot, and as President Obama himself stated in a press conference with Chinese president Xi Jinping, "a strong, cooperative relationship with China is at the heart of our Pivot to Asia."[33] By building such a relationship with Asia's largest economy, the United States signals not only to China but also to China's neighbors that our China policy is not intended to produce needless and unproductive friction that would not be in the interests of most Asian states.[34] Although some suggest that the Pivot resembles containment, this is an unfounded and confounding argument. Virtually no serious American policymaker supports containing China because the very concept of containment, which dates back to the Cold War competition with the Soviet Union, has little to no relevance to the complexities of an interdependent Asia in which most states have deep economic ties with China. Indeed, a chief challenge in constructing a durable Asia strategy for the United States is that most important nations in the region have strong commercial ties with Beijing and, simultaneously, important security relations with Washington. A better strategy is to work with China wherever possible, as well as to induce it to support international norms and contribute to global governance, while signaling resolve on issues of disagreement that are central to Asia's peace and prosperity. To that end the United States established and expanded the annual U.S.-China Strategic and Economic Dialogue, transforming what had once consisted of high-level and singular conversations about economic policy into a comprehensive set of meetings of strategic concern spanning many government agencies and efforts, thereby facilitating both broad and deep engagement. The United States also established the Strategic Security Dialogue, through which the two countries have held unprecedented high-level discussions on such sensitive matters as maritime security and cybersecurity.[35] The United States and China also institutionalized their first-ever regional consultations, which allow for greater clarity and transparency in the countries' respective strategies and approaches to Asia itself. The United States has sought to cooperate with China in a variety of different international institutions on a host of important global issues, including climate change, maritime piracy, and global economic management. Additionally, the United States is currently negotiating a bilateral investment treaty will that will help facilitate greater flows of capital between the United States and China, binding the countries closer together economically and improving Chinese growth. These are not the kinds of things that containment-minded hegemons do.

The US Pivot to Asia is of course also about communicating resolve on several matters central to Asia's future. Most criticisms of the Pivot gloss over this critical nuance. A few years ago, for example, many commentators pointed out that China had become bold and assertive after the financial crisis because it doubted US commitment in Asia. Then, when the Pivot was announced a year later to demonstrate US resolve in the region, many of these same critics suddenly complained that the Pivot was insufficiently reassuring and far too threatening to China.

If the United States is to dissuade China from provocative behavior against its neighbors or from the improper disregard of international norms, it cannot do so from the sidelines or alone. In recent years China has escalated territorial disputes, built artificial islands, harassed American vessels, and threatened its neighbors. In light of this assertiveness, former Australian prime minister Kevin Rudd argues that "the 'Pivot,' or 'rebalance,' to Asia… has been entirely appropriate." "Without such a move," he pointedly notes, "there was a danger that China, with its hardline, realist view of international relations, would conclude that an economically exhausted United States was losing its staying power in the Pacific."[36] In contrast, the Pivot arrested a dangerous perception of US decline and retrenchment that was fermenting in Beijing. Indeed, one study concludes that, at least for a time, the Pivot and its related policies also "appear to have motivated Beijing to moderate its approach to dealing with its neighbors."[37]

What critics of the Pivot all too often fail to realize is that an essential feature of a healthy and positive relationship between the United States and China is a clear and realistic recognition of our respective trajectories, and that the Pivot is a reminder not to write off US influence in Asia. While it is true that the Pivot was not Beijing's preferred US policy course, those who fret that the Pivot is confrontational must also admit that at least some amount of competition and tension in US-China relations is inevitable and perhaps even healthy compared to the alternatives—overlooking real areas of concern or preemptively conceding on matters of fundamental principle. Put differently, there are times for reassurance, but when allies are facing down Chinese territorial provocations, and when the South China Sea risks becoming a so-called "Chinese lake," policy initiatives should lean more toward signals of resolve that make clear American commitment to sustaining peace and stability. Military investments, improved bilateral security ties with others in the region, and occasional displays of force at times annoy Chinese strategists and nationalists, but they are also useful aspects of statecraft that make clear the potential costs of Chinese unilateralism. For this reason the aspects of the US Pivot to Asia that are related to China are perhaps best understood as a mixture of reassurance and resolve that underscore elements of cooperation and competition respectively.

Even in light of these arguments, many US critics continue to claim that the Pivot will frighten China as public and elite opinion sours on the United States, perhaps setting off a negative security spiral in the process.[38] There are reasons to question these ominous prophecies. First, according to a Pew survey, China's favorability rating for the United States in 2015 of 44 percent remains unchanged from 2011, the year the Pivot was first announced, suggesting it had less impact on public opinion and perhaps did much less to fan the flames of nationalism than some critics, such as Robert Ross, have feared.[39] Critically, the US favorability rating in China actually stands ten points higher now than during the Bush administration, when it hit a low point of 34 percent in 2007.[40] Second, the official Chinese reaction to the Pivot has been more restrained than many critics note. In his survey of Chinese leadership and elite responses to the Pivot in 2012, Michael Swaine of the Carnegie Endowment for International Peace found a relatively low-key reaction from those officials regarded as speaking for the regime.[41] In another survey of Chinese sources, Michael Chase of the RAND Corporation and Benjamin Purser, now of the Senate Foreign Relations Committee, found that Chinese analysts regarded the Pivot with neither panic nor indifference, and instead encouraged Beijing to "remain patient" as well as to "observe U.S. actions and stay its existing course."[42] For the most part, China's official response to the Pivot was no knee-jerk reaction driven by concern over US intentions but instead a reasonable and measured decision to wait and see how US policy would evolve.

Resources and Follow-Through

One of the most significant critiques of the Pivot is that it lacks resources and follow-through. As Mike Green and Dan Twining cautioned at the Pivot's outset, "Without resources the big talk will quickly seem hollow to friends and foes alike."[43] Writing more recently, Aaron Friedberg worried that "many in the region and elsewhere, including the United States, have begun to suspect that the Pivot may not live up to its advanced billing."[44] In particular, concerns about US spending cuts and a potential diversion of focus to Eastern Europe or the Middle East animate a belief that the implementation of the Pivot may yet face serious obstacles.

Some of these criticisms are sound—the Pivot is a work in progress and there is simply no doubt that the United States needs to do more to implement it. It is also true that the unrelenting demands of the Middle East place claims on finite American resources. At the same time, these criticisms about follow-through often focus inordinately on security considerations, because those are tangible, thereby ignoring the reality that the Pivot to Asia is as focused on less visible diplomatic and economic initiatives as it is on military ones.

With respect to security, the United States has enhanced its presence in the region in ways that are far from trivial and sometimes unfairly criticized. Even in the face of the sequester, the United States can implement defense cuts in a way that does not harm its presence in the Asia-Pacific. Indeed, the United States is shifting 60 percent of its fleet to the Pacific and the air force and army are implementing their own regional rebalance, with the former deploying many of its fifth-generation fighters to Asia. The United States has also intensified its security partnerships with its allies, agreeing on new defense guidelines with Japan, discussing plans for the transition of wartime operational control with South Korea, signing a new Force Posture Agreement with Australia, and completing a new Enhanced Defense Cooperation Agreement with the Philippines.[45] With respect to other major partners, the United States has signed the Joint Vision Statement on Defense Relations with Vietnam, the ten-year Defense Framework Agreement with India, and the Joint Statement on Comprehensive Defense Cooperation with Indonesia. These are serious steps, and with them have come a series of important displays that show the Pivot is far from just words in a diplomatic communiqué. The United States has conducted military exercises throughout the region and increased its presence in the South China Sea, sailing a guided-missile destroyer within twelve nautical miles of a Chinese-created island and flying a B-52 through a Chinese air defense identification zone (ADIZ) over the East China Sea to reassert the principle of freedom of navigation. The administration has also quite consciously advanced policy pronouncements designed to shape subsequent actions, such as when Secretary Clinton declared in 2010 in a regional forum hosted in Vietnam that freedom of navigation in the South China Sea was a matter of enduring strategic concern to the United States.

Outside of defense and security, the United States has spearheaded significant economic and diplomatic initiatives that are harder to measure or see but are nevertheless acknowledged and deeply felt within Asia. Many of these were discussed early in this introduction, but it is worth pausing to note that high-level time and attention in Asia has increased dramatically under Secretary Clinton, who has taken more trips to Asia than any of her predecessors. The United States has significantly engaged virtually every main Asian institution, and American diplomats are intensifying their bilateral ties with virtually every Asian state. An aggressive agenda of trade and investment negotiations is also under way.

There is still much more to do within Washington to prepare the government to handle the exigencies of pivoting eastward. Congress can ensure that key agencies and departments have appropriate funds, and provide guidance ensuring that Asia receives appropriate attention. The executive branch can also provide overarching direction to remind agencies that the Asia-Pacific region is a White House priority. Indeed, a more public and coordinated Asia-Pacific strategy emanating from the White House and directed at a domestic audience could be useful in mobilizing the public, in setting priorities in the interagency process, and in our overtures abroad. In this vein, the annual Defense Department report on its Asia-Pacific strategy, first issued in 2015, is a positive step, and it should be emulated by other agencies.

Outside of Washington the United States will need to ensure that allies and partners do their fair share to make Asia safe, secure, and prosperous—including by investing in defense capabilities and negotiating in good faith on economic and diplomatic agreements. But it needs to enlist this support within the larger context of an enduring American commitment to the region. An appeal to greater allied burden sharing in the midst of perceived US retreat risks repeating the experience of the announcement of the Guam Doctrine by President Nixon in the last days of the Vietnam War, which simply spiked regional concerns about American decline and withdrawal. Put simply, the United States cannot rebalance to Asia alone, and it will need to engage regional players as well as extra-regional partners, such as European states, to be effective. But it must call on this allied effort as part of a larger US commitment to the region.

To skeptics, the significant progress made in Asia so far, and even the adoption of most of the proposals above, might still seem insufficient. To the doubters of US fortitude, however, it is worth remembering that the United States has remained a great power in Asia for the last several decades, weathering the occasional hand-wringing and prognostications of American decline that have periodically arisen. Furthermore, the United States has long had a bipartisan consensus on the importance of the Asia-Pacific region to our foreign policy and national interests. For decades Democratic and Republican administrations alike, with congressional support, have built and maintained strong ties that bind the United States with countries across the Pacific by way of alliances, trade, values, and immigration. There is public support for these initiatives as well. Even though there remains a sizable slice of Americans who feel the country needs to enter a period of relative retrenchment following two decades of war, there nevertheless exist a large and growing number who understand Asia's importance to American security and prosperity. The 2014 survey by the Chicago Council on Global Affairs found that 60 percent of Americans favor rebalancing American commitments so that more resources are devoted to Asia, an increase from just over half in 2012.[46] Of the region's main powers, the American favorability ratings for Japan and South Korea are at all-time highs, while more than two-thirds feel the United States should undertake friendly cooperation and engagement with China. Of particular importance to a successful Pivot, which requires trade agreements and an expanded role for regional and international institutions, almost two-thirds of Americans say that globalization is a good thing for the United States, the highest level since the Chicago Council began asking the question in 1998. Seventy-two percent of Americans believe that trade agreements are an effective means of achieving American goals, a figure corroborated by another 2014 poll that found 80 percent of Americans supported the negotiation of trade agreements.[47] Put simply, American staying power in Asia is in large part a political choice, and the public is not nearly so allergic to it as critics might suggest.

Pivot, Rebalance, and Credit

An underlying context for the tug-of-war over appropriate terminology (you say *rebalance*, I say *Pivot*) was the occasional jockeying for credit between bureaucratic players in the executive branch. From the outset *Pivot* was seen as a State Department term and *rebalance* a moniker more to the liking of the National Security Council at the White House. The Pentagon was generally less focused on the early formulation and execution of broader Asia policy, given the unrelenting demands of Iraq, Afghanistan, and the larger Arab uprising, but tended to adhere to the *rebalance* convention in meetings and public discourse. Curiously, the president himself occasionally used the term *Pivot* in speeches and toasts, adding to the confusion. We would sometimes joke at the State Department that those of us who favored the

Pivot convention would one day be rounded up and sent to a camp for re-indoctrination. So acute was my sensitivity to the language surrounding the initiative that I would sometimes squirm in my chair during recitals when my six-year-old daughter's ballet teacher instructed all the girls in their pink tutus to "now pivot, girls." I would often think to myself, does she mean *rebalance*?

Every principal in government is interested in legacy and accomplishment, and President Obama's administration was no different in this regard. The Obama administration marked a period of remarkable centralization in the White House for policymaking, along with a tendency to diminish other actors as merely "implementers" of White House–developed strategies. A natural tendency in most administrations is to claim credit for foreign policy accomplishments, but this predisposition perhaps was even stronger than usual in the first-term Obama White House.

While both the White House and the State Department were intent on advancing a strategy that focused more on Asia going forward, there were the occasional discernible differences between their two approaches and the respective energies directed toward the region. Some of this is perfectly natural in any broad government endeavor. In particular, the White House was noticeably more exercised and energized by China, a great power with undeniable clout and strategic import. The policy focus was more on planning for intimate meetings with senior counterparts from Beijing, and seeking consequential bilateral understandings backing restraint on the Korean Peninsula or Afghan reconstruction. This approach undeniably resulted in some important successes, such as the Iranian sanctions regime, but the tilt at the top had unintended consequences. China was the big leagues, and rhetorical focus on a rebalance to Asia was manifested primarily as a deeper engagement of Beijing. The NSC most certainly did engage the wider region, but the practice of NSC diplomacy sometimes resembled a pinwheel—seek to get China right and the rest of the region can be dealt with by the other branches of government. However, during times of uncertainty in Asia over US staying power and resolve—such as during this period—intensified diplomacy with China had the unintended consequence of creating concern in the surrounding region, spiking fears that the United States might in a weakened position sacrifice critical interests in the hope of preserving smooth ties with China. Allies and friends in Asia also sought higher-level access and meetings in the White House, and quietly felt diminished while watching from a distance during the lavish festivities afforded visiting Chinese guests.

The approach advanced by the Clinton State Department had subtle differences. At the heart of the difference was an appreciation for the ongoing changes in Chinese aspirations and how the larger region was responding to these changes. At Foggy Bottom there was an appreciation that a greater degree of regional ambition animated Chinese actions in Asia, along with a more competitive approach to challenging long-standing American positions across the region. There was an unmistakable sense emanating from senior Chinese interlocutors that China's time was rapidly approaching on the international scene. Chinese think tank and strategic writings beginning at the time of the 2008 Global Financial Crisis were overflowing with analysis suggesting a precipitous American decline and a continuing Middle East preoccupation. It had all the makings of a gathering storm for the American position in Asia. Secretary Clinton in particular understood the vulnerabilities for the US in the region, and her numerous visits around Asia were intended to shore up regional relationships and respond to doubts about US staying power.

While substantial harmony and collaboration at the professional level between the White House and State Department were on display in the Burma opening, coordination over North Korean provocations, and the guiding of relief efforts in the wake of the tragic Japanese nuclear disaster, there were still unmistakable signs of bureaucratic competition. For instance, the original *Foreign Policy* piece for Clinton that State sent to the White House for clearance met with some initial resistance. One key NSC staff member thought it might be too "broad in scope." What was really needed was "a careful history of multilateralism in Southeast Asia," a remark interpreted by the Clinton team as a desire not to have strategy emanating from outside the White House—even if it had indeed been developed elsewhere. Inside the familiar halls of the department, this was jokingly referred to as the NSC's preference for the State Department to write the authoritative account of nutmeg production discrepancies in obscure localities of Indonesian Sumatra between 1845 and 1890. Also, the tension was evident between the White House and the State Department over Chen Guangcheng, the blind Chinese dissident—who was housed and protected for a tense time in the US embassy in Beijing—with the *New York Times* reporting anonymous high-placed White House sources critical of the way Secretary Clinton and her team were handling the complex affair, which successfully led Chen and his family to safety in the United States.

These intramural skirmishes are common in any administration, and the collegiality and good humor of the Asia professionals on both staffs helped enormously. But credit for foreign policy success is the coin of the realm in diplomacy, and maneuvering for that elusive perception of intrepid effectiveness is a regular blood sport in Washington.

Conclusion

During the first term of the Obama presidency, the United States substantially increased its economic, diplomatic, and strategic presence in Asia. It was motivated by a simple set of unrelenting truths: the lion's share of the history of the twenty-first century will be written in Asia; the path to progress on every major global governance challenge runs through Asia; and the dynamism of Asia's economies will be central to American economic prosperity for generations to come. The Pivot to Asia is built on the premise that these truths have not sufficiently guided US policy to date, which has often been preoccupied with other theaters. The Pivot is not an abrogation of commitments to these other regions, for, as Richard Haass notes, "Between disengagement and preoccupation are myriad policy choices."[48] It is not an attempt at containing China, because such an effort would be wrongheaded and futile, but in part an effort to engage it with a necessary determination that mixes reassurance with resolve, the better to strengthen ties and induce fidelity to international norms. It is not a political or partisan polemic, but rather an attempt to reorient the national interest to reflect bipartisan concerns and aspirations. Nor is it empty rhetoric that lacks resources and follow-through, though more of both are certainly needed. The Pivot is a policy formulated and implemented to preserve and extend American power, supported widely within the region, and acknowledged as essential by dozens of foreign policy commentators—and its time is long overdue.

CHAPTER TWO

The Stage for the Pivot

The Stakes and Dimensions of a Rising Asia

With the Pacific Century now fully under way, global momentum and energy are shifting to Asia minute by minute and on every measure. Asia is now beginning to lead the globe in almost every metric, often in ways that illustrate the region's potential and its challenges, and sometimes in ways that appear both surprising and contradictory. The region is home to the world's largest emitters of greenhouse gases, but also to its biggest investors in green technology. It houses the world's largest urban population, but most of its countries have some of the world's lowest urbanization rates. It is a region that uses more power than any other, but one-fifth of its population still lacks access to electricity. Despite the region's long and proud cultural history, plastic surgery to look more "Western" has run rampant, with thirty thousand double eyelid surgeries being performed annually in South Korea alone.[1] And while countries such as Indonesia top the global rankings in alcohol abstinence, four of the world's top five countries for alcohol consumption are located in Asia. China has undergone a second "red revolution" to become the world's largest consumer of red wine.[2] With regard to spirits, South Korea leads per capita consumption at 13.7 shots per week, beating out traditional heavyweights such as Ireland, Scotland, and Russia by more than double.[3]

In this chapter we will look at the facts and figures behind Asia's amazing ascent. China plays the greatest role in the reemergence of the region, but all countries have participated in the most extraordinary tale of growth and development in human history. The scale and scope of the region's dizzying development, which has lifted more people from poverty than at any other period in human history, will awe even the most cynical observers.

Asia's achievements to date are remarkable and the future is bright, but it is by no means assured. While statesmen and pundits have long marveled at its potential and spoken breathlessly of its colossal markets and teeming multitudes, the region still faces challenges to realizing its promise. As we will see in this chapter, in much of the region, poverty is pervasive, sanitation is poor, pollution is rife, infrastructure is inadequate, energy use is surging, populations are graying, and the threat of climate change looms large over the future. In light of these obstacles, and as China's economy slows, it is increasingly common to write that the Asian miracle is over, with prominent economists predicting that Asian growth will soon regress to its historical average.[4] While Asia's rise has certainly brought challenges, it has also endowed the region with considerable resources with which to address them, not to mention the world's biggest middle class and its largest economies. And while Asia's growth now may gradually fall from its breakneck historic pace, the region's rise is about more than the speed of its ascent; it is also about the quality and scale of its progress on metrics that range from public health to growing economic inequality and from cultural identity to environmental preservation. An important part of Asia's story, as with all good tales, is a struggle for success and progress in the face of challenge and adversity.

This is a story of great consequence to the United States. As the region has risen, the bonds that have long tied Americans and Asians together have grown tighter. As Barack Obama stated on his first trip to Japan as president:

> Asia and the United States are not separated by this great ocean; we are bound by it. We are bound by our past—by the Asian immigrants who helped build America, and the generations of Americans in uniform who served and sacrificed to keep this region secure and free. We are bound by our shared prosperity—by the trade and commerce upon which millions of jobs and families depend. And we are bound by our people—by the Asian Americans who enrich every segment of American life, and all the people whose lives, like our countries, are interwoven.[5]

This tapestry of relationships between the United States and Asia means that the great boon of development and progress in Asia stimulates and enhances progress here at home. Strengthening America's links to a region that is home to wondrous innovations and a surging middle class is especially important given the sluggish economic recovery following the financial crisis in 2008. Promoting and expanding American exports to the world—and particularly to Asia—will be central to a sustained recovery and the creation of high-quality US jobs. Asia's rise is vital to the health and progress of the American economy, but the potential benefits to be reaped from the Asian Century bring with them concomitant American responsibilities. And just as the region is critical to America's future, an engaged America is also vital to Asia's future.

In order to prepare ourselves for the geopolitics and economic dynamism of the future, we must understand the scope of what is taking in place in Asia today, appreciate its drama and dimensions, and consider what may yet change. To that end this chapter will illustrate in broad brushstrokes the scale of Asia's rise, with careful attention to both its potential and its challenges. It will focus on traditional economic indicators, such as urbanization and energy use, as well as critical measures of social development, such as health and sanitation. It will then dive deeply into some of the global industries that have been irrevocably changed by Asia's emergence. By examining some usual suspects—such as shipping activity, defense spending, and technology—as well as some more unusual ones—such as the film industry and art market—this chapter will illustrate the widespread nature and dramatic impact of Asia's transformation. Let us begin by quantifying this dynamism.

Facts and Figures

Discussing Asia requires using enormous numbers. Its economies are measured in trillions of dollars, its populations swell to billions of people, and its militaries are manned by millions of soldiers. These numbers elude easy comprehension. Evolutionary biologists have noted that our human brains evolved to understand best what we routinely encounter, and we rarely meet with a trillion of anything in daily life.[6] To better grasp the scale of such large numbers, a few concrete examples may be helpful.

Most of us know the rough dimensions of a dollar bill, so let us start by merely imagining a lot of dollar bills. Although one dollar alone is thinner than a standard piece of paper, a million dollars would stack up to the height of a thirty-story building, a billion dollars would reach seventy miles high and into outer space, and a trillion dollars would stretch one-quarter of the distance to the moon. There are five Asian economies larger than $1 trillion, and their aggregate nominal GDP of roughly $20 trillion would allow you to create five piles of stacked dollar bills each stretching from Earth to the moon.[7]

A second way to appreciate the scale of these numbers is to think in terms of time. If you counted one number every second, it would take seventeen minutes to reach one thousand, twelve straight days and nights of counting to reach one million, and thirty-two years to reach one billion. A quick head count of the Asian population, currently standing at over four billion, would take more than 140 years. Since sixteen people are born each second in Asia, the task is effectively unending.[8]

If these exercises prove one thing, it is that terms like *million* and *billion*, which are so casually bandied about, actually refer to quantities so vast that they resist easy understanding. Asia's scale is literally incomprehensible. The statistics in this chapter will be of amazing magnitudes and, almost without exception, refer to numbers that are predicted to continue growing at relatively high rates. To break down Asia's dimensions, we now turn to some of the facts and figures that illustrate the region's astonishing growth and dizzying scale. We begin with the fountain from which most of Asia's shocking statistics flow—the region's large population.

Population and Living Space

In 1958 Mao Zedong boldly commanded that "the whole people, including five-year-old children, be mobilized to eliminate the Four Pests." With that he launched the aptly named "Four Pests campaign," which was intended to wield China's enormous population as a bludgeon in a military-style mass-line campaign against mosquitoes, flies, rats, and sparrows. His goal was nothing short of remaking China's entire ecosystem in a way conducive to public health and improved agricultural output. Chinese citizens of all ages and occupations participated in what became a routine part of community life, presenting dead rodents and birds to local functionaries and receiving praise or promotion for ideological fervor. With several hundred million Chinese squashing and swatting away vermin, the campaign was quickly successful in dramatically altering the country's ecology. In two short years, sparrows were driven to the brink of extinction in China. The otherwise harmless birds had been targeted for their fondness for grain, but it turned out they had an even greater appetite for grain-eating insects. Their virtual extinction brought swarms of locusts that devastated Chinese crops and ushered in famine. Mao's "Four Pests" campaign, a profound failure, is nevertheless a testament to the power, potential, and peril of hundreds of millions of people mobilized to act in unison, and an illustration of the significance of Asia's colossal population.[9]

Asia's population, always the world's largest, has grown sharply. Between 1800 and 1900, Asia's population rose at a steady rate, doubling in size over the course of the century. Between 1900 and 2000, following improvements in public health and increases in life expectancy, that same population quadrupled in size.[10] Today Asia is home to more than four billion people, 60 percent of the world's population, and more than one-third of the world's middle class.[11]

Global Population over Time

Population by Region

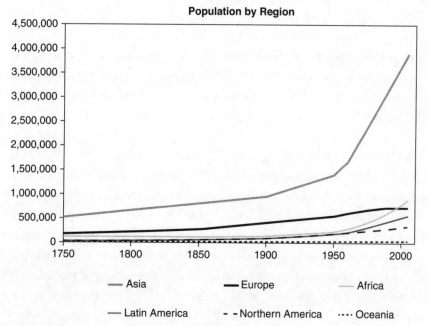

Angus Maddison Project

These enormous numbers are admittedly somewhat abstract, so to help make the scale of Asia's population somewhat more concrete, a small thought experiment may be helpful. Take the land mass of the United States, from sea to shining sea. By area the continental United States is roughly the same size as China. How much must we increase the American population to attain a population equivalent to China's? If the United States opened its borders and admitted every person from Canada, Mexico, Central America, the Caribbean, and South America, it would still fall short of China's population by roughly four hundred million. By adding in the populations of the United Kingdom, France, Germany, Italy, and Russia, we would finally have the same population as China, 1.4 billion, in roughly the same geographic area.[12]

This more populous America would face great challenges, with the average citizen possessing only one-fourth as much living space as today's average American, or about the same amount as an average Chinese citizen. At 367 people per square mile, China is considerably more densely populated than the United States. Although China has Asia's largest population, it is by no means the region's most densely populated country. The Philippines has 866 people per square mile, Japan 870, India 993, and South Korea an astonishing 1,303. The idea of personal space is understood very differently when people are forced to live so closely together. So too is the concept of resource scarcity.[13] James Fallows quotes a Chinese government official on this point: "Outsiders think of everything about China as multiplied by 1.3 billion. We have to think of everything as divided by 1.3 billion."[14]

Asia's colossal population unquestionably brings challenges, but it has also fueled the region's rise and undergirded global growth. Asian states are benefiting from what economists call the "demographic dividend." As fertility rates fall, the structure of the population changes profoundly as the working-age share of the population—those between the ages of fifteen and sixty-four—rises relative to both young and old dependents. This bulge of workers offers a window of opportunity for rapid economic growth, since output per capita is higher for workers than for the young and old, who tend to consume more than they produce. Since 1980, Asia's dependency ratio has fallen from 72.8 percent to just 47 percent in 2013, freeing up resources that can be used to fuel economic growth.[15] Of the fifteen countries with the largest working-age populations in the world, seven are in Asia and each has workers constituting more than 70 percent of its total population.[16] Malaysia and the Philippines, for example, have a median age of around 25, compared to 37.6 in the United States, and over 46 in Germany.[17]

The demographic dividend will quickly give way to a demographic deficit when what was once a large working class becomes a large retiree class with far fewer young workers to support it. For this reason the demographic dividend is a window of opportunity that comes only once. Some Asian states, such as India and Indonesia, are now entering this window, while others, such as China, are soon to exit it.[18]

For India the stakes are particularly high. The country will soon have one-fifth of the world's entire working-age population, and it will be the slowest-aging of all the world's major economies—in other words, the percentage of its population above the age of sixty-five will not climb quickly. If India is to harness its young workers, it will need to create jobs for them at a pace of roughly ten million a year, an enormous challenge. Even during the country's period of fastest growth, from 2004 to 2010, India created no new net jobs.[19] The country's world-beating firms in industries such as software and information technology employ relatively few Indians, and if the country is to employ its people, it will need to build an equally impressive manufacturing

Table of Asian Countries and UN-Calculated Window of Demographic Opportunity[20]

Select Asian Countries	UN-Calculated Demographic Window	Years Remaining as of 2016
China	1990–2025	9
Korea	1985–2030	14
Japan	1965–1995	0
India	2010–2050	34
Indonesia	2005–2040	24
Singapore	1980–2015	0
Vietnam	2005–2040	24

industry. Policymakers recognize the scale of this challenge, and that understanding forms the basis for Prime Minister Narendra Modi's "Make in India" campaign, which encourages manufacturers to relocate to India. Improved infrastructure, better regulation, and reformed labor laws would do much to attract those businesses, but unless India's own people are healthy and educated, India's window of opportunity may close before the country fulfills its potential.

Clearly, then, whether a state's population structure is a boon or a burden depends largely on what kinds of economic and social policies a government adopts within its window of opportunity. With the right policies, a prudent state can reap the demographic dividend; with the wrong ones, it will squander it. With that in mind we turn to focus on key metrics of social policy that measure the degree to which a state is investing in its people, such as poverty alleviation, public health, and education.

Poverty, Health, and Education

Over the last several decades, poverty in Asia has fallen dramatically, so much so that global progress on poverty reduction has largely been an Asian story. As the United Nations concedes, success on the UN Millennium Development Goals, which (among other things) challenged the international community to halve the worldwide proportion of people living on less than $1.25 daily, was "largely the result of extraordinary success in Asia, mostly East Asia."[21] Within the last two decades, absolute poverty has plummeted. Between 1990 and 2010, the proportion of poor dropped from 60 percent to 12 percent in China, 45 percent to 14 percent in Southeast Asia, and 48 percent to 22 percent in India—lifting approximately six hundred million people from absolute poverty in just twenty years.[22] For many international organizations and countries, the next goal is to eliminate absolute poverty by 2030 throughout much of Asia. If the first chapter of global poverty reduction was written in China, then the second will be written in India, where roughly one-third of all the world's poor reside.[23]

Liberating hundreds of millions from absolute poverty is no small feat, but it may be too soon to trumpet success. A poverty level of $1.25 a day, the level used by the World Bank, is seen by many as too low a figure to adequately represent poverty. The Asian Development Bank, for example,

Poverty in the Developing World

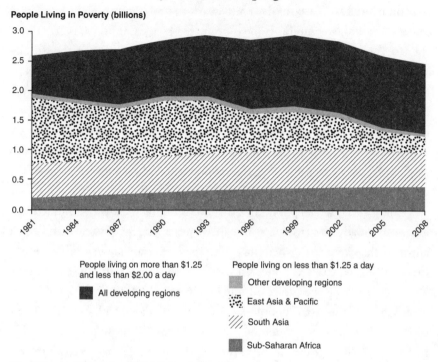

World Bank, *2013 Atlas of Global Development.*

believes that the level should be increased to $1.51, which would reclassify 50 percent of Asia as living in poverty.[24] And even a level of $2 is not necessarily appropriate, especially for city-dwellers who face steep rent and transportation expenses. When two upper-class Indians and recent MIT graduates together attempted to subsist on India's average wage of one hundred rupees a day, around $2 in 2011, they lost several pounds, complained of frequent dizziness, and suffered depression from a lack of food.[25] While extreme destitution is declining in much of Asia, there is still a long road to moderate prosperity.

Asia has also made tremendous strides in improving public health, with East Asia leading the way, Southeast Asia close behind, and South Asia facing continuing challenges. Between 1970 and 2012, deaths per 1,000 children under five years old plummeted from 111 to 14 in China, 161 to 31 in Indonesia, and 211 to 56 in India.[26] This is dramatic progress, but these Asian rates still tower over the Organization for Economic Cooperation and Development (OECD) average of five child deaths. Similarly, although the average maternal mortality ratio in Asia has decreased by a stunning 50 percent over the last two decades, it is still more than ten times higher than the OECD average—which is particularly depressing because maternal deaths are almost entirely preventable with good health care. One particularly bright spot is life expectancy, which due to improved nutrition, water quality, sanitation, and health care has risen in Asia from an average of fifty-seven years to roughly seventy-two years over the last four decades. Despite Asia's significant health challenges, its average life expectancy now sits only eight years shy of the OECD average—and the gap is narrowing.[27]

These successes in public health have brought their own unique challenges, as elderly citizens confront cancer, heart disease, diabetes, and other ailments that were rarer when life expectancy was much lower. For example, cancer rates in Asia are projected to reach 163 out of 100,000 people by 2030—overtaking the projected rate of 156 per 100,000 in the Americas.[28] Nearly half of the Asian population smokes, compared to less than 20 percent of the American population, and the incidence of lung cancer is skyrocketing.[29] Health-care expenditures will rise as these states struggle to deal with increases in expensive noncommunicable diseases.

Finally, Asian states have made considerable progress in education, which is critical to reducing poverty and kindling growth. Today more than 90 percent of school-age children in Asia are enrolled in primary or secondary school, most of the gains having been made in South Asia, which had only 75 percent of its children enrolled two decades ago.[30] Youth literacy is nearly universal in East Asia and Southeast Asia, though South Asia lags behind.[31]

Aside from basic education, higher education has grown rapidly in Asia due to government support, increasing privatization, and robust demand. The percentage of the college-age population enrolled in bachelor's programs has increased dramatically over the last twenty-five years, from 7 percent to nearly 70 percent in South Korea, 1 percent to 18 percent in Malaysia, and 5 percent to 37 percent in Thailand.[32] Today China and India have more than 10 percent of their college-age populations pursuing bachelor's degrees, and seven million Chinese and a similar number of Indians will graduate from college this year alone. A large college-educated population is an advantage, but the number of college graduates has outstripped the jobs available, with unemployment rates among recent college graduates in the double digits.[33] Many Asian universities suffer from a variety of challenges and fail to prepare these graduates for the workforce, but several are world class, including India's famous Indian Institutes of Technology and China's Peking, Tsinghua, and Fudan Universities.[34] Asia's growing human capital will be crucial if it is to solve the incredible challenges facing its swelling population, such as breakneck urbanization, poor sanitation, and hazardous air.

Urbanization, Sanitation, and Pollution

Asia has the world's largest urban population, yet it is far from the world's most urbanized region. Fewer than 200 million Asians lived in cities in 1960, but today the total is closer to 1.5 billion, an urban multitude surpassing that of any other region in the world.[35] Despite Asia's staggeringly large urban population, a majority of Asians nevertheless still live in rural areas. The percentage of the population living in the countryside is nearly 40 percent in East Asia, 50 percent in Southeast Asia, and 70 percent in South Asia, compared to roughly 20 percent in the United States and Western Europe.[36] Despite Asia's tremendous economic growth, its urban revolution has only just begun.

China is the paradigmatic case of Asian urbanization because of the size and speed of its vast transformation, and comparing it with the United States can be instructive. In 2012 just over half of China's population lived in cities—a level comparable to the United States circa 1920. The United States was home to just over one hundred million people then, with fifty million or so living in its cities during the Roaring Twenties. Today a population fourteen times that size lives in China's cities, and if China's urbanization rates hypothetically approach those of the West, China alone will boast an urban population of well over one billion. Asia's urbanization rate may be somewhat low, but that percentage reflects pure potential.

And yet Asia's cities are already gargantuan. The urban sprawl around China's capital, Beijing, is so great that talks are under way for integrating it with surrounding cities to create one massive conurbation of more than one hundred million people.[37] Shanghai, one of the world's largest cities with over twenty-four million inhabitants, has more than four thousand modern skyscrapers—twice as many as New York City—but had no such buildings as recently as 1980.[38] China's Pearl River Delta, the engine of its export economy, is home to nine major cities with a combined population of nearly sixty million, all within commuting distance of each other. This is as if New York, Los Angeles, Chicago, Houston, and Philadelphia all doubled in size and moved into an area roughly the size of Maryland. Asia is already home to fifteen megacities—that is, cities home to more than ten million people—including often-overlooked cities such as Dhaka, Jakarta, Karachi, and Manila.[39] Outside of these megacities, so-called middleweight cities with populations between 150,000 and 10 million are sprouting virtually overnight from the countryside. These cities, the Toledos and Milwaukees of Asia, are largely unknown to the world but will nonetheless contribute five times more to global growth over the next decade than megacities, according to the McKinsey Global Institute.[40] Few have heard of Foshan in China or Surat in India, but cities like them will likely determine the future of global growth.

While it will take decades for these middleweight cities to enter the global top tier, many Asian cities are already considered world class, rivaling New York, London, and Paris. The Institute for Urban Strategies publishes an influential Global Power City Index that ranks cities based on economy, research, cultural interaction, livability, environment, and accessibility. Today seven of the top fifteen cities are found in the Asia-Pacific: Tokyo, Singapore, Seoul, Hong Kong, Sydney, Beijing, and Shanghai.[41] Eventually other Asian cities will join them. A.T. Kearney's Emerging Cities Outlook, which measures a city's *future* potential to join the world's top tier, puts ten Asian cities in the top twenty.[42] The rise of these Asian cities, however, will not be entirely glamorous or graceful. For example, while cosmopolitan Mumbai is one of the world's largest and fastest-growing cities—home to Bollywood glitz, a booming financial industry, and twenty million people—almost half its population lives in slums. While Asia's leading cities may rank alongside those of the West, many of the region's rising cities face sharp growing pains that will affect the lives of millions of residents and the region's overall trajectory.

As tens of millions flood into Asia's teeming cities each year, government officials around the region grapple with basic but vital tasks, such as ensuring adequate sanitation and the appropriate disposal of human waste. Water contaminated by sewage threatens public health, exposing children to a "bacterial brew" that can cause sickness, malnutrition, and developmental setbacks even if they are well fed.[43] These challenges are acute in the region's slums, which lack running water and toilet facilities but are home to five hundred million Asians, or 30 percent of all the region's urban dwellers. At first glance these figures appear daunting; nevertheless, they are far from hopeless. Over the last two decades, the percentage of the urban population living in slums has fallen almost 40 percent throughout Asia, even as the urban population has skyrocketed, which proves that important progress is being made.[44] That progress is reflected in sanitation statistics, which show that the proportion of city dwellers with access to quality sanitation facilities grew from nearly 60 percent to almost 80 percent between 1990 and 2010.[45]

Still, sanitation remains a significant problem in many of the region's rural areas, especially in India, where nearly 75 percent of the rural populace defecates outdoors.[46] Most rural Indians lack access to toilets, so with Prime Minister Modi announcing that building toilets is even more important than building temples, the government put millions in villages that had never before had them, at a rate of one every second. Even as access to lavatories improves dramatically, old habits and cultural taboos against indoor defecation remain hard to change. Exemplifying this recalcitrance, one local villager dismissed the new toilet provided to her village: "Locking us inside these booths with our own filth? I will never see how that is clean. Going out there is normal."[47] Villagers are generally unaware that poor sanitation leads to digestive infection and malnourishment that can stunt child development, especially given India's high population density. Studies show that child mortality in villages where open defecation is common is much higher than in those where it is rare.[48] That this remains true nearly a century after the country's founding father, Mahatma Gandhi, declared that sanitation was more important than independence highlights the scale of the challenge facing India's leaders. And yet, by elevating the issue to the national stage for the first time since Gandhi, they are nonetheless making progress.

East Asia Now Has the Largest Number of People Living in Cities

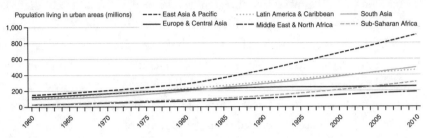

UN World Urbanization Prospects

Progress on Asian air pollution, however, remains another matter. Chinese air pollution is already the country's fourth-greatest risk factor for premature death and contributes to 1.2 million premature deaths annually.[49] The government has in the past attempted to hide from its poor environmental record, refusing, for instance, to release data on smaller particulate matter concentration in the air (PM 2.5), favoring instead the PM 10 readings that measure larger particulate matter but are less precise. It was not until the US embassy in Beijing began monitoring PM 2.5 levels in 2008 that the true extent of China's abysmal air quality became clear. Publishing daily on its dedicated Twitter feed, @BeijingAir, the service made headlines in 2010 when, on a scale that typically goes from 1 to 500, the pollution reading reached an astonishing 562, a figure literally off the charts. Humbled by the global publicity the story received, China has since increased transparency in its air monitoring data, including by publishing official PM 2.5 readings in 2012, and has undertaken a wide range of strategies to improve air quality. Nevertheless, pollution remains a chronic problem, with PM 2.5 ratings reaching a noxious 755 in January of 2013.[50]

While China has received the lion's share of global attention for its poor air quality, the world's worst air is actually in neighboring India. A World Health Organization (WHO) study of air pollution in 1,600 cities found New Delhi's air to be twice as hazardous as Beijing's, and that thirteen of the world's twenty most polluted cities are in India.[51] Hundreds of other Asian cities have air pollution levels at several times the WHO's acceptable limit.

Asia's cities face considerable challenges, but their present is not unlike the past of America or Europe. New York and London were themselves home to vast slum populations less than one hundred years ago, but development and prudent investments in infrastructure, transportation, and housing together created the glittering metropolises we see today. Western cities also suffered from crippling levels of air and water pollution, but careful regulation and improved technology produced the clean air and water we enjoy now. Asia's economic growth undoubtedly gives rise to challenges, but it also endows the region's governments with the resources to meet them. We consider the speed and scale of that economic growth in the next section.

Economy

The United States has been the world's largest economy since 1872, but its reign is coming to a close. According to the International Monetary Fund (IMF), China's economy surpassed the American economy in 2014, at least according to measures adjusting GDP for relative cost of living, known as purchasing power parity (PPP).[52] The measures were devised by the International Comparison Program carried out under the auspices of the World Bank. China was uncomfortable with the political challenges that come with being the world's largest economy; and unadjusted, nominal GDP figures show that the United States has a larger economy than China by $6 trillion and will continue to retain its paramount position until the mid-2020s.[53] Those involved with the World Bank project note that Beijing waged a rearguard effort for at least a year to undermine the methodology and data on which the work was based. For all the Chinese efforts, only a single line was inserted into the report to address its concerns: "The National Bureau of Statistics of China has expressed reservations about some aspects of the methodology."[54] China's reservations, however, were serious enough to block all coverage of the country's ascendance to the summit of the global economy within its domestic media. And while China is right to note that purchasing power parity adjustments are hardly an exact science, and that by many measures China is *not* the world's largest economy, all of Beijing's backroom maneuvering and domestic censorship cannot hide the obvious fact that economic power is moving inexorably toward Asia.

When pundits write that that the world's economic center of gravity is shifting eastward, they are almost always speaking metaphorically. The McKinsey Global Institute, however, sought to investigate whether the claim was literally true. Its economists attempted to find exactly *where* the world's economic center of gravity actually lies by weighting the center of each country's landmass by its GDP. Based on their calculations, the world's center of gravity is already in Asia, where they show it has been for twenty of the last twenty-one centuries. Today it is moving eastward at pace of roughly 140 kilometers a year, or faster than ever before in human history.[55]

Evolution of the Earth's Economic Center of Gravity, 1 to 2025 CE

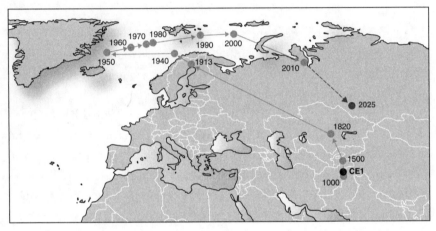

McKinsey

Even the conservative, nominal GDP figures that deny Chinese preeminence nevertheless reveal the precariousness of America's position as the world's leading economy. The chart below makes clear that Asian, and particularly Chinese, ascendance is likely even using numbers more charitable to the West. If the US economy continues to grow at 2 percent, then unless China's growth dips to a dismal 4 percent, it will likely overtake the United States in nominal terms by 2030.[56] Another striking trend is India's and Indonesia's ascendance on these global rankings. By 2030 they become the world's third and ninth largest economies in nominal terms respectively, having failed to appear on the list at all in 2010.

Ten Largest Economies by Decade

	1990	USD (tn)*	2000	USD (tn)	2010	USD (tn)
1	US	5.9	US	10.3	US	15.0
2	Japan	3.1	Japan	4.7	China	5.9
3	Germany	1.7	Germany	1.9	Japan	5.5
4	France	1.2	UK	1.5	Germany	3.3
5	Italy	1.1	France	1.3	France	2.5
6	UK	1.0	China	1.2	UK	2.3
7	Canada	0.6	Italy	1.1	Italy	2.0
8	Spain	0.5	Canada	0.7	Brazil	2.1
9	Brazil	0.5	Brazil	0.6	Canada	1.6
10	China	0.4	Mexico	0.6	Russia	1.5

	2020	USD (tn)	2030	USD (tn)
1	US	23.5	China	53.8
2	China	21.9	US	38.5
3	Japan	6.1	India	15.0
4	Germany	5.1	Japan	9.3
5	India	4.5	Germany	7.4
6	Brazil	3.9	Brazil	6.3
7	France	3.9	UK	5.8
8	UK	3.7	France	5.7
9	Italy	2.7	Indonesia	4.7
10	Russia	2.6	Russia	4.6

*Trillions of US dollars

Source: Standard Chartered Research

If we return to purchasing power, these figures appear much less surprising. China became the world's largest economy in 2014, India became the world's third-largest in 2008, and Indonesia broke into the top ten in 2011. The IMF estimates that by 2020 they will be the world's first, third, and sixth largest economies respectively, with a combined GDP twice the size of America's.

Top Ten Countries by GDP (PPP) in Billions of USD, 1980–2020

	1980		2020 (estimated)	
1	US	2,862.48	China	28,229.14
2	Japan	996.736	US	22,488.62
3	Germany	866.544	India	12,708.36
4	Italy	594.926	Japan	5,521.73
5	France	578.363	Germany	4,500.57
6	Brazil	572.139	Indonesia	4,155.46
7	UK	490.517	Brazil	3,977.90
8	Mexico	389.33	Russia	3,975.74
9	India	386.157	UK	3,240.20
10	China	298.397	France	3,159.79

Source: IMF World Economic Outlook, 2015

Because of their size, China, India, and Indonesia often receive more attention than Asia's other rapidly growing economies, but the region's smaller states are likewise growing at enviable rates. In 2014 Mongolia grew at 9.1 percent, Burma at 8.5 percent, Laos at 7.4 percent, Cambodia at 7.2 percent, Sri Lanka at 7.0 percent, the Philippines at 6.2 percent, Bangladesh at 6.2 percent, and Malaysia at 6 percent.[57] These are remarkable numbers compared to the anemic American rate of 2.4 percent and Europe's turgid 1.4 percent.

This breakneck growth has led to the creation of a large and increasingly influential middle class, which stood at 525 million in 2009 and is expected to jump to 1.75 billion by 2020, at a time when the North American middle class continues to shrink. In just six years, the North American share of the global middle class will fall to just 10 percent, while the Asia-Pacific share will account for almost 55 percent, and a staggering two-thirds by 2030.[58] Even if Asia's growth begins to slow, the concentration of so many of the world's consumers in Asia will reshape dozens of industries as businesses around the world compete to export to the world's largest middle class. Already one-third of the world's middle class is located in Asia.

Many macroeconomic factors undergird the growth of Asia's middle class. As discussed previously, Asia is benefiting from a demographic dividend with a large working population and relatively few dependents. At the same time, it boasts an unemployment rate of 4.6 percent, lower than that of any other region.[59] Investment is at record levels as Asian nations direct billions annually into sophisticated and vital infrastructure projects. Chinese domestic and foreign investment continues to fuel industrialization throughout the region, which in turn creates new markets for global products. Gross capital investment in the developing nations of East Asia and the Pacific has also far surpassed that of all other developing regions—rising from roughly $500 billion in 1995 to nearly $1.8 trillion in 2010.[60]

Investment Growth in the East Asia and Pacific Region

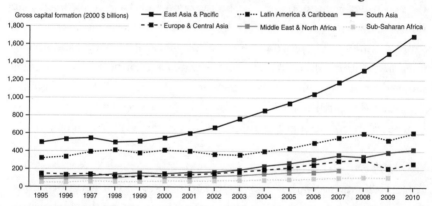

Note: For the Middle East and North Africa, last year of data available is 2007; for Sub-Saharan Africa, it is 2009.

World Bank, *2013 Atlas of Global Development.*

The World Bank and the International Finance Corporation jointly publish an annual report on the ease of doing business worldwide. Asia has several representatives in the top thirty, including Singapore, New Zealand, Hong Kong, South Korea, Australia, Malaysia, Taiwan, Thailand, Mauritius, and Japan.[61] These countries are of course the exception. Twenty-one other Asian states place in the bottom half of the list, including China, India, and Indonesia.

One reason many Asian states have been unable to ascend is corruption. When a country is corrupt, cronyism runs rampant, bribes are commonplace, business confidence is reduced, outsiders are reluctant to invest, and small businesses often face prohibitive start-up costs. The nongovernmental organization (NGO) Transparency International found that 64 percent of the Asia-Pacific region scored below 50 (out of 100) on its annual Corruption Perceptions Index, which measures how corrupt the public believes the government sector to be.[62] While the region includes high-scoring nations such as New Zealand and Singapore, many score abysmally, including Burma, Cambodia, and almost all of South Asia. A low score on the Corruption Perceptions Index indicates a significant drag on economic growth.

The question of how to root out corruption is a complicated one, especially since social factors may play a central role. Francis Fukuyama, for example, suggests that low levels of interpersonal trust and social capital tend to increase the prevalence of corruption.[63] Within the politics of Asian countries, corruption is an ever-more-salient issue. In India, anticorruption campaigns have galvanized millions of Indian protesters and become central to local and national elections. Within China, President Xi Jinping's anticorruption campaign has targeted previously untouchable members of the ruling Politburo Standing Committee, though it remains unclear whether the campaign is motivated by a desire to truly root out corruption or to weaken Xi's political opponents.

Infrastructure

Asia's economic ascent has been swift and marked, but if it is to continue, Asian governments will need to overcome a significant potential bottleneck: infrastructure. In 2009 the Asian Development Bank published a shocking and widely cited report that found Asian countries needed a collective $8 trillion of infrastructure investment within the next ten years alone to sustain fast-paced growth. The region's surging population, rapid urbanization, and breakneck industrialization were creating significant domestic demands for infrastructure spending. At the same time, the report argued that Asia's complex intraregional supply chains were only as strong as their weakest link, and needed greater regional investment in connectivity and transportation if they were to continue serving as the foundation for regional growth. Several Asian states have invested heavily in infrastructure, giving rise to a narrative that the region is home to glittering skyscrapers, luxurious airports, and daring architecture. While there is much truth to that narrative, Asia is a complex region, with some of its states erecting modern marvels and others grappling with infrastructure projects mired in red tape.

East Asia, and China in particular, is the home of Asia's most ambitious and astounding infrastructure projects. China aspires to be the land of infrastructure superlatives. It is building or has finished the world's largest airport (Beijing), largest wind farm (Gansu), largest dam (Hubei), largest port (Shanghai), largest building by area (Sichuan), largest theme park (Shanghai), largest museum (Beijing), largest mall (Guangdong), longest bridge (Qingdao), longest gas pipeline (Shanghai to Xinjiang), longest subway system (Shanghai), and highest bridge (Hubei).[64]

Much of China's infrastructure investment has been plowed into transportation projects. In less than two decades, China built the world's largest high-speed rail system, with trains hurtling forward at two hundred miles per hour on ten thousand miles of track, integrating most of the country's largest cities and twenty-eight of its provinces. If Amtrak traveled at Chinese speeds, travel time between Boston and Washington, D.C., would be cut from eight hours to just two. China seems unconcerned that its high-speed trains already carry twice as many passengers as its airlines and cut into airline profits, since it is proceeding with plans to construct eighty airports and expand over one hundred in five years.[65] In the last fifteen years alone, China expanded its limited-access expressway system from seven thousand miles to seventy thousand miles—it is now roughly 50 percent larger than America's.[66] Home to dozens of cities with over one million residents, China has decided to build or expand more than forty different subway systems in five years.[67] All of this is impressive, but it overlooks the hundreds of ghost cities, empty office parks, and silent stadiums that have failed to attract residents, businesspeople, and spectators. China's infrastructure investments have come at considerable expense, with half a trillion on high-speed rail alone, raising concerns that its projects will fail to pay for themselves, ultimately destabilizing the country's financial system and stunting China's growth.

While China is the clearest case of Asia's massive—and at times excessive—infrastructure investment, other Asian states have likewise invested in infrastructure that outclasses its Western equivalents. China, Japan, South Korea, and Taiwan all have advanced high-speed rail networks, which the US currently lacks. Singapore has been ranked by Mercer

Consulting as having the world's best infrastructure of any city, and the new Terminal 4 of Singapore's Changi Airport is a futuristic marvel with biometric checking, digital boarding, and virtual concierges.[68] Even Malaysia, not yet as developed as South Korea or Taiwan, is ranked twenty-fifth in the world for infrastructure—above Italy, Ireland, and Norway—due to decades of consistent and prudent investment.[69] In many cases Asia's emerging infrastructure is quite beautiful. The Helix Bridge and Henderson Waves bridge in Singapore, the Langkawi Sky Bridge in Malaysia, the Yongle Bridge in China, and the recently redesigned Banpo Bridge in South Korea are all stunning masterpieces of modern construction and art. If you can, I recommend putting the book down for a moment and searching for these bridges online to appreciate their sheer beauty. They are modern wonders of the world and signs of Asia's growing and sophisticated infrastructure investments.

Of course, while some Asian states have been quite successful in improving their infrastructure, much of the region is still in dire need of greater infrastructure spending. A comparison between China's infrastructure development and India's can be illuminating. For example, while India has a total of roughly 1,500 kilometers of limited-access expressway, China built nearly ten times that length in just *one year.*[70] In the last four years alone, China has laid more track for its railways than India has since its independence nearly seventy years ago.[71] Even if India can improve its transportation infrastructure, it still faces challenges on other fronts, such as housing, which will require India to build thirty-five thousand new homes *every day* for the next eight years in order to keep up with demand.[72] And India is hardly alone in facing these challenges. Most Asian states sit at the bottom of the World Economic Forum's infrastructure rankings, such as Vietnam (81), India (87), Cambodia (107), and Burma (137). Many of these states are wisely choosing to invest vast sums in infrastructure development. Indonesia boosted its infrastructure budget by 53 percent in one year, and India plans to spend $1 trillion on infrastructure over the next five years.[73]

Of course challenges abound because funds remain tight, land acquisition is often fraught, and implementation is generally undermined by corruption. Progress, however, is nevertheless being made. Road density is currently increasing annually at 5.8 percent in Asia compared to the worldwide average of 3.5 percent.[74] South Asian countries on average doubled their road networks between 1990 and 2008, though half of India's roads remain unpaved. China and India are beginning to focus heavily on commercial rail, with haulages that increased by 42 percent and 35 percent respectively from 2006 to 2011.[75] Meanwhile countries throughout the region are investing in port projects—often with Chinese commercial assistance—as container port traffic has surged faster than the global average.[76] Asia's infrastructure challenges are no doubt significant, but they are also considerable opportunities for increasing Asia's growth rate. In India's case, one widely cited estimate suggests that improving India's infrastructure would by itself increase the country's economic expansion by 1 to 2 percentage points annually.

Asian states are also making tremendous strides with respect to digital infrastructure. The United States may be the birthplace of the Internet, but Asia is its future. Asia's Internet population is already the world's largest, exceeding the combined Internet populations of Europe and the Americas. With more than six hundred million Internet users, China has an Internet population that is more than twice as large as America's, and India and Indonesia together have an Internet population larger than that of the UK, France, Germany, Spain, and Portugal *combined*. And yet Asia's Internet penetration rate is abysmally low, suggesting that the digital era is only now arriving within the region. Only about 37 percent of Asians use the Internet, in contrast to nearly 77 percent of Europeans.[77] Two of Asia's most populous countries, India and Indonesia, have penetration rates of a mere 15 percent. With the explosion in cellular devices and smartphones in the last twenty-five years, these penetration rates will grow dramatically in the near future. Asia is already home to more than half of the world's cellular subscriptions, and a growing percentage of its four billion cellular phones are Internet-enabled.[78] Although many of these phones are *not* smartphones, which occupy the higher end of Internet-enabled cell phones, smartphone usage in Asia is also exploding—with some estimating that there are roughly seven hundred million smartphones in the region today.[79] As more and more Asians access the Internet, through either their computers or their mobile phones, the distribution of the world's Internet users will begin to reflect the distribution of the world's population, perhaps irrevocably and profoundly altering the Internet.

Importantly, as Asia's Internet population surges, its digital infrastructure is able to keep up and, in an increasing number of cases, outclass the West's. South Korea, Japan, and Hong Kong have the world's three fastest

connection speeds, while the United States fails to break into the top ten.[80]
The United States may have invented the smartphone, but Asia's mobile networks are far faster than America's, with half of Australians and Chinese and
75 percent of Japanese and South Koreans receiving speeds of more than four
mbps, compared to less than 40 percent of Americans. While the West takes
steps to fully adopt 4G connectivity, countries like South Korea are already
experimenting with efforts to deploy 5G networks by 2017—purported to
deliver speeds a thousand times faster than those of the most sophisticated
networks available today.[81]

Of course not all investments in Internet infrastructure are designed
to enhance connectivity and access. China, for example, has spent tens
of billions to censor foreign websites, monitor traffic, and hire Internet
commentators—members of the *wumao dang* (fifty-cent party), as they
are pejoratively known—who receive fifty cents for each message they post
that is favorable to the ruling party and for each message they delete that
is deemed critical of it. Whether Asia's Internet users are able to access the
global Internet or will be cloistered away behind an insular domestic one will
be a crucial question not only for the region's political evolution, but also for
its economic growth and innovative potential.

Energy

Just as infrastructure expansion remains one potential bottleneck for Asian
growth, so too does energy. Asia's swift rise simply cannot be sustained unless
the region is able to secure vast and growing amounts of energy. Today Asia
consumes barely one-third of the world's energy, but within only twenty
years, it will consume well above half.[82] Asia's sharp upsurge in energy
demand is the inescapable result of increased standards of living and a growing convergence between Asian and Western per capita energy consumption.
Today the average Asian consumes only one-sixth as much energy as the
average American.[83] Despite this relatively low rate of per capita consumption, China alone uses more energy than the United States and more than six
times as much as the entire African continent.[84] As Asia's energy needs swell,
the future of the global energy market will be determined increasingly by the
habits of the region's consumers, the requirements of its businesses, and the
policies of its governments.

Asia is almost certainly unable to meet its rising energy requirements on its own and will need to rely heavily on imports, especially for oil, which is primarily used to power Asia's booming fleet of motor vehicles rather than to generate power. Today the region imports eleven million barrels of oil a day, a number that will almost triple to thirty-one million by 2035.[85] This is an appetite so staggeringly large that the entirety of the Middle East's oil exports will not be enough to satisfy it, with the International Energy Agency (IEA) projecting that even far-off regions like Latin America will increasingly supply more than half of their oil to Asia, the inevitable center of gravity for the world's oil trade.[86] Because Asian countries scarcely produce their own oil, and since their refineries are designed primarily to deal with the light crude exported by Middle Eastern states, the region's economies are highly vulnerable to oil shocks. The twin forces of rising energy insecurity and the shifting geography of the global oil trade are already pushing Asian states to invest heavily in blue-water navies, which they hope to use to protect oil shipments far from home. Conflict over oil shipment in the distant waters of the South China Sea, Straits of Malacca, Indian Ocean, or Strait of Hormuz is far from inconceivable to the region's military leaders. And as other regions of the world become more crucial to Asia's energy security, strategic transport routes through Russia, the Caspian Sea, and the Americas will also become increasingly crucial, altering the world's strategic geography.

While Asia suffers from a dearth of oil for its vehicles, it has an abundance of cheap coal for its plants that could provide several decades of power generation. Coal is obviously polluting, in terms of both particulates and carbon content, but with one in five Asians—or roughly 620 million people—still without power, many Asian states find they have little choice but to turn to one of the world's cheapest energy sources.[87] According to IEA projections, even if Asia dramatically expands the role of renewables in its energy mix, its will continue to burn more and more coal every year to generate power. To understand just how addicted Asia is to coal, consider the fact that China, India, and Indonesia derive 76 percent, 72 percent, and 45 percent of their power respectively from coal, and that the IEA expects these ratios to remain or rise above 50 percent for the next twenty-five years even under the most optimistic forecasts for renewable and nuclear energy.[88] Today China alone uses as much coal as the rest of the world combined, India uses more than the European Union, and the countries have plans to build 363 and 455 new coal plants respectively.[89] Even as coal's share of power generation will fall in China and India, it will actually rise sharply in Southeast Asia as the region builds hundreds of new plants. These plants will obviously produce gigantic amounts of carbon dioxide, dramatically worsening global warming, and more than offsetting reductions in the developed world.

Asian states are aware of the dangers of focusing solely on nonrenewable forms of energy and are investing aggressively in renewable energy sources such as wind, solar, and hydropower. Already Asia generates more power from renewables than any other region in the world, with China alone generating more than twice as much as the United States after six years as the world's top investor in renewables.[90] And yet, despite these landmark achievements, considerably more investment is to follow. The IEA estimates that, over the next twenty-five years, renewables will account for 40 percent of new Indian generation, 60 percent of new Chinese generation, and more than 66 percent of all new Japanese power generation.[91]

Although China is the world leader in renewables, other large Asian states are no longer content to be left behind. The meltdown at the Fukushima Daiichi Nuclear Power Plant in 2011 pushed Japan's leadership to shift away from a substantial reliance on nuclear energy toward renewables, especially wind and solar. Japan may soon be the world's largest market for solar panels and is already the world's second-largest generator of solar power, with plans to generate one hundred gigawatts of power a year from solar energy by 2030—the equivalent production of thirty-nine nuclear plants.[92] With little land available, Japan has innovatively turned to floating large and beautiful solar arrays on the surfaces of several of its reservoirs to generate power.[93] As impressive as Japan's achievements are, India generates even more power from renewables than does Japan. Although much of India's renewable energy comes from hydropower, the country is investing in wind and solar. Currently two of the world's three largest wind farms are in India, which is also home to the world's largest solar photovoltaic (PV) power plant.[94] Asia's largest economies are not the only ones committed to a greener future. Southeast Asia has emerged as a surprising leader in the field, with 20 percent of the region's power derived from renewable sources.[95] Burma is among the countries going all in on solar power. It already derives most of its electricity from hydropower and expects to have online two 150-megawatt solar energy plants that will provide up to 12 percent of its total power generation by 2016.[96] Meanwhile, Bangchak Petroleum of Thailand is one of the world's largest biofuel manufacturers and the Philippines is the world's second-largest generator of geothermal energy. Nuclear energy is also surging, particularly in China and India, while natural gas is an increasingly important part of the energy mix throughout the region. Already Asia is home to eight of the ten largest natural gas plants and five of the ten largest nuclear plants. Together these investments signal progress in the battle against climate change.

Despite Asia's impressive efforts in diversifying its energy mix to renewables, nuclear energy, and natural gas, for the next several decades, the region will nevertheless derive the majority of its energy from coal, according to estimates by the IEA.[97] It is perhaps a uniquely Asian irony that the continent is likely to be the greatest source of new greenhouse gas emissions while also leading the world in renewable energy. With that we turn to Asia's contribution and vulnerability to climate change, and the natural disasters the planet's rising temperature may bring in its wake.

Climate Change and Natural Disasters

After decades of growth, Asia now contributes more to greenhouse gases than any other region in the world. The Asia-Pacific alone accounted for 50 percent of the world's total carbon dioxide emissions in 2009, up from 38 percent in 1990.[98] China itself emitted 6.8 billion tons of carbon dioxide that year, 1.1 billion tons more than all of North America. On a per capita basis, however, the North American emission rate was three times that of China, a gap that is likely to close as urbanization continues in Asia and brings increased levels of pollution.[99] The West has made strides in reducing emissions, with new fuel standards for passenger and heavy-duty vehicles that will almost certainly lower American oil consumption in absolute terms. Even then, every barrel of oil eliminated from Western consumption will be replaced by two additional barrels of Asian consumption.[100] In the war against climate change, Asia is quite simply the most important battlefield.

The Asia-Pacific is particularly vulnerable to climate-related catastrophes. Researchers from the Intergovernmental Panel on Climate Change (IPCC) have noted that millions will suffer the effects of coastal flooding due to global warming, especially in crowded cities. Sea levels could rise by three feet by the end of the century, effectively submerging Kiribati, Fiji, the Maldives, Tuvalu, and other island states.[101] Continental Asia will not be spared either, and low-lying countries like Bangladesh, where nearly a quarter

of the land lies within seven feet of sea level, may be devastated.[102] Conservative estimates predict that tens of millions of the world's most impoverished
and vulnerable people are likely to be displaced by rising waters by as early as
2050.[103] IPCC researchers note that although much of this damage and disruption will be global, the "majority of it will be in east, south-east and south
Asia."[104] Aside from coastal flooding, climate change will also cause deadly
heat waves and increase the spread of disease. Finally, although the IPCC has
said very little that is definitive about the impact of climate change on Asia's
monsoons or its Himalayan water flows, the possibility that these could be
adversely affected is alarming because billions in China, India, and Southeast
Asia have depended on these systems for thousands of years.

The situation is serious but it is not bleak, especially because Asia can
take steps to mitigate the damage from climate change. The Asian Development Bank calculates that East Asia might need to spend only 0.3 percent of
GDP annually to protect infrastructure, coastal areas, and agriculture from
climate change.[105] Asian states, however, face far more than the risk of coastal
flooding, including the spread of infectious diseases, the shrinkage of lakes
and the loss of estuaries, large changes in migratory patterns for wildlife,
and a host of other serious issues. For that reason, investments in technology and policies to reduce greenhouse gas emissions will be as important as
infrastructure protection. For example, China hopes to increase forest cover
by forty million hectares and is piloting the type of national cap-and-trade
plan that failed in the United States Senate.[106] The city of Beijing has even
announced that it will ban coal use by 2020 despite the fact that coal currently provides roughly a quarter of the city's power.[107] Japan's government
is aggressively pushing policies to reduce the cost of imported solar panels,
while India's government seeks to harness the country's abundant sunlight
and powerful Indian Ocean winds through subsidies and accelerated depre-
ciation allowances for renewable investors.

Climate change and warming ocean waters will almost certainly increase
the cost and frequency of Asia's natural disasters, largely by strengthening
the devastating typhoons that batter the region every year and increasing the
coastal and river flooding that have afflicted the region for millennia. These
increased risk factors plague a region that is already considered by the United
Nations to be the world's most disaster prone, with much of its population
living in urban slums or coastal and river flood zones.[108] Asia has long suf-

fered disproportionately from disasters. From 1980 to 2009, the region had 61 percent of the world's population but 86 percent of the total population affected by natural disasters; meanwhile it generated 25 percent of world GDP but suffered 42 percent of worldwide economic losses due to disasters.[109] Today Asia is home to nine of the top ten countries in terms of casualties attributable to natural disasters, and its people are twenty-five times more likely to be affected by a natural disaster than are Americans or Europeans.[110] The loss of life in recent tragedies has been staggering. The 2004 tsunami claimed 230,000 lives and the 2008 earthquake in Sichuan, China, killed 87,000. The economic cost of these natural disasters, roughly $62 billion annually, is often borne by those who can least afford it, small farmers and poor urban households.[111] And with the region's economies increasingly interconnected, disasters like Japan's horrific meltdown at Fukushima, which cost the region up to $300 billion, can spiral outward and undermine those economies not directly affected.

Clearly, then, Asia's natural disasters are a shared problem that requires a shared solution, but the track record for regional cooperation so far is weak. When Typhoon Haiyan struck the Philippines in 2013, it killed six thousand people, displaced four million, and destroyed half a million homes.[112] The international community immediately mobilized to help. Japan and Australia each pledged $10 million in assistance, with Japan also sending a helicopter destroyer and smaller landing platform dock to assist in recovery efforts. The United States pledged $20 million and sent warships, including the USS *George Washington* aircraft carrier, with its five thousand sailors and eighty aircraft. The various offices of the Red Cross also sprang into action. However, an all-too-familiar sequence of events soon played out as other regional powers offered a less effective response. The navies of the ASEAN countries lacked the capacity to provide useful assistance. China, the world's second-largest economy, initially pledged just $100,000 in immediate assistance and an additional $100,000 through the Chinese Red Cross, its stinginess stemming from territorial disputes with the Philippines over the South China Sea.[113] Many states in the region still lack the necessary minimum capabilities to help themselves or each other following such tragedies, and many large economies are still reluctant to show the leadership and beneficence warranted by their economic size and success.

To make the world's most disaster-prone region safer, all of the region's countries will need to come together not only after tragedy strikes, but also in the years before. Better ecosystem management, land-use planning, supply chain management, and information sharing will be important steps in this direction. In addition, the region will need more coordination and cooperation among its military organizations, combined with prudent investments in joint humanitarian and disaster relief capabilities, in order to respond promptly to the next crisis. Together these efforts could save the lives and livelihoods of millions and remove one of the largest risks to Asia's prosperity and development.[114]

Sector Deep Dives

It is routine now to open a newspaper and read about some uniquely Asian development that will dramatically affect the world: record-breaking construction, stunning carbon dioxide emissions, or even the emergence of a new cultural practice. China's "Singles' Day" is an example of the latter—a recent tradition that, because of the scale on which it is observed, affects the entire global economy. It is held annually on November 11 (11/11 having been deemed the most appropriate date to celebrate singles because it resembles several "bare sticks," a Chinese term for singles), and the online retailer Alibaba reported 402 million unique visitors on that day in 2013—more than a third of China's adult population—and processed $5.75 billion in sales, more than two and a half times the proceeds of Cyber Monday in the United States.[115] Even though it only recently sprang into existence, China's Singles' Day is already able to dramatically affect the supply chains and marketing plans of major global retailers. This is related to both Asia's scale and the speed of its ascent, and these two factors likewise influence the evolution of dozens of other global economic sectors.

In this chapter we will analyze a range of diverse sectors, from shipping and defense spending to the art and film industries, in which Asia is increasingly emerging as the economic center. Each sector serves as a microcosm of the effects of the region's unprecedented growth on global industries and as a reflection of Asia's own transformation.

Shipping

While the international shipping industry receives little attention from the press and policy worlds, it is the foundation for the vast majority of global trade. At least 90 percent of the global goods trade is carried by the sea, from food to fuel to manufactured products.[116] Recent research suggests that the introduction of the standard shipping container, which allows efficient transportation from ships to cranes and onto trucks, revolutionized the global economy and increased trade more than every trade agreement signed in the last fifty years combined.[117] Since then, the shipping industry has continued to grow and today exists on a scale that strains comprehension. A modern shipping vessel is the length of three football fields, the height of a ten-story building, and able to unload enough cargo onto trucks to create a line of traffic sixty miles long.[118] If all the shipping containers of just one company, Maersk, were put end to end, the line would stretch halfway around the world.[119] Despite its immense scale, the shipping industry has been all but invisible in the press and policy worlds, and yet it is indispensable to the global economy.

Asian prosperity is truly the rising tide lifting all ships when it comes to trade and commerce on the world's waterways. Nearly half of all the world's cargo is loaded or unloaded in Asia, dramatically more than in any other region, and together it is worth trillions of dollars.[120] For example, US waterborne trade with Asia is worth roughly $775 billion and is twice as large as American trade with Europe.[121] Asian states have upgraded and expanded their infrastructure to facilitate the flow of commodities and manufactured goods through their ports. Nine of the top ten busiest ports in the world are located in Asia: seven in China, one in South Korea, and one in Singapore. Many of Asia's other countries also host some of the world's largest ports. Klang and Tanjung Pelepas in Malaysia are the thirteenth and twentieth largest in the world respectively, Keihin in Japan is ranked number eighteen, Tanjung Priok in Indonesia is ranked twenty-second, and Laem Chabang of Thailand is ranked twenty-third. Each of these, and three more Chinese ports, are bigger than the Port of New York and New Jersey, the twenty-seventh largest port in the world.[122] Asia's prosperity has certainly benefited the shipping industry, and the region's dominant position in maritime commerce means that the fortunes of a modern shipping company rise and fall largely with decisions made in Asia. For example, several shipping lines expanded over the last five years on the assumption that Chinese coal imports would continue to rise. But when Beijing chose to reduce coal imports as part of a broader plan to wean itself off the cheap and dirty fuel, the decision drove shipping prices to their lowest levels in twenty years.[123]

Despite China's about-face on coal imports, the fact remains that more commodities and manufactured goods are being shipped worldwide than ever before, and this has required the upgrading of existing fleets and the creation of new ones. So great has trade with Asia become that Maersk, the largest container ship operator in the world, contracted Daewoo Shipbuilding of South Korea to build twenty Triple E class transport ships for use on its Europe-Asia routes. At close to a quarter-mile long each, the Triple E vessels are the world's largest cargo ships ever, each able to transport enough sneakers for 111 million people, roughly the population of Mexico.[124] But even the gargantuan Triple E is dwarfed by the *Prelude* FLNG, built by Samsung Heavy Industries, also of South Korea. It is longer than the Willis Tower in Chicago (formerly the Sears Tower), and almost two football fields longer than the USS *Enterprise*, America's largest aircraft carrier. It is so vast that it displaces the same amount of water as the six largest aircraft carriers combined.[125] It is no accident these large and sophisticated vessels were built in East Asia. Today East Asia dominates the global shipbuilding business, with the combined market share of China, Japan, and South Korea exceeding 90 percent.[126]

Asian states are increasingly becoming maritime economies dependent on free and open sea-lanes for their own prosperity. Disruption to the flow of goods, whether by nation-states or pirates, would lead to major economic insecurity, and Asian states therefore view the stability and security of their maritime commerce as fundamentally intertwined with their national security. Combating piracy at sea also provides an opportunity for the world's navies to work together against common threats. In October 2012 the United States and China conducted their first joint counterpiracy exercise in the Gulf of Aden, and have repeated such cooperation numerous times since. Japan operates two warships in the Indian Ocean tasked specifically with providing antipiracy support, and India carries out similar operations.[127] Multilateral efforts include Combined Task Force 151, comprised of ships from Australia, Pakistan, South Korea, Turkey, the United Kingdom, and the United States. Ad hoc cooperation between states such as Indonesia, Malaysia, Singapore, and Thailand has also been successful in policing the

Straits of Malacca. As a result the region, which in 2004 accounted for 40 percent of worldwide piracy, registered just fifty incidents in 2006, and just a solitary attack in 2013.[128] Cooperation on nontraditional security threats such as piracy, natural disasters, and trafficking illustrates that militaries can work together and is a useful mechanism for training and enhancing interoperability during peacetime.

The magnitude and importance of shipping in and across the Asia-Pacific is one reason provocative actions in the South China Sea are so significant. By some measures of tonnage and value, these waters are the world's most important trade and energy transport artery. More than half the world's annual merchant fleet tonnage passes through the South China Sea, as does half of global liquefied natural gas (LNG) trade and one-third of global crude oil flows.[129] Attempts to circumscribe freedom of navigation and to extend maritime sovereignty claims beyond Law of the Sea interpretations have the potential to upset the operating system on which the region's prosperity depends. These contests for power and position in distant and obscure areas of the ocean may seem peripheral, but their outcome will shape every dimension of Asian life in the period ahead.

Defense Spending

Compared to the Middle East, we tend to think of Asia today as a region at peace. Under the surface, however, there lie bubbling tensions, national rivalries, and rising defense spending. Region-wide, Asia overtook Europe in defense spending in 2012, and is predicted to spend more than the United States beginning in 2021.[130] While many countries have cut their defense spending in recent years, reducing global defense spending by 1.9 percent, Asia as a whole saw an overall rise of 3.6 percent in 2013, which included a 5 percent increase in Southeast Asia and a 7.4 percent rise in China alone. Overall the region's expenditure has increased by 62 percent over the last decade.[131] While many countries are driven by security considerations, others see the acquisition of the newest military technology the same way they see the acquisition of the newest high-tech infrastructure—as a way of signaling that they are modern and advanced. But when more of a state's tools begin to look like hammers, more of its problems can begin to look like nails. Rising military investments, along with historic suspicions and contemporary territorial conflicts, can increase the likelihood of accidents, miscommunication, and miscalculation, with potentially catastrophic repercussions for the global economy and for American prosperity.

China's growing military spending in particular has caused consternation both within the region and in the West. Despite this spending's generally increasing in line with economic growth, China spends three times more on defense than India, and totals more than Japan, South Korea, Taiwan, and Vietnam combined.[132] This preponderance of defense spending, coupled with China's increasingly antagonistic actions in the East and South China Seas and on its border with India, has caused alarm. Assistant Secretary of State for East Asia and Pacific Affairs Daniel Russel recently referred to growing regional concerns when he spoke of Chinese efforts to assert control over the seas "despite the objections of its neighbors and despite the lack of any explanation or apparent basis under international law regarding the scope of the claim itself. China's lack of clarity with regard to its South China Sea claims," he concluded, "has created uncertainty, insecurity and instability in the region."[133] These concerns fuel increased military procurement by other regional actors. More military spending by all parties means the deployment of more ships, planes, and people—and potentially more costly misunderstandings and deadly mistakes.

Asia's continued growth in defense expenditure is therefore a real cause for concern, with China's swelling defense budget leading the way. China will account for 60 percent of the overall nominal defense spending increases across the region predicted between 2013 and 2017.[134] It is increasingly able to project power at longer distances, with stealthy nuclear submarines, advanced destroyers and frigates, replenishment vessels, and the recent commissioning of its first aircraft carrier, *Liaoning*, a rebuilt Soviet *Kuznetsov*-class carrier primarily used for training. While concern has been raised about Chinese military transparency, China was more than happy to show off *Liaoning* to Secretary of Defense Chuck Hagel on his visit to China in April 2014. Although the *Liaoning* is just a starter carrier with limited capabilities, China is in the process of building two brand-new carriers and has plans for two to four more.

China is not the only regional power focused on blue-water operations. Concerned in part by the Chinese navy's frequent forays into the Indian Ocean, including its antipiracy operations and high-profile port calls in

South Asia, India has been modernizing its own navy. Like China, India is also pursuing its own sea-based nuclear deterrent, which adds to the strategic complexities of the region's arms race. India is also developing next-generation stealth frigates and destroyers, designing its own nuclear submarine, deploying the world's fastest long-range antiship cruise missile, and expanding its carrier force from two to three. Other Asian states also have blue-water ambitions. Thailand has its own modest aircraft carrier, while Australia, Japan, and South Korea are investing in amphibious assault ships and helicopter destroyers. Vietnam, meanwhile, concluded a $2.9 billion deal with Moscow in 2009 to deliver six Kilo-class submarines, ideal for conducting area-denial operations in the South China Sea against Chinese naval deployments.[135]

Asian states are also modernizing their air forces, with many of the region's states developing or manufacturing some of the most advanced jet fighters in the world. China has developed a carrier-based aircraft—the Shenyang J-15—and become only the second country in the world, after the United States, to have two flight-tested fifth-generation fighter aircraft, the Chengdu J-20 and Shenyang J-31, the latter likely to be adapted to also serve on aircraft carriers. Other Asian countries are also investing in fifth-generation fighters. South Korea and Indonesia have partnered on their own fighter program, Japan rolled out its Mitsubishi X-2 Shinshin stealth fighter in July 2014, and India continues to work on a program that will complement the Sukhoi/HAL FGFA that it is developing with Russia. To put these programs in perspective, these jets will be more advanced than some of Europe's leading aircraft, such as France's Dassault Rafale and the Eurofighter Typhoon. In addition, the United States and Russia will lose their monopoly on the production of the world's advanced fifth-generation fighters.

As Asia becomes the center for naval and air power in the world, the world's largest military manufacturer, and the biggest market for defense exporters, an important question remains: What is the purpose of all these expensive weapons? For many states, investments in military modernization are driven by a desire to deter or hedge against potential Chinese aggression or coercion. While China's rise is a major reason that most Asian states are investing in their militaries, other factors play an important role as well. In Southeast Asia, Indonesia, Malaysia, the Philippines, Thailand, and Vietnam are all upgrading their naval assets in order to better assert their claims for territorial, fishery, and energy exploration rights. Long-standing conflicts between India and Pakistan, unrest in neighboring states such as Burma, maritime presence requirements for coastal states, the desire for prestigious technology, and generous defense budgets following years of breakneck growth have also pushed countries to pursue greater arms buildup.

China's intentions, in contrast, have long been shrouded in secrecy and subject to speculation. According to the US Department of Defense, China is implementing a long-term plan to build a modern and comprehensive military program that will "improve the capacity of its armed forces to win short-duration, high-intensity regional contingencies."[136] In essence, China is developing the ability to quickly and effectively win any potential conflicts that emerge in the Taiwan Strait, East China Sea, or South China Sea. While China's comprehensive military modernization is unsurprising for a growing power, the development of many of its high-end systems is certainly a response to US capabilities, with an eye toward potential conflict scenarios in the region. These capabilities, which grouped together constitute a "counterintervention" strategy of military development, seem aimed at ensuring that, in the event of a regional conflict, China would have the ability to prevent the United States or other third-party actors from intervening. Such anti-access/area-denial (A2/AD) investments include advanced short- and medium-range ballistic missiles, land-attack and antiship cruise missiles, long-range surface-to-air missiles, small missile boats, submarines, counterspace weapons, and military cyberspace capabilities.

China's military has also begun to look past its immediate territorial concerns. Each year China is more capable of operating beyond its shores, as evidenced by the global tours of its hospital ship, the successful evacuation of Chinese citizens from Libya in 2011 and Yemen in 2015, routine participation in counterpiracy exercises in the Gulf of Aden, frequent deployment of warships and nuclear submarines in the Indian Ocean, and important contributions to UN peacekeeping missions around the world. China's defense spending is not only about offsetting American power in Asia, it is also driven by an explicit desire, often articulated in Chinese-language press and official government documents, to protect investments, citizens, and trade flows.[137]

For the United States, China's military modernization program has in fact had some salutary effects. China's neighbors are moving to embrace a US presence to counterbalance China's improving capabilities. After a grueling decade of war in Afghanistan and Iraq, conversations with Southeast Asian nations that now enthusiastically welcome a sustained US military presence on their territory represent a departure from the suspicion of US military power more common in the past. Discussions with Australia and Singapore resulted in tangible outcomes, with plans for up to 2,500 marines in Australia and up to four littoral combat ships in Singapore. The tone of these talks and the welcoming response from Southeast Asian states and India is directly linked to anxieties about China's rise.

While Asia is becoming the center of global defense spending, the potential for even more military investment remains great. Even as the region's defense budgets rise at a record pace, they nonetheless remain small as a percentage of GDP. China and India both remain under 2 percent of GDP for defense spending while, for comparison, between 2009 and 2013, US defense spending averaged 4.4 percent of GDP.[138] If Asian powers were to devote the same proportion to defense spending as the United States, the region would quickly become even more dangerous.

Technology

Asia has not only caught up to Western rivals in electronics; in many cases it is surging past them. Today Asia is home to the world's largest TV maker, largest computer maker, largest automaker, largest tablet maker, second-largest appliance maker, and second- and third-largest smartphone makers.[139] It has fast become the global center for technology manufacturing, with American companies such as Apple and Microsoft choosing to do much of their assembly and manufacturing in the region.[140] Although famous for its cheap labor, Asia in fact offers global companies much more: proximity to the world's largest consumer electronics market, advanced infrastructure, well-trained workers, and unimaginable scale.

There is simply no American equivalent to Foxconn City in Longhua, China, a sprawling complex where Apple, Sony, Microsoft, and Nintendo assemble many of their products, and it is highly unlikely that there ever could be. Such massive manufacturing centers can do things that are simply impossible anywhere else in the world. With much of the supply chain in one location, there is no delay when plans are changed or more material is needed. According to one Apple executive, "You need a thousand rubber gaskets? That's the factory next door. You need a million screws? That factory is a block away. You need that screw made a little bit different? It will take three hours."[141] This flexibility can be of the utmost importance in the fast-moving world of consumer technology. When Apple decided to alter the screen design on one of its iPhone models at the last minute, necessitating an assembly line overhaul, new screens began arriving at the plant the same day. The process, as described by the *New York Times*, is unthinkable in the West:

> A foreman immediately roused 8,000 workers inside the company's dormitories.... Each employee was given a biscuit and a cup of tea, guided to a workstation and within half an hour started a 12-hour shift fitting glass screens into beveled frames. Within 96 hours, the plant was producing over 10,000 iPhones a day.[142]

Asia provides a skilled workforce quickly and on a scale inconceivable in the West. Apple's executives estimated that finding enough industrial engineers to oversee its production line could take as long as nine months in the United States, but in China it took just fifteen days.[143] All this comes at a human price. While many of the leading factories offer relatively stable jobs, additional training, subsidized housing, and even college courses to their employees, they often make the news more for difficult conditions, monotonous work, and human rights abuses rather than their production runs or benefits. At Foxconn City alone, 24,000 people quit every month due to the working conditions.[144] With China's labor market tightening and its workers increasingly demanding better pay and benefits, low-skill manufacturing—such as textiles and footwear—is traveling to poorer Asian countries such as Bangladesh and Vietnam. It remains to be seen whether a similar trend will manifest in consumer electronics.

Asian companies are not simply successful manufacturers for Western firms, they also research, design, and develop their own innovative products. Today Asian global brands abound, particularly in consumer electronics and automotive manufacturing. Sony, Samsung, Toyota, Honda, Hitachi, Subaru, Nikon, LG, and Tata are readily recognizable and successful Asia-based multinational companies, each of which manufactures modern and innovative technology. India's Tata Motors, which owns luxury brands like Jaguar, also competes at the lower end with the Tata Nano, the world's cheapest automobile. Once intended for India's middle classes, the

Nano is now also marketed as a "smart city car" for Western consumers.[145] For Toyota, the constant pursuit of perfection in production and assembly, known as the Toyota Production System, *is* the innovation. Toyota is also making inroads into greener vehicles, following up its widely popular hybrid electric Prius with the Mirai, a fuel-cell electric car that will hit the American market in 2016. Similarly, both Honda and Hyundai have announced plans to release their own hydrogen cell cars in the coming year. Even though questions remain about the commercial viability of such technologies, it is clear that Asian competitors will continue to disrupt and push the boundaries of the global auto industry.[146]

Asia's success in technology depends increasingly not only on its prowess in hardware manufacturing, but also on its versatility in working with software. For example, while India has largely missed out on the electronics manufacturing revolution that propelled Japan, the Asian tigers, and then China to wealth, it has found success as a world leader in IT services and software. Indian companies like Infosys and Wipro, with market capitalizations in the tens of billions, compete in markets around the world.

Software has also revolutionized manufacturing in consumer electronics. While Japanese technology companies like Panasonic, Sharp, and Sony once ruled the electronics industry, they have suffered from sharp competition from upstarts in South Korea, Taiwan, and China who have taken better advantage of the digital revolution to create smartphones, tablets, and computers that marry user-friendly software with manufacturing. Apple, Samsung, LG, and even Chinese companies such as Xiaomi and Huawei are now leaders in consumer electronics. As Hiroaki Nakanishi, the president of Japan's Hitachi, noted after selling off the company's consumer electronics businesses, "Digital technology changed everything.... We could not adjust to such an environment. So that is why I gave up those segments."[147] Nakanishi refocused Hitachi rather successfully on high-quality manufacturing for heavy industry, such as turbines, nuclear power plants, and high-speed trains, which the company now sells to India and others in sore need of improved infrastructure.

Long considered a region filled with factories and laborers rather than innovators and entrepreneurs, Asia has evolved into something more. Its companies have found success in a wide range of technology businesses, from software to consumer electronics to heavy industry. Although the region faces daunting challenges—including environmental degradation, infrastructure shortages, and pervasive malnutrition—its innovative and efficient enterprises can have a major role to play in overcoming them.

Film Industry

One growing but perhaps underappreciated area of Asian influence is in the global film industry, which is increasingly a lever for Asian governments hoping to exercise soft power. Success in the Asia-Pacific market has become essential for global movie executives. Asia is now the top region for international box office receipts, with $12.4 billion in 2014 alone—more than Europe, the Middle East, and Africa combined—and a 72 percent increase since 2009.[148] China and Japan bring in the most in international box office receipts, with India, South Korea, Australia, Taiwan, and Malaysia also making the world's top twenty. Asia's purchasing power in the global film industry has sent ripples into Hollywood, whose moviemakers increasingly adapt their films to appeal to the tastes of Asian viewers and accommodate the sensitivities of Asian governments.

Captain America: The Winter Soldier, for example, in which the eponymous hero is still adjusting to life after waking up from being frozen for the previous sixty years, includes a to-do list to help him become a more modern man. This list, shown briefly on screen, includes watching the TV show *I Love Lucy*, learning about the moon landing, the construction and destruction of the Berlin Wall, and the life of Steve Jobs and Apple, and experiencing disco music. In South Korea, however, Captain America makes a note to catch up on the 2002 World Cup, which was jointly held in Korea and Japan, and to specifically research the most decorated Asian footballer in history, Park Ji-sung, who was at the time playing for Manchester United. Likewise, *Iron Man 3* included an extra four minutes of footage producers hoped would appeal specifically to Chinese fans, such as longer scenes with local actors Fan Bingbing and Wang Xueqi.[149]

These efforts are made not only to enhance a film's appeal to Chinese audiences, but also to comply with China's strict guidelines on foreign films, which in some cases dictate that 30 percent of the investment and workers (on- and offscreen) come from China and that the movie reflect a Chinese theme or cultural context.[150] These demands would be scoffed at by Hollywood producers were it not for the fact that China accounts for nearly $5 billion in annual earnings.[151] Increasingly, therefore, Asia is being given a more prominent role in Hollywood movies, with blockbusters such as *Looper, Skyfall,* and *The Wolverine* including many scenes filmed in Asian cities and resorts.

A lot of the time, such script accommodations will make little sense to the film's plot. The extra scenes in *Iron Man 3* included an incongruous explanation for how Iron Man revitalizes his power, evidently by drinking Gu Li Duo brand milk.[152] Similarly, *Transformers: Age of Extinction* offered product placement to many Asian companies, regardless of whether it affected the movie's integrity. One Chinese viewer asked on Weibo, the Chinese equivalent of Twitter, "Why would a middle-aged man in the middle of the desert in Texas take out a China Construction Bank card to withdraw money from the ATM?" Other confusing placements included American actors drinking Chinese versions of Red Bull and Shuhua milk, which led to this graceful dialogue in a previous *Transformers* installment:

Jerry: May I finish my Shuhua milk, Donny?
Wang: I don't care about your exotic milk! I care about respect!

The US film industry considers access to the Chinese box office so essential that significant changes are now made even without overt pressure from the Chinese government—as in the case of a 2012 remake of *Red Dawn,* where the original Chinese aggressors were switched to North Koreans.[153] The villain in *Iron Man 3,* instead of being a traditional Iron Man foe called the Mandarin whose comic-book history tells of his life in a Chinese village and his family ancestry going back to Ghengis Khan, was played by Sir Ben Kingsley to avoid controversy in China.[154] The makers of *World War Z* similarly removed potentially disparaging references to China, while Chinese villains were edited out of *Pirates of the Caribbean: At World's End* and *Men in Black 3* altogether. Such efforts may increase in future Hollywood productions as the Asian market grows ever more influential. Since the end of 2012, the number of movie theaters in China has increased by more than the total number of screens in all of France, with ten to thirteen new cinemas opening every day.[155] Trouble in the Asian market can mean the difference between profit and loss. The power of money was perhaps explained best by the director James Cameron, currently in coproduction with China for *Avatar 2*, who maintained that "as an artist, I'm always against censorship," but agreed to remove certain scenes from *Titanic*'s 3D rerelease, claiming that "this is an important market for me."[156]

So great is Hollywood's desire to please China that changes have even been made in the types of movies studios are willing to produce. Fans of US comedies will likely despair at the effect of the rising importance of the Asia market. While comedies made up 44 percent of all of 20th Century Fox's output in 2010, their lack of appeal to Chinese audiences meant that this number has dropped to less than 10 percent, with other companies, such as Disney, not releasing a single comedy in 2014.[157] Asia prefers big-budget, explosion-laden, action blockbusters in its imported films, which is good news for Michael Bay, but not for fans of Will Ferrell or Zach Galifianakis. The one ray of light for those unhappy with this change in emphasis is that China's own film industry is looking to soon usurp Hollywood. Local films saw ticket sales rise by 144 percent in 2013, while those for imported movies fell by 21 percent. According to producer Zhang Zhao, "U.S. studios are too big and too slow.... Maybe China can now make a meaningful contribution to world cinema."[158] This could be a welcome change, as, according to Hong Kong–based director Peter Ho-sun Chan, "Audiences in China no longer care about the director; they just want to know what the story is about."[159] The growing power of China's studios was on full display during Chinese New Year in 2016, when a surge of Chinese moviegoers generated half a billion dollars for domestically produced Chinese movies like *The Monkey King 2* and *The Mermaid* in roughly a week. Four of the world's five top-grossing movies in that period were Chinese films—a testament both to the size of China's market and to the stunning success of its once-fledgling filmmakers.[160] The rise of China's own domestic film industry may bring the age of Michael Bay–style blockbusters to an end.

So too may the surprising success of other Asian film industries, which with slimmer budgets and far fewer explosions are nonetheless increasingly able to displace big-budget Western films within China. Bollywood's *PK*, a comedy about religion starring Indian megastar Aamir Khan, held its own against *Tomorrowland*, a $190 million George Clooney sci-fi movie that cost fifteen times more to produce. Meanwhile the $35 million Japanese animated film *Stand by Me Doraemon* performed as well as Dwayne "the Rock" Johnson's *San Andreas*, which had a $110 million budget.[161] For these reasons, many of Asia's established film producers are finding ways to partner with Chinese studios and movie stars. For example, Katrina Kaif, one of Bollywood's biggest actresses, will soon collaborate with Jackie Chan on an action-comedy coproduction called *Kung Fu Yoga* that will be released in both markets.

Asia's film industries are maturing into critical successes. Bollywood, which makes more movies than China and the United States combined, dramatically outgrosses Hollywood within India and has a long and celebrated critical tradition, with its movies having won several awards at the Cannes Film Festival and Vienna International Film Festival over the last seventy years.[162] Long popular in South Asia, Central Asia, and the Middle East, India's movies are now increasingly finding success in the rest of Asia as well. And of course India's own market, with nearly three billion in annual ticket sales, may eventually follow China to become one of the world's most important for Western moviemakers.

Although South Korea's population is small relative to India's, the country's film industry punches well above its weight, consistently outgrossing American imports and garnering international recognition from such prestigious film festivals as Cannes, Berlin, and Venice. The latter awarded the South Korean drama *Pietà* the festival's best-film award in 2012. South Korean directors have even begun to make English-language movies to compete with Hollywood, such as Park Chan-wook's *Stoker*, Kim Jee-woon's *The Last Stand*, and Bong Joon-ho's *Snowpiercer*, which scored 95 percent on Rotten Tomatoes. With these indigenous successes, and as American companies increasingly make films in partnership with Asian studios, the moviemaking business is transforming into a truly globalized industry and changing both the styles and the concepts of the movies we watch.

The Art Market

Asian success in technology and heavy industry is increasingly matched by the region's growing prominence in high culture. The art market in particular has been energized and transformed by the massive wealth recently created in Asia. World-class auction houses like Christie's and Sotheby's now have offices throughout Asia, while Hong Kong has become the third-largest art market by auction sales.[163] In 2008, for reasons including its tax-free status, mature financial services, and direct access to Chinese markets, Christie's and Sotheby's consolidated their Asia sales to Hong Kong to be squarely at the center of the art world in Asia.[164] In October of 2013, Sotheby's marked its fortieth anniversary in Hong Kong with a record-smashing series of sales that totaled $538 million, far more than the presale expectations of $370 million.[165]

Hong Kong has become one of the world's most vibrant art centers thanks to several important galleries and auction houses. In 2013, Art Basel, one of the world's preeminent stagers of modern and contemporary art, added the Hong Kong International Art Fair to its portfolio of shows, which includes Switzerland and Miami Beach. It is now one of the largest art shows in the world, attracting over two thousand artists and incorporating more than 250 art galleries. The demand from buyers was so great in 2014 that many dealers sold out of their paintings before the fair had even begun. French art dealer Edouard Malingue recalled that after selling all seven works by Chinese painter Yuan Yuan, he spent the rest of the fair calming angry buyers who had been beaten to the punch. "Some of my clients got really upset with my staff and I had to intervene," he recalled.[166] Within the fair's first three days, another dealer, Victoria Miro, sold all eighteen of her works by Japanese artist Yayoi Kusama despite their being priced at as much as $2 million each.[167]

For the last four years, China has been the leading country in terms of sales in the art market, taking in a total of $5.6 billion in 2014 alone.[168] And it is not only Western auction companies that are benefiting from the rise in popularity of Asian art. Of the top ten auction houses by sales volume, six are Chinese, a rise that has caused the market share for Christie's and Sotheby's to fall from 70 percent in 2008 to 55 percent in 2013.[169] Asian cities are quickly becoming the most dynamic centers of the contemporary art world. While New York remains the epicenter, seven of the top ten cities by auction turnover in 2014 are now Asian, with Beijing forcing London into third, and Paris being relegated to sixth behind Hong Kong and Shanghai. The latter is rapidly gaining a reputation as the Berlin of Asia thanks to the thousands of emerging artists selling their work in the growing network of local galleries that have popped up across the city.[170]

Much of the major growth in the art market in general is from China, which now makes up 40 percent of the global market, up from just 5 percent in 2006.[171] Two Chinese artists, Zeng Fanzhi and Zhang Xiaogang, appear on the list of the top ten living artists whose works sell for over $10 million each, a fact that would have been inconceivable in the art world just five years ago.[172] Meanwhile, Ai Weiwei has been ranked in the top ten of *ArtReview*'s list of the contemporary art world's most powerful figures for several years, reaching number one in 2011.[173]

Even more remarkable is the recent shift toward Asia in the list of highest-grossing artists at auction. The following chart shows that the top ten highest-grossing artists in 2006, 2007, and 2008 were Western, and mostly European. In 2009, Qi Baishi appeared at number three, marking the beginning of Asia's modern art ascendance. From then on we see Asian artists (shown in light gray in the table on p. 78) competing for and then dominating the top spots.[174] Individual artists trend differently depending on what comes up for sale each year, but the movement from an all-Western top-ten list to a list on which half the artists are Asian has been enough to startle critics and entrepreneurs around the globe.

Chinese artists are some of the world's most successful, but increasingly works by artists in other Asian countries have also received critical acclaim and fetched handsome prices. Pieces by Indian painters such as V. S. Gaitonde and Tyeb Mehta are sold for millions of dollars, and the leading auction houses now view India as a significant potential market.[175] Southeast Asian art is already booming, with the region widely expected to be the next breakout tiger of the Asian art market. Malaysia had few art galleries in 2010, with little outside interest in its indigenous artworks. Since then, however, Kuala Lumpur has attracted four large international auction houses. It has been estimated that buyers and auction attendees in Malaysia have more than doubled in the last four years.[176] In 2011, Ronald Ventura of the Philippines set the record for a contemporary Southeast Asian artist when his painting *Greyhound* sold for $1.1 million. His success has stimulated greater interest in Filipino artists, with the market now ranked twentieth in the world, ahead of Russia and Switzerland, and gaining recognition from top museums throughout the world.[177] In 2013, New York's Solomon R. Guggenheim

Museum exhibited work from throughout Southeast Asia, with Filipino artists heavily represented, while the USC Fisher Museum of Art in Los Angeles ran an exhibit in 2014 titled *The Triumph of Philippine Art.* The Philippines even has its own art fair, Art Fair Philippines, which has been held annually for the last three years to great success.

Top Grossing Artists by Year

	2006	2007	2008	2009
1	Picasso	Warhol	Picasso	Picasso
2	Warhol	Picasso	Bacon	Warhol
3	Klimt	Bacon	Warhol	Qi
4	De Koonig	Rothko	Hirst	Matisse
5	Modigliani	Monet	Monet	Mondrian
6	Chagall	Matisse	Giacometti	Giacometti
7	Schiele	Basquiat	Richter	Léger
8	Gauguin	Léger	Degas	Degas
9	Matisse	Chagall	Fontana	Raphael
10	Lichtenstein	Cézanne	Klein	Monet

	2010	2011	2012	2013
1	Picasso	Zhang	Warhol	Warhol
2	Qi	Qi	Zhang	Picasso
3	Zhang	Warhol	Picasso	Zhang
4	Warhol	Picasso	Qi	Basquiat
5	Giacometti	Xu	Richter	Qi
6	Xu	Wu	Xu	Bacon
7	Matisse	Fu	Li	Richter
8	Modigliani	Richter	Rothko	Lichtenstein
9	Fu	Bacon	Bacon	Zao
10	Lichtenstein	Li	Fu	Monet

Source: "The Art Market," New York Times and ArtPrice.com, based on fine art sales at 4,500 auction houses worldwide.

Other emerging markets include Indonesia, which has spawned a number of well-respected artists using all types of media. Video artist Reza Afisina, for example, uses his own face as a canvas by slapping it black and blue to simulate the effects of interrogation while reciting passages from the New Testament that speak against hypocrisy and for the importance of truth and confession.[178] Arin Dwihartanto Sunaryo combines resin with different materials, such as in his 2012 work using ash gathered from the 2010 eruption of Indonesia's Mount Merapi. Those who appreciate Indonesian art have gone beyond the contemporary to laud also the work of previous generations. The work of Sindoesoedarsono Soedjojono set an auction record for a posthumous Southeast Asian artist when his oil on canvas, *Our Soldiers Led under Prince Diponegoro*, sold for a staggering $7.5 million in 2014.[179] Not only has Asia's recent prosperity benefited Asian artists, it has also left the region awash in art collectors. According to art historian Simon Soon, "The strength of the art market in Southeast Asia lies in the fact that most collectors are from the region....Their collections are more focused...[and they] are very knowledgeable about the development of art in the region."[180] Indonesian collectors, for example, have become so knowledgeable about the country's work that they are highly regarded for their expertise by scholars, auction houses, and art professionals.

Asia's prominence in the art world has had global effects. In October 2014 the Vancouver Art Gallery announced plans to create an Institute of Asian Art to allow the institution to tap into this new and popular source of material. That same month Australian television, not known for its focus on programs about the arts, began a ten-part series called *A Journey through Asian Art* to help guide students, teachers, and the generally curious through the region's art up to the modern day. Exhibitions of contemporary and modern Asian art, largely unheard of ten years ago, are now being held in museums across the world. The Asian Art in London festival is an annual event that in 2014 exhibited art from across the Asia region in numerous galleries and museums throughout the city, including the British Museum and the Brunei Gallery at the School of Oriental and African Studies. Similarly, New York City's Asia Week art fair sold over $200 million in Asian art in locations such as the Metropolitan Museum of Art.[181]

Conclusion

Asia is a region of vast potential accompanied by serious challenges. It is home to the world's largest urban population but some of its lowest urbanization rates, and while it uses more power than any other region, one-fifth of its people lack power altogether. A surging economy has lifted more people out of poverty than ever before in human history, but also given rise to the world's greatest environmental challenges. Asia's booming population of eager young workers has fueled the region's growth but also strained its resources, and some of the region's countries risk growing old before they grow rich. Perhaps the most fitting illustration of Asia's progress and its challenges is that many of the region's countries have the world's largest and most powerful economies but also the lowest per capita incomes. As far as Asia has come, it still has a long journey ahead.

Asia is not only a land of challenges and contradictions but also a region of profound consequence for every major American policy priority. Its vast scale and broad dimensions ensure that the history of the twenty-first century will be extensively written in the Asia-Pacific. Today the prosperity and stability of the American-led order rests in part on how Washington manages Asia's intensifying security competition and China's historic rise. The path to a greener world runs through Asia, which generates more carbon than any other region worldwide. In the global war on poverty, Asia is the defining battlefield, home to more than 60 percent of the world's poor. To those who advocate a return to medieval Islamic traditions in the Middle East and Africa, Asia offers a powerful rejoinder as the home of several successful and moderate Muslim countries, though as recent attacks in Indonesia attest, it is also a battleground for hearts and minds that terrorist extremists seek to exploit. Its cities and resorts have also been targets in attacks staged by violent jihadists. For American businessmen Asia is an indispensable market, supplier, and partner, and the center of gravity for countless industries such as shipping, defense, technology, film, and fine art. Already the economic fortunes of every American are intimately intertwined with developments in Asia. Clearly, then, the United States can ill afford to neglect this vital region.

Americans have been captivated by Asia since the earliest days of the republic and have involved themselves in Asian affairs for at least as long.

And yet the history of American engagement in Asia is not well understood. As we will see in the next chapter, American involvement in this consequential region has been marked by cycles of attention and neglect, enchantment and disappointment, as well as warfare and peace. To fashion an effective strategy for tomorrow's Asian century, we will turn first to the successes and failures of yesterday.

CHAPTER THREE

Patterns Preceding the Pivot

Historical Themes in American Ties to Asia

It has been said that a person ignorant of history is like a leaf that is unaware it is part of a tree.[1] That aphorism can be quite helpful in thinking about contemporary American policy in Asia, which is only the most recent strand in a tapestry that has been woven by Washington for more than two centuries. If policymakers are to succeed today, they must better understand the origins and biases of yesterday's policies and discern the ways in which their own plans fit into the rich fabric of yesteryear. To that end, this chapter will focus on the enduring historical themes that have animated American involvement in the Asia-Pacific.

Rather than restate boilerplate factual information on more than two centuries of American engagement, this chapter will instead call attention to eight influential themes that have steered America's past and present engagement in Asia—and that are almost certain to shape the contours of its future actions. In adopting such an approach, I seek to situate the current American Pivot to Asia in its broader historical context by highlighting the patterns that precede present policy.

The first historical theme that has shaped relations between the United States and Asia is the "tyranny of distance." The challenges posed by the vast ocean that separates our two lands have historically hindered the growth of commerce, communication, and accordingly sound, regularized diplomatic relations with the far and unfamiliar lands of the East. Before the advent of modern air travel and telecommunications, the raw physical distance between the United States and Asia precluded the type of close connections and cultural commonalities that the United States enjoyed with Europe. This geographic distance from Asia also led to a second theme in American diplomacy with the region, a cultural distance that made Asia both alien and alluring but often incomprehensible to Westerners. All too often this lack of understanding has bred misperceptions about Asia that are often stereotypical and dangerous, comprised in equal parts of myths of Asian indulgence, mockery of Asian abilities, and fears of an Asian menace. From images of luxury, high elegance, and ancient wisdom to beliefs about untrustworthiness, inferiority, and foreignness, the American perception of Asia, rather than the reality, has unfortunately shaped a considerable share of interaction and engagement.

While the great geographic and cultural distance between Asians and Americans has at times kept them apart, Americans have often been lured eastward by the pursuit of economic relations and the expansion of missionary work, the third and fourth themes of American engagement respectively. Traders and missionaries alike saw untapped potential in Asia's teeming multitudes, and the possibility of selling a million shirts or saving a billion souls helped forge the first links between the two continents. Trade may have tied American prosperity and interests to Asia, but it was the work of missionaries who took the time to learn local languages and customs that provided the scaffolding for subsequent American diplomatic and commercial architecture within the region.

As American interests in Asia grew, so too did the possibility of being embroiled in the region's conflicts. America's long history of costly victories and traumatic defeats constitutes the fifth theme in US relations with Asia, with the region's present prosperity paid for in part by the sacrifices of American lives and treasure. Within seventy years the United States fought four major wars in the region against the Philippines, Japan, North Korea and its Chinese ally, and Vietnam respectively. Each brought unintended consequences, with effects that linger to this day and lessons that hold relevance for tomorrow.

Although the United States has defended the region from the forces of nationalism, imperialism, and Communism, American diplomacy has rarely received the level of attention paid to diplomacy in Europe or the Middle East. A sixth theme in American relations with Asia is that the region has been considered a "secondary theater," with an American legacy of engagement that has often been reactive, episodic, and ambiguous, leaving behind a sense of uncertainty and a job half-finished. The United States has frequently surged into the region and then just as quickly retreated, leaving costly and unresolved problems in its wake. An important by-product of this lack of focus is an inability to commit adequate resources and personnel to the region, which is the seventh theme in American engagement with Asia. With the United States often short-manned and underequipped, it has in many cases lacked the necessary resources to follow through on US strategy or to handle an unanticipated crisis.

Finally, although Asia has been witness to disheartening American setbacks such as Vietnam, it has also been home to the soaring success of American promotion of democracy in Japan, South Korea, and Taiwan. While often overlooked, the legacy of democracy promotion—the eighth theme in American Asia policy—is richly illustrative of the abiding American passion for the expansion of liberty and freedom throughout the world.

Altogether these eight themes have contributed to the complex legacy that is the relationship between the United States and Asia. Together they provide the context in which the Pivot is planted. Some themes have reinforced engagement, others have undermined it, but all have been influential in shaping American history in this vital region. This chapter will examine each in greater detail and assess how the United States might continue to affect relations as we enter the Asian Century. It will close with a comprehensive synthesis of all eight themes that explores the major objectives and challenges of American strategy over the past two centuries.

The Tyranny of Distance

The United States has been blessed by its geography, insulated by two vast oceans and bordered by two close allies and a smattering of nearby islands. For much of its early history the country benefited from a degree of geographic isolation that allowed it to remain relatively removed from continental gambits abroad and to expand across the vast American landmass unopposed.[2] In contrast, the close proximity of European nations to one another fueled that region's history of state conflict and power politics, the specter of which now looms again with the Russian intervention in Ukraine.

Geography may have divided the United States from Europe, but cultural kinship imparted a level of understanding and familiarity that partly transcended distance. Personal links, religious history, and shared reference points ensured a high degree of economic and political connectivity as well as trust and understanding—so much so that the United States was sometimes referred to as the west coast of Europe. This camaraderie continues today, with the United States enjoying strong relationships with most Western European powers. British prime minister David Cameron talks passionately about the close relationship he has with President Obama, and how the president often refers to him as "bro," much to his pleasure.[3]

Such intimacy has generally been absent in American relations with Asia. Asia is twice as far from the United States as Europe and considerably more distant culturally, and it was therefore considered alien and mysterious from the outset. Efforts to reach Asia have been made since the dawn of the republic, but at first they were exceedingly slow and fraught with danger. The first American ship to sail to China, in 1784, took almost fifteen months to complete its trade mission, three to four times longer than comparable Atlantic crossings of the time. It was not until 1805 that Lewis and Clark finally reached the West Coast, and even then most American attention was devoted to domestic exploration rather than engagement with such faraway lands. With the invention of speedy clipper ships in the 1840s, sailing times were reduced considerably. In 1846 the *Yorkshire* broke the record for a journey across the Atlantic, arriving in New York just sixteen days after leaving Liverpool, England.[4] The record for crossings of the Pacific was broken four years later but, at eighty-one days, the trip still took a considerable time and proved a barrier to engagement with a region that did not have a shared culture or history.[5]

Despite the distance, American traders still coveted the riches of the Far East, but only the most adventurous and well-equipped trading companies could pursue them. Gradually, and with an eye toward promoting and expanding trade with that bountiful region, the United States began to expand its presence in Asia. The necessity of ports at which trading ships could dock en route to Asia led to the opening of relations with Pacific islands such as Fiji and Samoa, as well as more substantial bases in conveniently located Hawaii, the Philippines, and Guam.

Yet despite the development of island stopovers, travel to Asia remained restrictive throughout the nineteenth century and for much of the twentieth. As a result Asia remained largely unknown to the majority of Americans beyond vague myths and stereotypes. Even to those with great interest in the Pacific region, it took enormous effort to conduct anything approaching sustained diplomacy. President Theodore Roosevelt, enamored with improving relations with Asia and not known for admitting defeat or taking half measures, approached Asia in his typical full-throated style. Rather than pursue diplomatic engagement through the slow and inefficient process of sending one or two officials to Asia at a time, he ordered the dispatch of the largest diplomatic delegation in American history.[6] In the summer of 1905 the members of this diplomatic mission climbed aboard the SS *Manchuria* and embarked on a historic journey. It consisted of Roosevelt's own daughter, Alice, a leading celebrity of the time, one secretary of war and future president in William Howard Taft, seven senators, and twenty-three congressmen. With the accompanying military and civilian officials, as well as support staff, the party consisted of upwards of eighty people. After taking a cross-country train from Washington, D.C., they sailed from San Francisco to Hawaii and then on to Japan, the Philippines, China, and Korea. Transport and meals alone cost the equivalent of roughly $12 million in today's money, and the high-ranking delegation spent more than two months away from Washington.[7]

While Theodore Roosevelt overcame the sometimes daunting geographic distance in his own inimitable style, that distance nonetheless remains formidable to this very day. Modern aircraft can reach London in six or so hours from New York City, time that passes quickly after a good meal and a short nap. Yet even leaving from the West Coast of the United States, flights to Beijing still take more than eleven hours, and even longer if departing from New York or Washington, a dishearteningly long period to be trapped inside a metal tube. And this says nothing about the jet lag that inflicts sleepless nights on even the most seasoned travelers, who, based on my own personal experience, invariably have to endure groggy business or diplomatic meetings in the days that follow.

The enduring problem of distance has not only hindered the development of relations with Asia, it has also long exacerbated feelings of unfamiliarity and bred powerful misperceptions that linger to this day. These influences on US engagement in Asia have been deep, pervasive, and enduring.

Myth, Mockery, and Menace

On the silver screen and across television, in print media and behind closed doors, Asia and its peoples have been unfairly subjected to misperceptions born of geographic distance and cultural unfamiliarity. These misperceptions have been varied, comprised in equal parts of myths of Asian indulgence, mockery of Asian abilities, and fears of an Asian menace. They have found influence in matters wide-ranging, including government policy, movie castings, and, in one prominent case, business investments in the nation's capital.

In 2004, above the railroad tracks of the southwest quadrant of Washington, D.C., and alongside the western edge of Maryland Avenue, a $155 million, four-hundred-room hotel first opened its doors. The Mandarin Oriental Hotel boasts views of the monuments and is perfectly situated to take advantage of the cherry blossoms along the Tidal Basin, a gift from Japan over a hundred years ago. Its rooms combine Asian and American design elements arranged under the principles of feng shui, the ancient Chinese philosophical system of harmonization. The five-thousand-square-foot Oriental Ballroom serves as a popular reception venue, while the hotel's spa includes a "Zen" relaxation space that even offers two-hour Thai massages for the more adventurous guests. Promotional materials describe the hotel restaurant as providing an "Asian feel" that combines local produce "with the distinctive flavors of South-East Asia."[8] In all, the hotel is one of the newest and grandest examples of a tradition that has existed for centuries in the West, and especially in the United States—one that taps into the myth of an alluring, opulent, and indulgent Asian culture.

The lure of the exotic has long been a staple of the American vision of the Far East, and enterprising folk have been quick to capitalize on and exploit its mythology. The Mandarin Oriental Hotel is one of a number of similar hotels owned by the Mandarin Oriental Hotel Group chain. Located throughout the world, these Asian-themed luxury accommodations promise a sense of the exotic and the "magic of the orient."[9] The theme is pan-Asian but not faithful to any particular culture; as one commentator has put it, the hotels provide "a Western aesthetic with Asian characteristics."[10] The romanticized version of the "Asian experience" generated revenue of nearly $1.4 billion in 2014, and before-tax profits of almost $116 million.[11] Other companies that also promise the Asian fantasy or supposed Zen luxury are similarly rewarded. Cathay Pacific and Singapore Airlines advertise their "high standards of care and service," with the former offering a "Marco Polo club" for loyal members and the latter anointing as its mascot the "Singapore Girl," symbolizing "the epitome of Asian grace and hospitality."[12] These airlines serve only international destinations, catering solely to those most taken in by the Asian fantasy—such as Western businessmen. The reality of Asian air travel is shown in glaring contrast by the region's domestic carriers, which are far more like the no-frills cattle-herding varieties of the West, often overcrowded, with overstuffed overhead compartments and uncomfortable seats with little legroom.

The view that Asia is a land of indulgence and elegance is a mythology maintained in part by Western media. One journalist notes that her colleagues are "tempted and encouraged" by their editors to write about a "mystical, exotic world of difference" because "that is what sells books and articles back home."[13] Over time, she notes, through media and entertainment, Asia in the Western mind has become

> an exotic land of graceful allure, of swaying sugar palms and soaring bamboo, of servants, silks, and sumptuous feasts. In the mind's eye we can envision its mystical charms, its incense-shrouded temples and opium dens; its appeal to the despot in all of us, lying on a divan's satiny cushions, tended by beautifully beguiling Orientals. It is sensual and decadent, enticing and thrilling in its forbidden temptations. This has long been our Western fantasy of The Orient— antiquated, perhaps, but still shockingly influential.[14]

The myth of an exotic and luxurious Far East has expanded to include stereotypes of Asians that are utterly untethered from reality. Asian women have been described as submissive, obedient, and obliging. Such romanticized stereotypes surface at times in works such as *Madame Butterfly* and *Memoirs of a Geisha* and are taken to be emblematic of the region as a whole. When not shown as submissive, Asian women are depicted as the reverse—a strict, socially conservative stereotype made famous in the movies of Anna May Wong in the 1930s. More recently this stereotype has been found in the characters of Ling Woo in *Ally McBeal* and Mrs. Kim in *Gilmore Girls*, and propagated by Amy Chua in her book *Battle Hymn of the Tiger Mother*.[15] In many cases these stern Asian women are considered dispensers of age-old wisdom. In an episode of the popular American comedy show *Seinfeld*, George Costanza's mother receives advice from a woman called Donna Chang after the phone lines get crossed when she is trying to call her son. When it turns out Donna Chang is actually Donna Changstein, a blonde-haired Jewish woman, Mrs. Costanza exclaims, "Well then, that changes everything! I thought I was getting advice from a Chinese woman. She's not Chinese. I was duped. I'm not taking advice from some girl from Long Island!"[16] Ultimately these two extremes—the exotic submissive and the wise and strict disciplinarian, demanding perfection of herself and her children—are almost the sole examples of Asian women shown in the West. Very rarely are Asian women portrayed to be just "well-adjusted mothers and professionals."[17]

In addition to the myth of Asian extravagance and luxury, mockery has played a prominent and at times dangerous role in American perceptions of Asians. Asian males, for example, have suffered from stereotypes based on cultural and physical differences. These have ranged from visions of wise old men and martial artists to figures of derision based on physical differences and difficulty in assimilating to Western life. Such stereotypes have long been a standard tool for Western writers hoping for a cheap and easy laugh. Examples include Mickey Rooney's portrayal of I. Y. Yunioshi in *Breakfast at Tiffany's*, the famous restaurant scene in *A Christmas Story*, and the character Han Lee in *Two Broke Girls*. In sports, Jeremy Lin, the Taiwanese American basketball player who gained fame from his performance in a series of jaw-dropping NBA games, nevertheless faced continued and shockingly widespread public skepticism about his physical abilities and even endured racial slurs on ESPN. Condescending mockery has even affected how the United States has historically approached Asia. Paternal racism was evident, for example, when then governor-general of the Philippines William Howard Taft referred to Filipinos as our "little brown brothers," a view shared by William McKinley and Theodore Roosevelt before him.[18]

These pernicious perceptions played a role in the intrinsic underestimation of Asian capabilities in wars with Japan, North Korea, and Vietnam. Americans were caught by surprise after Pearl Harbor, in part because it was scarcely to be believed that the Japanese had been able to execute such a daring and sophisticated attack. The prevalent belief, despite proven Japanese successes against Russia, was that they "were a little yellow people incapable of waging a war effectively against a modern Western power like the United States," and many senior members of the administration initially believed that Germany had encouraged or facilitated the attack.[19] American leaders continued to underestimate Asians subsequently, assuming that the United States could handily defeat the North Koreans or Vietnamese. In the latter conflict, the common view, famously enunciated by President Lyndon Johnson, was that Vietnam was merely a "raggedy-ass little fourth-rate country." In virtually every single case of combat, the United States was surprised by the fighting ability of Asian nations.

Despite clear demonstrations that dismissing and demeaning Asian countries can be dangerous, stereotypes remain prevalent, especially in regard to North Korea—a country repeatedly mocked and underestimated but that has proven itself to be dangerously resourceful. Margaret Cho's crude portrayal of a North Korean general at the 2015 Golden Globes was the latest in a long line of such efforts and bore a distinct similarity to that of I. Y. Yunioshi some fifty years earlier.[20] *The Interview*, a raunchy comedy that skewered North Korea, was tinged with racial humor and mockingly emasculated Kim Jong-un by tapping into offensive stereotypes about Asians and their perceived lack of masculinity. North Korea ostensibly responded to the movie by launching crippling and embarrassing cyberattacks against the studio that had produced it, Sony Pictures. The widespread surprise in the Western media and among the public that a country like North Korea could have the capability to hack Sony's e-mail system demonstrated the continuing legacy of underestimation.

But the region is not without a few positive role models in the West. Bruce Lee's career is still celebrated in part because he too had to endure racism and a lack of opportunity in the United States. By overcoming these setbacks, Lee made his ultimate legacy not only his martial arts prowess but the determination, courage, and perseverance that allowed him to defy prevailing caricatures. "I think of Bruce in my worst moments—when I am discriminated against, when I am underestimated, when I am wronged," wrote one Asian American commentator in 2014.[21]

Today there are buds of change in American perceptions of Asians. In February 2015 a new prime-time television show about an Asian American family, *Fresh off the Boat*, debuted on ABC to an audience of almost eight million, beating more established shows such as NBC's *Parks and Recreation*. The show has received rave reviews for moving beyond stale stereotypes and fantasized notions of Asian life. But in many ways, progress remains too slow. The clothing store Forever 21 recently celebrated the Chinese New Year by dressing mannequins in Asian conical hats, better known as paddy field hats. These stereotypes not only offend, they also affect the lives and careers of Asian American citizens. Even in the worlds of business and technology, Asian Americans today are confronted with what many term the "bamboo ceiling" (another inappropriate racial reference) because of stereotypes that suggest they lack leadership potential. Despite the highest educational attainment of any demographic group in the United States, Asians have some of the lowest rates of representation in upper management.[22]

Cultural differences, which have driven myth and mockery for almost two centuries, have at times driven something even darker—panic and alarm. At many times in American history, Asians have been regarded as a looming menace that threatens American culture and tradition.

As Americans rushed to tame the West in the early to mid-nineteenth century, Asian laborers were allowed into the United States, enticed by the promise of jobs, higher wages, and a better standard of living. These predominantly Chinese immigrants worked on the railroads and in gold mines for years, but as California's mines ran dry and jobs became scarcer, these poorly assimilated immigrants became convenient scapegoats for the dismal economic climate. By 1852 anger against Asian immigrants was so widespread that the populist California governor John Bigler publicly blamed the Chinese for depressed wage levels and urged the government to intervene to "check this tide of Asiatic immigration."[23] That racial and cultural prejudices played a role is clear. After all, Asians were small in number compared to other immigrant groups, and hundreds of thousands of white European immigrants were welcomed during the same period, with many states actively competing for the privilege of attracting and settling them.[24] Even

Irish immigrants—who had to struggle to achieve their own acceptance—
led anti-Chinese protests without fear of stirring a backlash.[25]

Hostility toward Asians culminated in the Chinese Exclusion Act of
1882, which prohibited all immigration of Chinese laborers and banned those
already in the country from gaining US citizenship. Later amendments in the
1920s set quotas on the number of Asian immigrants that were far stricter
than on those from European states, in order to "preserve the ideal of American homogeneity" in the face of panic over Asian immigration.[26] The quotas
remained in place until Congress finally revised the act in 1952 and removed
exclusions based solely upon country of origin. Even today, however, if you
look up chapter 7 of Title 8 of the United States Code, you will find the
heading "Exclusion of Chinese" featured ignominiously.

The poor treatment of Chinese in the United States had a lasting
diplomatic impact on US relations with China. In 1899, shortly after the
announcement of the Open Door Policy intended to protect Chinese independence, the Chinese government lambasted the United States instead of
offering words of gratitude. The Chinese minister to the United States, Wu
T'ing-fang, railed against the treatment of Chinese immigrants in America
and the "utter disregard of the American government for the friendly relations which should exist between the two governments."[27] China's leadership
correctly perceived a double standard: while China was forced to grant equal
treatment and certain privileges to Westerners, its own people were denied
reciprocal treatment in the United States.[28]

American anxiety toward Asians was not only codified into law but
also ingrained in film, most notably in the creation of characters such as
Fu Manchu in the early twentieth century.[29] With his trademark mustache,
the criminal mastermind was featured in books, films, and television series.
In one particularly offensive installment, Fu Manchu is seen rallying stereo-
typically garbed Indians, Arabs, Persians, and other Asian groups to "kill
all the white men and take their women."[30] Fu Manchu was so offensive
to Asians, especially Chinese, that by the time of the Second World War
the State Department had asked MGM not to make any more episodes
because they were harmful to the alliance between the United States and
China.[31]

A poster made by the American Federation of Labor, 1902.
Source: John Kuo Wei Tchen and Dylan Yeats, "Yellow Peril: 19th-Century Scapegoating,"
Margins, *March 5, 2014. http://aaww.org/yellow-peril-scapegoating/*

While the war made allies of the Chinese, it made enemies of another Asian country whose people swiftly replaced the Chinese as the most menacing Asian group—the Japanese. After Pearl Harbor, stores removed Japanese merchandise, museums hid away Japanese artifacts, Cleveland renamed a street that had formerly been called Japan Street, and a man in Washington, D.C., sawed in half four of the grandest Japanese cherry trees and marked them with the words "To Hell with the Japanese."[32] Other actions were not simply about appearances, especially on the West Coast, where 90 percent of Japanese Americans lived.[33] In contrast to German Americans, Japanese Americans were seen as inherently sneaky and treacherous, and a potential national security threat from within, regardless of how long they had been living in the United States or whether they were American citizens.[34] Even Earl Warren, the liberal lion who later became the chief justice of the United States Supreme Court and whose ruling in *Brown v. Board of Education* helped end segregation, demanded that the government turn its attention to this new and insidious domestic threat. Fearing a fifth column, he warned that "the Japanese situation as it exists today may well be the Achilles heel of the entire civilian defense effort."[35]

Roughly 120,000 Japanese Americans—the vast majority of whom were US citizens—were interned in camps for the duration of the war, without charge, evidence of wrongdoing, or due process. In contrast, of the more than ten million German Americans in the United States, including the one million or so born in Germany, scarcely any were interned. Chinese immigrants and Japanese Americans were the unfortunate victims of standards that were not applied to more racially similar and culturally familiar Europeans. Indeed, Americans generally found Germans less menacing. As *Time* and *Life* publisher Henry Luce wrote, "Americans had to learn to hate the Germans, but hating Japs comes natural."[36]

After the war anti-Japanese sentiment slowly tapered away, but returned as Japan became an economic rival in the 1980s.[37] At its core, however, remained the same old view that Japan and its people were inherently different and alien. Americans were critical of Japanese economic protectionism and feared that the country's people were superhuman workers who could outcompete Americans.[38] The Japanese even returned as antagonists in the American imagination, occasionally replacing Soviets as the enemy du jour. Michael Crichton's novel *Rising Sun* epitomized this view by portraying Japanese as intrinsically different, dangerous, and menacing. As one commentator lamented,

> Its portrayal of the Japanese as inscrutable, technologically proficient, predatory aliens who communicate through telepathy, subsist on unpalatable foods, manipulate *everything* and *everyone*...will be more influential in shaping opinions on Japan and the Japanese than any of the more thoughtful and insightful books recently published.[39]

Compounding this fear, the book was later turned into a blockbuster movie starring Sean Connery and Wesley Snipes. Even American marketers were complicit in fearmongering. A General Motors commercial in 1990, for example, asked viewers to picture the world in the year 2000:

Imagine, a few years from now. It's December and the whole family is going to see the big Christmas tree at Hirohito Center.

Go on, keep buying Japanese cars.

The commercial concluded with two words printed in large letters on a black screen: "Enough Already." That "Hirohito Center" was viewed as less American than the German-named Rockefeller Center once again points to double standards for Asians and Europeans and the ease with which entertainers and salesmen could play on the prejudices and anxieties of so many Americans.

Edward Said wrote in 1978 that Western views of the Orient were created through brief encounters and experiences with the unfamiliar lands of the East. Today, however, there are greater opportunities for in-depth engagement and understanding than ever before.[40] Some twenty-five years after General Motors' offensive commercial, the United States is a country transformed. Already Asian Americans make up over 5 percent of the US population and are the highest-earning, best-educated, and fastest-growing demographic group in the country.[41] America's demographic evolution and its growing contacts with Asians abroad will gradually extricate the country from the prejudices of the past. As myth gives way to reality, mockery to respect, and menace to reassurance, the United States will gradually move beyond the clichés and stereotypes of the past. Yet still American diplomats and policymakers must remain on guard so as to avoid slipping into old habits.

To Sell a Million Shirts

Since the earliest days of the republic, trade has often served to bridge the daunting geographic and cultural distances between Americans and Asians. On George Washington's first birthday in an independent America, February 22, 1784, the *Empress of China* left New York bound for the then mysterious lands of the East on a mission to commence trade with China. After a fifteen-month round trip, she returned laden with tea, silks, nankeen, porcelain, and other commodities of great value to the newly formed United States. The voyage's success encouraged other merchants to follow suit, and with that the Old China Trade route was begun.

For Americans and Europeans, Asia's reluctance to engage in large trade volumes posed a considerable challenge. Initially China and Japan were afraid of cultural contamination, disinterested in Western wares, and loath to relax their mercantilist and protectionist policies. According to its rulers, China was the center of the universe, favored by heavenly authority, with no need to concern itself with foreign lands of lesser importance.[42] The Mandarin word for China, *Zhongguo* (中国), literally translates to "Middle Kingdom," the center of everything. When the outside world came to China, the court dismissed its traders and missionaries as barbarians. To manage their arrival and limit their influence on Chinese culture, China restricted foreign trade to Canton (now Guangzhou), the port farthest from the capital of Beijing.[43] Other Eastern countries, such as Japan, followed similar policies in relation to the outside world. The United States, however, was successful in at least some of its early commercial diplomacy. In 1833 it organized trading relations with Thailand and was one of the first outside nations to begin the process of opening up a hesitant continent to the international community and global economy.

What the United States attempted to accomplish relatively peacefully was pursued much more violently by European states. Britain colonized India and large portions of Southeast Asia, but had less influence in China, with whom it ran a dreadful trade imbalance. Britain imported vast quantities of tea and porcelain but a largely self-sufficient Chinese economy was in little need of British manufactures or commodities, and accepted only gold and silver as payment. One American trader estimated that between 1805 and 1825, years of still relatively small volumes of American trade with China, a massive $62 million was transferred from the United States to China, and likely far more from the coffers of Great Britain.[44]

Unwilling to continue this imbalance, the British began trading with opium instead of gold and silver, even in the face of opposition from the Chinese authorities. Opium, a highly addictive drug derived from the same plant as heroin, was relatively rare in China until the British East India Company began to use its vast poppy fields in India to supply the country with it. With imports of opium into China increasing exponentially, opium itself quickly became the most valuable commercial crop in the world.[45] By 1838, Chinese authorities were alarmed by reports that nine out of ten people in the provinces around the port of Canton were addicted to the drug.[46] In response China banned the import and trade of opium, arrested almost twenty thousand Chinese workers believed to be involved in the drug trade, and destroyed £2.5 million worth of opium held in Western factories.[47]

The reaction was immediate. After accusing the Chinese of barbaric and criminal acts, the British fleet arrived and inflicted a swift and devastating defeat on the Chinese in what became known as the First Opium War. Despite being heavily outnumbered, Britain dominated the conflict with its more powerful ships. Only sixty-nine British lives were lost compared to the deaths of over twenty thousand Chinese in a war that demonstrated the sheer military superiority of Western equipment and technology over China.[48] Britain's modern rifles easily bested China's matchlock muskets, while the first steam-powered iron warship wrought havoc against China's crude junks. China's inability to defend against the far more advanced military and naval capabilities of the Western powers began a "Century of Humiliation," with Western powers able to extract demand after demand from the weakened Chinese government. The first was the Treaty of Nanking in 1842, which ended the hostilities, rewarded Britain handsomely, and allowed it access to ports beyond Canton, thereby destroying the Chinese system of restricting foreign interactions.

The United States too sought greater economic ties with China, but was able to achieve them through diplomacy rather than by force. Soon after the British had forced their terms on the Chinese, US envoy Caleb Cushing successfully negotiated the Treaty of Wanghia, giving the United States commercial benefits comparable to those of the British, plus a dedicated diplomatic line to the reclusive Chinese government by granting American officials the ability to communicate directly with the court rather than its regional emissaries. This more peaceful approach, along with American efforts to restrict the opium trade, boosted the reputation of the United States in China and convinced Imperial Commissioner Kiyeng that "of all the barbarians of the West... only the United States is noteworthy.... [Others] do not come up to the recent status of the said country."[49]

It was the attainment of these economic rights that drove American policy toward Asia and made the region a vital area of commercial US engagement. While American policy toward Europe at this time may have been considered isolationist, no such charge could be leveled against its relations with Asia. The Treaty of Wanghia gave the United States valuable commercial opportunities, the security and expansion of which became top priorities for American foreign policy. Their protection, however, demanded that Chinese independence and sovereignty be shielded from the growing number of imperial powers wishing to absorb the country into their own personal spheres of influence. The United States therefore made clear to its competitors that any violation of Chinese independence would be resisted. The policy was buttressed by the growth of the East India Squadron of naval ships, which later became the Asiatic Squadron and, ultimately, the Asiatic Fleet, giving the United States a powerful voice in Asian affairs.

The United States adopted its military presence in the region to protect its economic and missionary interests and not, like other Western countries, to establish traditional colonial outposts. In general, the flag quite literally followed American trade. In 1825, President John Quincy Adams declared that the "flourishing of commerce and fishery extending to the islands of the Pacific and to China still require that the protecting power of the Union should be displayed under its flag upon the ocean as upon the land."[50] By the mid-1850s, American sea power had expanded and the United States had become an important player in the region's affairs. Its merchants were granted greater protection and new markets were swiftly opened. In some cases trade followed the flag, such as when Commodore Matthew C. Perry navigated his heavily armed black ships of the East India Squadron into Uraga harbor near Tokyo and refused to leave until Japan opened trade negotiations with the United States.[51] Militarily inferior, the Japanese had little option but to acquiesce. The resulting Convention of Kanagawa, signed on March 31, 1854, granted access to the Japanese ports of Shimoda and Hakodate, and Japan was slowly incorporated into the international economic system.

In response to these humiliations, Japan entered a period of internal reconstruction and social, political, and military modernization based largely on European models of development. By the end of the nineteenth century, Japan was so powerful that it could hold its own against Western aggression and even began its own policy of regional expansion in competition with European powers. These new capabilities were on display in 1895, when Japan secured its own victory over China and joined the Western countries in wringing concessions from the stricken Asian giant. The race by Japan and several European powers to obtain exclusive trading rights in China prompted the United States to take action to protect its own commercial interests.

In 1899 the American position on the sovereignty of China was made clear by Secretary of State John Hay, who succeeded in cajoling great powers to sign on to what became known as the Open Door Notes. A rudimentary precursor to the World Trade Organization (WTO), these notes underlined America's interest in global free trade and equal access, as well as offering protections for Chinese independence.[52] The Open Door Policy illustrated the American desire to continue unfettered trade with the region while also reasserting the country's opposition to European and Japanese colonialism. That other powers reluctantly agreed to limit the exploitation of Chinese land under their control was a testament to growing American power.[53] The agreement protected Chinese sovereignty at a time of its greatest vulnerability, and not a moment too soon. Russia had already carved off Manchuria, Japan had taken ownership of Taiwan, Germany had seized land in China's Shandong Province, and Britain had annexed parts of Weihai on the northeast coast and occupied control of the Port of Hong Kong and the surrounding Kowloon Peninsula.[54] The Open Door Notes demonstrated the American alternative to colonialism, a vision based on a liberal world order and free trade. This period and process has been described as the first step in transforming the logic of international relations in Asia from European to American principles.[55]

Elsewhere, American principles of capitalism and free trade were threatened by incessant conflict among the various powers competing for influence in Asia. After using its diplomatic powers to protect the independence of China, the United States next assumed the role of peacemaker to create a safer environment for the expansion of its commercial endeavors. The highlight was President Theodore Roosevelt's Nobel Peace Prize, awarded for bringing Russia and Japan together following the outbreak of war in 1904. To this day the medal adorns the Roosevelt Room in the West Wing of the White House, an abiding symbol of the positive role the United States has played in the region. The ensuing Treaty of Portsmouth recognized Japan as a rising power in East Asia but also forced Russia to abandon its policy of expansion, both of which helped maintain the peace for another thirty years.[56] This benevolent, trade-based approach to Asia continued during the Progressive

Era as the United States looked to increase cultural and educational relations with China and promote the establishment of a new political order following the collapse of the Manchu dynasty in 1911. The movement was later coordinated by Woodrow Wilson, who linked the promotion of economic and cultural reforms and development abroad to the furtherance of America's own national interest. Increasing global trade and supporting new trading partners directly benefited the US economy and was the signature element of American policy toward the Asia-Pacific as World War I broke out.

While the United States worked to stamp out the embers of conflict in Asia, the conflagration in Europe illustrated the need for greater cooperation and integration to prevent similar crises from occurring elsewhere. Asia was racked with several potential sources of conflict—European great power competition, a rising Japan, instability in China—that threatened to damage American trade interests. To secure the region, the United States promoted a multilateral system of norms based on common trade practices and limits on military expansion, with the ultimate goal of protecting commercial interests and avoiding conflict. With the relevant powers invited to the United States to sign the agreement, these norms became known as the "Washington System," a series of treaties and conferences adopted in the early 1920s. A multinational system of cooperation between both Western and Asian states, it included not only political and economic agreements but also, in the Washington Naval Conference of 1922, the first arms control regime in history. Organized by the administration of President Warren Harding, the system was meant to ensure peace in the Pacific during a time of increased naval buildup. The protection of China was also high on the administration's list of priorities and, in the Nine-Power Treaty, the major European powers, the United States, and Japan reaffirmed the country's independence and agreed to maintain equal economic opportunity rather than pursue individual imperialist aims. With the protection of China now an international norm, the Open Door Policy was effectively internationalized and American trade was allowed to continue in a more secure environment. The United States had committed itself to the formation of a stable and internationally incorporated Asia at an early stage—very different from American policy in Europe at the time, which initiated but then ultimately renounced similar efforts such as the League of Nations.[57] Ultimately the Washington System in Asia protected trade and limited conflict for the next fifteen years, enabling the

United States to establish a large and valuable commercial foothold in the region during the interwar years.

While World War II shattered the Washington System, economic activity returned after the war's close, especially as the United States worked to rebuild Japan and integrate Asia into the global economy. Once devastated by atomic blasts and extensive firebombing, Japan rose from the ashes to become one of the world's fastest-growing economies in the second half of the twentieth century, expanding at a rate of over 10 percent a year between 1950 and 1970 by plugging itself into the American economy through exports. Its success became the model for other regional economies, including Hong Kong, Malaysia, Singapore, South Korea, Taiwan, and Thailand. By the 1980s Asia appeared to be a land of economic miracles, interdependence, and double-digit growth. South Korea in particular, a country that had historically suffered from the encroachments of its larger neighbors, used American security and markets to move from being one of the poorest countries in the world to being one of the world's ten largest economies.[58] The East Asian development model, based on the promise of inexpensive and skilled labor for American and European companies, allowed the region's states to expand their economies rapidly to become powerful and influential in their own right.

With American influence, support, and access to its markets, Asian economies evolved to become some of the strongest and most dynamic in the world, with still far greater potential for the future. The region's countries have gone from having protectionist policies that limit trade to being state-managed export economies and vast manufacturing hubs, and finally major purchasers of American products. Throughout this evolution the United States has promoted and incorporated Asian countries into an international economic system intended to benefit all its members. For nearly seventy years, America's strategic role as balancer and ultimate guarantor of peace and stability in the region, secured during the Second World War across bloody battles in the Solomon Islands, Peleliu, Okinawa, and Iwo Jima, has allowed the region to blossom. The result has been Asia's ascent and the greatest accumulation of wealth and prosperity in world history. The US pursuit of its own economic interests, and its dedication to a liberal and open economic order, has been one of the longest, most enduring, and most successful American traditions in Asia.[59] It is a tradition that the US Pivot to Asia is designed to continue.

To Save a Billion Souls

American engagement in Asia has not been driven solely by material concerns such as trade and investment, but by spiritual ambitions as well. Writing in his diary in the 1830s, the missionary Dr. Peter Parker wrote that "China contains three hundred thirty-three millions of idolaters, but the land is yet to be possessed by Christ."[60] Like the traders before them, American missionaries were drawn to Asia by its untapped potential, seeing an extraordinary opportunity to expand the Christian faith in lands untouched by the Gospel.

The desire to proselytize became an early fixture of American policy. The emergence of missionaries to Asia dovetailed with an evangelical revival in the United States known as the "Second Great Awakening."[61] The lands of Asia grew to be of great importance to American churches, and it was the passion and determination of their early missionary workers in Northeast Asia that opened a region initially unwelcoming of foreigners and allowed the United States to build a more intimate relationship with many of its countries. In this regard the United States was unique. While Britain was the dominant power in the region, it did not pursue a similar policy of evangelism. The British East India Company preferred the locals to be subservient and backward and forbade missionaries from traveling to Asia on its ships because of their propensity to support education and build hospitals.[62] American traders did not share this view, and the numbers of American missionaries grew quickly.

Economic interests may have motivated a growing American role in Asia, but it was the work of missionaries that facilitated it. The Canton system in China restricted the movement of foreigners and forbade locals from teaching them Chinese languages or customs, a practice that inhibited trade but made missionary work entirely impossible. Unsurprisingly, missionaries proved the most determined, imaginative, and energetic in overcoming such hindrances. They became the first Westerners to learn Asian languages and were often later employed by their respective countries' diplomatic missions to aid in translation and outreach. The recollections of these early missionaries provide fascinating insights into the dangers of cultural interactions under the Canton system. One reported that his language teacher would bring shoes to every lesson so he could claim to be just another shoe seller if suspected by the authorities of breaking the law. Another would carry a bottle of poison, preferring instant death to capture and subsequent torture.[63] Even after missionaries acquired fluency, obstacles remained. Attempts to spread the word of God to a population ordered to pay no attention to foreigners led to some very strange conversations indeed. Missionaries reported that the Chinese would often look to change the conversation to "the price of your jacket," or "the size of your nose" rather than discuss the Gospel.[64] In other instances American evangelicalism led to increased antagonism, with numerous antimissionary riots breaking out in the late nineteenth century.[65]

Although the missionaries largely failed in their mission to convert the billion Asian souls to Christianity, they were successful in opening up the region and assisting in its modernization. With the United States largely content to simply ensure the safety and expansion of its trade and religious missions in Asia during the nineteenth century, it was left to American missionaries to forge personal links with Asians and improve conditions on the ground.[66] Many sought to transform society as well as to spread the Gospel, often by promoting equality and human rights. Some, such as Young John Allen, the "great Mandarin of the Methodists," even crusaded for the education of women.[67]

American missionaries left an enduring legacy across the region, helping to start what are today some of Asia's most successful institutions. One shining example is the Scudder family from New Jersey, whose patriarch, the physician and reverend John Scudder Sr., established the first Western medical center in Asia in 1819. Forty-two of his descendants across four generations, including all of his eight children, gave a total of 1,100 years of service to India.[68] His granddaughter, Ida S. Scudder, founded the Christian Medical College and Hospital at Vellore, India, in 1900, now one of the foremost medical and educational centers in the country.[69] In China, John Leighton Stuart, born in Hangzhou to missionary parents, became the first president of Yenching University, an amalgamation of several missionary-founded universities. Stuart bought old Qing imperial gardens and adopted Chinese architecture for the campus, and turned Yenching into one of China's premier institutions, with close ties to American universities like Harvard and Princeton.[70] The university, in its own words, sought "to mediate to China the finest values of Western civilization" while enabling students to preserve "the best features of their national heritage."[71] Although the school was closed after Chairman Mao established the People's Republic of China

(PRC), its legacy lives on in China's most prestigious institutions, Peking and Tsinghua Universities, which have adopted most of its departments and its campus. The links established with Harvard have also endured. Today the Harvard-Yenching Institute continues to advance the cause of higher education in Asia under the leadership of Harvard professor Elizabeth Perry.

Missionary sons also became central figures in the realms of government, diplomacy, and commerce, thanks to their often firsthand experience of the region. John Leighton Stuart himself became US ambassador to China. John Paton Davies Jr. and John S. Service, both born in Sichuan, China, became valuable members of the State Department and made history in leading the efforts to open the first official relations with Mao's Communist Party in the mid-1940s. Davies and Service were among the earliest to recognize the power and influence of the Chinese Communist Party relative to Chiang Kai-shek's Nationalist government, and yet, ironically, they also suffered the blame for losing China when the Communists were victorious.

Over time, in part because of their good works, American missionaries became more accepted in Chinese society. During some of China's darkest days, such as the 1937 Rape of Nanking, when Japanese forces in China conducted a seven-week campaign of brutality and terror in which somewhere between forty thousand and three hundred thousand people were murdered, foreign missionaries played a leading role in sheltering and protecting terrified citizens. In return, a thankful Chiang Kai-shek lifted the ban on compulsory religious courses in China's mission schools, allowing the missionaries greater freedom to continue their work.[72] But Mao's assumption of power in 1949 ended missionary work in China. Mao himself publicly accused John Leighton Stuart of being at "the vanguard of cultural aggression."[73] Work continued elsewhere in Asia, however. In Taiwan, for example, missionaries doggedly promoted democracy and human rights despite decades of martial law.[74] And as the United States gradually rebuilt its relations with China, Western proselytizing was quietly tolerated even though it remained officially illegal.

Numerous American churches still devote considerable resources and attention to Asia in the hope of drawing its nearly two billion souls to their faith. The United Methodist Church, for example, has operations in twenty-five Asian countries, from China and India to Fiji and Tonga. Gospel for Asia, headquartered in Texas, supports thousands of missionaries throughout the region who work to spread their faith and combat poverty. The Catholic Church is also heavily invested in Asia, with its spokesman calling it "one of the great frontiers of the Church of our time."[75] While his predecessor failed to travel to Asia, Pope Francis has already visited the Philippines, Sri Lanka, and South Korea. In January 2015 he also appointed three Asian cardinals, including the first from Burma, a country that has slowly begun to open up to outside influences.[76] As Catholicism declines in Europe, the Church has launched its own pivot to Asia, where its numbers are rising and its adherents still face persecution.

While many countries are now welcoming of missionaries and support or tolerate freedom of religion, the region is not free from dangers for those who wish to spread their faith or perform good works. American citizen Kenneth Bae, for example, was held in a North Korean labor camp after being arrested in November 2012 for spreading religious material. And in a return to the past, Chinese authorities are once again targeting missionaries under President Xi Jinping.[77] American missionaries have of course long faced such restrictions and risks in the region, and it is indeed remarkable that generations of believers nonetheless overcame those obstacles to leave a powerful legacy, forging early and enduring links between Americans and Asians. Today their legacy lives on in some of the region's finest institutions and in the best traditions of America's modern diplomacy.

The Costs of Conflict

From its earliest encounters with the region, the legacy of conflict has defined the American relationship with Asia almost as much as trade and faith. While gunboat diplomacy opened up commercial relations with Japan without the need for actual military engagement, other involvements in Asia have been more deadly. After defeating Spain and gaining its Pacific possessions in 1898, the United States subsequently fought four costly wars in the region—against Filipino rebels, Japan, Korea, and Vietnam—and also took part in several smaller skirmishes and demonstrations of military strength, including during the Boxer Rebellion, the Russian Revolution, and various crises in the Taiwan Strait. Each conflict brought unintended consequences, with effects that still linger today and lessons with relevance for tomorrow. We now turn to examine each of these four major conflicts, beginning with the costly legacy of a spectacular victory.

After defeating Spain in 1898, the United States became a powerful Pacific actor by assuming control over Spain's colonial holdings in Asia, including the Philippine islands. And yet President McKinley was initially unsure whether to adopt the islands, saying, "When I realized that the Philippines had dropped into our laps I confess I did not know what to do with them."[78] He was even unsure where to find them, confiding to a friend that he could not "have told where those darned islands were within two thousand miles."[79] Eventually, after consulting both maps and advisers, he decided to use the islands to further the work of American missionaries and promote American values in the region. In McKinley's words, the United States would "educate the Filipinos, and uplift and civilize and Christianize them."[80] The "natives," however, did not welcome the Americans any more than they had the Spanish. For two years before the American arrival, Filipino guerrillas had been fighting a war for liberation. Although some had supported the United States out of hopes for their country's independence, once it was clear that they would not receive it, these same rebels promptly turned their muskets on the United States.

While soon-to-be secretary of state John Hay called the defeat of the Spanish "a splendid little war," with little to no resistance against American forces, the ensuing war against impassioned Filipinos desperate for independence was anything but splendid or little.[81] Over one hundred thousand Americans were sent to the islands, of whom six thousand died—roughly the same number lost in the combined wars in Iraq and Afghanistan following 9/11.[82] Filipino casualties were much higher: roughly twenty thousand troops and over two hundred thousand civilians.[83] Some historians estimate that including deaths from disease and starvation, two direct consequences of that war, the death toll was closer to one million out of a population of only seven to eight million.[84] American governance in the Philippines stood in sharp contrast to previous American policy in Asia, which had emphasized trade and rejected imperial ambitions in the region.

Perhaps for that very reason, domestic opposition to the move was widespread, ranging from politicians such as William Jennings Bryan to philanthropists like Andrew Carnegie and writers including Mark Twain and Ernest Crosby. Twain in particular lamented how American policy had descended from its once-lofty aspirations:

[Creating] a government according to Filipino ideas...would have been a worthy mission for the United States. But now—why, we have got into a mess, a quagmire from which each fresh step renders the difficulty of extrication immensely greater. I'm sure I wish I could see what we were getting out of it, and all it means to us as a nation.[85]

In due course and on more than one occasion, *quagmire* would be a word often repeated in the annals of American conflict in Asia.

But first the United States had to become a Pacific power capable of projecting force. The year 1898 was a consequential one, as America stepped decisively in that direction. That year the United States gained not only the Philippines from Spain but also the strategically located island of Guam; in the same year, and through different circumstances, the United States also finalized the annexation of Hawaii. And so, in two swift strokes, a Pacific America was born.

While McKinley had hoped to use the Philippines to project American beneficence, his successor, Theodore Roosevelt, had more ambitious goals. "I wish to see the United States the dominant power on the shores of the Pacific Ocean," he said in 1900.[86] US installations and military assets in Hawaii, Guam, and the Philippines helped realize Roosevelt's vision. Before its victory in the Spanish-American War, the United States had no forward-deployed presence in Asia and scarcely used force in the region. Afterward America's assertive and forward-deployed posture would come to occupy a major role in its relations with the Asia-Pacific. Not more than two years later, the United States dispatched four thousand troops to China to help quell insurgents during the Boxer Rebellion, which threatened to restrict American commercial interests.

A result of greater American power and activity in the Pacific was that the United States was brought into direct competition with a rising Japan, a country also with growing regional ambitions. Japan's rise had been swift. After capitulation to Commodore Perry's black ships and the rapid reconstruction and industrialization during the late Meiji period, Japan entered the twentieth century a more developed, modernized, and ambitious nation.[87] Militarily the Japanese modeled their navy on the British and their army on the Germans, both seen as the best in class at that time, and very rapidly became a major power in their own right. This was demonstrated by Japan's stunning naval victory over Russia in the Battle of Tsushima Strait in May 1905, the first significant Asian victory against Western power since the Middle Ages.

Sensing a window of opportunity provided by a moribund China, Japan had already taken the Ryukyu Islands and also applied pressure to Taiwan and Korea. During the Meiji restoration of the late nineteenth century, Japan had held the United States in high esteem, with Yukichi Fukuzawa, a leading Japanese academic, calling it one of the wonders of the world.[88] The advent of competition in the Pacific between the two countries, however, soon altered this perception. After defeating China in 1896, Japan took over control of Taiwan and eagerly looked for more territory in which to grow. The swift American annexation of the Philippines, Guam, and Hawaii—combined with the existing holdings of European colonial powers—severely limited the possibilities for Japanese expansion. Fears of being muscled out of the region were manifested in Tokyo and led to heightened nationalism and a desire to confront the United States over the sovereignty of China.[89] Even after its intervention in the Boxer Rebellion, the United States was still seen as the main guarantor of Chinese independence, and Japan looked to test this commitment.

This circumstance bears some similarities to that of contemporary Asia. Then, a powerful and rising Japan demanded respect as a regional power, just as China does now. The US relationship with Japan during this period demonstrates the difficulty of managing changes in the balance of power while also protecting important economic and political interests.

The United States was slow to fully appreciate Japan's determination to become a dominant regional power, and racial condescension prevented policymakers from taking its growing capabilities seriously. Initially the United States sought to protect the region's status quo and American interests therein. In an attempt to set clear international norms regarding behavior following World War I, the major Pacific powers signed a number of treaties that together comprised the Washington System. These were designed to prevent conflict through diplomacy and to slow the budding naval arms race in the Pacific by adopting a ratio of ships of 5:5:3 for the United States, Britain, and Japan respectively. The United States further promised not to fortify the islands of Guam and the Philippines and was able to persuade the nine major Pacific powers to internationalize the Open Door Policy and affirm the sovereignty and territorial integrity of China. For several years this agreement successfully restrained an all-out arms race in the Pacific, and it was seen as a high point for the administration of President Warren Harding. At the final session of the naval conference it was said that "this treaty ends, absolutely ends, all naval competition."[90]

Such prognostications were premature, and within Japan the treaty was widely condemned. Japan's leadership chafed under the restrictions dictated to it by Western powers.[91] The 5:5:3 ratio was derided by nationalists as the equivalent of "Rolls Royce: Rolls Royce: Ford."[92] When this formula was included in a subsequent revision to the treaty, nationalist anger again erupted. Premier Osachi Hamaguchi, who had signed the treaty, was shot by a nationalist activist and died soon after.[93] As nationalists began to take over the main offices of power in Japan, the country became increasingly strident and determined to overthrow all restrictions on its expansion. In a 1935 article for *Foreign Affairs* magazine, Admiral Kichisaburo Nomura, who later became Japan's ambassador to the United States, complained that the United States and Japan had not negotiated "on a basis of equality" and that the treaty was "a decided blow to the self-respect of the Japanese people."[94]

Unsurprisingly, then, Japan began to retreat from the Washington Treaty System, occupying Manchuria in 1931 and renouncing the naval ratios in 1936.[95,96] The American-led system in Asia began to unravel, but rather than oppose Japanese assertiveness, the United States was occupied with the Great Depression and offered only the milquetoast response of nonrecognition of Japan's invasion of Manchuria.

As Japan's incursion into China began to widen, and with Japanese planes expanding their bombing raids to administrative centers closer to Beijing, Secretary of State Henry L. Stimson initially sought to place economic sanctions on Japan. With the American economy still suffering under the Great Depression, however, this was seen by others in government as a nonstarter and President Herbert Hoover made clear he would block any attempts to enact economic sanctions. According to Assistant Secretary of State William Richards Castle Jr., any sanction would be seen as an act of war to which Japan would respond with a blockade of all Chinese ports, impeding lucrative American trade routes. The United States would then have to choose between surrendering all rights in China, further damaging the American economy, or declaring outright war on Japan.[97] Nonrecognition was seen as the only feasible option at the time, and after being adopted by Stimson, was subsequently continued by Franklin Roosevelt, who was elected to the White House in 1933. Nonrecognition, of course, did not slow the Japanese army, which moved on to bombard Shanghai.

The United States had failed to take serious action against threats to the major pillars of the Washington Treaty System—limits on naval arms buildups, and the protection of Chinese sovereignty—and this temerity only emboldened Japan. In 1937 Japan launched a full-scale war on China, finally shattering the American-led system that had kept an uneasy peace and restrained Japanese ambition for fifteen years. In its place Japan sought to create an Asian "Co-Prosperity Sphere" free of European interference and under Japanese hegemony. This time Japan's brazen aggression against China finally provoked an American response. Provisions and materiel were dispatched to China and an embargo was placed on all iron and steel shipments to Japan. These efforts failed to deter Japan, and eventually the United States enacted a de facto embargo on oil exports to Japan, eliminating 50 to 75 percent of Japan's foreign trade and 60 percent of its oil supply.[98] These sanctions outraged the Japanese government, and its ambassador to Washington, Kensuke Horinouchi, objected strongly.[99] The oil embargo accelerated the descent into war, or, as Secretary of State Cordell Hull stated, "everything was going hellward."[100]

Meanwhile the US ambassador to Japan lamented American policy's failure to reach some form of accommodation with the region's rising power. To his diary, Joseph Grew despaired, "Why, oh why, do we disregard the experience and facts of history which stare us in the face?"[101] He felt the American response to the Japanese war with China would achieve only one thing: it would push Japan to adopt more extreme measures. He warned Washington that Japan was determined to continue its rejection of the Washington Treaty System and would pursue "an all-out, do-or-die attempt, actually risking national hara kiri, to make Japan impervious to economic embargoes abroad rather than to yield to foreign pressure."[102] As the Pacific Fleet was moved from its base in San Diego to Hawaii, and American military preparations began in the Philippines, war in the Pacific drew ever closer. Fighting in Europe, however, largely preoccupied most political and military leaders, despite the deterioration in relations with Japan. War plans drawn up in 1939 expected the majority of military attention to be given to the European and North African theaters of operation, and little substantive preparation was made for the East.[103]

In last-ditch diplomatic talks in 1941, the American and Japanese positions were as far apart as ever. The United States demanded the Japanese accept the Open Door Policy with China and withdraw all military forces from the country before the flow of trade and oil would be allowed to resume. This was untenable for the Japanese. The special envoy, Saburo Kurusu, angrily blasted the American position and the "Washington Conference treaties" which he concluded were "tantamount to meaning the end" of Japan.[104] Admiral Osami Nagano, chief of staff of the Imperial Japanese Navy, laid out the stark decision facing Japan's leadership: "Since Japan is unavoidably facing national ruin whether it decides to fight the United States or submit to its demands, it must by all means choose to fight." He continued, "Surrender would spell spiritual as well as physical ruin for the nation and its destiny."[105] On a day that has since "lived in infamy," December 7, 1941, the Japanese launched a preemptive attack on the American fleet in Pearl Harbor, and the United States promptly declared war against Japan. As Walter Lippmann noted, the Japanese intention at Pearl Harbor was not just to scuttle the US Navy, but to "sink our Pacific fleet because we were opposing them on matters that they were determined to carry through... [those being] the conquest of China."[106] The United States waged a costly war with Japan across thousands of Pacific islands and atolls, with the loss of over one hundred thousand American lives, in large part to prevent the disintegration and annexation of China and to preclude a regional hegemon's emerging to dominate the continent.

Today the United States once again faces a rising power in Asia with territorial ambitions beyond its borders. It will be more important now than ever to understand the failures of both deterrence and compromise that contributed to war in the last century, the better to ensure peace in the present one.

Power transitions naturally bring the possibility of misperception, but this is not the only potential pitfall that awaits the United States in Asia. In the classic film *The Princess Bride*, the Sicilian notes another as he celebrates what he thinks is his victory in the battle of wits against the Man in Black.

He laughs and taunts his adversary: "Ha ha, you fool! You fell victim to one of the classic blunders! The most famous of which is never get involved in a land war in Asia!"[107] The American wars in Korea and Vietnam proved the sagacity of this statement, with the former ending inconclusively and the latter in humiliating defeat, in contrast to the costly victories against the Philippines and Japan.

The Korean War began in 1950, only a few months after then secretary of state Dean Acheson gave a speech before the National Press Club in which he omitted the Korean Peninsula in discussing the US defense perimeter in Asia. At the time the United States defense perimeter was focused on maritime rather than continental Asia, and Acheson's omission likely emboldened North Korean leader Kim Il-sung to invade South Korea in an effort to reunite the two countries. Kim quickly worked to secure permission and support from Joseph Stalin, as well as a promise of reinforcements from Mao should the war go badly. In June 1950 he sent his forces across the 38th parallel—the artificial dividing line between North and South Korea—and launched a war that even to this day has not technically ended.

The United States reacted swiftly to North Korea's military advances and rallied UN support, fearing that if the Korean Peninsula were to fall to hostile forces it would imperil the safety and security of Japan. Although the operation in Korea was ostensibly a UN military action, the United States provided 90 percent of the troops to Korea and played a leading role in how the war was fought. General Douglas MacArthur, who had been a hero of two world wars, had overseen Japan's reconstruction, and enjoyed widespread political and public support, was chosen by President Harry S. Truman to lead the effort in Korea. Although initially short-staffed and underequipped, the UN forces under General MacArthur mounted a daring amphibious landing at Inchon, one hundred miles behind North Korean lines, and eventually succeeded in pushing the North Korean forces back across the 38th parallel.

With that status quo from before the war almost restored, US leadership grappled with the question of what to do next, which prompted one of the most significant crises in the history of US civil-military relations. Truman and MacArthur had differing views of the conflict, with Truman convinced the war was a distraction from Europe and MacArthur more focused on Asia as the defining Cold War battlefield. To discuss the war's next stage, they chose to meet at a location between Asia and the United States on Wake Island, a meeting some prominent historical accounts describe as tense, with MacArthur deliberately choosing to keep Truman waiting for roughly an hour.[108] As they talked about the war, MacArthur assured Truman that the chance of Chinese intervention was minimal and proposed that the UN forces advance northward to reunite the peninsula. Truman authorized MacArthur to proceed with this plan, but stressed that the United States should not take action against China and that only South Korean forces should be allowed to approach the Yalu River, which formed the border between the Korean Peninsula and China.[109]

Confident of victory, and in apparent violation of Truman's orders, MacArthur ordered his troops to approach the Yalu River, even as he received guidance from Washington prohibiting him from sending American troops into any Korean province bordering China.[110] His march toward the Yalu was a factor that prompted China's entrance into the war, with China concerned about American intentions and the potential emergence of an American military ally on the very peninsula that Japan had used as an invasion route into China. Beijing alone committed over 1.3 million troops to support the North Korean forces. Together with Northern Korean troops and Soviet air support, Chinese troops pushed American forces back to the 38th parallel, and by the spring of 1951, the war had reached a brutal stalemate. As David Halberstam writes in his marvelous history of the campaign, it "became a war of cruel, costly battles, of few breakthroughs, and of strategies designed to inflict maximum punishment on the other side without essentially changing the battle lines," a modern form of bitter trench warfare.[111] In the face of considerable public and political pressure, Truman reasserted civilian control of the military and recalled Douglas MacArthur for insubordination and his continuing habit of making public statements critical of the Truman administration. As the war dragged on, public opinion began to turn against it, with President Truman's approval rating plummeting to 23 percent in 1951—in part because of his then-controversial decision to replace MacArthur.[112]

With the United States unwilling to escalate the conflict, either by sending additional forces or by fielding nuclear weapons, the war remained deadlocked.[113] The United Nations forces thus settled on a draw, with an uneasy armistice in place across the 38th parallel. Over thirty-five thousand Americans had died defending South Korea—the fourth-bloodiest conflict in

American history to that point.[114] Despite the grave loss of life for all participants, the situation remained virtually unchanged from that before the war,
marking the first time the United States was unable to achieve its wartime
goals in Asia. Neither side viewed the Korean denouement as satisfactory,
and it has since remained a situation unfinished, unsettled, and increasingly
tense and spring-loaded. Today the heavily militarized "demilitarized zone"
(DMZ) separating North and South Korea is arguably one of the most heavily armed and dangerous places on the planet.

In the wake of the stalemate, a "Never-Again" club formed of those generals and politicians who saw American policy as profoundly misdirected. In
their minds the United States should not intervene ever again in Asia "unless
America was prepared to fight an all-out war, with the level of national commitment and mobilization necessary to accomplish the mission before public
support eroded."[115]

Opposition to limited war in Asia would remain influential, though not
always decisively so, as Communism spread.[116] Soon after the Korean War, a
standoff in the Taiwan Strait known as the First Taiwan Strait Crisis (1954–
1955) took place between Communist China and Chiang Kaishek's Kuomintang (KMT), threatening to draw the United States back into another
costly Asian conflict. Chinese forces began to shell the islands of Kinmen
and Matsu and seized the islands of Yijiangshan and Dachen. All of these
islands were closer to China than they were to Taiwan, but for that same
reason they were also crucial parts of the KMT claim to have sovereignty
over all of the mainland. President Dwight Eisenhower wished to avoid
committing forces to the conflict but also did not want to embolden China
by failing to demonstrate resolve over the crisis. Ultimately the Eisenhower
administration pushed for the Formosa Resolution, which would authorize
the United States to defend Taiwan and Taiwanese possessions in case of
attack. In addition, Secretary of State John Foster Dulles publicly stated that
the United States was considering using nuclear weapons to resolve the crisis.
These declarations were sufficient to force the issue to temporarily recede
from view, but it returned in 1958 when the Second Taiwan Strait Crisis
erupted unexpectedly.[117] After fierce Chinese shelling of Kinmen and Matsu,
the Eisenhower administration transferred weapons to Taiwanese forces,
increased the American naval presence near Taiwan, and circumvented a
Chinese blockade of the islands so that Taiwanese troops could be resupplied

by Taiwan. Eventually China stopped intensive shelling, ending the crisis, though both China and Taiwan reached a somewhat informal agreement to continue shelling each other's positions, often with propaganda leaflets, on alternate days until the United States normalized relations with the PRC in 1979.

With Korea resolved inconclusively and the question of Taiwan left to simmer, another conflict soon came to a boil. The collapse of the French proxy in Indochina in 1954, coming so soon after the loss of China and the stalemate in Korea, helped persuade policymakers that the United States could not stand idly by while Communism was on the march in Asia. President Truman had identified Indochina as a vital link in the worldwide containment line against Communism. With both American prestige and the region's future at stake, the United States gradually ratcheted up the number of American troops and advisors in Vietnam to signal resolve and determination, all the while aware of the perceived historical context of indecision in Korea and lack of resolution in the Taiwan Strait. What began as four hundred Green Berets in Vietnam in early 1961 increased to more than sixteen thousand troops by 1963, and over five hundred thousand by 1968.

If Korea was a costly draw, Vietnam was a resounding defeat that has traumatized America in ways obvious and subtle ever since. Korea had shaken American faith in its powers, but it was not until defeat against Vietnam that the United States realized the limits of its power.[118] As Marvin and Deborah Kalb describe, "Up until Vietnam, the United States had been a nation of unlimited vision and capacity. No goal was considered beyond its reach."[119] But after a war that lasted for seven years, in conditions that ranged from jungle warfare to hand-to-hand combat, fifty-eight thousand Americans had lost their lives, along with hundreds of thousands of Vietnamese.[120] The frantic escape by helicopter of the remaining American officials from the roof of the embassy in Saigon left an indelible mark on the psyche of the United States.

All presidents since have been haunted to some degree by the legacy of Vietnam, a legacy Bob Woodward has likened to a "bare 10,000 volt wire" that still runs through the White House.[121] The desire to avoid another Vietnam remains at the forefront of the American consciousness and has affected most presidential military decisions since. The American legacy in Vietnam has become a familiar touchstone that conjures visions of indecision, a lack of strategic resolve, the potential of devastating surprise, and the specter of national humiliation. It loomed in the background of Ronald Reagan's response to the bombing of US Marine barracks in Lebanon; Bill Clinton's unwillingness to send ground troops in response to unrest in Haiti, Kosovo, and Somalia; and President Obama's fears of another quagmire in Afghanistan and Syria.[122] Even today generals, politicians, and the media frequently talk about the dangers of conflict escalation and mission creep with a firm eye on the American experience in Vietnam. In recent years *Newsweek* has wondered, "Could Afghanistan be Obama's Vietnam?"; the *New York Times* has asked "Will Syria Be Obama's Vietnam?"; the *Washington Post* has conducted an analysis of "How Obama's Foreign Policy Team Relates to the Vietnam War"; and John McCain has remarked that President Obama's strategy to combat ISIS "is beginning to remind me of the Vietnam War."[123]

The history of US conflict in Asia at times casts a long shadow over US foreign policy. In a span of seventy years, the United States fought four major wars in the region against the Philippines, Japan, North Korea and its Chinese ally, and Vietnam respectively. Within the region the legacy of the Korean War and the Chinese Civil War remains with us in the form of a brutal, nuclear-armed dictatorship in North Korea and the risk of conflict with China over Taiwan. And yet America's costly victories and traumatic defeats have also shaped the region's future in positive ways. US victories against Japan safeguarded the region from imperialist domination, and US support for South Korea and Taiwan helped give rise to a prosperous and democratic government. To this day the American forward-deployed presence in Asia has brought peace and stability and underwritten Asia's dizzying economic ascent. It is in no way an exaggeration to suggest that a considerable share of Asia's present prosperity was paid for by the sacrifice of American lives and treasure.

Secondary Theater

For brief and infrequent periods, Asia has dominated American attention. At the end of the nineteenth century, the United States attempted to steer clear of European affairs and became increasingly engaged in Asia, following on expanding trade and missionary work. Asia was a paramount focus of President Theodore Roosevelt, who himself once stated that the American future "will be more determined by our position on the Pacific facing China than by our position on the Atlantic facing Europe."[124] These moments of concentrated focus on Asia, however, were rare and transient, and other challenges have often drawn American attention elsewhere. For this reason Asia has often been a secondary theater, and even been referred to at times as the "Forgotten Theater."[125] Although the United States fought long and hard to ensure Asia remained free from Japanese imperialism during World War II, swift disengagement soon followed, launching a flow-and-retrench pattern that continued throughout the twentieth century. As we will see in greater detail in the next chapter, American policy in Asia has been one of surge followed by retreat, and those retreats have often left unresolved problems in their wake that fester and then erupt, once again requiring a costly surge of American attention. America's cyclical approach to Asia has stunted the formation of a long-term and enduring commitment to the people and countries of the region, with Americans and Asians alike paying a high price for the periods of American whipsawing and neglect.

In the years preceding Pearl Harbor, the United States had paid comparatively little attention to affairs in Asia. Its gaze was focused on domestic economic woes, European instability, and Latin American revolutions. After the Japanese invasion of Manchuria in 1931, Secretary of State Henry L. Stimson reportedly wished people would stop "nagging" him about the conflict in Asia so he could address issues he deemed of greater importance elsewhere in the world.[126] Part of Stimson's exasperation came from various constraints leaving him unable to offer any significant response to Japanese aggression. President Herbert Hoover had rejected the use of economic sanctions and more coercive steps were off the table. As a result, and despite the brutality of Japanese conquest, the United States was willing only to publicly denounce Japan's Manchurian takeover.

The invasion of France by German forces led to an altogether different response from Washington. Materiel and provisions—including a gift of fifty aging destroyers by the US Navy in return for landing rights on British possessions—were quickly sent to Europe. In March 1941 the passing of the Lend-Lease Act provisioned $50 billion of military aid to nations fighting the Axis powers and, a few months later, the United States began an unofficial sea war with the *Kriegsmarine* in the Atlantic. Despite deteriorating relations with an increasingly ambitious Japan, American naval, air, and ground capabilities in the Pacific at this time received little in the way of material improvements or reinforcement until mid-1941.[127] The Japanese navy far outnumbered the US in cruisers, destroyers, and aircraft carriers. Defenses in the Philippines were neglected, allowing Japanese forces to quickly overwhelm the American defenders at the war's outset.[128] According to historian Harry Gailey, "Continual lethargy on the part of military and civilian leaders, combined with a lack of time to repair two decades of neglect [in the Pacific], cost the United States and its allies dearly during the first months of the war."[129]

After Pearl Harbor, American neglect was transformed virtually overnight into an overwhelming response. The United States had little choice but to respond with a massive military effort to rectify the grave situation in the Pacific. Even then Asia remained a secondary theater, with America pursuing a grand strategy to achieve total victory against the Axis in Europe before shifting full attention back toward the Pacific.

Ultimately the United States prevailed in Asia, but while it won the war it subsequently failed to secure the peace. The postwar demobilization and reduction in forward-deployed forces after Japan's defeat left the region once again deeply uncertain about its future. One of the main aims of the war, to preserve the status quo and Western-oriented China, were quickly forgotten as the United States focused on domestic issues and European reconstruction at the war's end. With the United States withdrawn, China quickly descended into civil war between Mao Zedong's Communists and Chiang Kai-shek's Nationalists. Besides a "modicum of financial and military support to the Nationalists" and the dispatch of a handful of senior American diplomats and officials, the United States did little to affect the situation.[130] Even Mao was shocked by the lack of American reaction to events in China, later confiding to Stalin that he had expected Washington to send a million troops to save the country and ensure its continuation as a Western ally.[131] Mao's surprise was understandable, since the United States had long been involved in China's affairs and had fought a bloody war with Japan in part triggered by concerns over Japan's invasion of China. As Communism enveloped China, America's trade relations and security arrangement in China collapsed and the Nationalists were pushed off the mainland. To General Eisenhower "the loss of China [was] the greatest diplomatic defeat in this nation's history" and was due in large part to American disengagement.[132]

Although China's loss should have shaken the United States from its complacency, it did not. The United States continued to postpone resolution of many of the thorny issues that lingered in Asia after the war's end, producing crises that plague the region to this day. Although the Allied powers had agreed to unify the two Koreas after the war, absent active American diplomacy, little progress could be made.[133] Meanwhile American officials hurriedly prepared expansive recovery packages to rebuild Europe, organized the partitioning of Germany, and constructed security alliances such as the North Atlantic Treaty Organization (NATO) to prevent a breakdown of order on the European continent. That Asia was deemed a secondary theater even after the loss of China was made explicit in January 1950. Before the National Press Club in Washington, D.C., Secretary of State Dean Acheson stated that the American defense perimeter in Asia ran in an arc through the Aleutians and Japan and down to the Philippines. For other countries, most notably Korea, Acheson stated that "no person can guarantee these areas against military attack," and that "should such an attack occur... the initial reliance must be on the people attacked to resist it."[134] Although Acheson mentioned that the United Nations would be called upon to defend all areas against aggression, the speech was viewed as a green light for North Korea to attack the South because of its suggestion that the Korean Peninsula did not fall under the American security umbrella. To Kim Il-sung, the autocratic North Korean leader, the Acheson speech and prior American inaction over China demonstrated that the United States was not committed to Asia and that he was free to make his move across the 38th parallel.

According to noted historian Philip Zelikow, the American decision to withdraw from an active role in Asia in preference for concentrating on the rebuilding of Europe "accelerated Soviet, Chinese, and North Korean planning to press the offensive."[135] It was not until North Korean troops marched over the border that the United States returned its focus to a region rapidly succumbing to Communist pressure. David Halberstam has called the Korean War one that President Truman didn't want, in a part of the world his national security team thought didn't matter.[136] Nevertheless the shock and embarrassment of the invasion, as well as its startling rapidity, "jolted the United States right back into the Asian commitments it had [previously] foresworn."[137] Thus continued the cycle of surge and retreat. The costs were great and the legacy of missteps enduring, as China remained estranged from the region for decades and an unpredictable and subsequently nuclear-armed adversary emerged in the North on the Korean Peninsula.

The erratic nature of US engagement in Asia continued, as the United States again pulled back following the Korean War and then surged into Vietnam a decade later. Retreat followed defeat in Vietnam, as failure to achieve American goals led to a reconsideration of American policy in the region as a whole. The failure of the most advanced and sophisticated military in the world to overcome a small and seemingly backward country, the political failure of a campaign without clear goals, and the loss of domestic support was a turning point for American policy.[138] President Nixon sought to extricate the United States from the quagmire through a policy of Vietnamization, attempting to replace American involvement through greater training and assistance for South Vietnam. This policy was then expanded regionally as the United States downgraded the American security guarantees that had underpinned security in Asia, and encouraged Asian countries to take greater responsibility for providing security for their own region. Known as the Guam Doctrine or the Nixon Doctrine, this new approach was intended to reduce America's active commitment in the world by supporting the self-reliance of regional military forces. At its core it was an attempt at sharing the burden of Communist containment by encouraging and supporting the buildup of its allies' defense capabilities. "The United States," Nixon explained, "has a right to expect that [the security problem in Asia] will be increasingly handled [by] the Asian nations themselves."[139] While it may have been a reasonable expectation for a country so stretched by existing military commitments to share the load, the perception among governments and commentators alike was that it was tantamount to an American withdrawal, and even a call to pull back from the world. The *Washington Post*, echoing the view of many, called it "a formula for an American retreat" that followed swiftly from American defeat in Vietnam.[140]

After Vietnam the United States began to turn its attention more firmly to other theaters, in large part because the Cold War in Asia suddenly became much quieter. China had played important roles in both the Korean and Vietnam Wars, but as US relations with China improved following rapprochement in 1972 and normalization in 1979, the prospect of another major land war in Asia continued to diminish. For the most part, American attention turned toward the grave threat of renewed and potentially nuclear conflict with the Soviet Union in Europe, with much of American strategic focus directed toward questions involving nuclear weapons, arms control, and conventional warfare against the Soviet Union and Warsaw Pact. The United States tended to its bilateral relationships within Asia, but otherwise remained focused on developments elsewhere.

Even with the Cold War's conclusion and the elimination of the risk of great-power conflict in Europe, US attention and resources did not immediately flow back to Asia. American foreign policy was not focused on any one region in the 1990s, with the United States fighting the First Gulf War in the Middle East and intervening to stop humanitarian crises in the former Yugoslavia. For a brief period in the late 1990s, it seemed possible that Asia would receive a growing share of US focus and attention as economic interaction intensified and new security issues surfaced, including the Third Taiwan Strait Crisis, North Korea's attempts to build a nuclear weapon, and the uncertainty surrounding China's rise. This was not to be, however, because the September 11 attacks forced the United States to turn its full attention to the wars in Afghanistan and Iraq and to counterterrorism. Asia instead remained a secondary or even tertiary theater, and although China was welcomed as a partner in the war on terror, the focus remained on what could be achieved in the Middle East and South Asia rather than in Asia as a whole.[141] With the United States preoccupied during this period, China made enormous military advances, expanded its regional trade, forged diplomatic ties within the region, engaged local institutions, and deftly applied its soft power in what many referred to as a "charm offensive." Rarely in history has a rising power made such prominent gains in the international system without any response from established powers. Those within the administration with a focus on Asia, such as Deputy Secretary of State Robert Zoellick, spoke of the need to "manage" China's emergence as a dominant power. With less focus and attention on Asia, the reality was that China was instead "managing" a period of US distraction, much to its success and perceived advantage.

Although the United States has shown a willingness to commit military forces to the region when crises emerge, its expenditure of political capital and its pursuit of sustained engagement has been episodic and, at times, insufficient. The present Pivot to Asia is intended to overcome a legacy of strategic oversight and inattention that will limit the US ability to fully shape the Asian Century. A new era in which relations with Asia are pursued in an intensified but stable fashion across multiple administrations will require sustained effort and demonstrated effect. Without it American partners and competitors will doubt the endurance of US commitments, and the United States will find itself—as it has numerous times in history—in a position of strategic disadvantage.

Short-Staffed

American policy in the Asia-Pacific is challenged not only by a lack of sustained focus, but also by a failure to provide sufficient resources to the tasks at hand. The United States often pays dearly for its inattentiveness when crisis emerges, such as in the early months of war with Japan, when years of inadequate American defense preparation were exposed by quick defeats. America's cycles of surge and retreat do not allow for long-term planning to build new core competencies, nor can painstakingly acquired capabilities survive in the lean years between neglect and engagement. The unfortunate result is that the United States has generally been short-staffed and under-equipped in Asia, which has thwarted American objectives over time. The story of Task Force Smith during the Korean War, and the State Department purges during the early years of the Cold War, are illustrative of the dangers of subtle lapses in attention, materiel, and expertise. A greater attention to the Asia-Pacific demands also the concomitant provision of adequate resources to get the job done.

Task Force Smith

In 1950, during the opening weeks of the Korean War, a small contingent of American troops on a ridge overlooking the main highway between Suwon and Osan watched the North Korean army move toward them. The approaching force had just taken Seoul and now rolled its way through South Korea in an attempt to unify the peninsula. Surprised and largely unprepared for the invasion, the United States had hurriedly sent an advance party of troops to slow the North Koreans before the main contingent of Western forces arrived. That was the mission of the roughly four hundred American troops in what became known as Task Force Smith, named after their commanding officer, Lieutenant Colonel Charles B. Smith. General MacArthur said they would be an "arrogant display of strength" that would make the enemy regret ever setting foot in South Korea.[142] Instead they illustrated the tragic result of a failure to adequately prepare for challenges.

As an approaching tank column came into range of the American guns, Task Force Smith opened fire with everything it had. Numerous rocket and howitzer shells slammed into the armored bodies of the tanks but failed to halt them in their tracks. Instead of there being an arrogant display of American strength, it was the North Koreans who "advanced arrogantly, seemingly unconcerned by the exploding...shells about them."[143] One task force member reported direct hits from twenty-two of his 2.36-inch rockets, but his rounds failed to impart any damage on the Russian-built T-34 tanks. Instead the North Korean forces trundled through the token resistance that Task Force Smith presented and continued on their way, refusing even to deem the Americans worthy of battle.

Looking down the road through his binoculars, Smith next saw the main North Korean contingent approach. It was a long column of tanks, trucks, and men that he estimated to be at least six miles in length—the Sixteenth and Eighteenth Regiments of the battle-hardened North Korean People's Army (NKPA) Fourth Division. Undeterred by their failure in the first skirmish, the Americans once again opened fire, but were just as ineffective. While the element of surprise caused initial chaos among the North Korean ground troops, they soon regrouped and outflanked the American position. Under heavy fire and taking many casualties, Smith and his men eventually made a rough and frantic escape down the ridge and away from the enemy. The next day's roll call accounted for just 185 men out of the over 400 that had initially made up the task force. While others would straggle back in the days and weeks that followed, MacArthur's arrogant display of strength, intended to delay the Korean advance before the main American forces arrived, succeeded only in delaying the Inmun Gun for a total of seven hours.[144]

"To any troops with solid training, armed with the weapons standard to any advanced nation at the middle of the century," wrote the historian T. R. Fehrenbach, who had commanded a company of troops in Korea, the North Koreans "would have been duck soup. But Task Force Smith had neither arms nor training."[145] Instead it had been a hastily arranged and understrength group that showed clearly the dangers of failing to prepare for even the most likely military gambit. The United States had turned its attention away from

Asia following World War II, underresourced its remaining outposts, and then compounded its weak position with an inability to respond quickly and effectively to new challenges. The inadequacy of the 2.36-inch bazookas that Task Force Smith used against the North Korean tanks had been well known since 1945, yet five years later US weaponry had still not been updated.[146] The conclusion of World War II had catapulted the United States to the status of the most powerful country in the world, and yet its lack of preparation meant that it was North Korea that dominated the early stages of the war. The Americans had the technological capability to dominate North Korea, particularly after the development of 3.5-inch rocket launchers that would easily have penetrated the Korean tanks. However, due to a focus on demobilization, these had been distributed neither to MacArthur's Far East Army nor to its South Korean allies, despite knowledge of the strength of North Korea's tank force. As a result the North Koreans were able to drive brazenly down roads in broad daylight, destroying South Korean placements with ease and opening "virtually unopposed paths for the infantry to follow."[147]

In just five years, the US military had become a shell of its former self, with troops at bases such as Fort Lewis even being told that their budget would cover the use of only two sheets of toilet paper per latrine visit.[148] Smaller budgets hampered American preparations in Asia, so much so that General Matthew Ridgway, MacArthur's successor in Korea, described the status of American forces in 1950 as being one of "shameful unreadiness."[149] As Halberstam notes, the United States was a country "trying to get by on the cheap, and in Korea it showed immediately."[150] Task Force Smith was the best a retrenched and redirected United States could muster to hold the line and signal resolve. The first month of American engagement in Korea has been called one of the worst periods in American military history, as the undertrained and outgunned troops, despite numerous acts of bravery and dedication, were overwhelmed by the North Korean forces.[151] As defense cuts again threaten the ability of the United States to respond to emerging threats, the men of Task Force Smith serve as tragic reminders of the legacy of inadequate preparation and the risks it brings.

The China Purge

In the early afternoon of Sunday, May 4, 1919, roughly three thousand students congregated by the Gate of Heavenly Peace in Tiananmen Square to protest the concluding rounds of the Treaty of Versailles. Although China had been an Allied power during World War I, German territory in China was to be provided to the Japanese rather than returned to China. This was the latest in a series of humiliations that China had been forced to accept, dating back to the Treaty of Nanking in 1842. This demonstration was a departure from China's more recent quiescence in the face of imperial predations, and as it quickly spread across the country, the May Fourth Movement was born. It marked the moment at which Chinese intellectuals drifted toward more radical political thought, and Mao himself referred to these protests as a major step toward Communist revolution.[152] The Communist Party of China was formed soon after, and six years later, civil war broke out between its supporters and the government forces of the Western-backed Chiang Kai-shek. It would prove to be a long and bloody conflict that claimed the lives of as many as six million people.[153] By 1949, however, Chiang and his followers had been pushed off the mainland to Taiwan, and China had become a Communist state. For Americans debating the recent turn of events, one question stood taller than all others: "Who lost China?"

It was in this atmosphere that the specter of McCarthyism and the Red Scare loomed large and enveloped the nation. The State Department was an immediate victim of a national paranoia regarding the infiltration of the government by Communist spies. Attention was focused on the State Department after the conviction in 1950 of Alger Hiss, a senior department official accused of spying for Communists. Unwilling to believe that China could have been lost without some form of nefarious conspiracy inside the United States government, many regarded Mao's victory as having been possible only with support from shadowy figures inside the State Department, particularly those responsible for China policy. Such accusations propelled the junior senator from Wisconsin, Joseph R. McCarthy, to national prominence. In February 1950 he shocked the country by delivering a speech in Wheeling, West Virginia, in which he waved in his "hand a list... of names that were made known to me by the Secretary of State as being members of the Communist Party and who nevertheless are still working and shaping policy in the State Department."[154]

No list actually existed, but the accusation provided a simple explanation for what had been complex and traumatic setbacks. The loss of China, and later the invasion of South Korea by the Communist North, were blamed squarely on the State Department, a place full of people McCarthy said were "loyal to the ideal and designs of Communism rather than those of the free, God-fearing half of the world."[155] Although resulting congressional hearings found no wrongdoing, the careers of many China specialists in the State Department's Division of Far Eastern Affairs were ruined. "China hands" like O. Edmund Clubb, John Paton Davies Jr., and John Service, among others, were forced out of government service by McCarthyite hysteria. The China purge at State stripped the department of virtually anyone who knew anything about China. The United States had often been short-staffed when it came to Asia experience, but now the levels of expertise plummeted to new depths.

With a generation of Asian experts dismissed, the United States lacked the necessary insight into a vital region and regime at a decisive moment in history. Policy invariably suffered, with enduring consequences. Senior officials thought China was led by fanatics who ruled recklessly and without reason, which delayed rapprochement.[156] Until 1979, Chiang Kai-shek's Republic of China, holed up in Taiwan, remained the only Chinese government recognized by the United States. The inability to identify the strained relations between Moscow and Beijing, which were of utmost strategic importance, prevented the United States for years from seeking to exacerbate the tensions inherent in the Communist alliance.[157] National Intelligence Estimates from as late as 1960 predicted no likely break between Moscow and Beijing in the foreseeable future, despite the fact that a rupture in the Communist camp was already well under way. Relations had been sharply strained ever since Stalin's death in 1953.[158] Mao despised Stalin's successor, Nikita Khrushchev, who in return felt little affection for Mao. Other dangerous misunderstandings mounted, as policymakers initially suspected that Chinese pressure had convinced Khrushchev to place missiles in Cuba, and that China's 1962 offensive against India was an entirely coordinated act meant to test the United States. In reality China had no input on the Cuban Missile Crisis and the Sino-Indian border war was a more complicated affair, with India's own "Forward Policy" playing a role in provoking Chinese hostility.[159] Ultimately, without the cadre of knowledgeable and effective China hands, American diplomacy in the Cold War years lacked expertise and was blinded by ideology. Fearing accusations of disloyalty, America's thin ranks of Asia experts largely kept quiet or were ignored.

The costliest result of a dearth of Asia experts, further exacerbated by the increased scrutiny of State Department China hands that had begun in 1949, came during the Korean War. After Allied troops had successfully pushed the North Koreans out of the South, China feared that the Allied forces would continue north, and the resulting incursion would manifest a Western outpost directly on China's borders. This would be a serious strategic threat to China and one it was determined to prevent. Chinese premier Zhou Enlai sent a clear message to the Americans through the Indian ambassador in October 1950, stating, "If the United States, or United Nations forces cross the 38th parallel, the Chinese People's Republic will send troops to aid the People's Republic of Korea."[160] As China expertise became increasingly politicized or inadequate, the United States failed to take seriously Chinese signaling. The threat was mistakenly regarded as a bluff, and policymakers assumed that China was merely a satellite state over which Moscow maintained close control. "The Russians were not ready to risk global war over Korea," concluded Omar Bradley, chairman of the Joint Chiefs of Staff; "therefore, there would be no Soviet or Chinese Communist intervention" in Korea.[161] Such conclusions were accepted by Washington as near certainties that did not warrant further reflection or testing of assumptions.[162] Allied troops, "intoxicated with the heady taste of triumph," crossed the 38th parallel and approached the Yalu River.[163] Soon after, China entered the war with overwhelming troop numbers, bringing the United States and China into conflict with each other and inflicting a heavy toll on the UN forces.

Many of these costly mistakes and misperceptions, which took the lives of thousands and fundamentally altered the future of the region and the American role in it, could have been avoided with better expertise and sufficient resources. The tragic history of Task Force Smith and the crippling purge of the State Department China hands illustrate the dangers of a United States policy that is not fully prepared for the Asian challenge, either materially or intellectually. Today, after nearly a decade of war in the Middle East and South Asia, the United States has a large and impressive cadre of experts familiar with the valleys and villages of Iraq and Afghanistan. It will need to develop equivalent levels of expertise on the intricacies of culture, history, and diplomacy in Asia if it is to avoid the pitfalls of the past and capture the potential of the Asian Century.

Democracy Promotion

Liberal democracy has taken root in many Asian countries, in no small part because the United States has been a firm advocate and promoter of a system intended to provide people with a means to decide their own future. The promotion of liberal values, the rule of law, and democracy have been long-standing and important themes in the story of American relations with Asia.

The Philippines was one of the earliest examples of American nation-building and democracy-promotion efforts. After taking the islands somewhat unexpectedly from a Spanish government eager to leave, the United States almost immediately declared its intention to return the country to its people, a goal supported by even avid expansionists such as Theodore Roosevelt. Before doing so, American leaders felt a responsibility to first impart knowledge of self-governance.[164] As Woodrow Wilson wrote in 1902, it was the American duty to "impart to [the Filipino people], if it be possible by contact and sympathy, and example, the drill and habit of law and obedience which we long ago got out of the strenuous processes of English history."[165] The United States quickly established the Philippine Commission, and through it set about building institutions that could effectively teach Filipinos how to pursue democratic rule in the future. Starting at the local level and gradually building up to the provincial and ultimately national level, the United States planned to depart the islands with a functioning democratic government in place. Of course Filipinos rejected such paternalism, waging their own war for independence against the United States until 1902. The awkward program of democracy building, which continued during the conflict, was ridiculed by one contemporary who felt American policy was like "going with a sword in one hand, a pacifist pamphlet in the other hand, and trailing the model of a schoolhouse after."[166]

Despite such criticism, the United States pressed on with its plans to make the Philippines an independent and modern democracy. Spanish judges were replaced by Filipinos, and American soldiers were required to teach children, distribute food, and rebuild local infrastructure.[167] By 1902, through a commission headed by future president William Howard Taft, the United States had established a judicial system, including a supreme court and a modern legal code, a civil service, and municipal and provincial systems of governance, and had extended the provisions of the US Bill of Rights to the Philippine islands. By 1907 the first elections for a national legislative assembly had been held and, after adopting the rules of the Fifty-Ninth US Congress, the Philippine Assembly was opened in October of that year. Although support for the Philippines' eventual independence was strong in the United States, it was finally formalized as a goal only in 1916, when the United States passed the Philippine Autonomy Act along with conditions for granting it. One of the main obstacles to independence was the fear, shared with many Filipinos, that independence would simply mean eventual conquest by Japan.[168] By the 1930s the United States had committed to granting the Philippines independence within ten years, and after Japan's defeat the islands promptly received it. In all, the American policy of "Filipinization" had allowed the country to gain experience and knowledge of self-governance so that, when independence finally occurred in 1946, much of the population had become accustomed to democratic rules and norms. While the dictatorship of Ferdinand Marcos undermined some of the country's democratic gains, democracy returned not long after and endures to this day.[169]

American policy in the Philippines stood in stark relief to that of other imperial powers in that, from the very beginning, America set as its ultimate objective the independence of the country it governed. Its attempts at nation building were also effective elsewhere in the region, most notably Japan. Before the Americans arrived, the country's Meiji restoration period of the late nineteenth century had included many reforms that transformed the country from a traditional autocracy to a modern twentieth-century constitutional government.[170] Japan slid into military dictatorship in the 1930s, but after its defeat in World War II, the United States was intimately involved in pushing democratization during the Allied occupation. After hopes that the Japanese would initiate the process of their own accord were dashed, the United States, under the leadership of Douglas MacArthur, supreme commander for the Allied powers, drafted a democratic constitution that remains a guiding force today. Army officers Milo Rowell and Courtney Whitney, with assistance from others, such as Beate Sirota, wrote the constitution in the space of a week after numerous drafts by the Japanese were rejected for not taking the drastic steps the United States felt necessary to create a more liberal and modern state. The document made the executive branch answerable to parliament rather than the emperor, introduced a liberal bill of rights, gave women the vote, and has largely remained a successful and effective document that has underpinned the growth and revival of postwar Japan.

While more ambitious plans for Japan—such as land redistribution and other democratic reforms—were ultimately abandoned for fear of weakening the country in the face of Communist encroachment, the United States was instrumental in reviving the fortunes of a country decimated by war and distraught by defeat. American-led reconstruction, political reform, and subsequent economic support laid the groundwork for the country's entrance into the global economic community and its eventual "economic miracle" of the 1950s and 1960s, which catapulted the economy forward to become the world's second-largest by the 1980s. The United States was supportive at every step, encouraging, for example, Japan's entrance into the Organization for Economic Cooperation and Development (OECD) in 1964.[171]

Another democratic success eventually followed in South Korea. The country has often been likened to a shrimp caught among the whales of China, Japan, and Russia, with each taking turns to invade and dominate it. As with Japan and the Philippines, the United States was drawn to the country by war. The American-led response to North Korean aggression precipitated a greater role for the United States in South Korean affairs after the war ended. While supportive of the anticommunist strongman Syngman Rhee, the United States was influential in establishing an atmosphere of independence and sovereignty in a country historically beset by conflict and occupation, although democracy remained lacking. With American financial aid and assistance, South Korea experienced rapid economic growth, improved its education levels, implemented vital reforms to its bureaucracy and military, and set the foundations for its eventual transition to democracy.[172] American action in Korea allowed the United States to serve as a democratic role model, and it also established "a desire to democratize among the Korean public" and the formation of what has been called "an internal and quite indigenous attachment to democratic principles."[173]

The Cold War delayed the onset of democratization in the country as the United States tilted toward preferences for stability and authoritarian leadership for fear of Communist inroads. Nevertheless, American values were disseminated and helped modernize Korean society during the 1960s and 1970s. A new generation of Koreans, many schooled in the United States, returned to their country determined to foster a society that combined loyal citizenry with greater individual freedom and prosperity. Economic success begat political development, which, coming as it did at a time of de-escalation in the Cold War, was once again supported by the United States. American quiet diplomacy under Jimmy Carter, and then Reagan, in support of liberalization soon turned into a roar when, in 1987, Assistant Secretary of State Gaston Sigur gave a high-profile speech calling for members of the Korean government to permanently "civilianize their politics" or face the withdrawal of American support.[174] With street protests against authoritarian rule emboldened, the Reagan administration leaned heavily on Chun Doo-hwan and, according to Selig Harrison, an expert in American relations with Korea, "played a major role in preventing the imposition of martial law."[175]

American action in promoting development, the rule of law, and a respect for democratic principles in South Korea has been called one of the most impressive and dramatic successes of the United States in the post–World War II era, on the level of the American Marshall Plan for rebuilding Europe.[176] Democratization in South Korea was swift and effective because of American support and the prior financial aid that had allowed the country to bounce back from the ravages of war. Other successes include Taiwan, where the United States supported the end of one-party rule and encouraged the emergence of opposition parties in the 1980s.

Democracy promotion has at times also led to frictions with states in the region. The United States sanctioned Burma after abuses by its military junta, Fiji after a military coup, and China after the Tiananmen Square massacre. In some cases the American concern for rule of law and democracy has clashed with more pragmatic interests in the Asia-Pacific and caused tension with autocratic states, especially China.

Importantly, there have also been times when a reversal in American policy from sanctions and toward engagement has had dramatic and unexpected effects. In 2009 the Obama administration reversed a Bush-era policy intended to isolate Burma and the repressive military dictatorship that had ruled the country for five decades. Instead the new more proactive policy emphasized greater direct communication with the military junta as well as cooperation on a variety of shared interests and concerns. These US overtures were meant to encourage Burmese reforms and were welcomed by Burma's government, which within a few months took bold and unprecedented steps in a more democratic direction. Since then Burma has written a new constitution, held elections, allowed the formation of a parliament, and freed countless political prisoners—including Nobel Prize–winning opposition leader Aung San Suu Kyi. While the country's ultimate trajectory remains unknowable, and although there remain obstacles ahead, the shift in Burma's political system has been striking and heartening, and may one day lead to a genuinely democratic form of government in a country with enormous diversity and promise.

The birth of each Asian democracy can change the region in ways that are subtle and yet profoundly important. As Samuel Huntington and others have noted, the establishment of democracy in even a handful of successful states can affect governance in other states, contributing to democratic waves.[177] Japan's democratic transition influenced South Korea's and Taiwan's, which in turn have influenced Indonesia's, and so on.

American democracy promotion in Asia has therefore had a long history and, although placed on hiatus for much of the Cold War, has nevertheless been a consistent theme in American policy dating back to the nineteenth century. The result has been a region that has grown steadily wealthier and more democratic for decades, forming an enduring legacy that the United States can build upon as it seeks to ensure the Asian Century is characterized by freedom and liberty for all.

Conclusion

The history of the United States in Asia has been a multifaceted and mixed story of achievement and sorrow, of victory and defeat, of deep knowledge and unhelpful stereotypes, and of certainty and indecision. The eight themes outlined in this chapter continue to shape not only our complex understanding of Asia but also the Asian perception of the United States. As we have seen, the tyranny of distance has left the United States both geographically and culturally distant from Asia. Across that vast space, misperceptions have at times festered and prejudiced judgments hardened, often to the point of influencing policy. The myth of Asian extravagance has at times led business entrepreneurs to exaggerate the region's opportunities, mockery of its people has led policymakers to discount its dangers, and the irrational fear of an alien menace has sometimes led policymakers to abandon prudence and pragmatism. Across the geographic and cultural divide, the United States has been drawn to Asia, which has often been seen as a place to sell shirts, save souls, and spread democracy on a grand scale. For these pursuits—of trade, faith, and freedom—each with an uncertain trajectory, the United States has been willing to expend considerable blood and treasure. Afterward, however, American focus has tended to wane as challenges at home or in other regions beckon. For too long Americans have viewed Asia as a secondary theater, which is why the country's diplomats and soldiers often find themselves short-staffed and underequipped to deal with its sudden challenges. As we will see in the next chapter, US strategy in Asia has been remarkably consistent in its overall definition but often inconsistent in its implementation, for complex reasons and with serious consequences for the America's future in the region.

CHAPTER FOUR

The Pivot's Antecedents

The Recurring Elements of American Strategy in Asia

The previous chapter focused on the history of the United States in Asia, as well as eight broad features or motivations that have animated American policy since the earliest days of the republic. In contrast, this chapter distills that history to explore the more narrow topic of American strategy in Asia over the last two hundred years. Here I seek to situate the current Pivot to Asia within this larger and longer legacy and tradition of American strategic encounters with Asia.

Through most of American history, US strategy in Asia has had several enduring features. It has generally called for the use of diplomatic, economic, and military means in order to prevent the emergence of a dominating hegemon in Asia, thereby making the region safe for American pursuits like trade promotion, faith advocacy, democracy support, and territorial security. Despite the general coherence and consistency of this strategy across time, the United States has not always adhered to it, as unanticipated foreign crises, consuming domestic distractions, and insufficient investment in the means of American strategy complicated its implementation. For much of its history, the United States has thus pursued its Asian strategy in fits and starts, at times executing it vigorously and at other times neglecting it woefully.

This inconsistent approach is no longer suitable to the changing strategic realities of twenty-first-century Asia. For the most part, the rudiments of American strategy are sound. Long-standing American objectives like ensuring free trade and liberal values have not changed, nor has the reality that the way to secure these objectives is to keep the region free from hegemony. But the rise of a complex challenger like China and the emergence of numerous nontraditional, transnational challenges, from climate change to freedom of navigation to regional economic management, call for an addition to the historical focus on a balance-of-power approach. To address these issues, Americans will need to strengthen Asia's operating system—the complex arrangement of institutions, norms, and values that have facilitated cooperation and undergirded Asia's peace and prosperity. In important respects, key elements of this operating system cannot be imposed from the outside; they must be embraced first and then subsequently reinforced. What requires greater consideration in the period ahead, then, is *how* the United States can both keep Asia free from domination and also strengthen the region's essential operating system, two distinct but interconnected ambitions.

This chapter focuses first on the recurring features of America's Asia strategy, then on its often inconsistent application, and finally on the questions now central to the future of American statecraft in the twenty-first century. It concludes by noting briefly the ways in which the current Pivot to Asia marks a continuation of and evolution from these earlier antecedents of American strategy in Asia.

The Persistent Features of Asia Strategy

From Carl von Clausewitz and Niccolò Machiavelli in the West to Sun Tzu in China and Kautilya in India, for thousands of years generals, scholars, and historians around the world have wrestled with the riddle of strategy. Rather than wade through these divergent philosophies, which can at times be difficult to reconcile, it may be more useful to adopt the elegant and powerful theory of strategy that is used by the American military.

In this view, strategy is fundamentally concerned with ends, ways, and means: certain fundamental interests (ends) are achieved when policymakers combine the resources and tools available to them (means) with a theory or ordering principle of how those resources can best be used (ways). It is true that at times *ends*, *means*, and *ways* can bleed over and blend into each other in ways that make them difficult to differentiate. Still, by using this contemporary framework, it is possible to systematically explore the recurring features of American strategy in Asia. As we will see, the American approach to statecraft has often been implicit rather than explicitly defined or codified into doctrine; nevertheless, several remarkably consistent qualities over time give it a certain coherence.

US strategy in Asia has had four long-standing *ends* over the last two hundred years, though a few have grown in salience as others have receded. Three were discussed in detail in the previous chapter: (1) selling shirts, (2) saving souls, and (3) spreading liberal values. From the first US trading voyage to Asia, undertaken by the *Empress of China* in 1784, through to the negotiations surrounding the Trans-Pacific Partnership more than two centuries later, trade has been a central motivation of American Asia policy. For example, it was at the core of the earliest American treaty with the Qing dynasty, Commodore Perry's decision to open up Japan using his black ships, and John Hay's Open Door Notes. Ensuring the safety and protection of American missionaries has been also been a recurring goal throughout US history, often addressed in early American treaties. Although spreading Christianity is no longer official US policy, two hundred years of US missionary activity produced a reservoir of Asian experts who often served diplomatic efforts—from Dr. Peter Parker's work as an interpreter for the Treaty of Wanghia in the 1830s to Jon Huntsman Jr.'s service as US ambassador to China more recently. The focus on Christianity has been superseded by a third enduring end in American Asia policy, that being support for democracy and liberal values. This mission, so to speak, has a long heritage connecting early twentieth-century efforts to create constitutional democracy in the Philippines, later exertions to promote democracy in Japan, South Korea, and Taiwan, and contemporary endeavors to support Burma's democratic awakening. To these goals we must add a fourth additional interest that is manifest in American history—the protection of American territory in Asia, which once included the Philippines and today includes Guam and Hawaii.

How were Americans to achieve these goals? The *ways* employed by the United States have been fairly consistent. As Henry Kissinger writes, "For over a century...it has been a fixed American policy to prevent hegemony in Asia."[1] The American hope has long been that if Asia does not fall under the domination of another power, trade will flow more freely, religious freedom will grow, liberal values will flourish, and US territory will be safe from menacing powers. A belief in this particular approach animated the Open Door Policy of 1899, which was intended to prevent China's domination by imperial powers and to keep the country open for trade with other nations. It was also present in President Theodore Roosevelt's successful mediation of the Russo-Japanese War in 1905, which was motivated not only by daring American idealism on the global stage but also by a desire to maintain a balance in Asia that involved both Russia and Japan, as well as by a prophetic wariness of possible Japanese expansion southward. During the Cold War, the United States fought Japan to protect the region from Japanese domination. In the midst of that conflict, the United States pursued a balance of power by normalizing ties with China and working with Japan and its treaty allies to counter Soviet power in Asia. For Americans, then, the way to achieve enduring US goals in Asia has been to prevent hegemony there. Of course, as we will see, there have been long-standing debates on precisely how hegemony is prevented and balance achieved.

Having discussed the ends and ways of American strategy, we now turn to the *means* wielded to implement it. The United States has relied on three broad instruments of power in pursuit of strategy: diplomatic efforts (such as the direct use of emissaries or representatives, institution building, and treaties), economic statecraft (including trade and sanctions), and finally military force (its use and the threat of its use). Importantly, the United States has not always had a "tool kit" expansive enough to accommodate its broad strategy. In the early years of the republic, the United States lacked a Pacific navy and had no Pacific bases or coaling stations. In the twentieth century, having acquired territories like Guam, the Philippines, and Hawaii, and having built a robust forward-deployed naval presence, the United States had more chits that it could play on the Asian game board. The precise mix of American instruments of statecraft in Asia policy has varied over time. In some cases, the United States has relied on diplomatic instruments like the Open Door Notes, which initially were not backed by substantial American power; in other cases the United States has employed brute military force, including for rolling back Japanese aggression and the spread of Communism.

Through most of American history, US strategy has been implicit but fairly stable in its definition. American statecraft has worked to blend diplomatic, economic, and military *means* in order to prevent the emergence of a hegemon in Asia, which has been the key *way* to keep the region safe for American *ends* like trade, faith, democracy, and territorial security. As we will see, despite the overall coherence and consistency of this strategy across time, the actual practice of American strategy has been at times irregular and inconsistent.

The Inconsistent Application of Asia Strategy

A brief overview of American foreign policy in Asia reveals that there have been times when the United States faithfully implemented its implicit Asia strategy and other points when it most assuredly did not. It is worth asking not only *when* the United States pursues or distorts its Asia strategy, but also *why*.

As we will see, throughout the history of American involvement in Asia, there have been at least three broad reasons for the country's inconsistent adherence to a discernable Asia strategy. First, as we saw in the last chapter, the United States has often viewed Asia as a secondary theater to concerns in Europe, the Americas, and now increasingly the Middle East. As a consequence it often pursues its Asia strategy in fits and starts, exhibiting an accordion-like tendency to surge into the region and then retreat as concerns elsewhere drain away American attention. Second, in addition to foreign concerns, preoccupations within the United States ranging from economic malaise to political gridlock have often drawn the United States inward and complicated its ability to implement its Asia policy. Third, and closely related to these first two reasons, is the fact that US investment in the means of American Asia strategy has often exhibited a marked inconsistency, with policymakers in the region finding themselves short-staffed or ill equipped to cope with the region's challenges. This at times has brought unforeseen and difficult consequences, as the tragedy of Task Force Smith recounted in the previous chapter attests.

US Asia strategy began coalescing in the early eighteen hundreds as trade and missionary activity increased, but it remained shallow and vague because the United States lacked the ability to exert much influence in or over Asian affairs. Washington's goals were to protect the growing numbers of traders and missionaries operating in the East, but the absence of any appreciable naval presence caused those efforts to be lacking. The United States instead practiced a form of "beneficiary imperialism," in the words of the diplomat John Paton Davies Jr., reaping the benefits of treaties signed by the British and French with China and relying especially on the British navy to secure the high seas.[2] US Asia enthusiasts like the missionary-turned-diplomat Dr. Peter Parker, as well as naval enthusiasts like Commodore Matthew Perry, who used his fleet of black ships to open Japan in the 1860s, became vocal proponents of a more assertive American strategy in the Pacific. Their exhortations and lobbying for the cause of an enhanced American capacity went largely unheeded due to pressing concerns and opportunities elsewhere. The United States was still more concerned with continental developments, expanding into its own borders and then distracted by a civil war and the decades of internal reconstruction that would follow it. It could not yet play more than a passive role in Asia, nor could it practice in any meaningful way its Asia strategy.

Building the Foundations for an Asia Strategy

The first vigorous implementation of American strategy in Asia began in the 1890s, guided by a handful of visionary leaders who built the diplomatic, economic, and military means to pursue a more formidable Asia policy. They were spurred to action by the increasingly aggressive predations of European imperialists on China, as well as by China's defeat by Japan in the Sino-Japanese War of 1895, which imperiled American interests in promoting trade and faith. These concerns led the naval theorist Alfred T. Mahan, President Theodore Roosevelt, and Senator Henry Cabot Lodge to advocate "positive action in East Asia to protect American interests and maintain a balance of power."[3] The effort began almost accidentally, as the United States acquired an Asian presence through the Spanish-American War—as well as a new national interest: the territorial integrity of its Asia possessions. In the words of Mike Green, the capture of the Philippines and Guam, and the separate annexation of Hawaii, "created the canvas upon which [American strategists] . . . would paint the first American cohesive and integrated grand strategy for the Pacific."[4]

To maintain US interests in this period by preventing hegemony, American policymakers turned chiefly to diplomatic and military means. On the diplomatic side, the Open Door Policy of 1899 was intended to prevent hegemony in Asia and maintain free trade with an independent China. Roosevelt's mediation of the Russo-Japanese War was intended to keep Russia part of the Asian balance largely because of a fear that a rising Japan would threaten US territories. Later the Washington Naval Conference of 1921–1922 was organized by President Harding as European power waned in Asia after World War I. It sought to keep Japan at bay by forcing other major competing powers to commit to the Open Door Policy and by limiting the size, armaments, and tonnage of US, British, and Japanese fleet sizes. Although the United States wanted to keep Asia open and balanced through diplomatic means, Mahan rightly observed that "it remains obvious that the policy of the Open Door requires naval power."[5] So to these diplomatic components of America's Asia strategy were added military ones—coal stations, naval bases, and a fleet that grew in a few short years from the world's sixth to its second largest.[6] In 1907, Roosevelt dispatched sixteen white-painted battleships—nicknamed the "Great White Fleet"—to circumnavigate the globe and remind others of growing American naval power. At the same time, Roosevelt's concerns about Japanese power led him to order War Plan Orange, a series of secretly developed military plans for a potential conflict with Japan. Within three decades America's largely unarticulated Asian strategy was endorsed by top-level officials and implemented both vigorously and methodically by its leaders. The United States was now an Asian player, using its diplomatic and military might to keep Asia free from hegemony and to secure its long-standing interests in trade, faith, and territory.

Forgetting American Strategy

If the period from 1898 to 1929 constituted the first committed execution of America's Asia strategy, then the 1930s corresponded with its first major malpractice. With the arrival of the Great Depression and a swell in isolationist sentiment, a nearly three-decade surge of American attention gave way to neglect and retreat, revealing fully the accordion-like quality of American efforts in Asia. US strategy in Asia remained the same—securing national interests by preventing regional hegemony—but American attention was turned inward, the strategy was not practiced, and the means to implement it were allowed to wither on the vine. First, US diplomatic instruments were neutralized as Japan violated the terms of the Washington Naval Conference, expanding its navy, invading China, establishing the puppet state of Manchukuo, and even sinking the USS *Panay* in 1937—all without facing any meaningful economic or military response from the United States for several years. Second, the United States allowed its military instruments of statecraft to atrophy, and, perhaps clouded by prejudice and myths of Japanese inferiority and unsophistication discussed in the previous chapter, did not sufficiently invest in the assets called for by Plan Orange. The United States failed to upgrade or invest in new Pacific capabilities until the infamous events of 1941, in the process allowing Philippine defenses to deteriorate, and its own soldiers and sailors to soften through lack of training. During the run-up to hostilities, the United States found itself outnumbered by the Japanese navy in cruisers, destroyers, and aircraft carriers.[7] This lack of investment in hard power assets in turn limited its ability to discourage Japanese expansion. When the United States finally used one of its remaining instruments of statecraft, economic sanctions, they lacked the backing of military power—which almost certainly emboldened Japan as it responded with a violent quest for regional hegemony. In short, the failure to pursue a focused Asia policy in the 1930s resulted in a clear and unambiguous failure to secure American strategic objectives.

The United States briefly recommitted to Asia strategy after Japan's attack on Pearl Harbor, giving it full attention and employing every instrument of statecraft to defeat Japanese hegemony across the islands and military outposts of the vast Pacific. Even then, however, the Asia-Pacific remained a secondary theater. Shortly after the Japanese attack, the United States committed to a "Europe first" strategy at the Arcadia Conference, planning to first defeat Nazi Germany and then to turn its full attention to Japan.

This "Europe first" strategy continued even after the end of the Second World War, with the United States promptly losing its strategic focus in Asia and curtailing continuing investments in its Asia strategy. The United States was instead principally engaged with rebuilding Europe and securing its industrialized states from Communist expansion. Just as it had in the 1930s, this departure from a consistent Asia strategy led to swift and serious setbacks to American interests in Asia. As Philip Zelikow notes, "The 'Europe First' emphasis of the early Cold War, and the corresponding reluctance to confront Communist moves in Asia, ultimately produced considered U.S. decisions in 1949 *not* to defend Taiwan, South Korea, or Indochina with U.S. forces."[8] Crucially, it also led to the "loss of China" to Communism, which was shocking to many Americans because China's independence had been a central feature of US policy, integral to American interests in trade, faith, and freedom as well as vital to an Asian balance of power. These decisions demonstrated an abrogation of American strategic ends in Asia as well as the inconsistency of American commitments to Asia—especially since, after a bloody war with Japan, the United States sacrificed almost wholesale the interests for which it had fought, in order to attend to other pressing matters on the other side of the globe. Unsurprisingly, then, this period was not only a time of strategic distraction but also an interval when the United allowed the means of its Asia strategy to deteriorate dangerously. Almost prophetically, steep budget cuts left American troops in Japan perilously ill equipped for war in Korea.[9]

A More Muscular Asian Strategy

After effectively forsaking Asia strategy from 1945 to 1950, the United States dramatically elevated its importance after North Korea's attack on the South, launching perhaps the most comprehensive commitment to Asia strategy since the time of Theodore Roosevelt. The nature of American statecraft adapted in response to the rising Communist threat. In the past, US strategy had called for using its instruments of statecraft to preserve enduring interests by preventing the emergence of an Asian hegemon. Now the strategy was intended to prevent the collective dominance of a group of ideologically aligned states rather than the rise of one particular hegemon. Importantly, preventing these states from dominating Asia could not be accomplished only by sea. The United States would have to shift resources from the maritime domain (e.g., Japan, Guam) to the continental domain (Korea, Vietnam) in order to defeat Communism on the Asian mainland itself.

To achieve these objectives, the United States unsheathed and sharpened all the means of statecraft at its disposal. On the military side, it intervened on the Korean Peninsula, threatened China during the Quemoy and Matsu crisis when the Chinese military shelled Taiwanese islands, and fought a long and bloody war in Vietnam. It also maintained bases in Japan, South Korea, the Philippines, and even Taiwan. On the economic side, it used its enormous market and the creation of the General Agreement on Tariffs and Trade (GATT) to help bring prosperity to Asia's noncommunist states, seeking to reduce the appeal of Communist ideology to domestic populations through better prospects and higher wages. Finally, on the diplomatic side, it signed alliances with Japan, Australia, New Zealand, Korea, and Thailand—creating the hub-and-spokes structure that continues to serve as the foundation for US regional influence. Washington also launched the Southeast Asia Treaty Organization, a short-lived attempt at an Asian NATO that involved Australia, France, New Zealand, Pakistan, the Philippines, Thailand, and the United Kingdom—though it proved poorly aligned with changing conditions and divergent aspirations. Ultimately, the most defining initiatives from this era were the costly American exertions of the Korean and Vietnam Wars, the latter of which led to a strategic reassessment of American purpose in Asia.

A More Realistic American Strategy

The more muscular US Asia strategy that began with the Korean War was undermined by American failure in Vietnam and economic stagflation at home. These together led to a substantial renovation to core aspects of American statecraft. US Asia strategy was not abandoned, but it began to change in its key elements and applications rather substantially. In 1969, President Nixon announced the Guam Doctrine, which suggested that the United States would increasingly rely on its allies to contribute more to their own security. In other words, the United States would begin reducing investment in the means of its Asia strategy. With regard to military capabilities, the United States withdrew from Vietnam and reduced troop levels around the region. The United States also shifted its economic position away from buoying Asian economies and, beginning to see them more as commercial rivals, became embroiled in disputes with Japan, went off the gold standard, and veered away from key elements of Bretton Woods, the international monetary system forged after World War II. Most consequentially, Nixon changed a core assumption of American strategy to better accord with geographical realities. It also aligned with a more traditional American approach to power dynamics. Nixon's secretive and bold move toward rapprochement with China suggested a return to balance-of-power logic and a departure from the misconception that Communist states together comprised an Asian monolith. Under this more realistic approach to American strategy, and with the Soviet Union and China now openly antagonistic, the risk of Asia falling under hegemony seemed diminished, and less involvement in Asian affairs therefore seemed justified. Much of the Cold War conflict in Asia, including the wars in Korea and Vietnam, had involved China; once relations between China and the United States improved, the Cold War in Asia calmed considerably.[10]

From this point forward, through to the end of the Cold War, Asia policy was markedly less grand and sweeping, and focused much more on the hard work of managing existing alliances and partnerships—a task

Secretary of State George Shultz famously referred to as "tending the garden." US policymakers dealt with a wide range of concerns: human rights in allied states including South Korea and the Philippines; economic tensions involving Japan; continuing disagreements with China, largely over human rights; the clarification of commitments to Taiwan; and the debate over whether to work more closely with Japan or China in regional policy. These were extremely important issues, but they did not dramatically jeopardize US strategic ends or the region's balance of power. In contrast, the end of détente with the Soviet invasion of Afghanistan, the possibility of war in Europe, and the dangers of nuclear weapons occupied an enormous share of top-level attention relative to Asia. Indeed, during the twilight years of the Cold War, Asia became a quieter region of relatively low priority and less focus from American strategists. While it is important not to overemphasize the American role, during this period of relative calm, American power and action was often decisive in shaping outcomes.

Strategic Confusion, China's Rise, and Nontraditional Challenges

As the Cold War ended, and the threat of Soviet hegemony in Asia disappeared, US policy in Asia was set adrift. In many ways US strategy appeared to be a resounding success, but in other ways there were concerns over larger questions surrounding American purpose going forward. The region was increasingly democratic and prosperous, and through hard work and fortitude had transformed itself into a major pillar of the global economy. The region was also at peace, even while dark clouds loomed on the horizon. China's surging growth, its use of force against student protesters in Tiananmen Square, and its threatened missile blockade of Taiwan raised the specter of a long-term, illiberal great power that could dominate Asian politics and potentially undermine American interests. China's rise was in many ways the kind of traditional balance-of-power problem with which American strategy had historically dealt, albeit with some salient differences, particularly given China's size and its economic interdependence with the United States and with other Asian states, many of whom were staunch American allies. To this somewhat traditional challenge were added a host of new transnational and nontraditional threats, such as climate change, North Korea's nuclear program, and new diseases like SARS. In preparation for both traditional and nontraditional challenges, Joseph Nye in the Pentagon launched the aptly named Nye Initiative, which was meant to strengthen ties with key allies, particularly Japan. Both the United States and its allies were in search of a rationale for strategic cooperation in an uncertain period very different from the Cold War. As part of a diversified push in Asia, the United States also boosted its economic tools, in part by articulating a more significant role for Asia-Pacific Economic Cooperation (APEC).

After September 11 the United States was drawn fully into the conflicts of the Middle East and South Asia, and Asia was once again relegated to the status of a secondary theater. As we have already discussed elsewhere, these wars drew attention away from Asia during a period when China made enormous military advances, expanded its regional trade, forged diplomatic ties within the region, engaged local institutions, and deftly applied its soft power in what many referred to as a "charm offensive." The United States still attempted to pursue its traditional Asia strategy by preparing for China's rise. On the diplomatic front, it expanded and improved ties with treaty allies, and signed a civilian nuclear deal with India. On the economic side, the United States pushed for trade agreements with Singapore and South Korea. Its military focus was elsewhere, however, at a time when China's military investments intensified, including China's development of anti-access/area-denial capabilities. At the same time, the Bush administration understood the importance of coping with emerging nontraditional tasks and wisely undertook efforts to incorporate China into existing institutions as a "responsible stakeholder." However, with the global economic crisis humbling American prospects and the United States bogged down in the Middle East, there were serious concerns about the durability and resilience of American power across Asia.

The Asia Pivot and an Uncertain Future

The Pivot to Asia has marked an effort to once again elevate Asia in the councils of American policymaking. By returning American strategic focus toward Asia, the Pivot in Mike Green's words has constituted "a rejuvenation of strategic thinking towards the Pacific in the spirit of Mahan and Roosevelt."[11] Although the Pivot faces an uncertain future as administrations change and crises in the Middle East demand a substantial share of American attention, it has nonetheless seen serious accomplishments in its early years.

The Pivot to Asia has focused in large part on seeking to strengthen all the various means of American statecraft in the region after a period of distraction and investments elsewhere. The United States bolstered the diplomatic arm of American policy by joining ASEAN's Treaty of Amity and Cooperation and through engaging regional organizations like the ASEAN Regional Forum and East Asian Summit. The United States also brought Burma onto the international stage and intensified diplomacy with each American ally and partner as well as with China. With respect to economic statecraft, the United States passed the Bush-era free trade agreement with Korea, negotiated the Trans-Pacific Partnership, and is currently negotiating a bilateral investment treaty with China. India is increasingly engaged around shared Asia-Pacific objectives. Finally, the Pivot has seen the United States strengthen its military capabilities within Asia. The United States stationed 2,500 marines in Australia, dispatched littoral combat ships to the Straits of Malacca, and is now implementing plans to devote 60 percent of its naval and air forces to the Asia-Pacific—as clear a commitment as any that the United States seeks to bolster its military capabilities in the Asia-Pacific. Perhaps as importantly, senior officials from the president on down have sought to articulate a rationale for enhanced engagement buttressed by diplomatic, strategic, and commercial arguments.

The Pivot has reenergized the *means* of American strategy and also worked toward articulating a new concept of the *ways* in which these should be used to secure American *ends*. The way the United States historically secures its interests, by preventing hegemony in Asia, remains a core component of American strategy, but there are now questions about how this endeavor should be pursued and whether it is sufficient to achieve American aims. We now turn to the broad strategic debate on the future of US Asia strategy.

Revising Asia Strategy for the Future

For much of its two-hundred-year history, the United States has had an Asia strategy that has been largely consistent in its core tenets but inconsistent in its application. However, the changing realities of the twenty-first century, and the new strategic challenges of Asia in particular, demand an approach different from the one the United States has historically pursued. At a minimum the United States will need to apply its Asia strategy with more consistency than it has in the past—especially as the growing magnitude of new challenges, including China's rise, raises the costs of future failures. If the United States is to secure its objectives in the region, Asia can no longer be treated as "secondary theater," and Asia policy needs to receive more frequent top-level attention along with the necessary funding for civilian and military purposes.

For many considering contemporary US strategy, it is clear that this alone may not be enough. The United States will need not only to apply its strategy consistently but also to adapt it shrewdly to twenty-first-century realities. Admittedly, not all elements of preexisting strategy need revision. The *ends* of American strategy, for example, continue to be the maintenance of free trade, liberal values, and territorial security. As for the *means* of US strategy, economic, diplomatic, and military instruments of statecraft will continue to be important, though there remain questions about which elements should be stressed and what combination of them will be most effective. By far the sharpest lines of disagreement will pertain to the *ways* in which the United States wields its strategic instruments. In other words, how should the United States use its still-substantial power to achieve its ends?

For two hundred years, the consistent answer to this question has been that the United States should use its instruments of statecraft to prevent hegemony in Asia. Today this is unlikely to be sufficient, especially with the rise of a complex challenger like China and the emergence of numerous nontraditional, transnational challenges from climate change to freedom of navigation and nuclear proliferation—none of which can be solved by a simple balance of power. The question of how the United States should use its means to achieve favorable outcomes on these new and different challenges will be an increasingly important dimension of US strategy.

Since the end of the Cold War, various scholars and policymakers have grappled with this question and debated how to carry out US strategy in Asia for the uncertain period ahead. Their approaches can broadly grouped into five schools of thought.[12]

The "China first" school puts China at the center of American strategy in Asia, and holds all other bilateral relationships as secondary to building a strong and resilient relationship with Beijing. This is an approach taken in the past by key personalities in the White House, where the dominant features of China policy are traditionally formulated. This approach assumes that the United States can forestall or mitigate Chinese hegemony in the

Asian arena by co-opting China into a bipolar framework, perhaps through a "fourth communiqué" or a bilateral condominium with Beijing (e.g., a G-2). This kind of grand bargain would allow the two countries to jointly cooperate on regional challenges and perhaps even global challenges, thereby allowing for the management of new transnational threats. Perhaps the most serious objection to this way of pursuing American interests is that it may raise the specter of a spheres-of-influence alignment replete with "core interests" and international waterways transformed into closely guarded territorial waters. Undeniably this outcome would be contrary to the open and rules-based US order and raise destabilizing concerns among US allies and partners. Additionally, it may not even be possible to use a G-2 framework to convince China to respect global freedom of navigation or refrain from pursuing aggressive policies against US allies, especially if it believes its own interests are at odds with these objectives and that the United States lacks the capacity to object. Furthermore, such an approach could also imperil China's own national interests by potentially upsetting some of the key features of global commerce, transportation, and communication on which aspects of the Chinese miracle of growth have been built.

In contrast to a principal focus on China, the "bilateral alliances" school focuses on US security alliances and partnerships as the keys to solving complex problems, such as the strategic uncertainty surrounding China's rise or North Korean nuclear provocations. Its supporters, scattered around the Pentagon and the State Department, believe that alliances and partnerships can bolster US efforts to keep Asia free from domination while also providing benefits outside the realm of security. An article of faith among these practitioners is that when allies and partners agree on values like freedom of navigation or free trade, that shared consensus can elevate these principles and shape the behavior of recalcitrant emerging powers such as China.

While the "bilateral alliances" school still makes room for a cooperative relationship with China, the "China threat" school—a distinct third approach to organizing Asia in a strategic framework—stresses the competitive dynamic in the US-China relationship. Its adherents see China's enormous commercial potential as a distraction from its emergence as a "near peer" competitor of the United States. These hawks anticipate an ambitious hegemonic rise as well as increasing tensions, and focus on the need to prepare for (and thereby dissuade or deter) any future military clash with China.

For them, Chinese hegemony is best resisted through overtly pushing back on China's attempts to expand influence in Asia. The problem with such a strategy is that global and regional challenges that are hard enough to solve even with China's assistance will be impossible to solve without it, and an overtly adversarial strategy risks making any kind of partnership futile. Further, most US partners in the region want US resolve and fortitude, but they resist reckless efforts that threaten the region's hard-earned prosperity. A key challenge here is that virtually every one of America's security allies enjoys dominant economic relations with China. Any strategy that ignores this simple fact will fail by design.

Partnership, by comparison, is perhaps the defining feature of the "transnational challenges" school of strategic alignment. Its supporters believe that the biggest challenges facing the international system favor broad cooperation over narrow competition in US-China relations. Only through relative harmony between Washington and Beijing can these overarching and shared threats be seriously addressed. This school holds that multilateral mechanisms focused on common challenges such as global climate change, environmental degradation, infectious diseases, and renewable energy should take precedence over petty competitions. Importantly, this school is not focused simply on China but instead on building and strengthening institutional mechanisms involving a wide range of states. Its major drawback, however, is that it effectively punts on the question of preventing hegemony in Asia, with a hope that transnational questions will eclipse the traditional balance-of-power concerns.

Finally, there is an approach to Asia that is less well defined than a school or strategy, which could be called the "singular issue" approach. It consists of a focus on concrete issues or crises that are deemed so important that solving them supersedes a focus on wider regional imperatives. Elements of this approach have surfaced from time to time, drawing the full attention of several assistant secretaries of state for East Asian and Pacific affairs to what were then considered serious and pressing issues of the moment, such as Cambodian elections in the 1980s, tensions between Indonesia and East Timor in the 1990s, and North Korean provocations in the 2000s. There are of course times when grave and urgent developments do indeed require focused attention, but US Asia strategy as a whole suffers somewhat when it is driven more by the exigencies of short-term crises than the logic of long-term strategy.

The most promising of the strategies above, and the one that has been at the core of the Pivot, is to build upon a modified version of the "bilateral alliances" approach, one that extends beyond treaty allies to include US partners throughout the region, positive relations with China, and cooperation on transnational challenges. Those who practice this approach further seek to blend elements of the "transnational challenges" school along with the strong and determined parts of the "China first" school. This complex amalgam offers the best mix of strategies for American statecraft heading into the future. The United States has often been a gardener in the bilateral context, dutifully tending to the disputes and controversies that surface in its relationship with allies; in the period ahead, it needs to be more of an orchestra conductor, working not only to engage and manage partners but also to coordinate them in common cause to shape Asia's future. This comprehensive approach will allow the United States to foster a stable balance of power in Asia and to create shared agreement on sustaining and enhancing crucial elements of Asia's operating system. This nuanced and integrated diplomacy can also have an effect on the behavior of recalcitrant rising powers. For example, instead of encouraging the United States to pursue either a bilateral diplomatic "grand bargain" with China or an adversarial stance against it, this more encompassing policy, focused on engaging and coordinating allies and partners, holds that Beijing's behavior—as well as the behavior of other recalcitrant states—is best influenced through a truly regional and multilateral American strategy, one that embraces and engages Asian states and creates shared incentives for supporting the prevailing operating system and costs for undermining it.

How might we formalize the rather complex, all-in approach above into the language of American strategy? In simple terms, the United States should use its military, diplomatic, and economic *means* to prevent hegemony in Asia in order to achieve long-standing *ends*, like free trade and democracy. But preventing hegemony is no longer enough to achieve American interests, in part because a balance of power alone will not ensure Asian states adopt twenty-first-century rules on trade and navigation or join global efforts to prevent climate change. To address these increasingly pressing issues, Americans will need to *strengthen Asia's operating system*—the complex arrangement of institutions, values, and norms that have facilitated cooperation and undergirded the region's peace and prosperity—and this goal should become a core element of US strategy, along with preventing hegemony. The United States, then, should achieve long-standing interests using the major instruments of statecraft, and in concert with allies and partners, in order to prevent hegemony *and* bolster Asia's operating system. This is a strategy that may not fit on a bumper sticker, but it is one sophisticated and nuanced enough to address not only the highly complex relationship with China but also the emerging transnational challenges that are shaping global politics. Indeed, this approach is increasingly manifest in existing US policy, and has been a core component of the Pivot to Asia from its inception.

Conclusion

Through most of American history, US strategy has been implicit but fairly consistent. The United States has used diplomatic, economic, and military *means* in order to prevent the emergence of a hegemon in Asia. This has been seen as the key *way* to make the region safe for American traditional *ends* like trade, faith, democracy, and territorial security, but it is no longer enough, and American strategy will need to evolve to strengthen Asia's operating system. Although American strategy has been relatively coherent and stable in its definition over time, its actual practice has been marked by irregularity as foreign crises elsewhere, domestic distractions, and underfunded investments hobbled its implementation. These inconsistencies have occasionally frustrated American diplomatic efforts in the past, and avoiding them in the future would constitute a very good start.

The introduction of the Pivot to Asia marked a return of top-level strategic attention and resources to Asia, one that should be continued in successive administrations. Just as past distractions damaged American interests in Asia, so too will present bouts of inattentiveness or hesitancy, especially because Asia's swiftly changing strategic landscape is putting strain on American objectives. As we will see in the next chapter, Asia's trajectory is being pulled between a bright future consistent with American objectives and a darker one that is at odds with the operating system painstakingly built over generations. American strategy in Asia calls for a balance of power, but the region's power distribution is moving in the direction of a dominant China that easily surpasses and outshines its neighbors economically and militarily. American hopes for agreement on the irreducible features of a regional operating system require that Asian states support twenty-first-century norms and participate in global governance, and yet Asian states are also being pulled back to nineteenth-century spheres-of-influence attributes and act at times as selfish spoilers on transnational challenges. Finally, free trade and democracy have been long-standing ends of American Asia strategy, but they are strained by forces pulling Asia toward protectionism and repression. With Asia's future in flux, American success in securing its interests in an Asian Century will require not only steady focus and strong will but also sound strategy.

CHAPTER FIVE

The Pivot and the Asian Future

Guiding the Choices of a Changing Region

The Pivot comes at a moment of historic consequence, with a dynamic and rising Asia now grappling with matters that will reverberate throughout the region and around the globe. Dramatic transformations are well under way in the region's domestic politics, military capabilities, economic performance, and power distribution, and together they are throwing Asia's trajectory into question. On several matters that lie at the heart of Asia's evolution as well as US strategy, Asia is being pulled in two contradictory directions toward two contrasting futures—a promising one consistent with American objectives and a more perilous one at odds with US interests and intents. Because Asia will in many circumstances end up living somewhere between these two stark choices at opposite ends along a spectrum, a crucial and enduring component of the Pivot will be to bend the arc of the Asian Century more toward the imperatives of Asian peace and prosperity and long-standing American interests.

This chapter explores six crucial choices for Asia's future that are closely related to the prominent features of America's Asia-Pacific strategy identified in the previous chapter.

The first question Asia faces is whether it will drift more toward hegemony or more toward a balance of power, especially in light of China's economic and military rise within Asia and continued questions about the endurance of the US role toward the region. Asia has historically required the active participation of benevolent external powers to reinforce its peace and stability, and a long succession of strategists and practitioners underscore the importance of the United States' taking steps to ensure that the region is defined more by balance than by hegemony.

Second, Asia is being pulled between a more open twenty-first-century "operating system" and a return to the spheres-of-influence model of the nineteenth century. For example, China has articulated positions calling for an uncontested zone in the South China Sea, issued challenges to freedom of navigation, and made periodic appeals for reducing the role of external powers in Asia—actions that hark back to some of the practices of nineteenth-century power politics. For its part, US Asia strategy has been intended to guide Asia more toward agreement on the shared twenty-first-century values at the core of Asia's operating system—such as the peaceful resolution of territorial disputes through international tribunals, and respect for the principle of freedom of navigation—and away from actions and formulations that evoke an earlier, less rules-based era.

Third, Asia is home to emerging powers that must choose whether they will become stakeholders in the current system and join fully in common efforts to solve transnational problems or instead become spoilers or free riders concerned with their own narrow self-interests. On issues including climate change, arms control, nonproliferation, disaster response, trafficking in persons, piracy, and human rights, the action and especially the inaction of Asian states will provide indications of where the region is trending.

Fourth, after years of territorial disputes and military buildups across Asia's flash points, national grievances and mutual distrust are dragging the region toward heightened tensions while economic interdependence and military deterrence are pulling it back toward coexistence. Potential skirmishes in hot spots like the Korean Peninsula, the South and East China Seas, and the Taiwan Strait could trigger a larger conflict involving several states, with the potential for dramatic escalation. The United States then has an interest in facilitating dialogue between contenders, taking steps to reduce the threat of accidents and inadvertence, and, through its words and actions, dissuading adventurist behavior among contenders. This is perhaps the greatest American challenge: seeking to preserve peace and stability on the shifting seesaw of conflict.

Fifth, Asia's politics could become defined by greater domestic liberalization or more by democratic failure as its numerous transitional states, like Burma and Thailand, make consequential decisions about how they will be governed. A long-standing goal of US Asia strategy has been to encourage and incentivize the region toward democratic values and institutions, and in this effort the trajectory of Asia's transitional states will determine where Asia falls on the spectrum between democratic advance and retreat.

Sixth, Asia's dynamic economies must choose whether Asia's commercial order will be defined more by rules that protect free trade and intellectual property or more by practices that shield protectionism and discriminate against foreign-generated goods and services. Asian states, which long ago reduced tariffs on many goods, now must decide how they will treat issues central to the new economy, such as services, data flows and storage, intellectual property, and the role of inefficient state-owned enterprises. US strategy in Asia has consistently called for free trade across the Pacific, and American support for agreements like the TPP can help craft an Asian economic order that is more conducive to prosperity than protectionism.

As these six choices make clear, Asia's future is perched at a decisive moment of transition, one that is central to the shape of the twenty-first century but also amenable to American exertions. The American Pivot to Asia is designed to help shape the future of the Asian Century in ways overt and subtle so that on each of these consequential questions, the scales tip toward conditions conducive to Asian peace and prosperity, as well as to long-standing US interests. We turn now to consider those choices in greater detail.

Hegemony or Balance

Too much is made of the present hand-wringing about American decline and the inevitability of Chinese hegemony in Asia. If past prognostications about Asia's power balance are any indicator of the credibility of present ones, then today's pundits and would-be oracles are better off stressing the ambiguity— not the certainty—of Asia's evolving power distribution. Indeed, looking back over the last forty years, it is both fascinating and concerning how wrong much of the strategic commentary has been about seemingly inevitable power shifts in Asia. In 1975, Lee Kuan Yew mistakenly saw American defeat in Vietnam as the death knell of what had been a thirty-year period of American dominance in the region. Roughly ten years later, the US strategic community mistook Mikhail Gorbachev's "Vladivostok Speech" declaring a bold Soviet Asia policy as evidence of looming Soviet hegemony and coming American decline in Asia. Then, in the late 1980s and early 1990s, many in the United States and Asia saw Japan's stunning economic ascent and growing political influence as evidence that it would replace the United States as Asia's predominant military power at a time when the United States appeared to be sinking into postindustrial decline. As these past projections make clear, what is most certain about Asia's future power distribution is that it often remains uncertain and ill defined—and therefore amenable to American influence.[1]

Today Asia is a region undergoing profound economic and military transformation with significant, far-reaching, and as yet unclear consequences for the region's future. When we set aside the question of American power and look at Asia squarely on its own terms, it becomes apparent that the balance of power across the region has rarely been more uncertain. Although China stands tallest in Asia as the region's largest economy, its growth is slowing even as other major powers, such as India, are surging forward. Looking out into the period ahead, it seems premature to conclude that Asia will fall under inevitable Chinese dominance; instead Asia's eventual power distribution is likely to lie somewhere on a spectrum between Chinese hegemony on one end and an unsteady balance of power on the other. The question of where on the spectrum Asia's distribution ultimately falls will be determined by developments in Asian capitals and particularly in Washington over the next decade, and it is a matter of substantial relevance to American interests.

Asia is presently drifting out of balance because of surging yet uneven growth rates within the region. While readers will no doubt be familiar with the rise of China on the global stage, they may be less aware of its equally impressive rise *within* Asia. In what has long been the world's most economically dynamic region, China has grown the fastest, outpacing every other major Asian economy. It now surpasses its neighbors on almost every indicator of economic power. For example, China's share of Asia's combined GDP was a mere 7 percent in 1980; by 2020 that share will have risen to 50 percent, even as China's economic growth continues to slow.[2] Already China's GDP is double the combined size of the next two largest economies, Japan and India. If China alone occupied one end of a scale, it would take every other Asian state to bring that scale into economic balance.

The picture is increasingly similar on military metrics. As Princeton professor Thomas Christensen notes, "While Washington enjoys military superiority over China, it is increasingly the case that China enjoys military superiority over most, if not all, of the United States' regional friends and allies."[3] China's share of total defense spending in Asia rose by some estimates to nearly 40 percent in 2014, a year in which China also accounted for nearly two-thirds of all new military spending within the region—suggesting that its lead in Asian defense expenditures is still growing.[4] This has translated into hard power capabilities that are in most cases superior to those of its neighbors. China is developing several different fifth-generation fighters, advanced anti-access/area-denial weaponry, next-generation submarines and surface vessels, and a fleet of several carrier battle groups. For the most part, its neighbors lack these capabilities.

These complex new power dynamics will call for ever-greater American focus and attention. Stability in the region has traditionally been gained through the active engagement of purposeful, external powers, particularly the United States. In order to fulfill its historical role in the region and bend Asia's evolving distribution of power away from hegemony and more toward balance, Washington will have to work more closely with traditional allies and partners and engage China constructively and resolutely, as well as stepping up its commercial diplomacy with the region's emerging economies.

An important component of these efforts will be deepening Washington's historic commitment to bolstering economic opportunity and growth throughout the region. For example, by encouraging Chinese economic reforms, keeping its market open to Chinese goods, investing capital in Chinese companies, and helping maintain peace in Asia, the United States arguably did more to help facilitate China's rise than any other country has done. Now, by pursuing what Secretary of Defense Ash Carter calls an "everyone rises and everybody wins" approach within the region, the United States can turn its attention to assisting the region's many other emerging economies in reaching their potential, and, in so doing, help realize an Asian balance of power in a way that contributes to Asian prosperity and maintains relative harmony across the region.[5] However, the US role should extend beyond simply supporting market-opening liberalization and adherence to the rule of law. Increasingly the United States must also advocate more assertively for an increase in the export of American goods and services to the region's rising middle classes and emerging firms. This will create a further American stake in Asian prosperity and result in a complex interdependence that favors both sides of the Pacific.

Several Asian states could contribute to a more stable balance of power. India, a secular democracy with a population roughly the size of China's, has the potential to be an influential great power that reshapes the region's architecture. Indonesia, with a population twice as large as Japan's, a favorable geographic position, and abundant natural resources, could achieve the kind of growth that propelled the smaller "Asian tigers" into prosperity. Burma, Malaysia, Thailand, and Vietnam together have a population roughly as large as America's and dreams of lifting their citizens from poverty and playing a larger role in the global economy. Like China a generation ago, these countries all have young and teeming populations hungry for productive work, and just as Beijing harnessed its demographic dividend to fuel its stunning ascent, these countries will need to find employment for their large populations before their labor forces age—complicating efforts to kindle growth and bring Asia into balance. For too long these Asian governments have been reluctant or unable to take the steps necessary to undergo structural reforms and spur foreign direct investment, often delaying infrastructure investments, putting off labor market reforms, reneging on intellectual property agreements, opposing foreign investment, and underfunding education. It is on precisely such matters that the United States, offering enlightened counsel, targeted investment, generous technical support, and twenty-first-century trade and investment agreements, can enable its partners to make prudent choices. Indeed, these efforts—which have taken the form of initiatives ranging from the Trans-Pacific Partnership to regularized economic dialogues with several regional states—are a crucial part of the American Pivot to Asia.

Along with these economic efforts, the United States can facilitate a more stable balance of power within Asia by deepening its ties with the region's militaries and bolstering its presence within Asia. Asia suffers from territorial disputes, radical terrorist groups increasingly linked to the violence and carnage in the Middle East, maritime piracy, nationalist tensions, and the world's costliest and most devastating natural disasters. Improving the defense capabilities of Asian states through military exercises, training efforts, broad-based exchanges, joint defense development efforts, and sales of equipment is essential to ensuring that the region's states can attend to the variety of transnational challenges that afflict the region. Many of these tasks, and others, cannot be tackled alone; they require the constructive cooperation of numerous nations working together in common endeavor. In addition, by bolstering the military capabilities of Asian states and drawing them into a web of defense cooperation and joint planning, the United States can reduce the likelihood that Asia will become a region where powerful countries can dominate smaller ones through military coercion and intimidation. Finally, as it has since the end of the Second World War, a robust and forward-deployed US presence within the region can deter conflicts between major states and help safeguard American investments and Asian prosperity.

Together US economic and military assistance to Asia's emerging states can create a more balanced and stable Asia, but that possibility is bounded in part by time, and the fact that realizing these goals tomorrow will depend in large part on decisions that are made today. For example, whether Asian states ultimately achieve their economic potential will depend on bold economic reforms and prudent infrastructure investments made in the present. Similarly, the vessels and aircraft Asian states field tomorrow will be the ones that they are designing, saving for, and developing now. The foundations for both economic prosperity and military power are generally laid well in advance, which is what makes the next several years so vital to the shape of the next several decades. Asia is on the cusp, and the actions taken today will determine whether tomorrow's Asia will be one in which individual Asian states have a seat at the table and a voice in the process.

While economic and military balance may be necessary to secure a peaceful Asia, it is not sufficient. As Henry Kissinger argues, "Equilibrium works best if it is buttressed by an agreement on common values." Kissinger notes that while balance inhibits the *capacity* of a state to unilaterally rewrite the rules, it takes the adoption of shared values to inhibit the *desire* of that state to revise the existing order, and therefore to sustain regional stability.[6] As we saw in the last chapter, the promotion of shared values should become a more integral component of American strategy in the period ahead, which calls for a focus on efforts to bolster the operating system of Asia—that is, the complex system of norms, rules, and institutions that has undergirded the region's growth and prosperity. We turn now to the question of which values will shape Asia's future.

Twenty-First Century or Nineteenth

Asia is being pulled between an open and liberal twenty-first-century order and a return to the spheres-of-influence model of the nineteenth century. At stake are simple but time-tested principles that have brought the region prosperity, such as freedom of navigation, greater transparency, the peaceful resolution of disputes, the sanctity of legal contracts, and the promise of free trade.

In the nineteenth century, it was common for great powers locked in a struggle for mastery over a particular region to bargain over the unofficial boundaries of their domains, creating loose spheres of influence in the process. A great power would assume a level of control over the autonomy of those states, waterways, and peoples within its sphere, and other powers would be expected to implicitly respect that authority in exchange for recognition of their own spheres. In that era, and especially in the wake of the devastating Napoleonic Wars, European powers divided the continent and much of the colonial world into their own respective spheres of influence.[7] The United States itself announced its own Monroe Doctrine not long after, declaring that Europeans must refrain from meddling in the Americas and appointing the United States the guardian of the region's security and well-being. The American experience with the Monroe Doctrine is often cited by Chinese interlocutors as a precedent and rationale for Chinese actions in its own neighborhood, despite the general evolution of the international system in the past two hundred years.

Today there are those who propose a return to a spheres-of-influence approach to foreign affairs. Former Australian prime minister Paul Keating has declared the "Keating mantra," which says that "great states need strategic space and that if they are not provided some, they will take it."[8] Some suggest drawing a line down the Pacific, allowing China unparalleled authority west of Hawaii and requiring the United States to pull back east of it. Either explicitly or implicitly, supporters of these views propose that the United States should formally cede a sphere of influence to China as it rises in Asia. In such a world, the United States would withdraw its troops from Japan and Korea and abrogate the respective security treaties, Taiwan would be reabsorbed by the mainland, the South China Sea would become Chinese territorial waters, and the East China Sea would come under Chinese control. Asian trade would proceed on principles that favor the Chinese economy exclusively. Freedom of navigation would be relegated, with enormous consequences for the broader global economy. Beijing would be able to apply its military and economic instruments without reservation in negotiations with its neighbors, and Asia's smaller states would be trapped in a system defined by raw power. It is clear that this approach would be bad for much of Asia, but it is likely to be bad for China as well. Arguably the best forty years in China's long history were the last forty years, and while Chinese practitioners and strategists strain against elements of the operating system the country has risen within, it is also true that these very elements have been indispensable features of China's ascent. A return to nineteenth-century principles would undermine some of the critical components of China's own growth and prosperity. In this sense the United States resists efforts to embrace a nineteenth-century domain in Asia because of American interests *and* arguably Chinese interests as well.

Furthermore, consigning democratic states, friends, and allies in the surrounding region to a form of nineteenth-century imperium stands in stark contrast to long-standing American strategic interests and values. Indeed, the very notion that the world should be divided into spheres of influence is an outmoded and archaic concept in an era of profound interdependence, one from a time before free trade, freedom of navigation, human rights, international law, democracy, globalization, or sovereign equality—all the values that characterize a twenty-first-century global order. It runs contrary to Asia's emergence as one of the world's most economically interconnected regions, with a web of crisscrossing supply chains binding faraway countries together in shared economic partnership. Finally, a spheres-of-influence approach would be profoundly undemocratic and illiberal, leaving the fates of millions of people and dozens of states in the hands of a few great powers.

Increasingly the question of where Asia falls on the spectrum between the outmoded models of the past and the open and liberal model of the future will be determined in the decades hence.

While China pursued a careful strategy of "peaceful rise" for much of the last decade, in part to forestall encirclement by its wary neighbors, it has been increasingly bold and assertive since the end of the global financial crisis. It would be simplistic to suggest that China is either a status quo or a revisionist power. The truth is that China is both, a power that benefits significantly from Asia's existing operating system but one that seeks also to revise it in ways that in some cases are both nationalistic and outmoded. Notably, President Xi Jinping appears to be flirting with policy designations or approaches that approximate spheres-of-influence thinking. His actions have essentially undermined the principle of freedom of navigation, a bedrock concept incompatible with spheres of influence. He has sought no-go zones by escalating Chinese claims over the South China Sea, building and militarizing islands within it, declaring an air defense identification zone (ADIZ) over the East China Sea, and using China's military forces to harass or threaten planes and ships operating in international waters. This territorial touchiness has been reinforced by occasional calls for an "Asia for Asians" and mounting criticism of the role of foreign powers and American alliances in Asia.[9] As Professor Minxin Pei notes, "Xi's statement marked a significant departure from China's long-standing position on America's presence in the Asia-Pacific region," which was once one of "studied ambiguity regarding America's role."[10]

What Beijing and others in the region sometimes overlook is that the twenty-first-century values at the heart of Asia's operating system are not *American* values but are instead *shared* and even universal values. By working with regional allies and partners to stress that greater participation and representation, free trade, freedom of navigation, transparency, and other priorities are widely held, the United States can elevate them beyond points of contention in its bilateral relationship with China. In addition, the United States can enlist China in the twenty-first-century conversation on how to support the values and norms that have underwritten the most remarkable period of Asian prosperity in a thousand years and China's own rise.[11] A plan for how precisely this may be accomplished will be discussed in detail in the next chapter, but its core components involve persuading China of the advantages of the current system, as well as making clear that supporting the system in the main will generate benefits for China while opposing it will result in corresponding costs.

Whether Asia is drawn backward toward nineteenth-century practices or continues into the twenty-first century will depend in part on the ability of the American government to continue the Pivot, enlist the support of friends and allies in bolstering Asia's operating system, and implement a policy balanced judiciously between resolve and reassurance. Part of the challenge here rests with how the United States responds to efforts by China to remake elements of the international system. In more artful terms, the United States and other states must be prepared to be seen to support Chinese efforts to offer proposals for new features in the existing international system. For instance, the United States could have communicated earlier and much more effectively in the process of Beijing's Asian Infrastructure Investment Bank (AIIB) rollout that it was prepared to work with China to align the new institution with some of the existing features of the Bretton Woods system of international organizations.

Stakeholders, Free Riders, or Spoilers

Today's world is one of unparalleled challenges, and coping with them will require close cooperation with Asian states. Asia emits more greenhouse gases than any other region. It boasts the world's largest foreign exchange reserves and biggest economies. It is home to half the world's nuclear powers, three of which have mixed records on nonproliferation. Ultimately, the path to progress on any global issue—climate change, economic governance, nonproliferation, or any one of countless others—runs through this dynamic region and its rising states. Global challenges that are difficult enough to address with Asian assistance will be impossible to manage without it.

The question of whether Asia as a region is pulled toward nineteenth- or twenty-first-century modes of action is related to the question of whether its states become contributors to global governance. In the last two decades, Asian states have transformed themselves into major economies and global powers whose every action—and inaction—ripples through an ever more interconnected world. As they grapple with their newfound power and influence, Asian states now face a choice of profound global consequence: whether they become stakeholders in common efforts to solve transnational problems or free riders and even spoilers concerned solely with their narrow interpretations of self-interest.

Solving tomorrow's problems will require working through today's global system, which in turn requires ensuring that Asian states become invested in its success. That global architecture, made up of institutions and accepted practices, was built by the United States and its close allies and partners in the aftermath of World War II.[12] These institutions now include the United Nations, the International Monetary Fund, the World Bank, the

World Trade Organization, the World Health Organization, and dozens of others that address issues ranging from arms control to Internet governance. Many of these institutions have evolved to give Asian actors and voices a greater role. More can be done here to be sure, but the desire to reflect Asian perspectives in global architecture is growing and undeniable. The fate of this system, and with it many successful avenues for acting with common purpose to confront transnational challenges, will rest in large part on decisions made in Asian capitals.

At the same time, Asia is currently undergoing a period of remarkable and far-reaching institution building in its own right—much of it centered around ASEAN—that could also contribute to solving transnational regional and global problems. By working with Asia's nascent institutions, either as a member or as an interested observer, the United States can assist in integrating them into the existing network of global institutions that the United States and its partners have constructed over decades. Ultimately it is in the interests of the United States and the world that Asian states choose to become stakeholders in common efforts to solve global problems, whether through the global institutions built at the end of the Second World War or through the regional ones currently maturing in Asia. As one of the architects of the prevailing system, the United States is uniquely positioned to lead Asian governments in a broad conversation about cooperation and common international responsibilities. And yet it will face two broad challenges in this effort.

First, Asia's rising states are still developing countries and may not believe they should bear the same responsibilities for solving transnational problems as Western countries, which have per capita incomes that are four to ten times higher than those in Asia.[13] For example, China, India, and Indonesia—three of the region's most consequential states—respectively have per capita incomes equivalent to those of Ecuador, Uzbekistan, and Bosnia—and nobody is expecting these smaller countries to contribute greatly to global governance.[14] Since Asia's emerging states still face serious and immediate domestic challenges around welfare and basic development, they are at times unable to meet the requirements of Western organizations (such as the IMF) and unwilling to undertake efforts to mitigate transnational challenges (such as climate change), complicating efforts to get them to act as "responsible stakeholders."

Secondly, many Asian states find aspects of the current structure, built in the aftermath of World War II, unfair because it reflects a postwar world that has long since changed. India and Japan do not have seats on the United Nations Security Council, but the United Kingdom and France do, and this state of affairs appears outdated to many nations, both developing and developed. So too does the fact that World Bank and IMF voting shares have long been unreflective of Asian economic power, though this will likely change in the wake of recent congressional legislation that moves ahead with plans to increase the Asian vote share in the IMF. Nevertheless, frustration with the slow state of progress has already led several Asian states to create alternative parallel institutions, such as the BRICS Development Bank and the Asian Infrastructure Investment Bank, that better reflect their status.

On no other issue is both the importance and the challenge of sustained cooperation greater than on climate change. China and India are already the world's first- and third-largest source of carbon emissions respectively, Japan and South Korea are the fifth- and seventh-largest, and the region as a whole is responsible for more emissions than any other.[15] Soliciting the cooperation of Asian states will be crucial to any attempt at halting the rise in carbon emissions, but such efforts will be particularly fraught. Asian states argue that the problem faced today was not created by them but by the past practices of the developed world, which has already achieved prosperity and emitted considerable carbon in doing so. In their view the West is therefore more responsible for limiting emissions than Asia's developing economies. Moreover, they argue that although Asian states are now the world's largest emitters, their per capita emissions are much lower than those of developed states. For example, the United States emits two and ten times more carbon per person respectively than do China and India.[16] There is some merit to these Asian arguments, but even significant unilateral Western reductions will fail to solve the problem without Asian partnership. Clearly, then, the Asian focus on historical fairness and distributional equity lies somewhat at odds with contemporary concerns of practical efficacy. Even if the world's powers find ways to resolve these thorny questions, one significant problem remains—a stable climate is a public good and a nonexcludable good bedeviled by the "tragedy of the commons" logic.[17] Put simply, responsible stakeholders that limit their own emissions may pay high costs to stabilize the climate while spoilers or free riders, who pay no costs whatsoever, can relax and reap the benefits of the hard labor of others. This logic naturally compels states under even the best of circumstances to cheat or be averse to binding commitments for fear that other states will fail to honor their own commitments, thus complicating cooperation.

Progress is still possible, especially if some of the world's largest emitters are able to find a formula for participation that enables cooperation. For that reason the success of global climate change efforts may well begin with agreements between the two largest emitters, the United States and China. Leaders in both countries understand the significance of their bilateral relationship and have taken a number of promising steps. In 2014 the United States stated that by 2025 it would have reduced its emissions 26 to 28 percent from their 2005 baseline, while China committed to peak its carbon dioxide emissions around 2030. What made this agreement particularly important is that it appeared to overcome legacies of historical and distributional unfairness, marking the first time that a major developed country and a major developing country committed to limiting carbon dioxide emissions.[18] The next year the United States and China again signed a joint statement, wherein each side noted additional steps it planned to take, which included a cap-and-trade program in China's case and serious fuel efficiency and power generation regulations in both countries. These two bilateral agreements showed an international audience that the largest developed and developing country polluters could together surmount some of the disagreements that encumber cooperation on climate change, and thereby laid the foundation for the breakthrough agreement at the Paris climate summit in December 2015. That agreement, for the first time, committed nearly every country to lower greenhouse gas emissions and shows that global progress on climate change in many ways still remains profoundly tied to progress in Asia. Of course, these agreements are not binding, and sustained and significant progress will ultimately require all states—especially Asia's emerging powers—to become stakeholders rather than spoilers or free riders in these common efforts.

Aside from climate change, the United States will need the assistance of Asian states if it is to solve a number of prominent challenges. Asia is the region with the world's fastest-growing military spending, and no arms control efforts can be successful without Asian states. The Missile Technology Control Regime (MTCR), designed to stop the proliferation of missiles capable of delivering weapons of mass destruction, currently lacks China, India, Iran, North Korea, and Pakistan as members. The MTCR will need to evolve with the active support of these states and others in order to account for a new world of unmanned aerial vehicles and other related threats. Similarly, if the world is to develop mechanisms to deal with drones, autonomous weapons of war, cyberweapons, and a whole host of new capabilities, it will likewise need to secure the cooperation of Asian militaries that now develop and increasingly field these weapons and sell these technologies to others.[19]

Nuclear proliferation is a grave threat to world security. To safeguard the world from the risk of nuclear terrorism or war, the United States must join with other states to restrict the flow of nuclear technology to dangerous states, and Asian nuclear powers such as China, India, and Pakistan will be indispensable to such efforts. That alone, however, will not be enough to halt nuclear proliferation. The use of sanctions against states pursuing nuclear programs is an important tool, but its efficacy is undermined entirely if Asia's large and influential economies fail to accept its logic and refuse to cooperate with these efforts. The success of sanctions against Iran was in no small part due to Washington's ability to work out terms with major Asian purchasers of Iranian oil, such as China and India, so that the sanctions would actually put pressure on the regime.

A similar logic applies to development and good governance. If Asia's largest economies are willing to make unconditional loans to developing governments, either on their own or through new economic institutions such as the BRICS Development Bank and AIIB, then it will be increasingly difficult for the international community to use loans as a tool to promote positive, sustainable outcomes. For example, loans that are conditional on transparency and accountability in order to promote good governance, or that are conditional on sustainable and long-term growth in order to foster development, will not be effective unless international banks and major governmental lenders together uphold shared standards.

With respect to pressing the cause of human rights, coordination and cooperation with Asian states is vital to pressuring offending regimes through the UN Security Council and to ensuring the efficacy of economic sanctions. Asian states like China and India have been skeptical of human rights frameworks such as the UN's Responsibility to Protect that would weaken the norm of sovereignty and permit unilateral action—often undertaken by

Western forces—against governments thought to be guilty of or negligent toward human rights violations. The fact that many of the offending countries also have natural resources and contracts with resource-hungry Asian countries, especially China and India, is another important reason for occasional hesitancy on the part of Asian states in initiating sanctions or permitting the use of force. If the fledgling human rights regime born after the fall of the Soviet Union is to survive and grow, the United States will need to find ways to make Asian states stakeholders invested in its success.

Asia's rise poses a challenge not only to global governance, but also to the structure of the international order, as well as to prevailing international norms and principles in countless areas ranging from climate change to arms control. For decades no state could flout these rules without incurring consequences. In the wake of Asia's rise, several Asian states in some cases have the ability to effectively veto global measures on trade practices, proliferation activities, or climate change with which they disagree. Naturally the United States will have to address their concerns about the fairness of the current order, especially by giving them a larger stake in the institutions it has helped build. The rise of the G-20 is an example of how a more inclusive institutional model can emerge that gives many of the region's powers an important role in resolving global challenges. Fully nine of the twenty states in the new G-20 (along with frequent observers to the group, including Singapore) are Asia-Pacific players and have helped elevate Asia in emerging global councils. Even so, the pace of change is slow enough that Asian states are increasingly building institutions outside the current system. That trend, however, is far from irreconcilable with sensible American reforms to the current order. As John Ikenberry has written, what distinguishes the current system is that "unlike the imperial systems of the past," it is rule based, open, and multilateral—or, in other words, "easy to join and hard to overturn." In his view, "The most important benefit of these features today is that they give the Western order a remarkable capacity to accommodate rising powers."[20]

Of these powers, many of which are important, China is perhaps of greatest consequence. In fact, when Robert Zoellick first outlined the concept that Asian states should be "responsible stakeholders" in 2005, he was speaking about China in particular.[21] China's rise poses challenges for global governance not only because it is a global superpower with a tendency at times toward ambivalence and free riding on global matters, but also because the United States and China compete with each other in ways that could threaten cooperation on transnational problems. Henry Kissinger makes the stakes of this dynamic clear:

> A cold war between the two countries would arrest progress for a generation on both sides of the Pacific. It would spread disputes into internal politics of every region at a time when global issues such as nuclear proliferation, the environment, energy security, and climate change impose global cooperation.[22]

In other words, global governance is most likely to be effective when the United States and China cooperate, and yet the security relationship between them may cause mistrust and mutual antagonism that could hamper each side's willingness to work together. The tension that pervades the relationship derives in no small part from the very real possibility of conflict between the United States and China, and we turn now to examine that possibility in greater detail.

War or Peace

In 1520, Ferdinand Magellan carefully navigated the narrow strait that separates the South American land mass from Tierra del Fuego at the southernmost tip of the continent, becoming the first European to sail from the Atlantic Ocean into new waters. Taken by its stillness and favorable winds, Magellan named this new body of water *Mar Pacifico*, meaning "peaceful sea." In reality this vast ocean has featured several bloody wars and conflicts in the centuries since, and five hundred years after receiving Magellan's moniker, its waters remain far from peaceful.

A quick and easy way to stump scholars of international relations is to ask them what part of the world they believe is the most dangerous. It is a challenging question because these kinds of judgments are not straightforward, and as the world grows more complicated and interdependent, the list of qualifying locations continues to lengthen. Many scholars might reflexively say Kashmir, divided between nuclear-armed India and Pakistan, is the world's most dangerous spot. Others might hazard that conflict between Israel and one of its hostile neighbors, or perhaps the war under way in Syria, pose more significant risks to global peace and stability. To this list we must also add at least four zones in Asia that have the potential to drag the region from prosperity to penury through conflict—the Korean Peninsula, the Taiwan Strait, the East China Sea, and the South China Sea.

What makes these hot spots particularly challenging is that they are shaped by a variety of deeply unpredictable factors between countries with tense relationships, little military interaction, and few agreed-upon protocols for preventing minor incidents from escalating into major conflicts. Add to this toxic mix the palpable emotionality of historical grievances and competing nationalist sound tracks and the result is something dangerously combustible. For nearly forty years, most Asian leaders had the wisdom to overlook or downplay these problems, choosing to export them to future generations and joining instead in the common search for prosperity and growth. But now, for a variety of reasons related in part to China's rise and the anxieties that surround it, these narrow and intractable disputes are surging to the fore.

While Asia is often known as a region full of dynamism and commerce, it is also home to the very real threat of danger and conflict. With the region pulled by nationalism and mistrust toward war and by interdependence and deterrence toward peace, the need for American focus and action to tilt the scales toward comity and away from conflict is as pressing as it has ever been.

The Korean Peninsula

Known as the "land of morning calm" for more than two thousand years, Korea may well become the center of a future great-power competition and conflict.[23] The interests of several powerful states, including China, Japan, Russia, and the United States, have for decades been intertwined with the fate and freedom of millions of Koreans. The peninsula is a vexing place largely because of North Korea, a dangerous and opaque nuclear-armed state guilty of serial provocations. As Admiral Harry Harris, the commander of US Pacific Command, has said bluntly, "The greatest threat that I face on a day-to-day basis is the threat from North Korea because you have an unpredictable leader who is in complete command of his country and his military."[24]

Perhaps no Asian issue is more vexing or confounding than North Korea. Virtually every aspect of my professional experience involving North Korea has been frustrating and counterintuitive, and I have a record of North Korea prognostication over decades that is virtually unblemished by success. When I expected a new leadership in Pyongyang to test the waters of engagement with a friendlier South Korean government, it instead embarked on a risky course of confrontation. Conversely, at times when the United States and South Korea were ready for a showdown, Pyongyang abruptly switched gears and talked about peaceful relations. No country has played a bad hand more daringly, or more dangerously.

The North Korean regime's blatantly provocative and violent acts, including the sinking of the South Korean ship *Cheonan* in 2010, which killed 104 sailors, as well as its bombardment of South Korea's Yeonpyeong Island that same year, which wounded 19 civilians, caused worldwide concern and brought immediate condemnation. South Korean restraint was admirable in these instances, but no country can stand by as its citizens are murdered senselessly by a hostile government. In the future a similar North Korean provocation might well set off a major conflict with South Korea that draws in its treaty ally the United States, and even China.

In addition to threatening and outright attacking South Korea, the North continues to pursue nuclear weapons and advanced delivery systems. On three separate occasions, North Korea has tested nuclear devices. It has also conducted several missile tests, the most important of which took place in December 2012 and demonstrated that North Korea could successfully place a satellite in orbit, a capability that paves the way for an eventual intercontinental ballistic missile that could strike the US mainland. Put simply, North Korea's pursuit of these capabilities not only poses a grave threat to Japan and South Korea but could eventually pose an existential one to the United States as well. For now, its weapons tests have not only tried the patience of North Korea's neighbors but also enhanced ties between the US and its treaty allies Japan and South Korea.

During the Cold War, the United States and the Soviet Union could negotiate and take prudent steps to deescalate tensions. Negotiations with North Korea, while important, are not likely to be as effective in creating security. In my own experience with North Korean interlocutors, including formal meetings with the military in the 1990s, random encounters with "businessmen" (who were really part of the North Korean government) in Macao in 2002, and periodic meetings with the country's diplomats at multilateral events during my most recent time in government, I have found them consistently obstreperous. What has often been most striking is that no other country's representatives are on as tight a leash. For all the claims of Pyongyang's wanting to be "engaged" by the United States, in virtually every encounter I have experienced, my North Korean interlocutor was decidedly uncommunicative, either enraged over some supposed American perfidy or exceedingly cautious not to stray from state-sanctioned talking points. In essence, diplomacy has often been exceedingly difficult.

If there is one country that holds any influence over North Korea, it is China. The United States and China once fought a war on the Korean Peninsula after Mao backed the grandfather of the current leader in an invasion of the South. China has ever since been North Korea's chief patron. China has often been reluctant to use whatever leverage it has over North Korea and generally refuses to entertain the possibility of regime change. China is wary of precipitating a North Korean collapse that could send millions of refugees over the border into northern China. It fears a united Korea, democratic and allied with the United States, because that might undermine Chinese security and reshape regional politics by removing a useful buffer state between China and the American-led alliance system. No doubt a measure of caution also plays a role, since North Korean instability could trigger the intervention of outside powers—including both the United States and China—with the potential for grave miscalculation and even great-power war.

In addition to these three reasons for Chinese hesitancy, which focus mostly on the external implications of Korean instability, there is one large bilateral factor as well. There is a kind of revolutionary nostalgia that ties Beijing to Pyongyang, which is to some degree an ideological cousin of China. Stripping away North Korea's hereditary power transitions and the unique qualities of *juche*—North Korea's concept of self-reliance that verges on deprivation—reveals a state that resembles Stalin's Russia or Mao's China going through the horrors of the Cultural Revolution. Beyond this similarity, the Chinese military's intervention during the Korean War, which came at great cost to China, is richly celebrated as a moment when the People's Liberation Army stood up for the Chinese people in opposition to American imperialism.[25] A reversal on North Korean policy would implicitly cast aside the sacrifices of China's soldiers, indict Mao for his poor judgment, and require ideological and nationalistic gymnastics after decades of propaganda praising China's efforts in the Korean War. It may even meet with considerable domestic criticism. Ultimately, then, China is unlikely to abandon its twisted ideological cousin even though no other regime is perhaps as belonging on the ash heap of history as North Korea. Beijing will instead continue to counsel patience, gradual reform, and restraint—and, bluntly put, hope for the best.

While China is unwilling to destabilize North Korea, it has been more willing in recent years to take steps to express displeasure with some of its more provocative behavior, especially with regard to proliferation. China regularly calls for the denuclearization of the Korean Peninsula, and President Xi expressed public concern over North Korea's nuclear program after a meeting with South Korean president Park Geun-hye. Importantly, President Xi has met with President Park more than six times but has so far avoided meeting with North Korean leader Kim Jong-un. China's Ministry of Commerce even published a list of goods not to be sold to North Korea. Ultimately, although relations suffered in the early years of Xi's tenure, they seem to have rebounded slightly, with Xi sending a letter to Kim discussing steps for deepening bilateral ties.[26] After North Korea claimed to have tested a hydrogen bomb in January 2016, China reversed course and supported a UN resolution condemning the North Korean provocation and worked with the United States on drafting a new round of sanctions on the regime. For now, there is no sign that China's tougher line is a prelude to a break in relations between Pyongyang and Beijing, especially if such a break would accelerate a North Korean collapse that would lead to instability, a flood of refugees, and a united Korea allied with the United States.

Given China's relative unwillingness to pressure North Korea, and given the series of provocations engineered by Pyongyang in recent years—from nuclear tests to artillery fire—it is easy for critics to lambast US strategy. This criticism is often unwarranted. There are few good options on the Korean Peninsula, and although progress may seem unsatisfactory so far, the United States is playing a longer, more patient, and more strategic game than North Korea. It has demonstrated a willingness to negotiate with Pyongyang but not to budge on issues of strategic concern—such as North Korea's nuclear status—that would damage US positions, alienate the North's neighbors, or undermine global norms. It has worked hard with others to constrict North Korea's surreptitious exports of military items and missiles to Burma and states in the Middle East, restricting the flow of hard currency to the Pyongyang leadership. The United States has pressured and persuaded China to cooperate with some diplomatic efforts to constrain North Korea through the United Nations. Finally, Washington has worked to deepen cooperation with Japan and South Korea, as well as between them, and consistently reiterated its resolve to protect them.

American efforts on North Korea may not produce any breakthroughs, but nimble diplomacy and clear-eyed attention can reduce the risk of a catastrophe. If North Korea provokes a war with South Korea, or if its own internal contradictions lead to collapse, the region could easily spiral into war. Millions of refugees will need to be housed, nuclear weapons and other dangerous material will need to be secured, and South Korea will require the protection and support of the United States. China will need to decide whether it will intervene to prop up the regime, occupy part or all of North Korea and install its own government, or do nothing. The possibility of conflict between American and Chinese troops in such a frightening and fluid environment is very real. Given these dangers, one of the most important US tasks is to prepare for uncertainty or instability on the peninsula if or when dramatic changes unfold or disaster strikes by remaining vigilant, keeping allies together, and trying to make sure a level of communication and dialogue exists among all the various countries around the Korean Peninsula, including and especially China. North Korea may be an anachronism in the midst of remarkable prosperity, as well as one of the world's most backward states, but it nonetheless poses a serious challenge to a peaceful and secure Asia and warrants continued and long-term US focus and attention.

The South China Sea

A visitor brave enough to venture into the part of the Pacific Ocean in the waters enclosed by China, Malaysia, the Philippines, and Vietnam—an area known as the South China Sea—would witness an incredible sight: from a distance, trucks, cranes, and buildings appear to float on the water. If that visitor was able to elude Chinese patrol boats in the area and move in closer, he or she would see clearly that these installations lie on thin strips of reef resting barely above sea level. Usually submerged underwater except at low tide, these strips are now being built higher and higher by Chinese dredging and construction crews. Ships and dredgers are moving millions of tons of rock and sand from the ocean floor onto the reefs, then pushing them into place with excavators and cranes before firming them up with cement fortifications. Through this massive land reclamation effort, China has turned seven reefs into artificial islands, three of which are home to airstrips that enhance China's ability to project power within the region.[27]

China is not the only claimant in these waters. Brunei, China, Malaysia, the Philippines, Taiwan, and Vietnam lay claim to various islands within the region and at times have engaged in island building of their own; however, the scale of China's island reclamation completely dwarfs that of its rival claimants. In less than two years, China has reclaimed seventeen times more land than all other claimants combined over the past forty years—an amount that is equal to roughly 95 percent of all reclaimed land in the region. In addition to constructing runways there, China may also have stationed mobile artillery, according to recent US government reports.[28]

The disputes over the South China Sea are motivated by a variety of complex factors. For the claimants, considerations of honor and national prestige play an important role. So too do more tangible, material concerns. Underneath the waters lie large stocks of fish, which often lead to clashes between fishing vessels and security services ships; potentially rich energy deposits are also to be found there. The U.S. Energy Information Administration cites figures suggesting that the South China Sea may contain 11 billion barrels of oil and 190 trillion cubic feet of natural gas.[29] For China, the world's largest oil importer, the South China Sea offers the prospect of dramatically reducing its energy dependence and increasing the country's energy security.

It bears asking why competition over a number of uninhabited features in the South China Sea—some of which are not even islands—should matter at all to the United States. From the standpoint of American strategy and interests, freedom of navigation and overflight over the world's oceans has been a long-standing, enduring, and vital American principle dating back to 1801, when the United States went to war against the Barbary pirates for harassing US shipping. Though seemingly obscure, the South China Sea is by some measures of tonnage and value one of the world's most important trade and energy transport arteries, and freedom of navigation across its waters is a strategic and economic priority for Washington and the wider world. More than half of the world's annual merchant fleet tonnage passes through the South China Sea, as does half of global LNG trade and one-third of global crude oil flows.[30] By some estimates the value of goods traveling these waters annually exceeds $5 trillion. The South China Sea is by some measures more consequential than some of the world's more famous choke points, carrying three times more oil than the Suez Canal and fifteen times more than the Panama Canal. In Robert Kaplan's terms, "The South China Sea functions as the *throat* of the Western Pacific and Indian oceans—the mass of connective economic tissue where global sea routes coalesce."[31] If major powers like China could claim sovereignty over this vast body of water, it would seriously undermine the principle of freedom of navigation that has allowed global commerce to proceed largely free from state interference for more than seventy years and served as a foundation for Asia's economic miracle.

As those of the claimant with by far the largest economic and military capabilities, and a desire to enforce its claims both over the islands and over the water, China's claims are perhaps the most threatening to global freedom of navigation. Beijing officially staked its claim to the South China Sea in 1947, with a map that showed eleven dashes running from the Gulf of Tonkin, around Vietnam, and back up to China along the Malaysian and Philippine coasts. This has since been updated into a nine-dash line, often referred to as the "cow tongue" due to its shape. China's claims conflict with the United Nations Convention on the Law of the Sea (UNCLOS) which grants land-derived special economic maritime rights for all countries up to two hundred nautical miles from its coast. That treaty effectively turns the South China Sea into a patchwork of claims from numerous countries.

What makes this patchwork especially dangerous is the risk of conflict between claimants, which could disrupt maritime trade, raise shipping insurance rates and surcharges, escalate into a wider conflict, and even draw in the United States, which is a treaty ally of one claimant, the Philippines. The notion of potential violence is hardly far-fetched. In 1974, South Vietnam clashed with China over the Paracel Islands north of Johnson Reef, with the sides losing fifty-three and eighteen lives respectively. Fourteen years later Chinese and Vietnamese naval vessels took objection to each other's proximity to Johnson South Reef and fired on one another. Outgunned, Vietnam suffered over seventy casualties and pulled back. More recently, the possibility of violence between China and Vietnam returned in May 2014, when China provocatively placed a state-owned oil rig within Vietnam's declared exclusive economic zone and defended its placement with People's Liberation Army Navy (PLAN) warships. When Vietnam Coast Guard vessels attempted to ward off the Chinese, they were soon chased away by dozens of Chinese vessels, including frigates and patrol boats.[32] Three weeks later a nearby Vietnamese fishing boat sank after being rammed by a Chinese vessel. Throughout Vietnam, deadly riots against Chinese-owned factories and businesses triggered by Beijing's provocations claimed the lives of several Chinese citizens. China ultimately removed the oil rig in June, a month ahead of schedule, but the damage to its relationship with Vietnam, including in terms of lives and property, was considerable.

Now, with Chinese island construction proceeding at a brisk pace, and with militarization becoming ever more likely despite repeated Chinese pledges to discontinue such activities, the possibility of conflict continues to increase. All sides see their claims as legitimate and the other parties as duplicitous and dishonest, and it is within this emotionally charged framework that the actions of other claimants are perceived. The United States for its part walks a razor-thin line as it seeks to maintain peace across the South China Sea while demonstrating its resolve on freedom of navigation. On the one hand, if the United States does not challenge Chinese assertions of sovereignty over these waters, it will effectively concede that freedom of navigation can be sharply curtailed by powerful states. On the other hand, by insisting on its right to freely traverse these waters, the United States places its forces at risk of harassment by Chinese forces and risks a larger conflict between the two. Most recently, in 2015 and again in 2016, the United States sailed US Navy vessels and flew aircraft directly through the twelve-nautical-mile territorial zone claimed by China for its artificial islands, demonstrating its commitment to freedom of navigation. Such operational demonstrations of principle are necessary but also somewhat risky, and if they are not managed properly, they can lead to full-blown international crises.

One of the most famous examples of such a crisis occurred in 2001 during what has become known as the EP-3 Incident. The United States had for years used the EP-3, a US Navy signals reconnaissance aircraft, to perform electronic intelligence missions in international airspace above the South China Sea. In the course of these operations, the aircraft were routinely intercepted by Chinese fighters, which was neither out of the ordinary nor cause for concern. However, in the run-up to the EP-3 Incident, Chinese interceptions had become increasingly assertive. On one unfortunate day, a particularly aggressive Chinese pilot made two passes within ten feet of the

American plane, and on attempting a third accidentally collided with the EP-3. The Chinese pilot was killed and the US crew was forced to make an emergency landing at the nearest runway, on Chinese-controlled Hainan Island. For eleven days the American servicemen were detained and interrogated by Chinese officials. The subsequent tension in Sino-American relations was palpable and demonstrates how serious miscalculations can result from increased military presence and capabilities, particularly as nations in the region use military assets to actively assert disputed claims.

Over the last few years, China's military forces have been increasingly provocative when they encounter their American counterparts in the South China Sea. In 2009 a PLAN frigate harassed the USNS *Impeccable* while it was operating in those waters. A bridge-to-bridge radio broadcast directed the American ship to leave the area or "suffer the consequences," pieces of wood were dropped in its path, and another Chinese vessel used a grappling hook in an attempt to snatch its towed sonar array.[33] According to former secretary of defense Robert Gates, "It was a serious incident and a potentially dangerous one, both because of the Chinese actions and because the Chinese were asserting by those actions that we had no right to be in those waters."[34] This was hardly the last Chinese harassment. In 2013 a Chinese naval vessel in the South China Sea cut in front of the USS *Cowpens* and almost caused a collision, an action Secretary of Defense Chuck Hagel called "irresponsible." The next year, in a near repeat of the EP-3 Incident, a US Navy P-8 patrol jet flying a routine mission in international airspace was intercepted by a Chinese J-11 fighter jet that performed a ninety-degree pass across the nose of the American plane. It then returned to within twenty feet and performed an audacious barrel roll over the P-8, again risking collision.[35] The Pentagon complained that this was just "the most recent in a rising trend of nonstandard, unprofessional, and unsafe intercepts that we have observed since the end of 2013."[36]

Establishing a code of conduct for military encounters and a reliable and continuous line of communication between both militaries would reduce the risk of an accident's escalating into a conflict. During the Cold War, the United States and the Soviet Union had countless military encounters and were able to reduce the risk of escalation by adopting these kinds of measures. China has allowed for some modest steps in military diplomacy with the United States, such as the Military Maritime Consultative Agreement that is intended to moderate areas of dangerous military practice and thereby reduce risks of inadvertence. And yet Beijing has to date demurred about doing more, in large part for strategic reasons. China prefers to use uncertainty to deter US operations in the South China Sea, effectively forcing US vessels to accept the risk of serious crisis when they enter these waters. From this perspective, installing a US-China code of conduct for military encounters would be a bit like giving seat belts to speeders, effectively allowing the United States to manage risk and extricate itself from a crisis so that it can continue its freedom of navigation operations (FONOP) in the region.

The increase in Chinese military deployments, policy proclamations, provocative naval maneuvers, and rhetorical stridency calls for a revision in how American policymakers think about China's foreign policy objectives. The conventional wisdom has been that China needs a stable and benign international environment in order to focus on development, and that it is willing to settle or shelve territorial disputes to do so. Accidents and incidents have generally not been considered premeditated gambits. Under the leadership of Xi Jinping, however, there is the question of whether these more recent incidents should still be seen in isolation or whether they are part of a larger orchestrated strategy designed to push against the status quo in the maritime domain. "We say that this sea area has historically been ours," states one Chinese scholar, "but this alone is no use. It depends on whether we have actual control there. China's maritime monitoring must demonstrate its presence and express effective jurisdiction in the sea areas under its jurisdiction."[37] Xi appears to play a more dominant role in the formulation and execution of matters big and small than many of his predecessors— even small fishing boats receive communications and directives from senior authorities in Beijing. In light of that, the current set of provocations should be seen not as haphazard mistakes but as well-choreographed examples of China's acting on its own initiative.

The lack of crisis communication and effective operationally agreed-upon standards between the United States and China is but one potential source of conflict. With numerous countries all using military assets to press their claims, all ungoverned by a common code of conduct and unaddressed through military hotlines, the waters are increasingly dangerous.

In this environment the region's small examples of successful maritime cooperation shine brighter, showing the promise of resource sharing. For example, Japan and Taiwan signed an agreement in 2013 that divided fishing resources in their own disputed waters.[38] Indonesia and Malaysia had signed a similar agreement the previous year.[39] The key to such efforts is to come to agreements about how to jointly exploit resources in a manner that does not require an adjudication of or concession on territory.

The East China Sea

In the East China Sea, China is locked in disputes with Japan and South Korea over islands and the location of UNCLOS exclusive economic zones. The most dangerous source of tension surrounds a group of uninhabited islands that Japan calls Senkaku and the Chinese call Diaoyu. These small, barren islands lie northeast of the Taiwanese coast and are currently administered by Japan. Long regarded as irrelevant, they shot up in importance in 1968 when a UN survey suggested there might be significant amounts of petroleum deposits in the area.[40] These resource-related interests mix with uneasy questions of nationalism and history. China claims that the islands were captured by imperial Japan following the First Sino-Japanese War, and according to the Cairo and Potsdam Declarations from World War II, China is entitled to all territory seized from Beijing by imperial Japan, which therefore includes these islands. Japan argues that the islands were unclaimed rather than seized, and that China therefore has no historical claim on them. In recent years the islands have fueled nationalist tensions in both countries, which makes compromise and negotiation extraordinarily difficult.

These islands represent one of the few maritime disputes that could escalate to the level of a US-China conflict. The United States takes no position on the ultimate sovereignty of the islands, but it does recognize Japan's administrative control over them—the United States returned these and other islands to Japan as part of its postwar occupation in 1971. It also underscored that the US-Japan security treaty applied to these islands in circumstances involving armed challenges to the status quo. In 2010, Secretary Clinton was explicit that they were covered in the wake of a dispute over them. In 2014, President Obama himself told a Japanese newspaper that "The policy of the United States is clear—the Senkaku Islands ... fall within the scope of Article 5 of the US-Japan Treaty of Mutual Cooperation and

Security."[41] There is no question, then, that a Sino-Japanese conflict over the islands could draw in the United States.

There is a real feel of 1914 in the air and seas over and around these disputed islands, harking back to the complex European alliances and thick prewar tensions of the early twentieth century. That feeling is driven by the vehemence of national sentiment over the islands, the presumed righteousness of each side's claim, and the riskiness of recent provocations. In the last six years, three crises over the islands between China and Japan could have resulted in conflict.

The first took place in 2010, when a Chinese fishing boat captain rammed two Japan Coast Guard vessels and was subsequently arrested by the Japanese. The Chinese government demanded his release, the Japanese government refused, and the deadlock gave rise to a significant diplomatic incident. Several reports suggested that the Chinese government halted or reduced exports of rare earth minerals to Japan in response, though controversy remains over whether such an embargo occurred. Eventually Japan released the Chinese fisherman without charge, but not before serious harm had been done to the relationship.

The second major incident took place in 2012. That year Japanese prime minister Yoshihiko Noda purchased three of the disputed islands from a Japanese family that had a claim to them to prevent a nationalist group from doing so first and using the islands to take provocative actions. In confidential discussions between the United States and Japan in the midst of these deliberations, the United States urged Japan to engage directly with China over its motivations for purchasing the islands. In doing so Tokyo thought it had gained "understanding" from China, but that was not the case. The purchase promptly enraged the Chinese government and resulted in widespread rioting as well as an economic boycott of Japanese goods, which in turn led to a stark reduction in Japanese exports to China and a decline in Japan's industrial output by 1.7 percent, to the lowest level since the aftermath of the 2011 earthquake.[42] In the wake of the crisis, China increased patrols of the area; so too did the Japan Coast Guard. The United States tried carefully to facilitate dialogue and understanding and urged that cooler heads prevail, but to little overall effect. Afterward the two militaries almost came into conflict when a Chinese reconnaissance aircraft entered Japanese airspace, causing the Japan Air Self-Defense Force to scramble its own fighter jets.

Japan's Maritime Self-Defense Force reported that a Chinese frigate locked its firing radar on a Japanese destroyer the next month.[43]

A year later, with the relationship still at a very low ebb and with the possibility of clashes ever present, China brashly declared an ADIZ over the entire East China Sea and over the disputed islands, setting off the third major crisis over the islands. China required all aircraft flying over them to alert China before doing so, at risk of being shot down. Japan condemned the ADIZ and refused to comply with it, and the United States publicly challenged it by flying two unarmed B-52 bombers through the ADIZ without notifying Beijing.

These three incidents have left relations at a nadir from which they are unlikely to fully and fundamentally emerge anytime soon. Unless handled more judiciously by leaders in both Beijing and Tokyo, the next incident, either planned or inadvertent, could produce violence that would rock northeast Asia and dramatically harm the global economy. Now, as record numbers of Chinese maritime patrol vessels, fishing ships, fighter aircraft, and unauthorized landings are used to challenge Japanese claims, and as Tokyo responds by tightening its own patrols and scrambling fighters at the highest level in years, the risk of an incident has increased considerably.[44] Moreover, even if the tension abates, the actions of unpredictable third parties ranging from fishermen to Chinese activists could precipitate a crisis that neither China nor Japan would welcome and that could even escalate into a conflict that would draw in the United States. Even if such a conflict is avoided, there is no question that serviceable relations between Japan and China are a foundational piece of the modern Asian miracle. Without them the region will lurch into an uneasy and tension-filled future.

Clearly, then, the United States has important interests in ensuring that this dispute is peacefully managed and that steps are taken to head off a crisis. At risk is the possibility of conflict with China, the credibility of the US-Japan alliance and similar American commitments worldwide, and the region's future stability.[45] Like so many of Asia's other flash points, the East China Sea is poised among war, peace, and a gray zone of ambiguous and informal provocation. It will take focused and concerted American action to deter unilateral Chinese assertiveness, encourage both sides to refrain from provocation, support efforts to manage the dispute (perhaps through resource sharing), bolster military transparency, and encourage the development of rules of engagement between China and Japan.

The Taiwan Strait

The Taiwan Strait, though relatively tranquil in recent years, has long been one of the most dangerous flash points in the world. After Mao's Communists prevailed in the bloody Chinese Civil War, the defeated Chinese Nationalists (KMT) under the leadership of Chang Kai-shek retreated to the island of Taiwan, roughly one hundred miles east of the Chinese mainland. Although mainland China claimed sovereignty over Taiwan, the island instead remained under the control of the KMT, which declared itself the legitimate government of all China and represented it in the United Nations until 1971, all while harboring dreams of one day forcefully retaking the mainland.

Even as those dreams evaporated, the island remained a direct challenge to the Chinese Communist Party, especially after embracing democracy in the 1990s and subsequently flirting with the notion that Taiwan is a country altogether distinct from China. Since every Chinese leader has explicitly made reunification with Taiwan a paramount political goal, no Chinese leader can afford to "lose" Taiwan by allowing it to declare political independence. Much of this steadfast aversion to Taiwanese independence, like so much of Asia's politics, is rooted deeply in emotion and history. Taiwan casts a powerful psychological shadow over mainland Chinese, who see it as a lingering scar from China's "Century of Humiliation." For them Taiwan's separation from the mainland in 1895 is a historical aberration brought about by Japanese colonialism and then sustained by American support for the KMT. Taiwan is threatening because its very existence jeopardizes the legitimacy of the Communist Party, revealing that it has not completed the work of unifying the country and reversing the legacy of colonialism. Increasingly Taiwan also demonstrates the compatibility of Chinese culture with democratic traditions.

Taiwan is a particularly dangerous flash point not only because of this history but because of the way history intertwines with US security commitments. The United States once had a Mutual Defense Treaty with Taiwan, but when President Carter concluded normalization with China in 1979, the treaty was terminated and the US embassy in Taipei formally closed. From then on the United States would recognize China and maintain only an informal relationship with Taiwan. That same year the United States Congress passed and President Carter signed the Taiwan Relations Act (TRA), which created the domestic and legal basis for unofficial relations with Taiwan that have flourished in the years since. Importantly, it also committed the US to providing Taiwan with military equipment for defensive purposes and suggested, but did not make explicit, an American commitment to Taiwan's defense. This commitment is purposefully vague and constitutes a policy of "strategic ambiguity" intended to fulfill two policy objectives that lie in tension with each other: deterring China from using force against Taiwan and dissuading Taiwan from pursuing independence. This is a delicate balancing act, but the United States has a strong stake in getting it right, not least because crises and instability there could draw Washington into a war with Beijing.

Such scenarios are hardly fanciful. Over six decades the Taiwan Strait has been the focus of three serious crises that brought the region to the brink of war. The First Taiwan Straits Crisis (1954–1955) occurred less than a year after the Korean War when China shelled two Taiwanese islands far closer to the mainland than to Taiwan, Quemoy and Matsu. The islands were not covered by the Mutual Defense Treaty with Taiwan, but the initial barrage killed two American military officers.[46] China then invaded two smaller islands, Dachen and Yijiangshan. The conflict ended when President Eisenhower and Secretary of State Dulles threatened the use of tactical nuclear weapons in defense of Taiwan and when the Soviet Union, China's ally, began pressuring China to end it for fear of being dragged into the conflict as well. Although the United States and China were engaging in coercive diplomacy with no real intention of going to war, miscalculation could have led to a disastrous conflict involving Washington, Beijing, and Moscow, over insignificant islands far from Taiwan.

The Second Taiwan Straits Crisis (1958) was similar to the first in many respects. Once again China shelled Taiwan's offshore islands, killing nearly a thousand Taiwanese soldiers and civilians. This time Mao's intention was largely political: to induce the United States to resume talks with China. By the end of the crisis, both the United States and the Soviet Union had threatened nuclear escalation over the islands. In essence Mao had brought two superpowers to threaten nuclear war over islands that none of the parties, including China, believed carried much strategic significance.[47]

The Third Taiwan Straits Crisis took place after the Cold War and may bear the closest resemblance of the three Taiwan Straits Crises to a possible fourth one in the future. The roots of this particular crisis were buried in Taiwan's vigorous embrace of democracy, which began in 1987 after the elderly Chiang Ching-kuo lifted martial law and began to allow for liberalization. By 1994 constitutional reforms and universal suffrage had laid the foundation for a general election, and with it perhaps even formal independence. Lee Teng-hui had succeeded Chiang as the KMT's leader, and as the 1996 election approached, he began to take steps that contradicted the KMT's historical embrace of the "one China" principle—which stated that the mainland and Taiwan were part of the same China but had different views over who was its rightful leader. From Beijing's perspective one of his most provocative acts was a 1995 visit to his alma mater, Cornell, where he was to give a speech in an unofficial capacity. Lee's visit appeared to break with precedent, since the United States had not allowed a sitting Taiwanese leader to visit the United States since the normalization of relations with China. When Lee chose to make the visit semiofficial and then hinted in his formal remarks that Taiwan might be a separate country from China altogether, Beijing grew even more concerned about the possibility of Taiwanese independence.

In response China chose to make a show of force. It held missile exercises in July and August 1995, and then held additional exercises in November and December of the same year. In the run-up to the 1996 election, China attempted to intimidate Taiwan's electorate into voting against Lee by mobilizing one hundred thousand troops and firing missiles near Taiwan's Keelung and Kaohsiung ports, through which a majority of shipping to Taiwan passed, thereby suggesting China's ability to impose a missile blockade on Taiwan. The United States took issue with China's attempt to intimidate Taiwan through overt military displays and responded with one of the largest American shows of force in the region since the Vietnam War, sailing two American carrier battle groups toward the Taiwan Strait. China eventually backed down, but the political costs were indeed significant. Beijing's attempt at intimidation had been counterproductive, increasing support for Lee by such a significant amount that he was able to achieve an electoral majority rather than a mere plurality. China's behavior also provided a justification for continued US arms sales to Taiwan. Finally, the conflict made clear the new stakes in the Taiwan Strait: a nascent democracy was flirting with independence and China's leadership would risk war to prevent it. The United States, caught in the middle, would have a tremendous stake in ensuring that neither side unilaterally sought to shift the status quo.

Although there has not been another militarized Taiwan Straits Crisis since then, the Democratic Progressive Party (DPP) administration of Chen Shui-bian that followed President Lee was even more willing to provoke China on the question of independence than Lee had been. Chen broke assurances to Washington that he would not provoke the mainland and instead made a number of speeches suggesting that Taiwan was a sovereign and independent country. China was reassured by American promises that Washington would not support Taiwanese independence and chastened by its experience in the last Taiwan Straits Crisis, and decided to refrain from military exercises or overt coercion, even in the run-up to President Chen's reelection. But after Chen secured a second term, China drafted the Anti-Secession Law, which made explicit China's willingness to use military force in the event of Taiwan's independence. In addition China began massing short- and medium-range ballistic missile forces across the strait. Taiwan's provocations reached their highest level in 2008, when President Chen submitted a popular referendum that would allow Taiwan to apply for UN membership under the name Taiwan rather than the name Republic of China. This was largely a campaign tactic, and the US government was clear that doing so would constitute a unilateral change in the status quo that would threaten Taiwan's own safety and security. Chen was defeated in this campaign and Ma Ying-jeou, a conservative leader keen on deescalating tensions in the Taiwan Strait and opposed to Chen's proindependence maneuvering, came to power.

Under Ma's tenure tensions over Taiwan reached the lowest level since the end of the Cold War and relations with the mainland improved dramatically. Ma signed several major economic agreements with China, including the Comprehensive Economic Framework Agreement, and established direct commercial flights with China. Beijing, for its part, determined that influencing Taiwan through economic agreements might be more effective than doing so through overt military intimidation. The relationship reached a high point in 2015 with a historic meeting between Presidents Ma and Xi that marked the first time leaders of China and Taiwan had met since the end of the Chinese Civil War in 1949.

Toward the end of Ma's tenure in office, however, the Taiwanese public became increasingly concerned about the island's significant reliance on the mainland economy, with student protesters occupying parliament to show their opposition to a trade-in-services agreement negotiated between China and Taiwan, and public opinion polls reflecting flagging public support among Taiwanese for closer interdependence with the mainland. With Ma's approval rating at low levels, the DPP candidate, Tsai Ing-wen, won Taiwan's 2016 election. Since the DPP has historically pursued a more proindependence and anti-China line, and since Tsai was a part of Chen's administration, there are concerns in Beijing that this political transition could usher in greater instability in cross-strait relations if Tsai pursues proindependence policies or slows the pace of political and economic relations with the mainland.

The long-term trajectory of the relationship between China and Taiwan is thrown into doubt by Taiwan's evolving political identity. An important by-product of Taiwan's success as a modern democracy and prosperous economy, as well as the threats directed by the mainland against Taiwan, has been greater pride in a distinctive Taiwanese identity. An annual poll conducted by Taiwan's National Chengchi University shows that the number of people in Taiwan who see themselves as Taiwanese has risen from 18 percent in 1992 to nearly 61 percent in 2016, while the percentage who see themselves as Chinese has fallen from more than 20 percent to roughly 4 percent in the same period.[48] This shift is in large part generational, and it accompanies a growing opposition to unification with the mainland across all of society. As Beijing watches these trends, it may one day grow skeptical that unification can be accomplished through peaceful means and consider overt military or economic coercion. Recent turmoil in Hong Kong has also spurred very real but very different anxieties in Beijing and Taipei, and could well complicate the cross-strait relationship moving forward.

In light of the history of turmoil that surrounds US-China relations over Taiwan, and threatens to resurface again in current circumstances, prominent Asia specialists in the United States have occasionally suggested that the United States should effectively abandon Taiwan. George Washington

University professor Charles Glaser has argued that the "United States should consider backing away from its commitment to Taiwan," while the distinguished China specialist Chas Freeman has argued that our Taiwan policy is "oddly misguided."[49] Professor Bruce Gilley has proposed supporting the "Finlandization" of Taiwan, which would involve terminating the US-Taiwan security relationship.[50] Implementing such a policy would be antithetical to American interests and would indeed undermine the American position not only across the Taiwan Strait, but also within the wider region, by calling into question the credibility of American security commitments. It could even embolden China to pursue even more assertive policies throughout the region. As Bonnie Glaser and the late China historian Nancy Tucker have written, abandoning Taiwan would "prove to an increasingly confident China that Washington has become weak, vacillating, and unreliable," and will concede to Chinese demands in the hope that peace be preserved.[51] Finally, the symbolic value of a democratic Taiwan is profoundly important and often understated. The very existence of Taiwan's democracy is a signal to mainland Chinese that their government's claims that democracy is a Western phenomenon are baseless.

Instead of withdrawing, the United States needs to maintain a robust, unofficial Taiwan policy, the outlines of which are provided in the following chapter. For the purposes of this chapter, it is critical to note that the United States should remain deeply engaged as a stabilizing presence by supporting Taiwan's flourishing democracy, encouraging improved ties across the Taiwan Strait, and discouraging provocations on both sides.[52]

Democratic Advance or Retreat

Mongolia is one of the most beguiling countries in Asia. Sandwiched between two mammoth autocracies, China and Russia, and with no history of liberalism, Mongolia has nevertheless built a thriving democratic government. Once known for hordes of horsemen that conquered much of Eurasia, Mongolia is now a peaceful country with a small military that has supported roughly fifteen international peacekeeping missions in the last ten years and hosted a global gathering for the Community of Democracies. Mongolia's leadership and people deserve tremendous credit for the success of their democracy, but the United States too played a role. For years Washington has lavished attention on Mongolia to help it consolidate these democratic gains.

Indeed, as we saw in the last chapter, US commitment to democracy in Asia has been a long-standing component of US strategy. When one takes the long view, American success in these efforts has been unmistakable and profound. Although Washington waged war against Communism in Asia in Korea and Vietnam, the United States has generally refrained from inserting democracy into Asia through force or coercion, preferring instead a more subtle but effective route that involves supporting democracy through public pronouncements, institution building, legal assistance, people-to-people exchanges, and economic development. This is a policy that has produced great success, especially among close US allies and partners like Japan, South Korea, the Philippines, and Taiwan.

Looking out across Asia, it is clear that the region is home to a small number of stalwart autocracies, including China, Laos, North Korea, and Vietnam. It is home to a larger number of democracies, such as India, Indonesia, Japan, Mongolia, the Philippines, South Korea, and Taiwan. In contrast, and most importantly for the region's trajectory, it is home to an even larger number of transitional states that are moving either toward or away from democracy, including Bangladesh, Burma, Cambodia, Malaysia, Nepal, Singapore, Sri Lanka, and Thailand.

These fledgling transitional states in many ways define Asia's political future, and are currently in the process of making consequential decisions about how they will be governed. Depending on their political evolution, this massive region that is home to half the world's people and is now the cockpit of the global economy could become either a region of liberal advance and democratic community or a region characterized by painful democratic retreat. Indeed, Larry Diamond, a prominent political scientist, predicted in 2012 that if "there is going to be a big new lift to global democratic prospects in this decade, the region from which it will emanate is most likely to be East Asia."[53]

In the period ahead, the focus of US democracy promotion should be on supporting Asia's transitional states in their often-challenging journey to democracy, which in turn calls for a US strategy that is both patient and flexible. In essence, the most effective approach will involve the United States adhering to the principles of democracy and human rights without doing so dogmatically or in ways that would undermine US influence. Washington played an important role in encouraging former transitional states like the

Philippines and South Korea to embrace democracy, and it may be able to reprise that role with several of the region's other states. More recently I had the privilege of helping broker the opening of Burma, which until 2010 had hidden itself away from the world and relied almost exclusively on its commercial ties to China. Since then the previously totalitarian government has allowed the formation of a parliament, written a constitution, held elections, and freed Nobel Prize–winning opposition leader Aung San Suu Kyi, who is now more relevant and relentless than ever before. Although Burma still has far to go, with progress accompanied just as often by heartbreaking setbacks, the question for the country is not whether it will return to the past but how it will move into the future—and whether the United States will assist it as it does. If American policy in Burma and elsewhere is successful and Asia's transitional states embrace democracy, then the region could move toward one day becoming a democratic pillar of international order similar to Europe. This would have powerful implications for rules-based order, economic cooperation, peace and stability, and integrative international institutions.

One potential challenge to this vision, at least in the view of some, comes from the so-called Beijing consensus, which purportedly constitutes a coherent alternative to Western values. China's unique marriage of state capitalism, autocracy, and repression—although stalling now—has at times been able to kindle growth and bring development more rapidly than the American model. But those who would elevate China's system of government into some kind of exportable ideology dramatically overstate both its coherence and its attractiveness. Moreover, they forget that China itself is not an evangelical seeking to externalize its system, and although it supports autocracies and other states in global politics out of a belief in the importance of sovereignty and noninterference, it hardly seeks to overtly undermine democratic systems of governance in a fashion reminiscent of the Soviet Union or revolutionary China under Mao. Importantly, to view democracy as an American ideology in contest with a Chinese ideology misses the uniquely international quality of democracy today. The success of democracies worldwide and especially in Asia after the Cold War's close has made democracy an international norm, not a uniquely American export.

Indeed, in some cases democracy is treated as a Mongolian export. The country that only twenty-five years ago embraced democracy with Western assistance is now sharing its hard-won democratic knowledge and experience with states like Afghanistan, Burma, and Kyrgyzstan.[54] Perhaps one of the best measures of the success of American democracy is that the world's people no longer think of democracy as distinctively American.

Prosperity or Protectionism

For most of its history, support for free trade has been an important component of US strategy in Asia. As we saw in the last chapter, historians can draw a line between the first US trading voyage to Asia aboard the *Empress of China* in 1784 through to the negotiations surrounding the Trans-Pacific Partnership more than two centuries later. Today the continuance of free trade requires rules that facilitate the free flow of goods and limit the ability of states to enact protectionist policies. Washington was reminded of the importance of such rules during the Great Depression, when measures designed to protect domestic businesses in major economies set off a catastrophic spiral of escalating protectionism, ultimately producing a disastrous collapse in global trade and prosperity. After World War II, the United States and its allies and partners proposed rules to guide policymakers in order to keep markets open, and Asia was a direct beneficiary of this system. International organizations such as the World Bank helped Asian states modernize, while GATT and the WTO reduced trade barriers, resulting in a surge in intraregional trade and exports to the West that together underwrote the Asian miracle. The rise of Asia has been due in no small part to the prevailing system; now, with Asia as the dynamic center of the global economy, the very future of that system and of global free trade itself is increasingly likely to be written in Asia. For its part, Asia's economic system is being pulled between the high standards of the future and the low standards and soft protectionism of the past, and an important US priority in the period ahead will be to ensure the region moves closer to the former rather than the latter, for the sake of Asians, Americans, and the larger global economy.

Indeed, Asia is presently at the forefront of the twenty-first-century economy and the unique challenges it poses. Contemporary Asian trade bears little resemblance to the simple models of Adam Smith and David Ricardo, who theorized about how English textiles might be traded for Portuguese wine to the benefit of both. The region is instead now one of the world's most interconnected and interdependent. A tangled web of supply chains and capital flows string Asia's diverse economies together into "Factory Asia," a powerful engine for growth, job creation, and exports.[55] A simple pair of shorts might have buttons made in China, zippers made in Japan, yarn spun in Bangladesh, and stitching done in Pakistan—a cell phone or computer may have a still more complex lineage.[56] Although Asia is famous for its exports to Europe and the United States, nearly 56 percent of Asian trade is conducted within the region itself—a percentage second only to Europe, which has the benefit of a fully liberalized common market.[57] In contrast, Asia's states still have tariffs and a variety of nontariff barriers, not to mention lingering territorial tensions and security concerns, leaving what Evan Feigenbaum and Robert Manning have called "Economic Asia" in increasingly prosperous but uneasy coexistence with the military rivalries defining "Security Asia."[58]

While Economic Asia's emergence has been a boon to the region and pulled millions from poverty, Asia's future prosperity—and with it the future of global economy—is not automatically guaranteed. The region's states, including China, risk falling into the "middle income trap," especially if they fail to sustain growth or stumble in climbing the ladder into higher-value products. Asian states also face a new set of twenty-first-century challenges as the nature of the global economy changes. For example, many of the region's economies have captured the low-hanging fruit that comes from reduced tariffs on goods. Now they must find ways to reduce remaining nontariff trade barriers while also writing new rules to promote trade in services, as well as to deal with complex twenty-first-century questions on topics such as intellectual property, cross-border data flows, and the role of state-owned enterprises. Previous agreements, with their focus on commodities and manufactured goods, are not ideally suited for such concerns and require updating.

If sustaining Asian prosperity and autonomy requires new trade agreements and rules, the obvious question then is whose rules should form the standards for the twenty-first century. This is a question with implications far beyond Asia. Asia is a dynamic region that has transformed itself into the center of the global economy, and the rules that Asian states adopt will have a powerful impact on the shape of the larger global economy.

The system built by the United States and its allies that sustained Asian prosperity was based on the simple premise that economic rules should be designed to promote free trade and to discourage protectionism. Today the US hopes to ensure that free trade remains the bedrock of the twenty-first-century economy by updating older rules that no longer reflect an economy that is now substantially different from the past. To that end the United States has supported the Trans-Pacific Partnership (TPP) and the Transatlantic Trade and Investment Partnership (TTIP) as vehicles to create high standards that ensure free trade in the twenty-first century. The TTIP involves the United States and Europe. The TPP involves twelve Pacific Rim countries that together account for 40 percent of global GDP: Australia, Brunei, Canada, Chile, Japan, Malaysia, Mexico, New Zealand, Peru, Singapore, the United States, and Vietnam. The United States, however, is not alone in offering a vision for Asia's future. China—which is not a member of the TPP—supports its own low-standards approach through the sixteen-member Regional Comprehensive Economic Partnership (RCEP). This approach would do far less to promote free trade and would not address many of the issues that the TPP is intended to solve.

For many in Asia, both the TPP and the RCEP are way stations on the path to the ultimate destination, which is a massive though still distant agreement for the entire region, known as the Free Trade Area for the Asia-Pacific (FTAAP). Given the size and prosperity of the Asia-Pacific, the FTAAP would undoubtedly shape global trade for decades to come. Its content will be determined in part by whether TPP or RCEP standards become widely adopted in Asia, and since these agreements are being negotiated and finalized in the present, that means that the next several years will have an inordinately large impact on the shape of future global trade. Asia may well be the most important battleground in shaping the future of the global economy.

The United States has strong domestic interests as well in ensuring that free trade remains a bedrock global principle. President Obama, in outlining the case for the TPP, noted, "We've got to make sure we're writing those trade rules in the fastest-growing region of the world, the Asia-Pacific, as opposed to having China write those rules for us, in which case American businesses will lose and American workers will lose."[59] The United States, as a twenty-first-century economy, has a strong interest in putting forward twenty-first-century rules, not least because such practices help make the world safer for American exports of goods and services.

A discussion of such rules and standards can seem somewhat abstract, so it may be worthwhile to take a moment to discuss some of the key questions at stake. First, American negotiators are insisting on respect for patents, trademarks, and other intellectual property—principles that are threatened by piracy, counterfeiting, cybertheft, and indigenization and localization requirements in China and India that effectively require foreign companies to transfer technology to domestic rivals. When intellectual property is not respected, firms and entrepreneurs have no incentive to take risks or make investments in lifesaving drugs, movie franchises, or technology products. Second, the basic principle of free trade is reciprocity. All too often, however, states are happy to sell abroad but engage in soft protectionism at home by subsidizing or otherwise protecting their inefficient industries, erecting non-tariff trade barriers, or manipulating their currencies to gain trade advantages. These measures may skirt many of the trade rules that are currently on the books, but they also risk provoking the offended state to use sanctions as a way of evening the playing field, thereby producing the sort of dangerous protectionist spiral that could undermine global trade. Third, although economic agreements have long dealt with the goods trade, they have yet to comprehensively address the services trade. Services are the largest part of the American economy, half of the Indian economy, and the fastest-growing portion of the Chinese economy, and the potential economic gains from promoting an international market in services are truly enormous. Fourth, the emergence of Internet commerce has created a number of new trade questions. The United States generally supports allowing data to flow across borders and objects to Internet censorship, both for principled reasons and also because censorship can be employed as a shield to protect infant Web industries from foreign competition. Finally, a number of chapters in both the TPP and the TTIP are designed to deal with other difficult topics, including labor laws, government procurement, state-owned enterprises, and environmental provisions whose outcomes will play a central role in how the Asian Century moves forward.

Many of these provisions can seem burdensome for many Asian countries that, in contrast, may find the Chinese approach focused largely on goods to be simpler and less controversial. Moreover, because the United States is already so open, it has less economic leverage that it can use to induce others to sign onto its trade terms than a more protected economy like China. These difficulties are not insurmountable, in large part because the economic payoff of adopting a high-standards agreement would be truly enormous. A recent study showed an Asia-Pacific trade agreement with TPP standards at the core would bring in $1 trillion more in income gains than one built around RCEP standards, which, as Joshua Meltzer of the Brookings Institution notes, "will not achieve a level of ambition or comprehensiveness to provide a real alternative to the TPP."[60] In addition, a separate study showed that the TPP is also extremely beneficial to China. Two American economists and an economist at the China Investment Corporation found that the TPP would bring China income gains of $800 billion over the next ten years.[61] China's own economists may well have conducted similar calculations, and in recent years China has in fact shifted from hostility toward the TPP and begun to express some interest in even joining the agreement, suggesting that in the long run, the TPP's success could even induce China to adopt higher standards. TPP is an open-platform agreement that allows any country to join if it can meet the appropriate standards, and already Indonesia, the Philippines, South Korea, Taiwan, and Thailand have expressed an interest in joining.[62] In this important respect, the TPP is seen by central policymakers as not so much invitational but instead aspirational. The last time China signed on to a difficult trade agreement was when it joined the WTO, and after a period of costly but necessary domestic reforms, it benefited dramatically. As many in Beijing are likely aware, free trade can be painful short-term politics but it invariably ends up being gainful long-term economics.

Finally, geopolitics and economics often intertwine in Asia, with several smaller Asian states growing concerned that their significant dependence on China's economy exposes them to attempts at economic coercion by Beijing. These concerns are not merely paranoia, especially since China has in the past used its economic size to pressure the Philippines over fruit, Japan over rare earths, Norway over fish, and even the United States over aircraft. Understandably these smaller states believe it prudent to diversify their economic relationships and thereby increase their own freedom of maneuver.

Conclusion: Commitment or Retrenchment

On many issues central to Asia's future, the region is in a state of flux and uncertainty. Asia is being pulled between hegemony and a regional balance of power. Its operating system is drawn between twenty-first-century and nineteenth-century rules. Its great powers are deciding whether to become stakeholders or spoilers. Its militaries are drifting between war and peace. Its transitional states are deciding whether to embrace democracy or practice repression. And its economic structure is being pulled between high standards and soft protectionism.

At the heart of each of these questions that are so central to the shape of Asia's future lies a fundamental American choice: commitment or retrenchment. If the United States is to play a role in bending the arc of the Asian Century toward long-standing American interests and broad-based Asian peace and prosperity, it will have to be focused and engaged. In contrast, hesitance or inattention at this critical transitional moment may allow the most dynamic region in world politics to irrevocably drift in dangerous and counterproductive directions on many important issues. Success in guiding the choices of a changing Asia will require a "plan for the Pivot," and we now turn to a consideration of the strategy that the United States should employ in the Asia-Pacific.

CHAPTER SIX

The Plan for the Pivot

Fashioning a Ten-Point American Strategy for Asia

The United States has deep and enduring interests in Asia dating back to the earliest days of the republic. American power has long been a calming and welcome factor in the region, restricting the imperial ambitions of Great Britain, Japan, Russia, as well as currently providing reassurance during a more assertive period in Chinese foreign policy. Today, as the previous chapter made clear, Asia faces a decisive moment of transition on critical questions that are central to both American interests and the shape of the twenty-first century, but fortunately also amenable to American exertions. The Pivot can help ensure that Asian states pursue balance over hegemony, twenty-first-century rules over nineteenth-century pressure, global governance over parochial interest, peace and coexistence over costly conflict, democratic values over repression, and prosperity over protectionism. If Asia is to have a bright future, if its bounty is to bolster the prosperity and security of everyday Americans, then the United States will have to make a clear and unambiguous choice: commitment over retrenchment.

As the previous chapters have shown, American involvement in Asia has at times been inconsistent and unsteady, with policymakers all too often regarding Asia as a "secondary theater" less vital to American interests than the concerns of Europe and the Middle East. At times this haphazardness has led to unintended and even dangerous developments in one of the world's most vital regions. To achieve its interests in Asia and the wider world, the United States will need to sustain a consistent and steady Asia policy, even as administrations change.

This requires a coherent plan for the Pivot, one that demonstrates in ways big and small that the country has the unity of will, and the economic and political staying power, to continue playing its vital and leading role in the Asian Century. The many challenges and obstacles ahead require an approach to Asia that is diversified across the full instruments of American statecraft. To that end this chapter offers the broad outlines of a plan for the Pivot, composed of ten core elements.

First, the United States needs to clarify the Pivot and mobilize the American public behind it through clear and authoritative declarations of US Asia strategy. This domestic public diplomacy effort should elucidate the central tenets of the Pivot and why these initiatives are fundamentally in the US and global interest. This clarification should take the form of presidential speeches and statements as well as an annual strategy document articulating a whole-of-government approach to Asia. By better explicating the Pivot, the United States can persuade a public inclined toward retrenchment to more fully embrace Asia policy, while sending a clear statement to Asian states of US intentions, strategy, and resolve.

Second, a defining element of the Pivot is to focus on strengthening ties to our Asian allies, including Japan, South Korea, Australia, the Philippines, Thailand, and Singapore (a quasi ally). Through closer cooperation with the United States, and increasingly each other, these states can continue playing a significant role in the Asian Century. US alliances are the scaffolding for American architecture in the region and contribute not only to an Asian balance of power but also to common efforts to bolster Asia's operating system—that is, the complex legal, security, and practical arrangements that underscore what is now four decades of Asian prosperity and security. Particularly at a time when the United States faces resource constraints at home and myriad foreign policy challenges in other regions, sustained success in Asian endeavors will call for the close cooperation of our regional allies.

Third, the United States will need to more consequentially shape the contours of China's rise. It can do this by embedding China policy fully within a larger Asia policy framework, as well as by refraining from adopting a "China first" strategy that focuses inordinately on communiqués and grand bargains and regards China as the key to all US efforts in Asia. Ties with China will continue to be a challenging mixture of competition and cooperation, and to simultaneously sustain Asia's operating system, find common ground on crosscutting global issues, and overcome the notorious

"Thucydides trap," the United States will need to understand the drivers behind China's assertive turn and craft a work plan to manage competition as well as foster greater cooperation on issues crying out for more partnership between the United States and China.

Fourth, the United States will benefit from increasing ties with long-standing partners like Taiwan and New Zealand, as well as new partners including India, Vietnam, Indonesia, Malaysia, and the Pacific island states. The development of these relationships will afford the United States influence over the direction of Asia's overall development and expand US influence beyond the traditional hub-and-spokes model of bilateral alliances.

Fifth, the United States should look to integrate the Asia-Pacific both regionally and internationally through the expansion of free trade agreements and economic interaction, including through the passage of the TPP. Asia is the cockpit of the global economy, and the economic rules it adopts will influence global economic governance for the century ahead. For this reason the United States will need to firmly advocate for twenty-first-century, high-standards economic agreements.

Sixth, the United States has enduring interests in engaging the development of the region's proliferating and increasingly integrative international institutions. These multilateral bodies have the power to shape and shore up the rules and norms in the region on issues of profound consequence to US interests and the maintenance of Asia's operating system. The United States ought not to deny itself, or allow other powers to deny it, a seat at any table where Asia's future is discussed. For this reason US policy should favor helping build trans-Pacific institutions and capacities over pan-Asian groupings that do not include the United States.

Seventh, the United States will need to update and modernize its military capabilities in the region. These form the backbone of US alliances and the foundation for the region's peace and stability. It is imperative that the United States find ways to cope with emerging high-level challenges, such as China's anti-access/area-denial capabilities, as well as lower-level "gray zone" provocations in territorial disputes involving paramilitary and other forces. At the same time, the United States must prepare for evolving cyberthreats and ensure that it retains the capability to maintain its presence and attend to regional crises, humanitarian and otherwise, in part by increasing access and basing in Southeast Asia and the Indian Ocean. Greater military and defense cooperation to deal with the region's natural disasters is of paramount importance.

Eighth, the United States is a liberal power, one with an enduring commitment to freedom and democracy. Values are a core part of US policy and objectives in the region, and with a prudent and flexible approach, the United States can support Asia's transitional states on their democratic journeys and advance civil society and nascent representation developments.

Ninth, people-to-people ties can effectively humanize the otherwise abstract and impersonal pillars of American engagement. In this process, exchanges and educational opportunities can help break down barriers of misperception, create enduring personal connections, and build a wealth of area-specific expertise that together can have profound consequences for US engagement in Asia. The United States will need to strengthen people-to-people ties through new programs, engaging partner countries in high-level diplomatic efforts to boost such ties, and it will also need to make concrete efforts to include the influential and prosperous Asian American diaspora communities in policy.

Tenth, the United States need not Pivot to Asia alone. Most of the important American action on the international stage has been taken in concert with its European allies, and there is no reason why the Pivot should be an exception. European states have the potential to support and expand our shared interests in the world's most dynamic region, from macroeconomic and trade coordination to the pursuit of democracy promotion and the resolution of human rights concerns. This calls for a more integrated transatlantic approach to the region's challenges that combines complementary strengths to achieve shared interests.

Without a sustained and integrated, all-of-government commitment on these ten fronts, a successful Pivot will prove exceedingly difficult to carry out. With the right concentration and effort, as well as the correct combination of subtlety and strength, the United States can play a decisive role across the region that will mutually benefit all parties. This chapter will explore these main areas in greater detail in the hope of providing a blueprint for future American efforts in this most important of regions.

Clarifying the Pivot and Mobilizing the Public

"Although the Obama administration has issued a series of speeches and documents on the rebalance," a recent report notes, "there remains no central statement of the U.S. government's rebalance strategy."[1] Those few documents that have emerged tend to be from individual agencies and have limited and parochial perspectives. This lack of an authoritative and central-level explication of the Pivot is a reason not only for the initial confusion surrounding the term *pivot* but also for continued uncertainty and confusion among allies, partners, and the American public as to the Pivot's purpose and promise. If the Pivot is to be successful, this state of affairs will have to change. The United States will need to clarify the strategy behind the Pivot to domestic and foreign audiences, while also mobilizing its public in broad support of the initiative.

As a first step in this effort, the United States should produce an annual strategy document coordinated by the National Security Council that articulates a whole-government and interagency strategy for the US Pivot to Asia. This document would contain a clear enumeration of the ends of American strategy in Asia, a theory of the ways in which these ends can be achieved, and a discussion of the means available to American policymakers. Unlike some previous documents that have focused largely on security considerations, this document would be broad in its focus and discuss important regional developments, a program for American allies and partners, and economic, military, and diplomatic instruments of statecraft. The effort might also articulate a kind of scorecard from year to year to track areas of improvement and lagging initiatives. The publication of a comprehensive and coherent Asia strategy document would go a long way in clarifying elements of the Pivot.

Second, American administrations should better explain the Pivot's purpose and strategy abroad. US diplomats and alliance managers will need to directly communicate US regional strategy to their counterparts in Asia, and in this regard presidential speeches and an official strategy document could be profoundly clarifying, not only by broadcasting a clear and coherent signal directly to Asian states, but also by creating an internal consensus on US strategy that transcends agencies. This kind of message discipline could reduce confusion about the Pivot among Asian states. For close allies and partners, these efforts could together help allay fears of US abandonment and set an affirmative agenda for bilateral cooperation. For others, including China, such authoritative and high-level clarifications of the Pivot could reduce the risk of miscalculation by reassuring Beijing that the Pivot is not a form of containment, while also signaling US resolve to remain active and engaged in Asian affairs.

Third, the United States will need to mobilize domestic support for the Pivot and for Asia policy more broadly. American administrations should engage in outreach to Congress in order to secure sufficient resources for the Pivot's execution and to reduce the likelihood that the Pivot will be held hostage by partisan wrangling.[2] In addition, and perhaps more fundamentally, the Pivot's success will call for modest public mobilization for Asia policy. This will prove a challenging task, with the Iraq War and global financial crisis having reduced the American public's appetite for international engagement and economic globalization and created a public mood of more modest international ambitions. An American president will not be able to undo this sentiment overnight, but to begin turning the tide, presidential leadership is necessary to make the case for why Asia is important to American interests. This will involve reminding Americans that Asia is the world's fastest-growing region, boasts many of the world's largest economies, is the destination for the largest percentage increase of American exports, and features the world's largest middle class—and that any effective strategy for American economic renewal and renaissance will need an affirmative Asian agenda. The case for Asia should also emphasize that the path to progress on several American priorities, from climate change to nonproliferation, runs through Asia's rising states. Finally, Americans jaded by hostility and anti-Americanism in the Middle East would benefit from hearing that Asia is not like the Middle East; instead it is a region that is largely welcoming of an American influence and presence and one where American political, strategic, and economic investments can yield tangible returns for American policymakers. If these arguments are made by top-level political leaders, it may be possible to secure sufficient popular support for Asia policy. So far, although President Obama has given speeches on Asia policy abroad, he has yet to give a speech in the United States outlining and justifying a robust Asia policy. This stands in contrast to numerous policy speeches and high-profile proclamations on the Middle East over the past fifteen years. The Pivot's domestic underpinnings are a critical component of its overall success; indeed, without domestic support, US policy in Asia is likely to be episodic, inconsistent, and ineffective.

Bolstering and Integrating Alliances

For over half a century, the United States has brought order and stability to Asia through what former secretary of state John Foster Dulles indelibly termed a hub-and-spokes system of bilateral relationships. This system fixed the United States as the center—and its Asian allies as the spokes—on the wire wheel of regional stability. In contrast to Europe, where Western states joined with the United States in multilateral security arrangements such as NATO, Asia at the time required a bilateral system, given the region's unique security challenges, lack of comparable military partners, and very different cultures—not to mention deep historical distrust among those cultures. Together these factors bedeviled attempts to replicate the multilateral infrastructure being built in Europe.[3] A hub-and-spokes approach, US officials concluded, would provide the best solution to problems that required close regional relations to stem Communist advances. This approach also allowed Washington to dial up and back the level of engagement in various situations over time. It also allowed the United States to direct and support each of its allies.[4]

The first spoke was fixed in 1951 when the United States and Japan signed a security treaty in San Francisco. By 1954 the United States had also entered into formal alliances with Australia, New Zealand, the Philippines, South Korea, Taiwan, and Thailand. Washington tied many of these alliances together through the Southeast Asia Treaty Organization, a weak and short-lived organization meant to serve as an Asian NATO. It highlighted the difficulty of multilateral security cooperation and reiterated the importance of the US bilateral alliance structure. Since this short burst of so-called "pact-o-mania," as Eisenhower and Dulles's treaty proclivities were termed, the structure of US alliances in Asia has remained largely intact over decades.

Indeed, despite the end of the Cold War and the collapse of Communist ideology, these American alliances have endured and remain, in the words of John Ikenberry, "the single most important anchor for regional stability."[5] America's alliance commitments have been more than just scraps of paper—they have helped to maintain the sovereignty and independence of close partners and have deterred conflict. They have anchored the US presence in the region and provided the United States with the opportunity to shape Asia's operating system on questions such as the balance of power, freedom of navigation, the promulgation of a thriving trading and commerce regime, peaceful resolutions of disputes, greater transparency, and the endurance of liberal values. These features of the alliance structure are all the more crucial at a time when, as the previous chapter has demonstrated, Asia stands at a precipice on several issues central to the future of Asia as well as that of the larger world. In short, these security guarantees are symbols of US commitment in Asia without which American leadership would be devalued and diminished.

While the hub-and-spokes system will continue to serve as the core for American efforts in the region, the model also calls for modernization and refurbishment. Contemporary security problems in Asia are no longer based on the exogenous threat of menacing Communist advance but are characterized instead by deepening regional uncertainty surrounding territorial and maritime disputes, rising nationalism, lingering distrust, and China's more assertive foreign policy. Interconnected and transnational issues including terrorism, proliferation, piracy, refugees, and cyberthreats also call for greater attention and a coordinated approach. The multitude of challenges ahead requires the United States to adopt a two-pronged approach to its critical partners by (1) strengthening individual ties to allies, and (2) seeking to link allies together in common purpose.

First, the United States should continue to strengthen its defense ties with each of its allies. With security at the core of these relationships, the United States should pursue closer defense cooperation—such as military exercises, strategic dialogue, weapons sales, and cooperation in military industry—with each of its allies. For example, the United States is working with Australia to develop the latter's amphibious capabilities and has sold naval vessels and helicopters to the Philippines so that it can police its maritime domain. In many cases US bases and access agreements with treaty allies can bring with them a variety of complex political challenges; indeed, there are few things more challenging politically than stationing US troops on the sovereign, democratic soil of another country. Senior US policymakers will need to continue investing top-level time in some of the mundane and tedious—yet often surprisingly combustible—issues of alliance management, such as status of forces agreements and consultation mechanisms. This may seem an obvious point, but it is often easy for the United States to take its historical alliances for granted and to forget that alliance management is an active rather than passive task. Former secretary of state George Shultz famously described alliance management as gardening: it requires patience, the careful tending of sensitive issues, the routine weeding out of thorny ones, and the farsighted planting of new sources of cooperation. That said, it is nonetheless crucial that the United States and its allies not allow alliance management issues to consume the bilateral agenda, and that it work with each ally to develop and articulate a broader vision for the alliance that looks to the horizon and addresses the nature and complexity of emerging twenty-first-century challenges. In addition to strengthening security ties, the United States will need to widen each relationship so that it rests more sturdily on the additional pillars of economic, diplomatic, and people-to-people ties rather than the sole pole of shared security interests. This can help inoculate an alliance against swings in public opinion and changing strategic circumstances, thereby putting it on more solid ground for the future. Finally, the United States should take care to engage its Asian allies in regular high-level diplomacy with all the bells and whistles of protocol and statecraft, as it does with other key countries, such as China. Without such an inclusive and multifaceted approach, the United States risks giving other Asian nations the impression that high-level diplomacy with China essentially checks the box for the continent as a whole.

Second, the United States will best be able to manage Asia's emerging challenges if its allies and partners more effectively work together. This means that, in addition to playing the role of gardener in the bilateral context, the United States also needs to act more as an orchestra conductor in these multilateral forums (small gatherings of states), at times coordinating the increasingly independent activities and programs of its allies and partners in common cause. The five American defense treaty allies in the Asia-Pacific—Australia, Japan, the Philippines, South Korea, and Thailand—can increase their responsibilities and regional leadership not only independently but also in unison. While some may see such an approach as a return to Nixon's Guam Doctrine, which suggested that the United States would step back from its commitments in the region while others would do more, this comparison is poorly suited for modern circumstances. This approach is not Nixon-era retrenchment but twenty-first-century network building; in other words, the addition to the hub-and-spokes model of a tire that links allies to one another without interfering with their strong ties to the US hub.

In many cases cooperation is already proceeding without the United States at the center. Common interests are compelling allies and partners to construct the "tire" around the hub-and-spokes strategy all on their own, developing closer economic, military, and political ties between them. Japan is a standout example of such efforts. For instance, Tokyo is bidding on a contract to provide Australia with advanced diesel submarines, signed an agreement on defense cooperation with the Philippines in 2015, and is rapidly deepening defense ties with India—a close US partner—through exercises and weapons sales.[6] For its part, India has strengthened ties with Australia, the Philippines, and Vietnam, while Australia and South Korea have committed to a blueprint for closer defense ties. Of course, much work remains—notably on improving cooperation between Japan and South Korea—but a web of interconnected Asian allies and partners is clearly coalescing in Asia. The question for the United States is how to encourage and harness the organic emergence of these connections between allies and partners.

As a start, the United States could consider elements of what some call a "federated approach," which pushes for deeper integration of allied defense industries and capabilities. As Mike Green, Kathleen Hicks, and Zack Cooper write, "Federated approaches would connect allies and partners with one another, *often with the United States in the background*…through training, logistical support, tactical development, and, potentially, operational missions."[7] Aside from strategic cooperation, another component of this approach would be US encouragement for closer economic and diplomatic ties between US allies and partners where independent initiatives are lacking—and here the paradigmatic case would be ties between Japan and South Korea.[8] The United States is working to encourage Japan and South Korea to take increasingly prominent roles in joint operations, and pushing both sides to conclude agreements on sharing military intelligence.[9] More broadly, the United States can act as a convener in efforts pulling regional states together, especially through regularized multilateral initiatives. At the 2014 G-20 Leaders' Summit in Brisbane, for instance, the leaders of the United States, Japan, and Australia agreed to deepen trilateral ties and defense cooperation.[10] Similar trilateral efforts, including US-India-Australia, US-India-Japan, and US-

Japan-Philippines, among other formations, will be crucial to building a more integrated network of alliances and partners.

Ultimately, if these integrative efforts are successful, they will hold significance not only because they will manage regional tension and uncertainty, but also because they could provide a foundation for knitting together a still-nascent Asian security community. Many of these groupings should also seek to involve China in shared efforts to address common problems. Indeed, only by acting in concert, linked by common purpose, can the United States and its allies create a sustainable security order that extends confidence across the region, promotes interregional ties, fosters economic advancement, ameliorates conflicts between major powers, keeps sea-lanes open, combats extremism, and addresses nontraditional security threats. To that end the United States will need to expend care in reaching out diplomatically, economically, and militarily to forge closer ties with and between our treaty allies. To best formulate such a strategy, we now turn to each of our treaty alliances (and one quasi alliance). We discuss briefly the strategic setting and relevant history of each alliance, the comprehensiveness of the bilateral relationship, and finally challenges and recommendations for advancing the partnership into the future.

Japan

The US-Japan alliance dates back more than sixty years and has weathered the Cold War, North Korean provocations, and now the strategic uncertainty accompanying China's rise. The truly remarkable historical evolution of US-Japan ties began with the postwar occupation of Japan following its surrender at the end of the Second World War. Washington and Tokyo established their formal alliance through a 1951 security treaty and its subsequent 1960 revision. These agreements granted the United States military bases in Japan, which are today the backbone of the US forward-deployed presence in Asia, and in exchange obligated the United States to defend Japan in case of attack. Most importantly in the contemporary context, as President Obama and others have noted, these obligations cover the Senkaku Islands that are administered by Japan and claimed by China, and any hostilities over them will invariably draw in the United States.[11]

For much of the Cold War, the alliance was truly asymmetric—Japan's pacifist constitution and commitment to "defensive defense" meant that the

United States guaranteed Japan's security and Japan engaged in relatively little defense cooperation. Washington and Tokyo have since strengthened the
alliance through a series of defense guidelines (in 1978, 1997, and 2015), however, that established a framework for military cooperation and expanded the
alliance's scope. Over the course of that process, Japan has gradually taken a
greater role in the alliance and additional responsibilities for its defense, playing modest roles in recent Middle East conflicts. The United States, in turn,
has also rendered support during moments of crisis. In the aftermath of the
Tohoku earthquake and tsunami and the resulting nuclear disaster at Fukushima, the United States dispatched 24,000 service members, 189 aircraft,
and 24 naval vessels to assist in relief efforts, an unprecedented US commitment at a time of nuclear peril.[12] This alliance evolution most recently
culminated in Japan's 2015 security legislation, which will allow it both to
engage in deeper alliance cooperation and to begin to become a more active
security partner to the region.

The US-Japan alliance is on firm ground not only because our strategic interests overlap, but also because it is broad-based: our economies are
deeply intertwined, our diplomatic initiatives are generally coordinated, and
our commitment to shared democratic values and a liberal world order are
constant and guiding. Decades ago the United States opened its market to
Japanese exports, helping Japan to rebuild a country shattered by the Second
World War and to become one of the world's largest and most advanced economies. Today Japan and the United States are each other's fourth-largest and
second-largest trading partners respectively, Japan is the second-largest investor in the United States, and both countries are members of the Trans-Pacific
Partnership.[13] With respect to diplomatic ties, the United States and Japan
cooperate and coordinate in multilateral organizations both at the global
level (e.g., UN, G-20) and also at the regional level (e.g., APEC, ARF). Japan
is an enthusiastic stakeholder in the global structure Washington and its
allies built after World War II and is second only to the United States in contributions to the UN budget.[14] Like the United States, Japan is also a strong
supporter of democracy, human rights, and rule of law worldwide, and has
been active in international peacekeeping efforts.

Over the course of this postwar history, alliance managers have seen a
variety of issues emerge that challenge the relationship. First, the need to
properly address difficult issues arising from Japan's World War II conduct is

a persistent and nagging problem that has not been resolved to the satisfaction of many Chinese and South Koreans, despite the efforts of successive Japanese administrations. This often frustrates coordination between Japan and South Korea and sometimes exacerbates tensions with China. Second, concrete issues, especially the maintenance of large US Marine bases in Okinawa that support the US forward-deployed presence in Asia, at times threaten the domestic stability of the relationship.[15] Third, Japan's ability to play a more active role in Asia is imperiled by its own domestic situation, especially its anemic growth and aging population.[16]

Perhaps most fundamentally, Japan appears to be entering a new period. Japan's history has been marked by long periods of constancy, abbreviated by infrequent episodes of profound change. After recent "lost decades," it is possible that we are now in the midst of one of these periods of change. The fundamental shift in attitudes and the attendant politics are best exemplified by the landslide election and return to power of the Liberal Democrat Party in December 2012, followed by victory in the December 2014 snap elections. Under Prime Minister Shinzo Abe, Japan has since implemented a bold set of macroeconomic and structural reforms (nicknamed Abenomics) designed to jolt the nation out of its generation-long lethargy. Tokyo is also pursuing a more robust defense policy, reinterpreting aspects of Japan's constitution so that the country can take part in collective defense and select foreign missions. Tokyo is also investing in defense modernization, developing new security partnerships across Asia, and pursuing defense sales throughout the region. As Japan continues to evolve, the United States should stay close to Tokyo, providing steady counsel on how best to chart an uncertain course toward becoming what some Japanese strategists longingly describe as a "normal" country. This path offers risks and uncertainty, but is the best way to help preserve one of the most important bilateral relationships in Asia. Accordingly, here are elements of a work plan to help advance critical elements of the bilateral relationship.

First, the United States will need to encourage and assist efforts to revitalize Japan's economy. After decades of spectacular growth following the Second World War, Japan abruptly plunged into recession in 1991 and has struggled to sustain positive economic growth ever since, suffering four recessions in the last five years as public debt climbed to over 240% of GDP.[17] Until Japan is able to liberate itself from its economic torpor and once again achieve moderate growth, Tokyo will not be able to play a more active role in Asia or in the world over any sustained period. Efforts to resuscitate Japan's economy through "Abenomics" have been mixed but have not yet changed Japan's growth trajectory. In the period ahead, Japan's government will need to focus more on economic issues than on foreign and defense policy, as well as supplementing fiscal and monetary stimulus with long-overdue structural reforms. By offering support for these efforts, technical assistance, and opportunities to link structural reform to trade agreements like the TPP, the United States may be able to help Japan to prime its long-dormant economic prospects.

Second, the bilateral alliance has been unbalanced for much of its history, with the United States expected to bear much of the defense burden, and its long-term health and relevance will call for both sides to agree upon terms for a more equal partnership. Japan has historically been a subordinate power, somewhat ambivalent about taking on a major role in its own security, while the United States has subsidized Japan's defense and taken a lead role in addressing regional threats. This situation is changing, with Japan aspiring to become a more active partner. Japan has lifted a ban on weapon exports, passed a law that makes it easier for Japanese forces to fight overseas, pursued defense cooperation with other states, and signed defense guidelines with the United States that would allow Japanese forces to support the United States in conflicts in Asia's contemporary flash points. During this time of transition and occasional uncertainty, Japan needs US assurances that Washington is comfortable with independent initiatives in Tokyo's foreign and security policies, such as its outreach to India and even some diplomacy with Russia, and that Washington supports a Japanese foreign policy that is not simply derivative of ties with the United States. This trust in Japanese independence will be rewarded with greater trust in and partnership with the United States.

Third, one of the most prominent obstacles to Japanese influence in Asia is its World War II history—and the United States should work with Japan to overcome it. From Japan's perspective Tokyo has apologized publicly for its transgressions and also provided funds and overseas development assistance (ODA) as a form of atonement, and it views—with some justification—the stoking of anti-Japanese sentiment in China and South Korea as a crutch in the domestic politics of both countries.[18] Japan is now taking active steps to put its World War II history in an appropriate context, with Tokyo and Seoul having reached what both sides termed a "final and irrevocable" agreement in December 2015 over the issue of Korean "comfort women" who were forced into sexual slavery by the Japanese Imperial Army, seeking to remove the long-standing issue that has done the most to prevent closer coordination between these two US treaty allies.[19] The United States can support similar efforts at reconciliation by discouraging China and South Korea from employing anti-Japanese sentiment for domestic purposes and by dissuading Japanese officials from historically revisionist statements and from public visits to the Yasakuni Shrine, which commemorates the service of Japanese soldiers—including fourteen Class-A war criminals—and visits to which invariably raise criticism from China and South Korea. In addition, the United States can work to combat some of the misunderstandings surrounding Japanese efforts at defense reform. For example, Japan's passage of a state secrets protection law was erroneously criticized in China and South Korea as a sign of Japanese militarism; in reality the agreement was an important step for greater cooperation with the United States, which demands that classified information be protected and remain secure.[20] Similarly, working closely with Japan's Self-Defense Forces on peacekeeping or antipiracy operations can help reassure neighbors of Japan's benign intentions and forestall nationalist criticism and controversy. Fundamentally, the United States must assist Japan in talking much more about the last seventy years of its history, during which it has been a model nation with a sterling international reputation, and much less about the tragic years leading up to and including the Second World War.

Fourth, the United States and Japan will need to actively and creatively develop an alliance that is politically and operationally capable of dealing with the full range of emerging challenges in the region. Both countries need to cope with China's development of anti-access/area-denial capabilities that threaten the American forward-deployed presence in Korea, Guam, and Japan itself. This calls for serious discussions and innovations with Japan that will touch on everything from force structure to new capabilities, military budgets, and hardened facilities, among other matters. Both countries will need to discuss how they will ensure the United States' ability to continue to use its bases and to maneuver around Japan. They should also consult on how Japan can invest in asymmetric counter-A2/AD capabilities of its own that complement US efforts. Both countries need to focus more on cyber and would also benefit from intensifying cooperation on ballistic missile defense, especially in light of North Korea's nuclear and missile programs. Finally, given the lingering possibility of a Sino-Japanese clash over the Senkaku Islands, the United States should continue to underscore its commitment to preserving peace and stability and take the necessary steps politically and operationally to reassure Japan of its intentions to abide by its treaty obligations.

Fifth, US alliance managers should take care to be respectful when engaging Japan on sensitive issues. The United States sometimes forgets that we are Japan's sole treaty ally, and that Japan at times feels concerned about overdependence on the United States. When the United States runs roughshod over Japanese interests or fails to give its leaders "face"—that inescapable constant in engagement across Asia—our influence in Japan and the wider region languishes. Similarly, Japan is well attuned to how the United States treats Japan in comparison to China. These concerns are best addressed by the United States through more high-level dialogues with Japan, more consultation on US efforts in Asia, and more discussion of those issues that affect Japan. In some cases officials on both sides would benefit from remembering that an inordinate focus on complex and important issues like Okinawa is no substitute for strategy and can undermine broader discussions of the alliance's strategic direction. By taking care to build trust and respect with our interlocutors, but focusing all the while on a proactive and affirmative bilateral agenda, we can keep the US-Japanese alliance on solid ground and modernize it for the twenty-first century.

South Korea

The US–South Korea alliance was born in 1954, when the two countries signed the Mutual Security Agreement following the Korean War. Like Japan, South Korea was bonded to the United States through American recovery assistance following a bloody and costly war, one that claimed the lives of more than 36,000 American and 137,000 South Korean soldiers. The alliance is rooted in this shared history of sacrifice. South Korean troops fought with the United States in Vietnam and supported US efforts in Iraq and Afghanistan; meanwhile the United States remains committed to the defense of South Korea, with 28,000 US troops stationed there. Initially a bulwark against Communism, the alliance is now focused on the threat of a nuclear-armed North Korea, with its history of dangerous provocation. In 2010, North Korea shelled Yeongpyeong Island and sank the *Cheonan*, a South Korean corvette, and in 2015 and 2016 it tested new missiles and claimed to have detonated a hydrogen bomb. In the words of Defense Secretary Ash Carter, these are a chilling "reminder of how tense things are on the Korean peninsula... [and] a further reminder of the importance of our alliance."[21]

Beyond the military challenges that bind our two countries together, the US–South Korean relationship is increasingly diversified across a variety of dimensions. With American assistance, South Korea rose from an economy with per capita incomes that were among the world's lowest to become one of the largest and richest economies on the planet, with dynamic and innovative industries from information technology to infrastructure. The economies of our two countries are increasingly interdependent. Washington and Seoul signed a Korea-US Free Trade Agreement (KORUS) that went into effect in March 2012, and since then bilateral trade has increased 15 percent—with exports of US automobiles increasing 140 percent by value.[22] In international diplomacy, the United States and South Korea cooperate and coordinate their positions in global and regional institutions, and the two countries are also tied together by support for liberal values and efforts to solve common transnational problems.

Despite this remarkable trajectory of progress, Washington and Seoul will still need to take some concerted steps to strengthen and broaden this alliance for the twenty-first century. These should focus on security, which is the indisputable core of the alliance, as well as on broader economic and diplomatic concerns.

First, the defense relationship between the United States and South Korea would benefit from closer cooperation and integration. Both countries should boost military exercises, training, and exchanges, as well as continuing appropriate technology transfers and technical support to offset South Korea's purchase of US F-35 aircraft. Following North Korea's February 2016 missile test, the United States and Korea announced they would begin formal talks about the possibility of deploying the Terminal High Altitude Area Defense system (THAAD) in South Korea, which could help protect the South from North Korean ballistic missiles. While the United States has already provided Aegis-equipped warships and Patriot missile batteries to South Korea, Seoul has historically been reluctant to consider deployments of THAAD batteries because of firm and strident Chinese opposition, though recent polls suggest the South Korean public is increasingly supportive of such deployments.[23] A face-saving solution will likely involve allowing United States Forces Korea to deploy THAAD batteries rather than requiring South Korean forces to purchase and operate them. In addition to facing a threat from North Korean missiles, South Korea also now faces the risk of cyberattack. North Korean hackers were likely responsible for paralyzing three of the biggest banks in South Korea and two of its main broadcasters in 2013, and these attacks call for a greater focus on cyberthreats in the bilateral alliance.[24]

Second, one of the most important questions in the bilateral alliance is whether the United States can promote greater cooperation between South Korea and Japan. A functional trilateral relationship involving Washington, Seoul, and Tokyo will permit a more effective response to a North Korean attack on the South as well as coordinated approaches to China's anti-access capabilities, disputes in the South China Sea, and North Korea's nuclear and missile programs. Tensions between South Korea and Japan all too often sabotage cooperation. Indeed, when North Korea launched an ICBM in February 2016, US and Korean and US and Japanese Aegis systems were in communication, but Korean and Japanese systems were not. In 2012 both sides were prepared to sign a fairly routine agreement on information sharing, which would have facilitated such communication, as well as a separate agreement on facilitating the reciprocal provision of supplies. Unfortunately, domestic opposition in South Korea scuttled both of these important arrangements, demonstrating that nationalism and tensions over history run directly contrary at times to national interests.[25] As yet another example, when South Koreans learned their peacekeepers in South Sudan had asked the neighboring Japanese forces for ammunition, they demanded their troops return the ammunition to Japan, suggesting that "popular antipathy toward Japan is more powerful than the desire to ensure that one's own troops are adequately armed."[26]

The United States will be indispensable in efforts to bring South Korea and Japan together. The long-term vision should be to build a functional trilateral relationship, one that becomes a core part of the US security structure in Asia and makes the Tokyo-Seoul linkage a nearly equal leg of the trilateral relationship. This will call for structuring, regularizing, and enhancing opportunities for strategic dialogue and operational engagement. An important step in this effort will be to increase diplomacy at the leader level, which often requires behind-the-scenes US encouragement and prodding. For example, it was not until US officials invited both South Korean president Park Guen-hye and Japanese prime minister Shinzo Abe to a joint meeting on nuclear issues in March 2014 that the two leaders actually met for the first time. By holding a leader-level trilateral annually on the margins of a major international summit such as APEC or the East Asia Summit (EAS), and by calling for more ministerial trilateral and minilateral meetings, the United States can use its position as a convener to regularize top-level ties between Japan and South Korea. Private counsel also has a role to play in the relationship, and the United States should take active steps to dissuade Korean politicians from using anti-Japanese sentiment as a domestic political tool. Moreover, since much of the opposition to closer ties is at the public rather than the elite level, the United States can seek to make cooperation more visible, especially through exercises or peacekeeping operations. Doing so may produce short-term tensions, but over the longer term it will serve to acclimate the public of each country to news stories on defense coordination between Japan and South Korea. Such coordination should also be expanded to address a diverse North Korean threat spectrum, in part through a greater focus on intelligence, surveillance, and reconnaissance (ISR) coverage, more efforts to increase interoperability, and more frequent military exercises. Beyond security, people-to-people exchanges and closer economic ties, useful in strengthening US ties with China, could also be employed by both Seoul and Tokyo to help bring their two countries closer together. The effort to repair the fissures created by a shared but bitter history will take time but, if successful, will bring greater security and stability to the region and profoundly advance US interests.

Third, one of the most vital tasks for the United States and South Korea is to prepare for instability and uncertainty in North Korea through greater contingency planning and coordination. On this question of profound change occurring suddenly on the Korean Peninsula there are only two options for the alliance: being ill prepared and being very ill prepared. The United States and South Korea should always strive for the former through exercises, planning, and frequent dialogue on the full range of possible North Korean provocations—from artillery strikes to nuclear contingencies—as well as on the various follow-on repercussions, which could include North Korean collapse, massive refugee flows, and Chinese military intervention. Finally, if war does break out on the Korean Peninsula, US and South Korean forces will fall under the bilateral Combined Forces Command (CFC), which is led by a US general and gives the United States wartime operational control (OPCON) of the South Korean military. Although some South Korean politicians have expressed a desire to dismantle the CFC and transfer OPCON to the South Korean military, the status quo should be maintained. The prevailing arrangement has served both countries for decades and a transfer could reduce cooperation and create confusion in the midst of crisis. Any attempt to negotiate a transition will inevitably be perceived as a US retreat from the region and a diminishment of support for South Korea, even though it would be inspired by the desire to give greater regard to Korean capacities and national sensitivities.

Fourth, the robust economic relationship between the United States and South Korea could be strengthened further by support for Korea's eventual accession to the TPP. South Korean president Park Geun-hye has stated that South Korea is interested in joining, and through consultation and technical assistance, the United States can assist it with meeting the agreement's high standards, a fairly straightforward extension of the Korea-US Free Trade Agreement.[27]

Fifth, the bilateral alliance should continue in its efforts to "go global" and for Washington to support greater South Korean activism not just within Asia, but also outside it. South Korea is a robust democracy and one of the world's fifteen largest economies, home to global companies like Samsung and Hyundai, and it needs to take more proactive steps to decouple North Korea from its foreign policy goals and assert its own unique identity and interests on the global stage. South Korea is also an emerging player in providing foreign assistance and development support. In this context the United States and South Korea can cooperate on a variety of global challenges, including maritime piracy, humanitarian assistance and disaster relief (HADR), peacekeeping, foreign aid, climate change, and global economic governance.[28] Finally, greater South Korean activism regionally and globally will require closer ties with all the world's major powers, including China. Washington can do much to support South Korea's global profile and its interests on the Korean Peninsula by embracing closer ties between Seoul and Beijing.

Australia

The US-Australian alliance was codified in 1951, but the history of shared sacrifice begins much earlier. Australia is one of America's closest partners and it has stood shoulder to shoulder with the United States in every major twentieth-century conflict, including the First and Second World Wars, the Korean and Vietnam Wars, and now recent conflicts in Iraq and Afghanistan. This bilateral alliance is the gold standard for cooperation, with Australia playing a critical role in military operations in the Middle East as the largest troop contributor to operations after the United States. While Australia hosts no formal US bases, the security relationship received a significant boost when Australia agreed to host 2,500 marines in the port city of Darwin in northern Australia. In addition, Australia offers the United States access, acting as the southern anchor of an American Indo-Pacific strategy that stretches from the Indian Ocean to the Pacific Islands.

The relationship with Australia is mature and well-rounded beyond questions of security. With respect to economics, both countries signed a free trade agreement in 2005 and are members of the TPP today, with trade in goods and services at upwards of $60 billion annually.[29] In addition, the United States is the second-largest source of foreign direct investment to Australia, and Australia is one of the ten largest sources of investment in the United States.[30] Australia coordinated with the United States in a variety of multilateral forums and shares with it a strong belief in democracy, rule of law, and human rights. Public polling in both countries consistently shows high levels of support for the alliance.[31]

First, although the United States and Australia have a strong defense relationship, with the United States now rotating marines through the port in Darwin, there remains room for still closer cooperation.[32] Of crucial importance will be efforts to inject more vision into the conversations about the future of the alliance in order to prepare for a more complex future. Given Australia's favorable geographic position, strategic depth, long coastline, deep waters, and highly developed infrastructure, the country can play an important role in expanding US presence within Asia and facilitating a much-needed rebalance of US force posture toward the south.[33] The United

States and Australia would benefit from examining possibilities for additional US basing within Australia, especially for naval vessels, which would afford both countries the ability to respond more quickly and effectively to regional crises and bolster bilateral defense ties by creating new opportunities for improving cooperation and interoperability. Indeed, although the 2,500 US Marines rotated through Darwin do not constitute an overwhelming troop presence, this arrangement and future ones like it will allow the United States and Australia to expand the scope and number of their combined exercises to ensure the alliance is preparing for all manner of regional contingencies. Finally, given the proliferation of ballistic and cruise missile technologies in East Asia and the wider Indo-Pacific, both Australia and the United States will need to develop strategies for coping with the related A2/AD challenges, including through deepening recent cooperation on missile defense.[34]

Second, Australia is America's gateway to the Indo-Pacific, a maritime region home to the world's most important economic and energy waterways, which are of critical importance to the twenty-first century. The waterways and surrounding regions stretch from the Arabian Sea and Bay of Bengal through the South China Sea and into the Western Pacific, a superregion drawn together by oceanic commerce into a critical transportation and an increasingly linked commercial system.[35] Both the United States and Australia have an opportunity to cooperate and coordinate within this broader region. This effort might begin with the formalization of a joint Indo-Pacific security concept for the alliance that outlines shared interests and possible bilateral initiatives for this wider region in the period ahead. Beyond the bilateral relationship, the United States and Australia would benefit from pursuing a trilateral meeting with India focused on the Indo-Pacific. Indeed, India and Australia are two of the cornerstone countries of the Indo-Pacific, and efforts to improve their relationship that began with Australia's decision to lift a uranium export ban on India in 2011 have continued with leader-level visits in 2014. Encouraging both states to pursue enhanced trade relations, people-to-people links, and wider defense cooperation will advance US interests and Asian stability.[36] More broadly, the United States should work with Australia, as well as India, to hold multilateral meetings with Indo-Pacific states; draft new operational concepts and campaign strategies for the wider region; and bolster shared efforts at intelligence, surveillance, and reconnaissance (ISR) across the vast Indian Ocean. In addition, both countries could work together with India to increase security cooperation with states in the Indian Ocean through routine military exercises, HADR, and efforts to boost maritime domain awareness.

Third, Australia has interests not only in the Indian Ocean to its west but also in the smattering of Pacific Islands that neighbor it to the east. This region, historically Australia's backyard, beckons for closer cooperation between the United States and Australia as it confronts a range of serious challenges, from rising sea levels to obesity and economic stagnation. Australia is the largest donor to the region, with the United States a distant second that is at times only episodically engaged in Pacific affairs. In contrast, both Australia and New Zealand are in many ways central to the region's future and will be indispensable in supporting its small states, which calls for Washington to more actively cooperate with them on regional policy. All three countries will need to enhance trilateral dialogue on the very diverse challenges of the Pacific island nations, better coordinate their aid policies, undertake joint diplomatic initiatives, and more consequentially engage the region's diplomatic organizations, such as the Pacific Island Forum (PIF), in order to better address the region's unique challenges.[37]

Fourth, Asia is in the midst of an unprecedented and important period of institution building that will shape the future of Asia's operating system. As Asian organizations mature in their collective endeavors, advance a more ambitious region-wide agenda, and build brick-and-mortar headquarters and acquire permanent staffs, the United States and Australia should coordinate their agendas and advice in order to more effectively shape the development of these organizations so that they better support twenty-first-century values. Australia has at times played a significant role in defining and strengthening core regional organizations such as the East Asian Summit, the ASEAN Regional Forum, the Pacific Island Forum, and APEC, and in many respects Australia has shaped Washington's decision making when it comes to more active participation in various regional forums. The United States should continue to encourage Australia to take prominent leadership positions within Asia and vice versa, such as when Canberra took responsibility for the search for Malaysian Airlines flight 370 in March 2014. Finally, Australia's neighbors, especially in Southeast Asia, sit astride several vital sea-lanes and expansive maritime domains that are difficult to monitor and prone to natural disasters. The United States and Australia can work together to train regional militaries in HADR and maritime domain awareness through regional institutions like ASEAN.

Fifth, some notable Australian commentators argue that Canberra should do more to balance its ties between Beijing and Washington as China continues to rise. Indeed, when surveyed on the question of whether the United States or China is likely to be the most prominent regional power in ten years, Australian opinion is evenly divided.[38] This sentiment may prove to be a challenging consideration in the bilateral alliance, one that requires careful US attention. The United States should reassure Australia that politics in Asia are not zero-sum games and that Washington supports and appreciates Australia's unique role as a bridge country in Asia with close ties to both countries. China and Australia signed an FTA in 2015, and these efforts advance American objectives by demonstrating to China that US alliances are not focused on containment but important parts of an effort to create an inclusive and rules-based Asian economic order open to China.

Finally, by supporting and encouraging Australia to build ties with US allies and partners, the United States will bolster the hub-and-spokes alliance system. One of the most important efforts in this regard, which we will discuss in greater depth later in this chapter, will be increasing political dialogue and operational engagement among the United States, Australia, and New Zealand on issues ranging from counterterrorism to intelligence sharing as well as the Pacific Islands and the Indo-Pacific. Aside from New Zealand, the United States welcomes Australia's closer ties with Japan and that process should continue. In recent years Australia and Japan have become a "poster child for spoke-to-spoke collaboration."[39] Former Australian prime minister Tony Abbott was the first foreign leader to address Japan's newly formed National Security Council, Japan hopes to sell Australia advanced diesel-electric submarines, and the two countries signed a bilateral FTA in 2014. Finally, as discussed previously, the United States can encourage Australia to pursue similar efforts with other treaty allies, as well as close partners like India, and facilitate closer ties through trilateral initiatives and meetings.

Singapore

Singapore is perhaps the most defining example of a country that has stretched the definition of *partner* by providing uncommon capacity and support to the United States. Singapore is a uniquely strong partner that offers the United States strategic advice and military access. It is firmly committed to close relations with the United States, and Prime Minister Lee Hsien Loong has frequently declared that he believes the United States will continue to play a defining role in Asia's strategic leadership in spite of declinist arguments to the contrary.[40]

The strategic partnership with Singapore has a long history. The United States and Singapore had a close relationship throughout the Cold War. After the Philippines pushed the United States out of Clark Air Base and the Subic Bay naval base in 1991, Singapore offered the United States rotational access to Singaporean facilities such as Changi Naval Base. Today this small state is home to a US Navy logistics command unit that is crucial to naval operations within the region, and also hosts several littoral combat ships and P-8 Poseidon aircraft. Outside of the region, Singapore has supported US efforts in Iraq and Afghanistan and was the first Southeast Asian state to join the US coalition to combat ISIS. Bilateral defense cooperation is not a one-way street, and the United States supplies advanced weapons to Singapore, including F-15 and F-16 fighters, trains more than a thousand Singaporean military personnel each year, and hosts a number of exercises with Singaporean services. To commemorate the sixtieth anniversary of the relationship, the United and Singapore signed a Defense Cooperation Agreement in 2015 that identifies further areas of defense cooperation and dialogue. In simple terms, the defense relationship between Singapore and the United States is indispensable to both parties.[41]

Beyond robust defense and strategic interactions, the United States and Singapore have strong and healthy economic and diplomatic ties. Singapore was the first country in Asia to sign an FTA with Washington, in 2004, and both countries are members of the TPP. As of 2014 the United States has invested more than $180 billion in Singapore, six times more than it has invested in India, while Singapore has invested $21 billion in the United States.[42] On diplomatic matters Singapore has long pulled the United States deeper into Asian affairs, offering useful diplomatic advice, working with the United States in Southeast Asian regional organizations, and serving as an occasional intermediary for high-level US-China communication. It even urged the United States to join the P-4 trade group that eventually became the TPP.

The United States should further nurture this vital relationship. Singapore is a powerhouse island economy with close historic ties to Washington, and it has a deep and broad relationship with the United States spanning a variety of issue areas. Singapore also acts as a regional diplomatic fulcrum, in that it maintains positive relations with China and a leadership role in ASEAN. These ties make Singapore all the more valuable as a US partner, and Washington can more actively advance this relationship in several ways.

First, the United States and Singapore would benefit from more regularized and institutionalized high-level meetings and political engagement. As a general matter, Singapore does not receive the kind of strategic attention from top-level American policymakers and cabinet officials that is warranted for a vital partner that is increasingly indispensable to the US position in Southeast Asia. Although we launched the first United States–Singapore Strategic Partnership in 2011 to enhance bilateral ties, an initiative that I twice cochaired with the Singaporean foreign minister, it has not always been held annually, and the inability to schedule these sessions has occasionally been a sore spot for Singaporean interlocutors. There is still room to both broaden and deepen this initiative, ensure that it is held annually, and secure the participation of higher-level US officials. Doing so will send an important signal to Singapore that affirms the value of the alliance to Washington.

Second, although Singapore and the United States have a robust security partnership, it could nonetheless benefit from some targeted expansion. The United States could train more Singaporean military personnel each year, host additional exercises with Singaporean services, sponsor more defense exchanges, and potentially station additional American assets in Singapore to assist in antipiracy and maritime domain awareness. On the operational side, Singapore conducts a significant number of HADR efforts each year, and both countries could benefit from more frequent cooperation in these efforts when disaster strikes. Finally, Singapore and the United States should occasionally elect to multilateralize certain aspects of their defense relationship—especially with regard to training, capacity building, and HADR—by inviting the participation of other ASEAN states.

Third, in addition to offering the United States access to its facilities, Singapore also offers frank and sophisticated advice on Asian affairs that can be supremely helpful to Washington policymakers. In particular, Singapore's high-level political ties to China allow it to offer American officials a penetrating lens into Beijing's opaque politics and decision making and to serve as a useful go-between for Washington and Beijing. Singapore also has close elite-level and educational ties with Indonesia and can furnish key insights for American policymakers on Southeast Asia's largest and most populous country.

Fourth, the United States and Singapore should continue to coordinate agendas in the Southeast Asian multilateral forums that will shape Asia's future. Both countries have strong interests in twenty-first-century rules like freedom of navigation, the peaceful resolution of disputes, and free trade, and can advocate for them in concert through the ARF, EAS, APEC, and other forums—including those in which the United States still lacks membership. Through these kinds of multilateral forums, or through more ad hoc multilateral arrangements, both countries can work together to support regional efforts on regional challenges including piracy, narcotics, terrorism, pollution, and disaster relief. Singapore also sees itself playing a key role in the use of multilateral diplomacy to manage and resolve the South China Sea disputes, and its counsel on these complex and delicate matters is invaluable. Progress on all of these issues in Southeast Asia will require greater maritime domain awareness. The United States should support Singapore's leadership in the Information Fusion Center, which in part helps to integrate shipping and air traffic across the region, along with information about smuggling and piracy activities, and the two should cooperate to jointly boost the capabilities of Southeast Asian states in this regard.

Fifth, as Singapore enters a period of long-term political transition, Washington will need to expand its relationship across Singaporean society and embrace a broader range of citizens, civil society, and opposition. Singapore's success has been driven by its relatively stable politics and its government's ability to implement rational policymaking, at the domestic and international levels, in steadfast service of Singapore's national interests. The country's ruling party, the People's Action Party (PAP), faced a setback in the 2011 elections as it received a record-low 60 percent of the popular vote, due in part to frustration with the government's immigration policies and with rising costs of living, which led some senior ministers to step down.[43] In 2015, Singapore held its first election in which all parliamentary seats were contested, and although the PAP won 70 percent of the vote and performed well, these political changes suggest that the country's policymaking will begin to reflect its changing domestic landscape. According to Ernest Bower of CSIS, as Singapore changes, the United States should "reach out beyond official counterparts and interlocutors to engage a broader and more diverse range of Singaporeans.... Doing so will add depth and balance to the bilateral relationship and position Americans as trusted partners."[44]

The Philippines

The bilateral relationship between the United States and the Philippines is better than at any point in the last two decades. Although Filipinos are increasingly supportive of the alliance, there remain complex attitudes toward the United States that are a mixture of respect and nationalistic wariness owing to the complicated history between the two countries. The United States annexed the Philippines from Spain in 1898 and suppressed a Filipino independence movement shortly thereafter, and then spent five decades paternalistically building the rudiments of constitutional democracy in preparation for Filipino independence. Roughly a year after Americans and Filipinos fought together against Japan in the Second World War, the United States granted the islands independence. Since then the two countries have had a close strategic partnership. The Philippines allowed the United States to maintain facilities at Subic Bay and Clark Air Base, fought with the United States in Korea and Vietnam, and supported US efforts in Iraq and Afghanistan. For its part, the United States helped the Philippines defeat domestic Communist guerrillas and Islamic terrorists. Although the Philippines asked the United States to vacate Subic and Clark in 1991 at a moment of rising nationalism, its recent territorial disputes with China in the South China Sea have led it to favor an increased American presence. In 2014 the two countries signed the Enhanced Defense Cooperation Agreement (EDCA)—one of the most important agreements in the alliance's history—which will allow the United States to rotate troops, planes, and ships through eight different Philippine bases as well as pre-position supplies and build necessary support facilities.[45] This increased presence will allow the United States to play a more active role in regional security and to assist with Filipino military modernization efforts. It will also provide the United States with a more active point of departure for increased operations in Southeast Asia.

Although the US relationship with the Philippines has an increasingly firm strategic foundation, the relationship is not as broad-based as US ties with other allies. The Philippines has a large population and an average growth rate of 6 percent, yet economic ties between the two countries continue to lag. Goods trade has been virtually stagnant over the last twenty years, barriers to investment remain, and the economic relationship remains less developed than those between the United States and other Southeast Asian nations.[46] While the two countries have long-standing people-to-people and diplomatic ties due to shared history, there is still much room for expansion and improvement.

For now, though, strategic issues remain the core of the relationship and will occupy the most attention. The Philippines views China's territorial encroachments in the South China Sea as one of its most pressing concerns. In 2012, for example, the Philippines' ten-week standoff with China ultimately resulted in its loss of the Scarborough Shoal, which is claimed by both countries. After protests and attempts by China to put serious but unofficial pressure on Filipino agricultural exports, the Philippine government brought its dispute with China to the International Tribunal for the Law of the Sea (ITLOS). The United States remains neutral on the underlying sovereignty dispute but supports the Philippines' use of international law to adjudicate its maritime claims. The case will be decided in mid-2016 and its ultimate resolution holds tremendous import for the legitimacy of UNCLOS.

To more effectively deal with the South China Sea uncertainties and other issues, the United States and the Philippines need to bolster their alliance through a variety of shared initiatives.

First, in the wake of the recent completion of the EDCA, it is now time to regularize visiting procedures and update legal provisions to account for the increase in rotational US forces operating in the Philippines. The United States currently has a Visiting Forces Agreement with the Philippines that applies to US troops that are temporarily in the country, but both Washington and Manila may be able to put the relationship on firmer ground by revisiting or revising the agreement to make sure it accounts both for the change in the defense relationship currently under way and for ever-present Philippine sensitivities.

Second, given the complicated colonial history between the United States and the Philippines, the two countries will need to build a stronger base of public support and understanding for the alliance so that it can endure the occasional crises in bilateral ties that may surface in the period ahead.

Although Filipinos have highly favorable views of the United States, Filipino nationalism, lingering sovereignty concerns, and occasional disputes relating to the conduct of American military personnel at times buffet the relationship and factor into domestic politics. These dynamics, which played a role in the Philippine government's decision to ask the United States to leave Subic Bay and Clark Air Base in 1991, need to be better managed by both sides. The United States should take pains to treat the Philippines as an equal partner; Philippine political leaders should better explain the benefits of the alliance to the public and refrain from stoking anti-American nationalist sentiment when bilateral crises emerge. Fundamentally, this new period of closer security coordination must be distinguished from the earlier episodes of more paternalistic partnership.

Third, both countries should redouble efforts to deepen military cooperation and reap the full benefits of the EDCA. The Philippine armed forces have long been focused on a counterterrorism mission and seriously neglected, and the Philippines simply cannot modernize them on its own. As the United States rotates more forces and military assets through the Philippines under the auspices of the EDCA, it can use this opportunity to dramatically increase the pace and depth of military exercises and training with Philippine counterparts, including training to respond to contingencies in the South China Sea. Similarly, the United States can make use of its authority under the EDCA to construct facilities on Philippine bases not only to support US forces, but also to support Filipino forces by providing them with improved infrastructure. By upgrading facilities at Philippine bases, transferring surplus vessels and aircraft to the Philippine military, and increasing Foreign Military Financing (FMF) to the Philippines,[47] the United States could speed up the country's defense modernization. The Pentagon has announced a $425 million partner capacity-building initiative for Southeast Asia, and Manila will be one prominent recipient of this aid.[48] Because of the poor state of the Philippine military, however, the United States will need to work to ensure that the Philippines is making the best use of equipment and training, and will also want to help coordinate on the related parameters of partner capacity-building efforts with countries like Japan. Finally, because the Philippines are a vast archipelago with a large maritime domain, the country needs US assistance in developing maritime domain awareness and HADR capabilities that can be sustained into the future.

Fourth, although both countries are strengthening their security ties, economic ties in particular remain below their potential and require greater attention. It is promising that the Philippines has publicly expressed a desire to join the TPP, and the United States can support it as it undertakes the reforms necessary to meet the agreement's high standards. Washington should also encourage Manila to lower barriers to foreign investment that stand in the way of a closer economic relationship between the United States and the Philippines. Economic measures to deepen trade and investment with the United States (and other Asian states) will not only deepen the bilateral alliance, they will also provide the Philippines with greater resilience in the face of possible Chinese economic coercion in the future.

Fifth, the United States and the Philippines have been responding to Chinese incursions into the South China Sea on an ad hoc basis and in a "semi-permanent crisis management mode," and should instead work together to establish a coordinated long-term strategy.[49] Any such strategy should outline goals, examine strategic capabilities, and take into account possibilities for joint development agreements in which sovereignty questions are shelved so that parties can jointly harness disputed resources. The United States has begun to assist the Philippines in developing the capacity to monitor its extensive maritime exclusive economic zone (EEZ) through its Coast Watch system, and should continue transfers of military equipment, training, and better integrated intelligence sharing to this end.[50]

Thailand

Thailand is America's oldest treaty partner in Asia, and the only one in Southeast Asia that successfully avoided colonization or rule by an external power. For much of its history, Thailand was ruled by leaders who were masters of balance. During the colonial era, Thailand successfully played British expansion to its west off French designs on the east by becoming a buffer state between the two imperial powers, all while European states carved up China in the north. Surrounded by colonies on nearly every side, Thailand's leaders hastened to remake the country into a modern state with a strong military and clear borders. Through a sophisticated approach to balance-of-power politics, as well as self-strengthening and tactical concessions, Thailand maintained its independence against enormous odds.

It was in the midst of this period of European colonial expansion that

Thailand and the United States began their friendship. Thailand was the first Asian country with which the United States established diplomatic relations, and today it is America's oldest Asian ally, with official ties dating back to the time of President Andrew Jackson. Thailand fought with US forces in the Korean War, the Vietnam War, and both Iraq wars. It now offers the United States military generous and nearly unfettered access to its strategically located facilities, and US agencies like the United States Agency for International Development (USAID) and the FBI have established hubs there for regional operations in Southeast Asia. In 2003, President George W. Bush designated Thailand as a major non-NATO ally, which qualified Bangkok to receive special aid and assistance for weapons purchases. With regard to economic ties, the United States is one of Thailand's largest investors and its third-largest trading partner, with bilateral trade valued at roughly $44 billion annually.[51]

Thailand is now the American ally that is perhaps in greatest need of immediate American assistance, and also that facing the most perilous of prospects. Going through profound internal changes while facing a complex external environment, Thailand beckons for an increasingly deft and subtle US approach. The bilateral relationship has strained in recent years, especially after Thailand underwent a military coup in 2006 and a more recent one in 2014. Frustration with the US response to these events has reawakened some of the antecedents of Thai strategic culture, leading its military junta to turn closer to China for support as a way of balancing Thailand's external relations. China has embraced Thailand's generals and even sold Thailand three attack submarines in 2015. The fact that these purchases require long-term support and maintenance from China raises concerns about the larger trajectory of our alliance with Thailand. If the United States cannot find a way to manage this chapter in Thailand's political evolution, it may risk losing influence over an important and long-standing American ally.[52]

Thailand's politics at present are complicated and concerning, and even the most astute observers are regularly caught off guard by developments there. It is hard to reconcile the image of rows of untouched ballot boxes laid out on February 2, 2014, with that of the surrounding crowd of cheering and nominally prodemocracy protestors proud of their achievement of having prevented any voting from actually taking place.[53] The opposition Democrats based in Thailand's more affluent south have essentially lost every national election since 1992 to candidates who have rural support in the north. Rather than building a competitive political opposition that would promote popular political and economic reforms, the Democrats and their supporters in the judiciary and military, as well as their whisperers around the royal court, have driven three democratically elected governments out of office since 2006. These reactionary forces—despite the changing labels and political configurations—are essentially the "yellow shirts" of old and it is their allies and foot soldiers who have stormed government ministries and prevented Thailand's successful transition toward a more reflective democracy.[54] In response to this growing instability, Thailand's military assumed control in a coup on May 22, 2014, and currently shows little sign of returning power to civilian hands. According to longtime political activist and historian Thongchai Winichakul, "Electoral democracy like what was seen before 2006 will not return for a while."[55] Amid this domestic turmoil, the United States will need a policy that is both nuanced and subtle and that is intended to engage Thailand while encouraging a return to democratic governance.

First, the United States can support Thailand in this challenging period by maintaining open lines of communication with senior-level Thai officials and encouraging deeper domestic talks between the political parties and military leadership. By preserving close ties not only to governing Thai officials and key opposition figures but also to the leading officers of the Thai military, the United States can continue to press the case for a return to democratic processes. A unilateral refusal to engage in high-level dialogue by the United States would, in comparison, prove counterproductive. All of Thailand's major institutions—including the country's political parties, military, and royalty—will need to be encouraged to jointly formulate and follow through on a reasonable timetable for the return of democratic elections.

Second, military and intelligence cooperation between Thailand should continue despite the country's political turmoil. Military assistance, exercises, exchanges, training, and intelligence cooperation with Thailand contribute to regional security and build US influence with Thailand's military government that can be used to encourage a return to a more democratic path. Although the United States may choose to downgrade some exercises and restrict some aid to Thailand until democratic governance is restored, it will be important that it not do so in ways that undermine the broader strategic relationship, reduce US access to strategic facilities, or raise concerns about the broader alliance that might push Thailand toward Beijing and other partners. Good relations between Thailand and China are to be encouraged, but Thailand's interests are best served by Bangkok's retaining some of its historic balance, including by maintaining strong contacts with Washington and Beijing. In this regard, it will be important to restore high-level dialogue between senior military leaders, which has suffered in the wake of the coup. Finally, the United States should continue to participate in Thailand's Cobra Gold military exercises, which are the region's largest and involve twenty-eight countries. These venues offer powerful opportunities to observe and engage, and give the United States critical tools for military diplomacy.

Third, Thailand has historically been a leader in Asian multilateral bodies, especially ASEAN. For example, Thailand played a role in encouraging Burma's democratic transition, helped coordinate talks between ASEAN and China on a South China Sea Code of Conduct, and has generally worked to increase the profile of ASEAN-led institutions. Since the recent coup, Thailand has aligned itself closer to Chinese positions in these multilateral organizations, reducing its ability to serve as a bridge between China and those ASEAN states embroiled in territorial disputes with Beijing. But perhaps more worryingly, Thailand's once-active diplomacy in Southeast Asian affairs has largely disappeared during this period of domestic discord. The United States should work to encourage Thailand to again weigh in more directly on ASEAN diplomacy, including through coordinating positions within the organization and sharing thoughts on shaping its future evolution.

Finally, Thailand's political situation is volatile and uncertain, and the military government may remain in power into the near future. It will be incumbent upon the United States to manage its expectations for a return to democratic government and not to let setbacks or impatience undercut US influence—which is an indispensable ingredient in restoring Thailand's democracy.

Setting the Contours of China's Rise

The US-China relationship will be the single most consequential relationship of the twenty-first century and certainly the most challenging aspect of the Pivot, and yet little in American diplomatic history prepares us for the complexities of the China challenge. In comparison to the relatively black and white, forty-year Cold War between the United States and the Soviet Union, with its stark geographic and ideological lines of demarcation, the U.S.-China relationship is much like *The Wizard of Oz* when the cinematography is suddenly in full color: the mixture of profound integration with strategic distrust has created the most complex bilateral relationship in human history. Moreover, China has ascended faster than any other power in the modern era, and its rapid emergence marks the first time the US has faced a rising power and near-peer challenger with whom it must both cooperate and compete.

Cooperation is necessary in part because the American and Chinese economies are fundamentally linked and substantially interdependent. With China ranking as America's second-largest trading partner and the United States ranking as China's largest, open antagonism and a drift toward conflict would be very costly to the bottom line of both countries and disastrous to the commerce of the surrounding region.[56] A degree of common purpose and effort is also necessary because transnational problems such as climate change, nuclear proliferation, and economic governance that are already difficult enough to solve with China will be impossible to solve without it. As President Obama has declared, "It's precisely for this reason that it is important to pursue pragmatic cooperation with China on issues of mutual concern, because no one nation can meet the challenges of the 21st century alone."[57]

Competition too defines the relationship, and in this respect the last few years have revealed the seriousness of the task ahead. An increasingly assertive China under the bold and powerful leadership of Xi Jinping has posed an undeniable challenge to American regional leadership and prevailing international principles. China has challenged freedom of navigation, pursued expansive territorial claims against US allies and partners, engaged in economic coercion against neighbors, cracked down on dissent, and continued breakneck military spending. As the two countries confront each other over these differences, the tragic specter of the "Thucydides trap," named after the Greek historian who wrote about the dangers that surface when a rising power confronts an established one, looms over the relationship.

To step out from the shadow of the Thucydides trap, the United States needs a plan for US-China relations, one that sets tasks for the bilateral relationship and specifies, in Secretary Clinton's words, "how to find common ground and how to stand our ground" in dealings with Beijing.[58] This plan, however, should not supersede the imperative of broad-based regional engagement. Policymakers should avoid implementing the "China first" approach often pursued by US administrations, which is based on the flawed assumption that getting the bilateral relationship right is the key to getting Asia policy right. In theory, such an approach would focus on communiqués, condominiums, and grand bargains to return us to an era of comity and mutual understanding. Taiwan's status would be resolved and the United States would respect areas delineated by China as "core interests." In reality, such a big-power approach would simply unnerve US allies and partners in pursuit of a supposed "golden age" in US-China relations that actually never existed, especially for a relationship often defined as much by tensions and uncertainty as it is by cooperation.

The most effective China policy would instead be one grounded within a larger, more incremental regional framework. Under this approach the United States would use ties with close allies and partners as force multipliers for shared approaches throughout the region, strengthening norms on democracy, trade, and freedom of navigation and raising the cost for steps that undermine the operating system on which Asia's prosperity is positioned. A diversified strategy that coordinates economic, strategic, and diplomatic instruments of statecraft throughout the region would bolster this operating system and set the contours for China's rise. Such an approach, for which this section is named, informs the US Pivot to Asia.

Within this regional framework, the commanding mantra for the bilateral relationship is subtle and simple: the United States should preserve key national interests where necessary while sustaining a workable and sustainable relationship with China whenever possible. In hopes of fleshing out such an approach, this chapter will offer a US work plan for relations with China. It will begin with an exploration of the drivers behind Beijing's assertive foreign policy. In the succeeding two sections, it will offer policy prescriptions for managing competition and fostering greater cooperation with China.

China's Assertive Turn

Beginning in the later years of Hu Jintao's tenure and continuing to today, there has been an unmistakable shift in Chinese foreign policy toward greater assertiveness.[59] Under President Hu, China departed from what many had called a "charm offensive" focused on building closer ties with China's neighbors.[60] It sharply escalated its territorial disputes with Japan, India, the Philipppines, and Vietnam. It began to harass vessels of neighboring nations in the South and East China Seas, as well as American warships like the USNS *Impeccable*. It even abandoned its wariness of using economic sanctions and began employing them (unofficially) against Japan, the Philippines, and Norway during disputes.[61] For many scholars this combination of economic statecraft and coercive bargaining under Hu marked the beginning a distinctive new era in Chinese foreign policy.

The emergence of President Xi has amplified these assertive trends in Chinese foreign policy. Xi has been willing to push a tougher line on virtually every front. In the East China Sea, Xi's government declared an air defense identification zone; in the South China Sea, Xi has taken the unprecedented step of reclaiming land and constructing artificial islands with airstrips, docks, and artillery. He has even expanded China's territorial challenges beyond Vietnam and the Philippines to Malaysia and Brunei, who have seen an increasing number of Chinese vessels in their waters. With respect to regional governance, Xi has created international institutions such as the AIIB that will invariably serve as tools for Chinese economic statecraft. In 2014 he boldly declared his desire for an "Asia for Asians" at an international gathering where he also criticized US alliances. These actions, among others, have raised concerns that China's long-term objective may include pursuing a form of regional hegemony in Asia and diminishing Washington's historic role in the region.

China's turn to a more forward-leaning foreign policy requires explanation and is often the subject of scholarly debate. The present assertiveness appears to be related to three major factors: (1) perceptions that the balance of power has shifted or is shifting in China's favor, (2) Xi Jinping's control over foreign policy, and (3) an increase in popular and elite-level nationalism.

First, around 2009, Chinese leaders began to see their country as ascendant while at the same time regarding the United States as reeling from the aftermath of the global financial crisis and mired in two costly wars in Iraq and Afghanistan. That year China began an internal discussion on the future of its foreign policy. Since the early 1990s, China's external behavior had been guided by Deng Xiaoping's twenty-four character dictum: "Coolly observe, calmly deal with things, hold your position, hide your capacities, bide your time, and accomplish things where possible." The purpose of what many have a termed a "hide and bide" strategy was to allow China to develop without drawing opposition from other great powers. With China's strength growing quickly relative to the United States, the party evidently concluded that Deng's admonition required updating and modification. The party decided to stress the importance of "actively" accomplishing things, and while this modification may seem small, it was nonetheless unprecedented and consequential. Roughly around the same time this new formulation was adopted, China began pursuing more assertive foreign policy to match its continuing economic ascent and military investment. China's economy measured by purchasing power is already larger than that of the United States, even if senior Chinese officials refuse to acknowledge it publicly.[62] At the same time, China's rapid military modernization and its pursuit of anti-access/area-denial capabilities have given leaders in Beijing greater confidence in their ability to deter the United States from entering into conflicts near their borders. These structural shifts in the US-China relationship are undoubtedly one major reason Beijing has altered its policy. As Thomas Christensen writes, "Many in China believe China is significantly stronger and the United States weaker after the financial crisis. Domestic voices calling for a more muscular Chinese foreign policy have created a heated political environment."[63]

Second, President Xi Jinping has fundamentally changed China's system of governance, weakening the consensus-driven and collective system established by Deng Xiaoping and granting himself greater autonomy in foreign policy decision making.[64] By many accounts Xi is the most powerful leader since Deng Xiaoping. His anticorruption campaign, implemented by his right hand Wang Qishan, has targeted former standing committee members such as Zhou Yongkang and senior generals including Xu Caihou, cowing rival elites who might oppose him. With this power Xi has centralized decision making to his office and the leading small groups he controls—especially on foreign policy, where he has diminished the role of the State Council, Foreign Ministry, and military and made most top decisions through the National Security Commission he himself created and oversees. This unprecedented control of the foreign policymaking apparatus has liberated him from the strictures of the more cautious bureaucracy. For example, Xi is intimately involved in committees to implement signature Chinese initiatives, including "One Belt, One Road" and the AIIB, and foreign policy under him will reflect his more assertive and clearly nationalistic inclinations.

A third and closely related factor is the impact of nationalism, at both the popular and elite levels, on the formulation and execution of Chinese foreign policy. With the collapse of Communist identity, China's legitimacy has been built on the twin foundations of economic growth and nationalist ideology. After Tiananmen Square, the party began to stoke nationalist sentiment through a "patriotic education" campaign in the country's schools that was supplemented by a steady barrage of chauvinistic propaganda, official media, television shows, and movies. The government's narrative has been that China suffered a "Century of Humiliation" beginning with the First Opium War in 1839 and ending with the victory of the Communists in 1949.[65] The Communist Party is cast as a savior that resurrected China, defeated the Japanese, kept out Western imperialists, and rebuilt the country into the great power it is today. In this retelling of Chinese history, the Communist Party's mission has not been to create a Communist utopia but to undo the legacy of China's humiliation, which remains manifest in the country's territorial disputes and continued separation from Taiwan. This narrative has built a deep well of resentment and grievance in China that may complicate a resolution of the region's territorial disputes—especially with Japan—and contributes to China's assertiveness. It is also a reservoir for political legitimacy. When Xi Jinping came to power, he declared that his main objective was the "great rejuvenation of the Chinese nation."[66]

These trends now intersect with a new wild card, China's slowing economy. China's thirty-year era of 10 percent annual growth appears to be ending, with official statistics placing gross domestic product growth below 7 percent and a number of major banks and respected forecasters arguing the true growth rate is far lower—and will remain below 5 percent for years.[67] China's historic growth had been based on the model of low-productivity agricultural laborers moving into low-wage but high-productivity manufacturing jobs, producing goods for foreign markets. Every component of this model is now strained, as the labor force shrinks, wages rise, productivity growth slows, and China's export markets become saturated.[68] China previously sought to recapture growth through record investments, but as investment's contribution to GDP growth has climbed to a record 50 percent, diminishing returns have set in. A dollar of investment now produces 40 percent less growth than it did a decade ago, and many of the investments themselves—such as empty apartment complexes and redundant infrastructure—will not generate returns.[69] Chinese leaders hope to rebalance the economy away from exports and investment and toward domestic consumption, but this is a complicated and precarious shift that will require substantial time, experimentation, and patience before its ultimate success or failure is readily apparent. Meanwhile, with the export and investment engines stalling, China's growth has already fallen to levels concerning to the Chinese Communist Party. Senior Chinese leaders, including former premier Wen Jiabao, have previously stated that 8 percent growth is needed to maintain social stability. China's economy is unlikely to recapture such growth, and party members remember keenly that past economic crises in 1986 and 1989 brought down two Chinese leaders, Hu Yaobang and Zhao Ziyang respectively, and led to the violence in Tiananmen Square.

Economists debate whether China will experience a "hard" or "soft" landing as its historic growth slows and it attempts to recalibrate its economic model. Even short of these extremes, however, the slowing economy and the risks of social unrest are likely to affect Chinese foreign policy, pushing it in a more assertive direction rather than to a tactical retreat. As the economic pillar of state legitimacy erodes, the party is likely to lean more heavily on nationalism. Xi Jinping may be the most powerful leader in generations, but he is also profoundly exposed, and will be held accountable for China's slowing economy. By emphasizing territorial disputes, pursuing grand diplomatic projects, and standing up to the West, Xi might divert attention from the country's uncertain economic woes and secure himself against nationalist criticism from the public or currently dormant rival elites.

One purpose of the Pivot to Asia is to respond to China's more assertive foreign policy. The Pivot addresses doubts in Beijing about US staying power by demonstrating that the United States intends to remain active and engaged in the region. At the same time, as President Obama has noted, "a strong, cooperative relationship with China is at the heart of our pivot to Asia."[70] Through cooperation on transnational challenges, military exchanges, and other confidence-building measures, the United States may not be able to completely cool China's heated nationalist passions, but it may be able to reduce the risk that the relationship will spiral into conflict and hopeless antagonism. We now turn to consider areas of discord in US-China relations.

Dealing with Discord: A Work Plan for Managing Competition

Even before China's turn to a more demonstrative foreign policy, there were already several critical areas where Chinese actions were calling into question core features of Asia's prevailing operating system that had long been supported by the United States. In recent years, as China has grown even bolder in its external behavior, these areas of discord have become increasingly pressing. Below we discuss five of the most significant areas of tension: anti-access/area denial, territorial disputes, hacking, economic disputes, and human rights. We also offer a work plan for dealing with them and managing the more competitive features of Sino-American relations.

First, from Washington's perspective, China's breakneck military modernization is transforming the strategic balance in Asia in ways that threaten to erode regional stability and exacerbate strategic competition. The PLA's development of anti-access/area-denial capabilities appears deliberately intended to undercut the ability of the US military to project power into East Asia and operate effectively in theater. PLA modernization is also tempting a classic security dilemma, that of inducing its neighbors to fear for their safety and invest in their own militaries, that would lead to a negatively reinforcing downward spiral. We discuss later in this chapter how the United States should contend with this changing strategic situation, but solutions will include new operating concepts and capabilities to maintain its non-negotiable freedom of access; long-range strike capabilities; more undersea assets; hardened facilities; robust C4ISR[71]; and, crucially, ensuring that similar steps are undertaken by allies and partners. These kinds of adjustments to US force structure and military strategy could bolster regional stability by reminding Beijing that, for all its confidence about trends in the balance of power, the US presence in Asia should not be tested or provoked in flash points like the East and South China Seas, the Taiwan Strait, and the Korean Peninsula.

Second, below the military threshold, China has taken a more proactive approach to advancing its maritime claims in the South and East China Seas, calling into question the bedrock principles of Asia's operating system like freedom of navigation and the peaceful resolution of disputes. Recent

Chinese activities have included increasing invasive patrols into disputed waters, establishing an air defense identification zone over Japan-administered territory, harassing US naval vessels, cutting the cables of foreign commercial vessels performing seismic exploration, seizing contested territory from the Philippines, dispatching an oil rig protected by eighty vessels 120 miles from the Vietnamese coast, and engaging in extraordinary and unprecedented land reclamation in the South China Sea.[72] Although from China's perspective these are legitimate activities to defend its rightful claims, the rest of the region, the United States, and key outside actors largely disagree. None of the other claimants have engaged in comparable behavior that approaches the scale and scope of China's assertive moves. As just one example, China's land reclamation accounts for more than 95 percent of all land reclaimed in the South China Sea; its islands are now home to military-length runways as well as mobile artillery.[73] In addition to leaning more heavily on military and paramilitary instruments in the South China Sea, China has shunned peaceful diplomatic mechanisms to manage its disputes. Beijing has dragged its feet on completing a binding code of conduct with ASEAN and has attempted to thwart the Philippines' efforts to challenge China's maritime claims through international legal arbitration. China's behavior is beginning to rub up against vital US national interests and to call into question its overall commitment to a peaceful rise.

An effective response to China's persistent maritime claims will require a subtle and nuanced mix of military and diplomatic initiatives. In the East China Sea, the United States will need to continue to periodically reiterate that the Senkaku Islands fall under Article 5 of the US-Japan Security Treaty in order to deter Beijing's adventurism and to remind China that the United States will oppose any efforts to change the status of the Senkakus by force. Washington can also strengthen the US-Japan alliance along the dimensions discussed previously in this chapter, especially by encouraging Japan's investment in maritime awareness and patrol capabilities. In the South China Sea, the United States can use training, military exchanges, and military assistance to support regional allies and partners in bolstering their maritime domain awareness. With new rotational access to the Philippines, the United States should also strengthen its presence in the South China Sea, in concert with allies and partners, through multilateral exercises and freedom of navigation operations (FONOP), such as when the USS *Lassen* sailed within twelve nautical miles of China's reclaimed Subi Reef in the Spratly Islands.[74] On the diplomatic side, the United States ought to redouble its efforts to marshal international support for freedom of navigation and advocate for a regional code of conduct that would halt militarization and reclamation activities (ideally through ASEAN). Following the Permanent Court of Arbitration's legal ruling in the *Philippines v. China* case, the United States can strengthen international norms by publicly supporting the judgment as well as other efforts to use international law to resolve maritime disputes. In these efforts, securing the support of a wide range of international partners can elevate US critiques of China's policies beyond the bilateral relationship, grounding them instead in an appeal to widely held and commonly favored international norms. For example, Australia and Japan explicitly supported the US FONOP near Subi Reef, while India and South Korea offered more oblique endorsements.[75] Finally, given the intractability of present disputes, the United States could improve the prospects for regional peace and prosperity by advocating for joint development agreements that shelve sovereignty questions and facilitate resource sharing. Ultimately, the United States should handle intractable territorial problems deftly, preserving flexibility so future diplomats can explore creative and sustainable solutions.

China's increasing assertiveness in cyberspace constitutes a third area of increasing bilateral tension. The FBI estimates that Chinese hacking, likely organized by the PLA and designed to assist China's state-owned enterprises, is costing US businesses billions of dollars per year.[76] Shadowy organizations with spy-novel-worthy names such as Unit 61398 have waged a pervasive campaign of commercial espionage. In addition, Chinese hackers have reportedly targeted US journalists, think tanks, civil society groups, and academics.[77] More brazenly, in April 2015, US officials discovered that Chinese hackers had compromised the records of roughly twenty million government employees stored by the Office of Personnel Management, compromising the identities of some US spies.[78] Diplomatic progress was limited after China canceled the principal vehicle for dialogue, the US-China Cyber Working Group, following a US Justice Department indictment against five PLA members engaging in illegal hacking activities. The September 2015 summit between President Obama and President Xi, however, concluded with an agreement by both sides not to hack critical infrastructure in peacetime and included a promise by Xi to refrain from hacking US companies for commercial secrets. Although compliance has not yet been forthcoming, some former officials like Evan Medeiros note signs of progress, and they attribute them to the fact that the United States has leaned more heavily on coercive diplomacy, including indictments and the threat of sanctions against Chinese companies.[79]

The United States should continue this approach but also remain resolute in following through with sanctions against companies engaging in or benefiting from cyberespionage if China fails to comply with its recent agreements. Both the United States and China would benefit from ensuring that bilateral mechanisms for discussing cyberissues, such as the US-China Cyber Working Group, can endure disagreements and tensions. On a multilateral level, the countries could conceivably cooperate to establish norms and rules of conduct for this newest frontier of the global commons.

Fourth, on economic issues, the US government and US businesses are concerned about China's protectionist behavior, including mismanagement of its currency, violations of intellectual property rights, an unfair anti-monopoly law, and restrictions on foreign investment. With these efforts China risks undermining the support of the American business community, the ballast in the ship of Sino-American relations. In dealing with them, the United States might consider using international law and trade agreements to resolve many of these disputes, working through the WTO dispute resolution mechanism when possible. In addition, the United States together with its allies and partners may be able to shape global economic norms in ways that incentivize Chinese compliance with twenty-first-century trade rules. For example, by promoting high-standards agreements such as the TPP in Asia and the TTIP in Europe, the United States can establish prevailing standards in international trade that, by virtue of being adopted by many of the world's largest economies, can shape the behavior of nonmembers, including China. Indeed, if China takes action to meet the high standards of these agreements, which its leaders have expressed a willingness to do, then the United States should encourage and welcome its eventual participation in the TPP. Finally, the United States would benefit from using negotiations on a bilateral investment treaty with China to address some of its economic concerns. Successful completion of this initiative may have salutary effects on China's willingness to pursue economic reforms and may create new opportunities for economic cooperation in both countries.

Fifth, human rights remain an enduring source of tension in the US-China relationship. While China bristles at what it views as US interference in its domestic affairs, the United States is increasingly concerned with a resurgence in Chinese targeting of religious leaders, journalists (foreign and domestic), political activists, artists, and others who in Beijing's eyes might challenge the legitimacy of the ruling regime. As prominent China human rights scholar Jerome Cohen has noted, a particularly concerning practice is the increasing willingness of the Chinese government to turn to collective punishment, targeting the families of political dissidents in order to silence them or compel their return to China.[80] China's draft law on NGOs is of serious concern because it could crush the country's budding nonprofit sector and force US organizations to close their doors. China has also demonstrated an interest in using big data to monitor its people, with tentative plans to introduce an Orwellian "citizenship score" that would function like a credit score, but one influenced by an individual's selection of library books, Internet searches, and video game purchases, and even the actions and records of friends and colleagues. Lest this seem far-fetched, it is worth noting that China's Ministry of Education recently proposed using big data to track the ideological views of students.[81] These efforts have implications well beyond China's borders. Almost entirely for domestic purposes, China is seeking to externalize norms of "Internet sovereignty" that would allow governments throughout the world to more readily restrict the flow of ideas and information.[82]

The United States admittedly has little leverage over China's human rights situation, but there are nonetheless some steps that may prove fruitful in the long run. Within the bilateral relationship, the United States has long been an advocate for those dissidents whom China has targeted or placed at risk, and it should continue to serve in this capacity in the period ahead, even as Beijing bristles at foreign interference. Tensions on human rights issues occasionally rock the bilateral relationship, and both sides could better manage by ensuring that an established venue for diplomatic dialogue on these issues remains a regularized feature of the bilateral relationship. In addition, China's most recent NGO law is particularly concerning because it could lead to the shuttering of domestic nonprofits and foreign aid groups. To more effectively make its case against the law, the United States would benefit from rallying the support of friendly states who have similar reservations. Although progress on China's human rights situation is likely to be modest in the short term, efforts to improve the rule of law could help lay the foundation for long-term reforms. In pursuit of that goal, the United States can sponsor a combination of legal exchanges and training for judges, prosecutors, lawyers, and police officers as well. Finally, the United States should continue to support the free flow of information across borders through the global Internet, and prohibit the export of Western technology and know-how that would assist China in the censorship or monitoring of its population.

Sixth, although the relationship between China and Taiwan has been relatively stable in recent years, characterized both by growing economic linkages and by rising people-to-people ties, several signs suggest there may be greater strains in the period ahead. We discuss US policy surrounding Taiwan in greater detail later in this chapter, but for now it is important to note that the victory of the Democratic People's Party (DPP) in 2016 and the continued growth of proindependence sentiment within Taiwan, combined with China's willingness to adopt more assertive policies toward Hong Kong, together raise the possibility of cross-strait tensions. Beijing and Taipei have long viewed China's fidelity to the "one country, two systems" framework that affords political and economic autonomy to Hong Kong as an important proxy for how Taiwan might be treated under reunification. Beijing's crackdown on Hong Kong protests in 2014, its issuance of a white paper the same year revising Hong Kong's autonomous status, and its apparent abduction of Hong Kong booksellers who routinely publish Communist Party materials, have together raised serious concerns about China's adherence to the "one country, two systems" formulation. China's apparent lack of concern about the effect of these policies on Taiwanese public opinion suggests China may be willing to adopt a tougher line regarding Taiwan, one that is perhaps less focused on persuasion and more oriented toward economic and strategic pressure. Should China adopt a more assertive policy across the Taiwan Strait, the United States will need to more actively and unambiguously support Taiwan, encourage continued cross-strait dialogue and exchanges, and remind both sides to refrain from unilaterally changing the status quo.

The purpose of articulating this litany of differences is not to express undo pessimism or point fingers at Beijing. To the contrary, it is to highlight the enormity of the coming task of setting the US-China relationship on a more positive course. Considerable commitment, patience, and creativity will be required to prevent any or all of these issues from pushing the relationship toward increasing levels of competition—and there are still good reasons to hope and believe that such an outcome is not predestined. But in addition to a strategy for managing competition, both sides also need a proactive and affirmative agenda for fostering cooperation if they are to avoid the famed Thucydides trap. We turn now to the challenge of that task.

Overcoming Thucydides: A Work Plan for Fostering Cooperation

Graham Allison has summarized the challenge facing the United States in reorienting policy toward Asia while maintaining good relations with China as the need to "escape the Thucydides trap." That is, can a rising power and an established power find accommodation with one another without resorting to war? In writing about the Peloponnesian War in 431 BCE, Thucydides observed that conflict between Athens and Sparta became inevitable due to the "growth of Athenian power and the fear which this caused in Sparta." Since 1500 CE, eleven of the fifteen cases of a rising state's intersecting with an established state have resulted in war, as dominant states resisted the rise of challengers and challengers resented the prevailing balance of power.

The present relationship between the United States and China bears some similarities to, but also has several crucial differences from, these previous cases. It is true that there are many reasons why China today would resent the prevailing balance of power. The United States has been a major factor preventing China from unifying with Taiwan, and US stances on territorial issues in the South and East China Seas also cause resentment in China. China nurses grievances over American alliances in Asia and Washington's pressure on Europe to maintain the embargo on arms sales to China, as well as the American dominance of the international economic order. At the same time, however, China is not a rising Germany. There is no Treaty of Versailles tying China down; on the contrary, the United States has welcomed China into the international order, opened its markets to Chinese goods, and invested heavily in Chinese manufacturing, facilitating the country's dizzying economic ascent. Although the two have had their strategic differences, the United States has often cooperated with China in global politics, waging war against its Japanese occupiers, balancing with it against Soviet expansion, and working with it against terrorism. Over the last century, the United States has been the country that has most consistently supported China's rise.

Perhaps the most serious impediment to a closer bilateral relationship is strategic mistrust. The legacy of history has created acute suspicions in China about the intentions of the United States, and many officials believe that the United States seeks to entrap and weaken China in order to disrupt its rise.[83] These suspicious extend to Western culture as well, with Xi Jinping's government having issued multiple directives that warn against the threat of Western ideas, including democracy and an independent judiciary, and order a greater focus on patriotism in response.[84] American officials regularly encounter the effects of this distrust when they deal with government elites. Meeting with the PLA's deputy chief of the general staff in Beijing in December 2011, then undersecretary of defense for policy Michèle Flournoy witnessed the intransigence of Chinese suspicion firsthand. It began when Chinese officials voiced the oft-heard complaint that American strategic-reconnaissance missions around China were a throwback to Cold War containment. In an effort to allay these perceptions, Flournoy noted that during the Cold War, such flights made up 80 to 90 percent of all US missions, whereas currently around China they comprised a single-digit percentage of operations.[85] Flournoy remarked later that, "I think for a couple of minutes, I had some cognitive dissonance going," as the Chinese officials nodded with understanding. "Then they snapped back into, 'No, no, this must be disinformation—of course you're containing us.' "[86] Any US official who has had the opportunity to engage with Chinese counterparts can relate similar stories of the difficulties of overcoming this distrust that is present even at the elite level, and the persistent narrative of containment.

Historical narratives are powerful, and to overcome the legacy of distrust, the United States should put together a work plan for US-China relations that uses shared interests and cooperative endeavors to build the foundations for stronger ties, based on the idea that the bilateral relationship is healthiest when it has a series of clear, identifiable tasks in front of it. This work plan should have six broad components: (1) clear statements of US strategy; (2) broader and deeper governmental engagement, especially at the leader level; (3) concrete projects for the bilateral relationship; (4) dialogue and cooperation on transnational Asian challenges; (5) common efforts to address global issues; (6) a closer military relationship focused on crisis prevention and disaster relief.

First, as discussed at this chapter's outset, the United States needs to make clearer statements outlining the US approach and strategy surrounding the Pivot. These statements, made by the president and high-level political leaders and fleshed out in an annual government strategy document, would be helpful not only for our allies and partners but also for Beijing's policymakers. A clear statement of US purpose and intentions would reduce the risk of miscalculation in the bilateral relationship by making clear that the United States intends to remain engaged and committed in the Asia-Pacific for decades to come, and by directly addressing fears that the Pivot is focused on containing China. These official pronouncements should also be crafted to reassure China of continuing US best wishes for economic growth, territorial integrity, and political stability. Although Chinese leaders may retain a certain degree of skepticism toward pronouncements that the Pivot is not a form of containment, over time and through repeated interaction, the two sides might establish a baseline of trust that reduces the probability of conflict.

Second, the United States should increase governmental ties with China at every level, which will require deeper and more regularized bilateral interactions than any other diplomatic endeavor in American history. Within these meetings, the United States should continue to send reassuring messages even as it advocates for its national interests. Specifically, the United States must make clear that the Pivot is not intended to weaken China, that Washington welcomes China's rise, and that the United States does not ask its allies and partners to choose between it and Beijing. As part of the Pivot to Asia, the United States established the annual US-China Strategic and Economic Dialogue, a comprehensive set of meetings chaired by the US secretaries of state and the Treasury and their Chinese counterparts. It also established the Strategic Security Dialogue, through which the two countries have held unprecedented high-level discussions on such sensitive matters as maritime security and cybersecurity. These are two efforts that have been taken to bring the United States and China together.[87] These efforts are major improvements, but there is still much more to be done.

The United States should support more, and more frequent, crosscutting dialogues with China, in which officials from a wide range of agencies can meet. Not all substantive government interaction need take place around the Strategic and Economic Dialogue. In addition to wider ties across the full range of government, the United States could also be more creative about how to get senior leaders more time together to engage on twenty-first-century challenges. Direct engagement with Xi Jinping is especially important now, given his increasing dominance of a decision-making process that is becoming more opaque and unpredictable. State visits are not always the best means of building closer leader-level ties, since they are cumbersome, involve perilously high stakes, and are loaded with symbolism. Meetings in multilateral settings are also often rushed and inadequate to the task. In contrast, both countries would benefit from focusing on more informal "working meetings" between leaders and a much smaller subset of aides that keep the diplomatic bells and whistles to a minimum. Obviously both sides want to avoid Cold War imagery, but the US and the Soviet Union held such meetings for decades in neutral locations such as Malta, Reykjavik, and Vienna, when it was deemed inconvenient to plan a home match. The first Obama-Xi summit at the Sunnylands estate in California is a good example of the type of informal, open-collar meetings that should come to define top-level diplomacy between the United States and China. If US officials are to better understand and influence Xi, and if both sides are to build strategic trust and establish rapport, then these kinds of meetings will need to become a regularized feature of bilateral diplomacy that is sustained even through the inevitable highs and lows of the relationship.

Third, within the larger bilateral relationship, the United States and China might benefit from setting clear goals and objectives that the two countries could work together to achieve. On the economic side, this might include targets for bilateral trade and investment as well as the finalization of new agreements, such as the US-China bilateral investment treaty (BIT). Similar efforts could be undertaken in people-to-people diplomacy, with both sides setting ambitious targets for bilateral visits to be undertaken by tourists, students, and businesspeople. The recent 100,000 Strong Initiative, which had a goal of sending 100,000 American students to China within five years, is a useful model of the kinds of cooperative people-to-people endeavors that could be adopted in several spheres. Partnership should also be extended to more heady and speculative pursuits, especially in science and technology. Just as the United States and the Soviet Union were able to strengthen their bilateral relationship through cooperation in space, notably through the famous Apollo-Soyuz missions, so too should the United States and China cooperate in high-profile and signature pursuits—some perhaps relating to the space program, but especially those pertaining to more terrestrial pursuits such as developing revolutionary green technologies or researching treatments for intractable diseases like cancer or Alzheimer's.

Fourth, since the regional level is likely to be where tensions between the United States and China will be most acute, both countries need to adopt more affirmative and cooperative dialogues. The United States and China have already established a US-China Working Group Dialogue on Asia but could benefit from establishing new, regularized opportunities for dialogue on a range of issues going forward, opportunities that promote active, constructive cooperation across the region. The purpose of many of these meetings would be to proactively search out projects for regional cooperation in order to build enduring habits of mutual cooperation and trust that could address mutual threat perceptions. As chapter 1 outlined, Asia is a region full of promise but is also plagued by several developmental challenges that call out for cooperative solutions among the leading nations. The United States and China could create mechanisms for systematic bilateral cooperation on development and infrastructure projects, disease prevention efforts, humanitarian assistance and disaster relief, regional economic management, and growing refugee flows.

Fifth, the United States and China in recent years have successfully worked together on a variety of global challenges. China has been involved in diplomacy aimed at constraining Iran's nuclear ambitions, has struck climate change agreements with the United States, has worked with the United States to combat piracy on the high seas, and has taken a more active role in shaping Afghanistan's future. The two sides need a positive and affirmative agenda for cooperation on other global issues. For example, the global economy is sensitive to the decisions undertaken by US and Chinese economic officials, and coordination on global economic governance will be increasingly important for sustaining global prosperity. Both countries are also threatened by nuclear proliferation and have powerful interests in restricting the spread of nuclear technologies both in Asia and worldwide. Both the United States and China oppose North Korea's nuclear and missile program, and China has grown increasingly critical of Kim Jong-un's provocations, going so far as to join the United States in calling for a UN resolution against North Korea following its January 2016 nuclear test. Less controversially, the two countries could coordinate efforts to bolster nuclear security worldwide through export controls and steps to safeguard nuclear material. Finally, as the two largest emitters of carbon dioxide, the United States and China will remain central to efforts to address global climate change. Their recent precedent-setting bilateral agreements are nonbinding and long-term, but both sides could advance global efforts by jointly announcing more concrete commitments, including renewable energy investments, green building codes, and green standards for infrastructure, among other goals. Overall, as China's interests and capabilities grow increasingly global, Washington and Beijing could well start to see more eye to eye on a variety of issues such as antipiracy, stability in the Middle East, the Afghan peace process, and counterterrorism.

Sixth, in order to avoid dangerous miscalculation and escalation and to build a much-needed reservoir of strategic trust that can be drawn on in times of crisis, greater military exchanges and defense cooperation will be necessary. Although the two sides seek to avoid conflict, the risk of an inadvertent incident or military accident is increasing. Both China and the United States are expanding their military presence in the Asia-Pacific even as conflict hot spots in the South and East China Seas, Taiwan Strait, and Korean Peninsula continue to simmer. Because of this, US and Chinese forces are "rubbing up against one another more frequently," in the words of one senior Defense Department official. This can end dangerously, such as when a Chinese fighter collided with an EP-3, leading to the death of a Chinese pilot and a tense standoff when American servicemen were detained by the Chinese government. More recently, the USNS *Impeccable* and USS *Cowpens* were harassed by Chinese naval vessels in the South China Sea. In order to ensure the next crisis does not end in conflict, an increasingly important dimension of US strategy in Asia going forward will be to pursue military diplomacy with China.

Efforts to build a strong military relationship have generally been beset by considerable obstacles and have so far failed to achieve the goal of creating greater trust and mutual understanding. One of these obstacles has been China's historical unwillingness to advertise its military inferiority for fear it would expose its vulnerabilities to potential foreign adversaries, though China's military modernization has now reduced the salience of these concerns. More fundamentally, while the United States has welcomed transparency as a means of limiting miscalculation and promoting trust,

China has preferred opacity and uncertainty to enhance deterrence. But the most fundamental obstacle to military ties has been the fact that both sides have seen severing such ties as a readily available means of signaling displeasure with other aspects of the overall relationship. For example, relations were suspended in 1989 following China's crackdown in Tiananmen Square. After a brief period of progress in subsequent years, they collapsed under the weight of high-pressure situations like the 1995–1996 Taiwan Straits Crisis and the accidental US bombing of the Chinese embassy in Belgrade during the Kosovo War in 1999. This pattern continued into the first decade of the twenty-first century, when China cut ties in response to US arms sales to Taiwan.

To achieve a stronger bilateral relationship, the United States and China will need to depart from the previous trajectory. Bilateral military exchanges have for too long been inconsistent, with a scope that ranges from exchanges of chefs and bands to matters of real strategic import. What is needed now is systematic, regularized, and substantive communication and cooperation between the two militaries at a variety of levels—but particularly at senior-most levels—that are robust against political crises.

First, senior military officials at the Pentagon and at US Pacific Command (PACOM) should engage in more frequent discussions with senior-level personnel in the People's Liberation Army (PLA). These discussions should focus on matters of substance that are central to military affairs, and could conceivably range from questions of doctrine to matters of contingency planning. Regularized high-level interaction on such topics helps dispel dangerous misperceptions and can even build a modicum of strategic trust, and forms personal relationships that could be useful in future crisis prevention.

Second, the US and Chinese militaries should work together on a variety of instruments and agreements that could prevent small incidents from expanding into full-blown crises. Due to China's continuing harassment of US aircraft and naval vessels, the risk of an incident remains high—especially with both navies operating in close quarters in the South China Sea. Admiral Wu Shengli, the PLA Navy's top official, has warned that "a minor incident" at sea or in the air "could spark war."[88] During the Cold War, the United States and the Soviet Union negotiated the Incidents at Sea Agreement to prevent such a crisis. Both the United States and China are parties to the Code for Unplanned Encounters at Sea (CUES), and both have recently signed two memorandums to establish "rules of the road" for aircraft and ship encounters, though these rules have yet to be fully implemented and there remains a need for a more detailed and formal agreement. In addition, both sides need more military hotlines at a variety of levels and covering a range of different functional areas. For now these are few in number, rarely used, and sometimes terminated by China in response to any perceived slight. The more these two militaries regularize their interactions, the less likely it is that an accidental encounter will result in an inadvertent clash.

Third, both countries should pursue opportunities for cooperation at the operational level within the contexts of humanitarian assistance and disaster relief, maritime piracy, and peacekeeping—especially when the views of both countries are in alignment. Both sides should also consider increasing the number of joint exercises between them. Cooperation at the operational level could build each country's familiarity with the standard operating procedures of the other's military, which could be useful in preventing miscommunication and crisis; additionally, these activities can bolster trust and confidence.

Finally, the United States should encourage China to engage in military diplomacy with its neighbors and partners as well as in broader international assignments, such as in the UN peacekeeping context. Better diplomacy between the region's militaries could bring a degree of transparency and stability to maritime disputes, especially in the South and East China Seas. If successful, these practices might even prevent crises from occurring and place a ceiling on the escalatory potential of minor incidents, thereby serving the interests of regional peace and reducing the likelihood of a conflict between China and a treaty ally that might pull in the US military.

Overall, as the preceding discussion has suggested, we are heading into a new era in US-China relations that is likely to be filled with more tension and some acrimony. This does not mean cooperation cannot progress. Indeed, if there is no tension in the relationship, it means someone is probably not doing their job. Both countries have challenging domestic agendas and at times conflicting international interests, but Washington and Beijing fully recognize the importance of their bilateral relationship. Only through deeper cooperation and understanding can the United States and China forge a relationship that will ensure a more peaceful and prosperous twenty-first century.

Building Partnerships

While the hub-and-spokes structure—with a new tire connecting the spokes—will remain the foundation of American Asia strategy, it is now time for the United States to expand it to incorporate both emerging and long-standing American partners. To that end the Pivot is designed to intensify US relations with virtually each and every state in Asia. These partnerships can not only bring greater balance to Asia, they can also help the United States promote twenty-first-century principles within the region, engage Asian states in global governance, enhance regional security and stability, advance liberal values, and maintain free trade. Several states in particular make for promising potential partners across a variety of initiatives. Below we pay particular attention to India, Taiwan, and several Southeast Asian countries.

India

India is the world's largest democracy, its second most populous country, and one of Asia's fastest-growing economies, with the potential to become a twenty-first-century power.[89] Although ties between the United States and India are currently fluctuating near a high point, they have often had an inconsistent quality and lagged behind and below their true potential. The present pro-American leadership in New Delhi offers an opportunity to put the relationship on a more consistent upward trajectory for the twenty-first century. This task is an important part of the US Pivot to Asia, but it will at times be challenging, requiring both sides to manage expectations and proceed with patience and commitment. As one sage architect of early US engagement with India commented, "The only thing more challenging in modern diplomacy than not having a relationship with India is trying to build one."

The history of US ties with India has often been rocky. After gaining independence from Britain, a strongly anticolonial India became a leader of the Non-Aligned Movement of third-world states that refrained from allying with the Cold War superpowers. Eventually, after the Non-Aligned Movement weakened, India drifted into closer ties with the Soviet Union as the United States supported China and Pakistan. More than one generation of bureaucrats and politicians grew up with this potent mix of anticolonial sentiment and Cold War–era suspicions of Washington, and these attitudes still resurface at times to complicate relations. Bilateral ties have nevertheless surmounted many of these obstacles to come a long way in a short time. Only sixteen years ago, the United States sanctioned India for its nuclear tests.[90] Since President Bill Clinton's visit to India in 2000 and the Bush administration's decision to end sanctions in 2001, however, the United States has steadily worked to build a closer partnership with India— culminating in the effort led by Ambassador Robert Blackwill to sign a civil nuclear deal with India in 2005, effectively legitimizing India's membership in the nuclear club.

Today the relationship is increasingly broad-based and diversified. On the diplomatic side, the United States supported India's entry into the G-20, UN Security Council, and Nuclear Suppliers Group. Both countries have worked to strengthen their military relationship through the 2015 Defense Framework Agreement, joint research and development of military technology, routine exercises, and military sales—with India being the largest purchaser of US weapons in 2013.[91] On the economic side, goods and services trade is over $100 billion and the United States is India's largest trading partner.[92] Investment levels are rising as well, though economic ties face numerous obstacles.

The outlook for the bilateral relationship is increasingly positive. Prospects were once hampered by a degree of historical suspicion, occasional misunderstandings, and a general lack of ambition, but with the arrival of pro-American prime minister Modi, India has increasingly shed the vestiges of nonalignment and more openly embraced US ties. At the same time, long-standing policy disputes are fading. India has had close ties to Iran, but disagreements with the US over Iran policy are fading in the wake of the US-India nuclear deal. Similarly, although the US and India were once at loggerheads in the WTO over India's food stockpiling, a recent agreement has removed that significant thorn in the bilateral economic relationship. Meanwhile the two countries are increasingly bound through a powerful strategic logic, with each recognizing the need to direct more effort toward aligning policies in the rising East. The US Pivot to Asia coincides nicely with India's "look East" policy, which is designed to enhance India's own role in the rising Asia-Pacific.[93] Both countries welcome a strong relationship with China but remain concerned about the implications of its rise and military modernization. For India these concerns relate to China's growing naval presence in the Indian Ocean, its support for Pakistan, the residue of bad feelings from the 1962 Sino-Indian War, and ongoing border disputes between the two countries. Finally, both the United States and India are also increasingly attuned to strategic developments within the Indian Ocean region and its critical waterways. The present confluence of strategic interests and supportive political leadership offers a window of opportunity to deepen and broaden the bilateral partnership, and the United States should hasten to take advantage of it.

First, the United States and India would benefit from broader, deeper, and more frequent government interactions involving a wider range of officials. Although it is promising that the two countries now hold the annual US-India Strategic and Commercial Dialogue, it is also important to facilitate even greater and more ambitious interaction outside of the timetable imposed by this initiative. More regularized and institutionalized bilateral meetings, especially on Asian and Pacific affairs, where the two countries have common perspectives and shared interests, are a necessity and could be held throughout the year. In these meetings the United States should be careful to view India in its own context, not through the prism of the hyphenated India-Pakistan or India-China relationships.

Second, the United States has an opportunity to promote and benefit from India's economic reforms and robust growth, and can create a sense of common effort in boosting India's economic trajectory. An important component of this effort will be assistance and encouragement for Indian investments in human capital and infrastructure, as well as for reforms to the country's labor market, intellectual property regime, and investment laws. It is critical that the United States push for India's entry into APEC, which is long overdue. For its part, New Delhi would especially welcome US support on efforts that are priorities for India's ruling government, such as the "Make in India" initiative, which boosts domestic manufacturing in order to create jobs for the twelve million Indians entering the workforce annually. India plans to invest more than $1 trillion to improve its poor infrastructure, in part through public-private partnerships, and US firms and companies could be partners in the effort.[94] India is one of the world's largest consumers of energy, and US exports of crude oil and LNG to India could be mutually beneficial. Finally, because bilateral investment flows into India still remain rather anemic, the United States and India could work to reduce barriers to foreign investment, perhaps through a US-India BIT. Broadening the economic relationship in these ways will enable US-India ties to weather occasional disagreements and create a larger political constituency favoring their advancement. Importantly, it will also help bring about an India that is economically vibrant enough to play an important role in Asia's politics.

Third, although the strategic relationship between the United States and India is developing apace, it can still be elevated, perhaps one day even to a level that approaches that of US ties with allies. For example, as India acquires more advanced weaponry and capabilities, the United States can extend military training and exercises into the specialized functional realms so that India can make better use of them. In addition, the United States could permit India to access US training schools and should also expand the opportunities offered through the International Military Education and Training program (IMET). Bilateral exercises, as Ashley Tellis argues, should also "become more complex and more routine, and they should involve the best combatant capabilities on both sides," as well as other friendly partners.[95] The United States and India would benefit from closer cooperation on regional HADR in the wider Indo-Pacific, and from improving interoperability. As a way of broadening the hub-and-spokes arrangement, the United States could encourage closer cooperation between India and US treaty allies and partners within the region by integrating India into US alliance diplomacy as well as military exercises, and by broadening the scope of some of its exercises with India, such as Exercise Malabar, to more regularly include other allies such as Australia.

Fourth, both countries can expand their cooperation on regional and global issues. The United States and India have shared interests in the broad Indo-Pacific spanning from Africa to East Asia and can coordinate efforts to combat piracy, pursue HADR operations, and enhance maritime domain awareness. Both countries would also benefit from coordinating their agendas in multilateral bodies such as the ARF and EAS, within which India can be an important advocate for twenty-first-century values in Asia, including freedom of navigation and the peaceful resolution of disputes. Finally, the United States should try to globalize the bilateral relationship by drawing India into discussions about important issues around the world in which

India's cooperation and participation are required, such as efforts to deal with climate change or address Middle East instability.

Taiwan

The American partnership with Taiwan advances US economic and security interests, is rooted in shared values, and will have a big impact on the way American partners and allies view the United States across Asia.[96] After the United States broke off formal diplomatic relations with Taiwan in 1979 and recognized the People's Republic of China, the US Congress passed the Taiwan Relations Act (TRA). For more than thirty years, the TRA, the Six Assurances to Taiwan, and the three US-China Joint Communiqués have guided US relations with Taiwan and China.

US policy, informed by these laws and agreements, is grounded upon a few core principles. The United States acknowledges the Chinese position that there is but one China and that Taiwan is part of China. It opposes unilateral attempts by either side to change the status quo, either through force or through a declaration of independence. The United States welcomes efforts on both sides to engage in a dialogue that reduces tensions and increases contacts across the Taiwan Strait, and insists that cross-strait differences be resolved peacefully, in accordance with the wishes of the people on both sides of the strait. The United States is also committed to preserving peace and stability in the Taiwan Strait. As part of US commitments under the TRA, the United States continues to provide Taiwan with defensive military systems based on its needs and following long-standing policy, without advance consultation with the PRC.

Although US-Taiwan ties are unofficial, the relationship has nonetheless grown quite close and diversified across diplomatic, economic, military, and people-to-people components. The United States supports Taiwan's diplomatic participation in any organization for which statehood is not a requirement, such as the WTO, the Asian Development Bank, and APEC. The United States also supports Taiwanese participation in other important international bodies that do require statehood, such as the World Health Organization and the UN Framework Convention on Climate Change. The economic relationship is especially robust. The United States and Taiwan signed the Trade and Investment Framework Agreement (TIFA) in 1994, and Taiwan is the tenth-largest US trading partner and an important export market. With regard to security, the United States is the main provider of Taiwan's defensive capabilities, and the two enjoy a vital military relationship. People-to-people ties have expanded since the United States admitted Taiwan into its Visa Waiver Program. Finally, although Taiwan was once ruled by a military dictatorship, it is now a robust democracy that has held several elections and that shares a US focus on liberal values. Taiwan's emergence as an economic powerhouse and liberal democracy is a testament to the fortitude of the people of Taiwan and the success of US policy.

The United States should continue to maintain close ties to Taiwan. In 2016 the ruling Kuomintang (KMT) party, which favored close relations with China, was defeated by the Democratic People's Party (DPP). The DPP has historically been more proindependence than the KMT and skeptical of the 1992 Consensus, an informal agreement between China and Taiwan that there is but one China and both the PRC and Taiwan are part of it. During the prior period of DPP rule, from 2000 to 2008, the US-China relationship was particularly turbulent because of fears that Taiwan would declare independence. It is as yet unclear how the current DPP tenure will evolve on matters related to cross-strait relations.

First, the United States can maintain and improve upon the bilateral security framework that the two sides have together established by continuing to fulfill its obligations under the TRA and the Six Assurances.[97] An important aspect of the Taiwan Relations Act is a congressional requirement that the United States maintain the wherewithal to respond to potential efforts to disrupt the status quo across the Taiwan Strait, and the continued forward deployment of US forces plays a critical role in preserving peace and stability. In addition, the Taiwan Relations Act calls for the ongoing provision of defensive weapons systems to Taiwan, which are not to be subject to any prior consultation with China. With respect to broadening the defense relationship, both sides could increase the pace of military exchanges, training, and especially exercises—which Taiwan has expressed a public interest in joining. Finally, as the military balance across the Taiwan Strait has shifted decisively toward Beijing, Taiwan has abandoned conscription, fallen short of military spending targets, and so far refrained from fundamentally revising its defense strategy. For this reason the United States should work to persuade senior Taiwanese officials to commit concretely to the island's own defense and to consider more asymmetric technologies, such as sea mines, as opposed to conventional military investments, to offset Chinese advantages.

Second, the United States can contribute to peace and prosperity across the Taiwan Strait by continuing to welcome efforts by both Taiwan and China to sustain and further increase economic, cultural, and people-to-people ties. These kinds of initiatives can reduce tensions, preserve stability, and increase contacts across the strait. In supporting closer cross-strait ties, the United States should continue to follow the Six Assurances, which among other commitments call upon the United States not to mediate cross-strait ties or pressure Taiwan into negotiations with the mainland.

Third, although Taiwan's economic relationship with China has brought economic prosperity and political stability, Taiwan's economy now faces the risk of overdependence on trade with the mainland. In order to help Taiwan build a foundation for sustainable prosperity and reduce its susceptibility to Chinese economic pressure, the United States should encourage Taiwan's efforts to diversify its external economic ties. To that end the United States should support and facilitate Taiwan's eventual entry into the TPP, which is a stated goal of current Taiwanese president-elect Tsai Ing-wen, as well as greater economic ties between Taiwan and other major economies.

Fourth, it is important for the United States to continue supporting Taiwan's membership in organizations where statehood is not a requirement, and to support efforts to find creative ways to facilitate Taiwan's unofficial or semiofficial participation when full membership is not possible. In these efforts, when possible, it is generally best to avoid establishing the precedent that Taiwanese participation first requires permission from Beijing. Because Taiwan is a major global economy, Taiwan's involvement in these organizations often makes them more effective. Taiwan's recent participation in the UN Framework Convention on Climate Change (UNFCCC) and the International Civil Aviation Organization (ICAO) was important both for combating climate change and for helping make air travel safer. Although Taiwan is a member of the WHO, APEC, and the Asian Development Bank, and is now able to participate in several other organizations, there remain countless more in which its voice cannot be heard. In those cases the United States can help Taiwan by advocating on its behalf and serving as an intermediary.

Fifth, since the United States does not officially recognize Taiwan, many of the procedures put in place since 1979 to facilitate informal diplomatic ties are now in need of updating so that the bilateral relationship can be put on more solid ground. There is little cabinet-level or senior government interaction with the Taiwanese, but there could be found creative ways of circumventing this problem to facilitate senior engagement involving a wider range of US agencies. In simple terms, American officials too often forget that Taiwan is a top-ten US trading partner and an economic powerhouse often worth engaging, and by making that point more often within the government and by modernizing procedures to facilitate greater ties, the United States can give Taiwan greater "face" within the bilateral relationship.

Finally, as the United States engages Taiwan, it should be careful not to interfere in the country's domestic politics. A close partnership with Taiwan should be robust despite changes in Taiwanese administrations, and this means a hands-off approach toward its future elections. Relatedly, the United States could facilitate cross-strait stability by encouraging China to develop contacts across Taiwan's political spectrum, not just with the KMT, so that leaders in Beijing are potentially not quite so anxious when power changes hands.

New Zealand

Although the United States and New Zealand are no longer allies, the two countries have a long history alongside one another on the battlegrounds of the twentieth and twenty-first centuries. Americans stood shoulder to shoulder with Kiwis in the First and Second World Wars and the conflicts in Korea and Vietnam. Practical alliance cooperation and close defense ties, which were formalized in a 1951 security pact, came to an unfortunate end in the mid-1980s when New Zealand adopted a policy barring nuclear-armed and nuclear-powered warships from visiting its ports. The strategic relationship saw new life after New Zealand's decision to deploy regular troops and special forces to Afghanistan after the September 11 attacks. In 2010 it received a major boost when Secretary of State Hillary Clinton visited New Zealand and signed the Wellington Declaration, noting that it served to "deepen and broaden and strengthen this important partnership" and symbolically turned the page on the nuclear dispute.[98] The Washington Declaration signed two years later allowed for a return to closer security cooperation, and in the years since, the United States has reopened US naval ports to New

Zealand vessels and New Zealand has joined the RIMPAC exercises and begun working more closely with the United States. Security ties are at their highest point in more than thirty years.

Even though the defense relationship between the United States and New Zealand suffered after the 1980s, other aspects of the relationship continue to progress, and the bilateral partnership is strong and diversified across several domains.[99] With respect to economic ties, both countries signed a Trade and Investment Framework Agreement in 1992 and are members today of the Trans-Pacific Partnership, with the United States currently New Zealand's third-largest trading partner. After the devastating Christchurch earthquake in 2011, the United States responded with financial assistance and disaster response teams, and was the single largest donor country for relief efforts.[100] In the region's multilateral organizations, both the United States and New Zealand effectively coordinate their positions to advance common interests and values, especially in the ARF, EAS, and APEC. They also align aid policies and other initiatives regarding the Pacific island states. People-to-people and cultural ties between the United States and New Zealand are strong and enduring and span educational, professional, scientific, and other programs. Although the relationship is close and has achieved significant gains over the last decade, there nonetheless remain a few important areas for improvement.

First, the United States and New Zealand should continue the momentum in their security ties. This will involve more exchanges, exercises, training, equipment transfers, and operational missions spanning from HADR to the monitoring of Pacific fisheries. One of the most crucial dimensions of closer ties will be naval engagement, which has not yet achieved its full potential and still remains under the long shadow of the 1980s nuclear dispute. It was not until 2012 that ships from New Zealand could visit US ports, and obstacles still hinder the participation of the US Navy in exercises or operations in New Zealand. Finally, both countries should work to enhance trilateral cooperation, interoperability, and operational connectivity with Australia in the Indian Ocean, Southeast Asia, and the South Pacific.

Second, while the partnership has set about successfully overcoming the thorny legacy of the past, it is now time to develop a broad and shared vision for Asia through closer political engagement. For now, the two sides lack sufficient regularized and institutionalized high-level political dialogue on mutual perspectives on Asia. At a time when Asia is undergoing dramatic changes, however, both countries would benefit from closer discussion of the region's strategic trajectory.

Third, along with Australia, New Zealand is one of the most important and influential countries in the South Pacific, and any US policy that is to be successful there will benefit from Wellington's input and support. New Zealand effectively borders these states, and as the region's fourth-largest aid donor and a full member of the Pacific Island Forum—in which the United States is only a dialogue partner—New Zealand has close people-to-people, diplomatic, and economic relations with these small island states. The United States and New Zealand should deepen cooperation within the region, including through military operations that help the region manage the rising threat of illegal fishing, which threatens the livelihoods of Pacific island states.

Finally, as a relatively small state, New Zealand especially benefits from a stable Asian operating system that depends on and defends freedom of navigation, regional transparency, free trade, the peaceful resolution of disputes, and other key regional norms and practices. To support that system, the United States and New Zealand should continue coordinating their positions in the region's many multilateral organizations and diverse forums. New Zealand's membership in the TPP has been critical to efforts to bring Asian trade in line with twenty-first-century standards, and its cooperation with the United States, Australia, and other states on shared values and norms for the Asian future will be especially important in shaping a region in the midst of transition.

Southeast Asian States

US policy in Asia has long been focused on Northeast Asia, and an important part of the Pivot to Asia is actually a refocus within Asia on the countries of the southeast. The combined GDP of this region is now over $2.3 trillion, larger than that of all the BRIC countries but China combined, and the region's total population of over six hundred million sits above all but China and India.[101] Crucially, Southeast Asia is also home to a number of promising potential partners with which the United States should develop closer ties, especially Indonesia, Vietnam, Malaysia, and Brunei.

Indonesia is the world's largest Muslim country, its third-largest democracy, and its fourth-largest country by population. Bilateral ties were strained during the Cold War and in the 1990s, especially due to human rights abuses, but relations began to improve under the Bush administration. President Obama, who lived in Indonesia as a child for four years, has ushered in a remarkable period of advances, beginning with the 2010 US-Indonesia Comprehensive Partnership. The two countries intensified security cooperation through expanded exercises, training, and sales—with Indonesia receiving C-130 transport planes, Apache helicopters, and F-16 aircraft. To continue the upward trajectory, the United States can further expand the scope of military exercises with Indonesia, incorporate it into more complex exercises with allies, increase funding for military modernization, regularize exchanges with military officers, and pursue defense industry cooperation. Indonesia is also increasingly concerned about Chinese assertiveness in the South China Sea, and given the archipelagic nation's expansive EEZ, the United States should work with it and other regional partners to improve maritime domain awareness and to coordinate on diplomatic initiatives relevant to freedom of navigation.[102] Finally, with trade and investment ties the weakest links in the relationship, both sides would benefit from greater economic interaction and from Washington's support for Indonesia's economic reforms.

Vietnam is more populous than any European country and is a fast-growing economy with a promising future. Relations between the United States and Vietnam, normalized in 1995, have long ago stepped out from the shadow of the Vietnam War. Close ties with Vietnam are an important component of the Pivot. Both countries joined the TPP, launched the US-Vietnam Comprehensive Bilateral Partnership in 2013, and have cooperated in security and diplomatic affairs, especially involving the South China Sea. China's aggressiveness in the South China Sea, including its harassment of Vietnamese vessels, island construction, and 2014 deployment of a drilling rig in disputed waters, have pushed Vietnam to deepen relations with the United States. Although US-Vietnam relations have come far in recent decades and are arguably at a high point, there is still room for improvement.[103] On security, the United States should increase exercises, exchanges, and training with Vietnam; bolster cooperation on HADR and maritime domain awareness; and soften or outright lift its ban on lethal military sales to Vietnam. The United States, currently Vietnam's largest export market, should also undertake negotiations with Vietnam on lifting its designation of Vietnam as a nonmarket economy. Finally, a sustainable and stable relationship with Vietnam will require a pragmatic approach to human rights. The United States should forgo public shaming in favor of dialogue, private counsel, and support for Vietnamese reforms.

Although Malaysia is only one-eighth as populous as neighboring giant Indonesia, it is a fast-growing, moderate Muslim country that punches above its weight. The United States' relationship with Malaysia was at times plagued by domestic anti-Americanism as well as disagreements over the Cold War and the Asian financial crisis. Relations have improved markedly under Prime Ministers Abdullah Ahmad Badawi and Najib Razak, culminating in the 2014 US-Malaysia Comprehensive Partnership and the first visit by a US president to Malaysia since 1967. The two countries enjoy a robust economic relationship, and Malaysia has the third-highest per capita income of any ASEAN state. It is the second-largest US trading partner in ASEAN, the United States is Malaysia's fourth-largest trading partner worldwide, and both are members of the TPP. While the economic relationship is strong, security ties have lagged because of Malaysia's focus on economic development and its concern about balancing relations with China. China's encroachments in the South China Sea around James Shoal, which is claimed by Malaysia, have pushed Malaysia to pursue deep but quiet strategic relations with the United States. Malaysia requested US assistance in building an amphibious force base near James Shoal and is considering providing access to US reconnaissance aircraft.[104] In this environment the United States should proceed carefully by attending to Malaysian sensitivities as it expands exercises (such as Cooperation Afloat Readiness and Training or CARAT), strengthens interoperability, helps improve amphibious capabilities, provides training, and assists in Malaysia's development of maritime domain awareness. Multilateral initiatives focused on HADR and maritime domain awareness, especially through ASEAN, may be less sensitive for Malaysia and useful means of expanding the partnership. Finally, the coming period will be challenging as corruption scandals create uncertainty around current pro-American prime minister Razak and as elections approach in 2018. The United States will have to be particularly careful in navigating Malaysia's uncertain domestic politics if it is to maintain progress and improve the relationship.

Brunei, a Muslim monarchy located on the island of Borneo, is one of the most overlooked Southeast Asian states and an important partner for the United States. Although its population numbers only about half a million, this small country welcomes closer ties with the United States, is a member of the TPP and ASEAN, and a claimant in the South China Sea, and therefore warrants closer attention. The United States has official ties with Brunei dating back to 1850, but the modern era in bilateral diplomacy began when Brunei gained independence from the United Kingdom in 1984. With respect to bilateral economic ties, Brunei hopes to diversify an economy that remains reliant on its energy industry, which catapulted the country into the ranks of developed countries, and its membership in the TPP will assist with those efforts. Brunei is also a significant international investor, including in the United States, and an importer of American high-technology goods such as helicopters and aircraft. Although the countries have close strategic ties, especially with regard to cooperation on special forces, this relationship has not yet achieved its full potential. Closer collaboration on military exchanges, training, and exercises, as well as efforts to boost Brunei's maritime domain awareness, will be important going forward. With respect to regional diplomacy, Brunei has helped facilitate closer US involvement in ASEAN. When Brunei was chair of the organization in 2013, it hosted three US secretary of state visits as well as visits from other cabinet officials, and hosted a HADR exercise involving both the United States and China. Closer cooperation between the United States and Brunei, especially in Asian regional organizations, will be important for both countries, especially as Brunei struggles with territorial disputes in the South China Sea.

US policy across Southeast Asia is a crucial component of the Pivot. As the United States improves economic, diplomatic, and strategic ties throughout the region, it will also have to attend to the fact that many states—Burma, Cambodia, Malaysia, and Thailand—are going through varying degrees of political turmoil that could alter their future foreign policies and priorities. If its regional policy is to be successful, as the chips fall, Washington should adhere to basic principles of democracy promotion and respect for human rights, but without doing so dogmatically or in ways that would reduce US influence. Rather than betting on winners, the best approach would be to focus on issues that matter most to people in the region no matter who is in power, such as education, poverty alleviation, and natural-disaster response. This being the case, more attention should be given to expanding the role of the Lower Mekong Initiative (LMI), which was launched by the State Department in 2009.[105] It has been effective in narrowing the development gap between countries in Southeast Asia as well as enhancing integration among states within this emerging region that has been historically underrepresented.

Finally, Southeast Asian states are all members of ASEAN and are at the center of efforts to build enduring and influential Asian institutions. As we will discuss later in this chapter, the United States will need to work closely with Southeast Asian states to coordinate shared positions on twenty-first-century values like freedom of navigation, regional transparency, the peaceful resolution of disputes, and free trade. As these organizations build secretariats, hire staff, and acquire new responsibilities, the United States can place itself at the center of the process as a partner in and supporter of Asia's institutional evolution.

Pacific Island States

When policymakers speak about the Asia-Pacific they too often neglect the *Pacific* element of the formulation. The fourteen sovereign states that sit astride this vast region are part of America's far western border and important to American security and our shared history of sacrifice in the Pacific theater of the Second World War. During the dark days of the Pacific campaigns seventy years ago, the United States and the people of the Pacific fought side by side to counter the Japanese imperial march toward Australia. The American identity as a Pacific power was, in many ways, forged on the beaches of the Pacific during World War II in battles like Guadalcanal and Peleliu that proved fundamental to shaping the future of Asia.[106]

The region is home to a diverse array of states. Papua New Guinea is by far the largest, wealthiest, and most populous Pacific island country, and it is endowed with rich natural resources. Fiji, the region's second-largest state by population, is an important transshipment and economic hub but saw a coup in 2006 and has resisted international pressure to restore democracy. In comparison to these two states, which have roughly five million and one million people respectively, the other states are all substantially smaller—ranging from Vanuatu with some two hundred thousand citizens to Niue with a mere two thousand. All of these states are members of the Pacific Island Forum (PIF), an important regional organization, and many global powers like the United States, Japan, and China are dialogue partners. Australia and New Zealand are full members of the PIF as well as close partners and major donors to most of the region's states. Australia is the region's largest aid donor, with the United States a distant second.[107]

The United States has especially close ties to three of the states in the region—Palau, the Marshall Islands, and Micronesia. These were once US territories and became sovereign states in the 1980s and 1990s. Through the Compact for Free Association, these states voluntarily maintain close ties to the United States, which provides them with over $200 million in annual assistance, access to over forty US federal domestic programs, security and defense assistance, and rights to work and live in the United States. These states, which promise to deny third-country military access, are also important to the US defense posture in Asia. They host the US Army base in Kwajalein Atoll and the Ronald Reagan Ballistic Missile Defense Test Site, and are near the sea-lanes that the United States uses to reinforce its forward presence in Guam and beyond.

In the period ahead, the United States should continue to engage this strategically important region and coordinate its policies with Australia and New Zealand, the largest and fourth-largest donors in the region respectively.[108] Closer economic cooperation with Papua New Guinea and Fiji, in many ways the most influential Pacific island states, will benefit the region as a whole, as will continued encouragement for an eventual return to democracy in Fiji. Many of the region's challenges could be better addressed through more focused and coordinated US assistance with other major countries, especially with regard to climate change mitigation, relief efforts for cyclone- and tsunami-related disasters, and efforts by these islands to monitor their vast maritime domains and control illegal fishing. Therefore continued cooperation with Australia, New Zealand, and France through the Quadrilateral Defense Coordination Group will be essential, especially because the group saves Pacific island states tens of millions of dollars by preventing illegal fishing. In addition, the United States can deepen people-to-people contacts by expanding programs like the Fulbright Program and the Peace Corps. Finally, Pacific island states and the United States together have shared interests in shaping the global agenda on climate change and freedom of navigation, and may be able to better coordinate their positions not only in the Pacific Island Forum but also in larger global forums.

Embracing Economic Statecraft

From the first US trading voyage to Asia of the *Empress of China* in 1784 through to the Open Door Policy of 1899 and now the Trans-Pacific Partnership more than a century later, trade has been a central motivation of American Asia policy. The Pivot to Asia builds on this rich history and is based on the assumption that economics and security are inextricably linked in Asia, and that military might alone is unlikely to be enough to sustain American leadership in this economically dynamic and interdependent region. Economic statecraft should therefore be elevated to the core of US foreign policy in order to both maintain US influence in the region and fuel our domestic economic recovery and prosperity at home. It must also be said that China's largesse in providing infrastructure support and project assistance across the region with very few strings in very short order presents a direct challenge to the United States to deliver in other tangible ways. While the private sector must lead this process, the US government has an important role to play in facilitating closer commercial ties across the Pacific through trade, investment, and other economic agreements.

The Trans-Pacific Partnership and Beyond

The Trans-Pacific Partnership (TPP) is a region-wide economic agreement among a dozen countries. Negotiations were completed in 2015, and its ultimate passage will be a signature achievement of the Obama administration.[109] The TPP's importance is difficult to overstate; it is the true sine qua non of the Pivot. The agreement began with four participating nations and had expanded to twelve by the end of 2013: Australia, Brunei, Canada, Chile, Japan, Malaysia, Mexico, New Zealand, Peru, Singapore, the United States, and Vietnam. Together the members will represent 40 percent of the world's GDP and a third of world trade, and will provide a high-quality twenty-first-century platform for effective economic interaction. The TPP will level the economic playing field for all parties and set the standard for all future trade agreements. It is an ambitious project, aimed at achieving a high benchmark across "the widest range of trade topics that have ever been included in a preferential trade deal."[110]

Indeed, the agreement has become the main vessel for a variety of urgent questions in international trade and—given its sheer size—the agreement's success or failure will leave an indelible mark on the future of the global economy. The TPP is intended to resolve many controversial questions, from the levels of conventional tariffs and quotas to more modern topics involving regulatory harmonization, cross-border Internet communications, rules of origin, disciplines on state-owned enterprises, technical barriers to trade, sanitary and phytosanitary measures, telecommunications, intellectual property rights, customs cooperation, labor standards, and environmental standards, among others.[111] Beyond this, the TPP will provide an enormous common market, with significant benefits and opportunities accruing to workers, businesses, and consumers from all signatory nations—including the United States, which will see its exports rise, its long-term growth prospects improve, and its own economic recovery intensify. The TPP will also be a living agreement, open to updates and expansion as appropriate to best address future trade issues and allow for the induction of new members—including China. Because of this it is important to underscore that membership in the TPP is not invitational but an *aspirational* undertaking at its core because it requires serious and committed domestic reforms in order for states to meet its high standards.

At the same time, as we saw in the previous chapter, the TPP is particularly important because it arrives at a time when the economic rules of Asia are in sore need of updating, with significant consequences for global economic governance. Other trade agreements, such as the China-led RCEP and the long-hoped-for FTAAP, have yet to provide guidance about rules that prepare the world for freer trade in a twenty-first-century economy that is dramatically different from that of the twentieth century. The success of the TPP will ensure that modern, fair, and pro-growth rules are adopted in Asia, which as the cockpit of the global economy is itself a vital battleground in setting the rules of the global economic order. President Obama himself made the stakes clear in his defense of the TPP: "When more than 95 percent of our potential customers live outside our borders, we can't let countries like China write the rules of the global economy. We should write those rules, opening new markets to American products while setting high standards for protecting workers and preserving our environment."[112]

Beyond the TPP's economic implications lie important diplomatic ones that have consequential meaning for the future of US influence in Asia. For example, the TPP will offer Asian trade partners more opportunities for growth and reduce their vulnerability to economic coercion by China or other large economies. In addition, deeper economic ties will also bolster stronger security ties. As Michèle Flournoy and Ely Ratner have explained, security arrangements "are at their strongest and most durable when military cooperation rests on a foundation of shared economic interests."[113] These economic linkages broaden the base of our alliances and partnerships, allowing for greater individual connections, shared understanding, and senior governmental interaction. They also create wealth and interdependence across the region, freeing up additional resources that can be expended on fulfilling security obligations and creating a solid foundation for regional stability.

Perhaps in part because of these diplomatic arguments, the TPP has been seen by some as an American attempt to contain China, especially since the TPP's standards are too high for China to meet at this juncture. This is not at all the case. While it is true that the United States may not endorse some of China's economic practices, the fact is that TPP standards have not been written to deliberately exclude China's participation but rather to promote a set of appropriate, twenty-first-century rules that advance a more level Asia-Pacific commercial playing field. China has already publicly stated that it is considering joining the TPP. For example, senior Chinese officials have fully acknowledged that many of the TPP's high standards are in line with reforms that China itself needs to undertake, and China's trade minister has publicly declared that China will investigate seriously the feasibility of participating.[114] President Xi Jinping even raised the possibility with President Obama at their meeting at Sunnylands.[115] If China were to take the necessary steps to set a course to join the TPP, it would set the tone for a more peaceful and prosperous Asian Century in which major states work in unison and in compliance with agreed-upon rules.

The TPP is a cardinal priority and a cornerstone of the Pivot to Asia. It would benefit the US economy overall and create a long-term trade system in Asia, robust against the threat of protectionism. Beyond these economic benefits, the agreement has significant diplomatic implications and serves as a symbol of America's commitment to and desire for deep and sustained engagement with Asia. The agreement's success in the period ahead will require the focus and concerted efforts of top-level leaders if it is to be successful.

First, the United States needs to pass the TPP, which has yet to be taken up for a straight up-or-down vote in Congress. An important part of this effort and future economic initiatives will be a public education campaign that persuades a skeptical American public increasingly wary of international economic engagement and nervous about Asian economic competition that the region is truly central to America's continued prosperity and job growth. Asia is the world's fastest-growing region, boasts many of the world's largest economies, and features the world's largest middle class, and the TPP harnesses Asian growth to the benefit of everyday Americans by opening up export markets, putting economic competition on an even playing field, and ensuring that Western rules and standards—not those of rivals and competitors—define the future of the global economy. This kind of message requires public and high-level support coming directly from the country's political leadership in both the executive and legislative branches.

Second, if and when the TPP is passed, the United States should work to encourage and assist in China's movement toward the realization of the TPP's lofty entry requirements, with an aim of ultimately welcoming China into the agreement. Because the TPP is aspirational rather than invitational, the United States should make it clear that China's entry will be welcomed as long as it can meet the agreement's standards.

Third, China is not the only major Asian economy that is considering joining the agreement, and the United States would benefit from encouraging other major Asian economies to join as well. Taiwanese president Tsai Ing-wen has stated that "there is an urgent need for Taiwan to participate in the Trans-Pacific Partnership" and noted that she has established a task force to ensure that Taiwan can meet its standards.[116] Similarly, South Korea has also expressed interest in the TPP, with President Park Geun-hye declaring, "I believe Korea is a natural partner for the TPP as well."[117] The United States should encourage both Taiwan and South Korea to take the necessary steps to join the TPP. The Philippines has also expressed interest in joining, and the United States should consider efforts to assist it so that one day it too will be able to meet the agreement's standards.

Other Economic Efforts

The TPP may be one of the most significant American economic endeavors undertaken in Asia, but other initiatives also merit attention. For example, the United States has signed a free trade agreement with Singapore and South

Korea and is currently negotiating a number of other important agreements with Asian states.

First, within the bilateral context, the United States should complete negotiations on a bilateral investment treaty with China, which enjoys the strong backing of American business leaders.[118] In addition, the United States can work to deepen its economic relationship with India. Although the two are currently negotiating a bilateral investment treaty, progress has stalled, and the two states still lack a free trade agreement between them. Negotiating such an agreement would be highly ambitious and complicated, but the rewards in economic bounty and diplomatic comity that could follow justify the investment of serious time and energy. The United States still lacks bilateral investment treaties with a wide range of Asian countries, including Indonesia, a country that would benefit from closer economic ties to the United States. Finally, the Philippines have stated publicly their interest in the TPP or a bilateral FTA with the United States in the event that their joining the TPP is not possible, and the United States can work with the Philippine government to explore both possibilities.

Second, with respect to multilateral economic initiatives, the United States should continue to champion APEC and use the organization to advance practical economic reforms, including by supporting expedited business visas and supporting trade promotion events by expanding the organization to Indian membership. In addition, the United States could lend its support to some kinds of indigenous multilateral agreements. For example, the Trans-ASEAN Gas Pipeline would help get sorely needed energy supplies across the region and to ASEAN states.[119]

Third, the United States now has the unique opportunity to leverage the US energy boom to expand its economic influence in Asia. Although the United States removed a forty-year restriction on the export of crude oil in 2015, licensing barriers for LNG exports can sometimes prove problematic for energy companies. The United States should help address any remaining obstacles in order to facilitate the export of liquefied natural gas and crude oil to Asia. Doing so would enhance the energy security of its Asian allies and partners and send a strong signal of US commitment to the region.

Finally, the United States can encourage forms of economic cooperation to practically reduce the risks of conflict in the region, namely the adoption of joint development areas in circumstances of disputed sovereignty. For example, recent agreements on fisheries between Taiwan and Japan and Taiwan and the Philippines allowed for resource sharing without making concessions on intractable questions of sovereignty. These kinds of agreements could be useful throughout Asia to reduce the risk of conflict, and for that reason the United States should work to encourage their proliferation.

Engaging Regional Institutions

Engaging with the Asia-Pacific's maturing multilateral institutions is an important element of the Pivot to Asia. These bodies, while relatively young, have the potential to help build and reinforce a system of rules and responsibilities in Asia on issues in which the United States has key interests, including free trade, freedom of navigation, regional transparency, and environmental protection, among others.

To fully grasp the promise of Asia's institutional evolution, it can be helpful to first consider the example of Europe. After the Second World War, Europe built institutions that played a remarkable role in sustaining dialogue between former adversaries and building prosperity on the continent. It is often forgotten that it took nearly a generation for what were once relatively "shallow" European institutions to develop into the "thick" and influential organizations they are now. Today Asia is in the early phases of a similar process, and it is home to a large and multiplying number of fledgling institutions. Asia's institutional future lies not in building thick new institutions from scratch, but rather in the gradual evolution of its shallow institutions, which are now beginning to put down roots by acquiring brick-and-mortar headquarters, higher-profile secretariats, permanent staffs, and new responsibilities.

Although the United States has often relied upon the hub-and-spokes system of bilateral alliances and partnerships to secure its objectives, this approach will need to be supplemented by efforts to shape and support the development of Asia's budding multilateral organizations that must increasingly affect US interests in Asia. For this reason, if the United States is to build agreement on common values and advance its interests, its strategy will have to involve engaging regional institutions.

When the United States participates in Asian multilateralism, it creates significant benefits for American Asia policy. Notably, it lends a circadian-like rhythm to regional engagement, creating a predictable timetable of high-level

US visits and a steady churn of lower-level meetings that in turn gives the region confidence in the endurance of the American commitment to Asia. But more fundamentally, engagement offers the United States a seat at the table where Asia's future is discussed, and opportunities to shape the Asian organizations, programs, and policies that will define the twenty-first century.[120]

Committing to Crosscutting Institutions

Of the region's growing number of crosscutting institutions, perhaps the most important is ASEAN. Although some strategic figures in the United States believe that the United States should not position ASEAN at the center of its multilateral diplomacy, the reality is that ASEAN has been empowered by the region's states to play the defining role in Asia's institutional development and evolution. Absent American engagement, the countries of ASEAN will be left to deal with the region's major powers on their own, which would threaten the institution's effectiveness and jeopardize the interests of ASEAN's ten member states across a variety of domains ranging from freedom of navigation to trade. A crucial goal for ASEAN states is to use the institution to engage and socialize a rising and increasingly dominant China into the region's norms. To assist in this effort and build a more integrative institution, ASEAN has welcomed American involvement, as well as the participation of Asia-Pacific powers spanning from India to Australia and Japan. This inclusiveness serves to help build an organization that could represent all of Asia and avoid regional balkanization.

Despite ASEAN's centrality, the organization has been neglected during previous periods of American statecraft toward Asia. Secretary Rice famously missed two meetings of the ASEAN Regional Forum, President Bush missed the US-ASEAN Summit in 2007, and the United States refrained from joining the ASEAN Treaty of Amity and Cooperation (TAC) for fear it would constrain US action on Burma. The Bush administration was skeptical of ASEAN while retaining a preference for bilateralism, and the administration's decisions prompted many in the region to doubt the seriousness of US commitments to regional diplomacy.[121] And even before this, American diplomats were skeptical about the usefulness and worried about the perceived frivolity of groupings like the ASEAN Regional Forum, with its penchant for after-dinner staff-led performances.

The initial years of the Pivot, in contrast, saw a restoration of US focus on and attention toward ASEAN. Secretaries of State Clinton and Kerry made attendance at regional meetings a priority.[122] The United States dispatched an ambassador to ASEAN, created a representative office at the ASEAN headquarters in Jakarta, signed the TAC, joined the ASEAN Defense Ministers Meeting, and secured funds for strengthening ASEAN's secretariat.[123] This kind of steady engagement culminated in 2011 in the United States' joining the East Asia Summit (EAS)—one of the region's premier annual gatherings of heads of state. This was an important step, in part because China had originally conceived of the organization without the United States as an active member. Nevertheless, after joining, the United States was able to use this organization and several others in Asia to shape the consensus surrounding political and strategic issues, including reforms in Burma, disputes in the South and East China Seas, and tensions on the Korean peninsula.[124] Most notably, it was at the 2010 ASEAN Regional Forum that Secretary Clinton announced that the US had a "national interest" in the peaceful resolution of disputes in the South China Sea, welcomed a multilateral solution, and would be willing to support multilateral talks.[125] Although the complex web of Southeast Asian institutions can at times be frustrating given their slow pace and emphasis on consensus—often termed the "ASEAN Way"—there is little question that they promote regional cooperation on vital issues and require American focus and attention.

First, engaging ASEAN is no longer a matter of choice, and under succeeding administrations the United States should continue to support ASEAN's various institutional cousins and spinoffs by being present. At a minimum this will mean sending top-level officials, including the secretaries of state and defense, to its far-flung meetings. The United States can also broaden its ASEAN engagement by encouraging high-level meetings on a wider array of issues that would involve other US cabinet members, such as the secretaries of energy, agriculture, and commerce. A failure to be present at important meetings will raise concerns about the American commitment to Asia and allow others to set the agenda, sometimes to the detriment of the United States. When President Obama missed an important ASEAN meeting in 2013 because of domestic wrangling over the debt ceiling, China used the opportunity to push its own plans for economic investment in Asia.[126] Over the long run, sustained American involvement in these important multilateral institutions is vital to achieving broad-based action on key issues throughout the region. It is important to remember that the critical advantage the United States enjoys in Asia is a collective desire, among Asians and Americans both, for an enduring American role in the region. As such, Asians are inclined to overlook short-term setbacks in favor of a long-term historic trend that points the US squarely in the direction of the Asia-Pacific century. To paraphrase Woody Allen, in our Asian diplomacy, 80 percent of success is simply showing up.

Second, the search for leadership and consensus with ASEAN brings both vulnerabilities and opportunities for the United States that call for a concerted US strategy for effective engagement of the organization. Progress on US policy interests will at times require developing closer bilateral ties with individual ASEAN states in order to create alignments within the institution on some of the more contentious and divisive matters facing the region. In addition, the United States should support the construction of a broader and more diversified ASEAN architecture that better integrates continental Asian states like Cambodia and Laos on the north-south axis and also includes states like India and Australia on the east-west axis.

Third, looking past ASEAN for a moment, the United States can diversify its institutional connections in Asia by working to build stronger relationships with Asia's other nascent organizations. For example, in September 2014, the United States joined the Singapore-based Regional Cooperation Agreement on Combating Piracy and Armed Robbery against Ships in Asia, known as ReCAAP.[127] Not only has ReCAAP been successful in reducing piracy in the waters around Asia, it has also formed linkages between countries based on its transparency and information-sharing abilities that have brought the region together against a cause that involves all countries.

Fourth, across the wider Indo-Pacific, the United States should also consider greater participation in a variety of regional bodies in South Asia and the Indian Ocean as well as the South Pacific. The United States could deepen its involvement with the South Asian Association for Regional Cooperation (SAARC)—where it is currently an observer—as well as the Indian Ocean Rim Association (IORA) and the Indian Ocean Naval Symposium (IONS). The Indian Ocean is a region of growing importance and its nascent organizations may prove influential platforms in establishing rules on issues ranging from piracy to military exercises and transit. With respect to the

Pacific, the United States would benefit from continuing high-level participation in Pacific organizations like Pacific Island Forum meetings, which Secretary Clinton visited in 2012.

Finally, as Asian organizations proliferate and multiply, the United States should as a matter of policy declare its determination to retain a seat at the table in those organizations and multilateral bodies that discuss Asia's future. If consequential discussions on economic, political, or security issues are taking place, the United States has an important interest in being involved, and ought to oppose the elevation or creation of organizations that deliberately exclude or do not invite the United States. Within this context Washington will need to continue stressing that transpacific institutions that include the United States should play the leading role in the period ahead, in part because they are better able to address the complexity and transnational nature of Asian challenges than organizations focused exclusively on Asian membership.

A Rules-Based Institutional Order

In addition to increasing US participation in Asia's multilateral forums, Washington will need to support the development of a rules-based regional institutional order in Asia if it is to bolster the operating system that has maintained Asian peace and prosperity.

First, the United States can support the principle of peaceful resolution of international disputes by continuing to publicly support and encourage efforts to use international law and arbitration to address sovereignty disputes, especially in the South China Sea. The Philippines has taken its competing claims with China to the International Tribunal for the Law of the Sea.[128] Washington can remain neutral on the underlying disputes while building an international consensus and calling on all states in Asia to publicly support this mechanism, since the tribunal represents a test of whether the region is prepared to manage its disputes through legal and peaceful means. Relatedly, and as discussed in greater detail in the previous section, the United States can support its interests in Asian trade that conforms to twenty-first-century principles by pushing for trade agreements like the TPP, as well as bilateral investment treaties, bilateral FTAs, tax treaties, and a variety of other instruments to ensure Asian trade conforms to twenty-first-century principles.

Second, the United States will need to pay close attention to the institutional efforts of other states, which in some cases may be detrimental to the goal of bolstering rules-based order in Asia. For example, China has sought to advance forums that do not include the United States, including the East Asian Summit years ago and the Conference on Interaction and Confidence-Building Measures in Asia (CICA) more recently. Establishing a rules-based order will at times require engaging with, rather than avoiding, the new programs and institutions that China has decided to create. Not all Chinese-initiated institutions should be seen as threatening. Indeed, it is preferable that China be bound by predictable rules and norms even if those are not US-initiated. This being the case, it was misguided for the United States to decline participation in Asia Infrastructure and Investment Bank (AIIB), especially when many of its allies and partners around the world joined it, because it deprived Washington of the opportunity to shape the organization from within. Now the United States will need to rely on its friends and partners that are bank members to ensure that the bank operates as a true multilateral institution rather than as an instrument of economic statecraft.

When organizations arise that can threaten twenty-first-century values or that exclude the United States, one way of responding is to strengthen alternative organizations. For example, it is in US interests to ensure that AIIB is not the only institution through which Asian states can receive infrastructure assistance, and to that end Washington should bolster USAID's focus on Asia, redouble its commitment to the Millennium Development Fund, and more closely support the Asian Development Bank, the World Bank, and the ASEAN Infrastructure Fund. It would be a shame if AIIB, for all its promise, lent money without taking into account good governance and sustainable development, or if it disbursed funds solely for parochial political reasons. By providing well-funded alternatives, the United States can give the region more choices.

Finally, it is long overdue for the United States to fully commit to a rules-based system by ratifying the UN Convention on the Law of the Sea (UNCLOS). This treaty defines the rights and responsibilities of countries with regard to the planet's oceans. To date 166 countries are party to the convention, including the majority of Asian states, among them China, Japan, and South Korea. The fact that the United States has not yet ratified it is therefore an anomaly that dampens our credibility in addressing maritime disputes with China in the East and South China Seas. As Ziad Haider has accurately stated, for the United States to be able to "call for a much needed rules-based approach to these disputes, it must formally adopt the rules."[129]

Ratification of UNCLOS has widespread support from the American government and business sectors. In June 2012 the Senate Foreign Relations Committee heard testimony from a twenty-four-star panel made up of four admirals and two generals, all of whom urged ratification of the treaty. That same month the US Chamber of Commerce and several major companies petitioned the Senate to sign the treaty to strengthen the American economy and create more jobs. So far opposition to UNCLOS has largely come from some congressional elements who have steadfastly refused to support the ratification, arguing it would negatively impinge on American sovereignty.[130] These arguments are specious, especially because since the formation of UNCLOS in 1982, the United States has already largely adhered to the agreement, even recognizing it as a codification of customary international law. In contrast, American membership will strengthen UNCLOS as an international norm while simultaneously improving the position of the United States to call for other states to adhere to its criteria. It will ensure that the United States can ground discourse over these disputes in international law rather than historical grievance. Supporting a legal framework, one that provides for a peaceful and rules-based solution to territorial disputes, could help reduce tensions in the long run.

Increasingly, a successful American foreign policy requires more than just dropping by for meetings and wearing garish shirts for the photo opportunity (a famous ASEAN tradition). Engagement in Asia requires greater dexterity across a number of fronts: diplomatic, political, economic, and security. There is a profound need to integrate every element of American power and to deal with matters with nuance and subtlety. In that effort the United States should highlight the emerging importance of international norms, laws, and institutions. Such a plan of action in the multilateral realm will reap diplomatic and political benefits for the United States across the region.

Diversifying Military Forces

One of the most important components of the Pivot to Asia is the creation of a geographically dispersed, technologically advanced military that undertakes a variety of missions including deterrence, disaster relief, and military diplomacy. Indeed, for the last several decades, robust US military capabilities have provided peace and security in Asia as well as a foundation for American global leadership. What is often underappreciated, however, is that American military power is not effortlessly maintained; rather it is mostly the product of constant and unyielding investments of time, attention, and resources; the steady cultivation of allies; the management of competitors; and perhaps most importantly, periodic doses of innovation. From World War II through the Cold War and into the war on terror, the United States has evinced an ability to adapt to changing strategic circumstances. Now, with the dramatic growth in China's military capabilities and the conclusion of grinding US wars in Iraq and Afghanistan, the United States once again faces a moment that beckons for a reassessment of US military strategy.

The United States has deployed eighty thousand US troops in the Asia-Pacific, concentrated mostly in Japan and South Korea with a small number in Australia and Guam.[131] It fields some of the most advanced weapons in existence, including the world's most sophisticated nuclear-powered submarines, fifth-generation fighters, and aircraft carriers. The US military has been a critical component of the "long peace" in Asia that has kept the region prosperous and secure.

Increasingly, however, the United States confronts growing challenges from new military technologies that complicate US power projection and must reckon with four treacherous paths to great-power conflict: the Korean Peninsula, the Taiwan Strait, the East China Sea, and the South China Sea. At the same time, US budget politics and Middle East engagements have complicated efforts to reimagine the tenets of US military strategy in Asia in ways suitable to addressing these new realities. If the United States is to perform its traditional post–World War II role in Asia, keep credible its alliance commitments, sustain Asia's operating system, and maintain the Pivot to Asia, it will need to reconceptualize and subtly shift its security strategy going forward.

There are several tenets of such a shift. As we have already discussed, the United States will need closer military ties with allies and with China. And as we will see in the next chapter, it must also overcome domestic challenges to consistent and flexible defense funding. In this section we will focus more narrowly on three specific military reforms: (1) diversifying focus and force posture to the south, (2) diversifying capabilities to cope with anti-access technologies, and (3) bolstering presence through HADR and military diplomacy.

Diversification in Strategic Focus: Southbound and Down

The legacy of the Cold War left the United States defense presence over-weighted in Northeast Asia in order to deal with threats posed by both the Soviet Union and North Korea. Today, while maintaining a robust military presence in the northeast, it is strategically necessary and long overdue for the United States to carefully rebalance and diversify its military posture southward to Southeast Asia and the Indian Ocean, a region beset by natural disasters but blessed with the world's most important commercial sea-lanes. To that end the United States will need new operational concepts that link the Indian Ocean to the Pacific, as well as strategies and training regimes that reflect Asia's new strategic geography.

The United States has taken tentative steps in that direction by basing marines in Darwin, Australia, and placing littoral combat ships in Singapore and P-8 Poseidon surveillance aircraft at Clark Air Base in the Philippines. Of course, US force posture need not consist only of permanent bases; access and status of forces agreements can also be useful in diversifying military posture to low-cost, small-footprint facilities while providing the United States the ability to respond nimbly to faraway regional crises. The Enhanced Defense Cooperation Agreement with the Philippines is one such example.

There are several benefits to diversifying US forces southward. First, although US military bases in Northeast Asia form the backbone of Washington's ability to project power, they are increasingly vulnerable to disabling missile attacks. The United States has its greatest concentration of troops and bases in Japan, but China's vast arsenal of short-range ballistic missiles (SLBMs) can increasingly put these at risk. Air-launched cruise missiles can strike bases as far away as Guam, crippling runways, destroying fuel facilities, and disabling aircraft on the tarmac. Disbursing US assets across a number of bases in different countries would not solve this problem entirely, but it would mitigate some of the danger posed by keeping US forces consolidated in a few locations. Importantly, it would also permit the United States to respond to crises in the South China Sea or the Straits of Malacca with greater ease.

Second, US bases in Northeast Asia are far from the increasing security challenges in Southeast Asia and the Indian Ocean, among them greater demands for humanitarian assistance and disaster relief as well as threats from piracy. Diversifying American force posture to the south will permit both prompt and comprehensive responses to the region's various crises while building deeper reservoirs of goodwill. The size and scope of US response to the 2004 Indian Ocean tsunami and to 2013's Typhoon Haiyan were praised throughout the region and contrasted favorably with China's relative inaction.

Third, a strengthened US presence in Southeast Asia will afford more opportunities to pursue military diplomacy with regional partners located in the arc that stretches from India to Vietnam. These militaries are eager for opportunities to train, exercise, and interact with the US military. In addition, US port calls and other visible demonstrations of presence can have a reassuring and positive effect on ties with the states of this region.

Finally, by diversifying its military forces throughout the region, the United States can create a more politically sustainable force posture. There is perhaps nothing so difficult as stationing one's military forces on the sovereign, democratic soil of another country. US bases in Northeast Asia, such as Garrison Okinawa and Yongsan Garrison, have at times been targets of protest over the actions of US personnel or the nuisance of US aircraft and helicopters. By diversifying its forces further south, including through an increased presence in Australia and possibly a return to the Philippines, the United States can reduce the risk that the sometimes volatile domestic politics of its partners will jeopardize the United States' forward-deployed presence.

Diversification in Military Capabilities: Maintaining Access

The technological edge the United States has for decades enjoyed over competitors and adversaries is not a given but instead the product of calculated investments in new capabilities and fresh strategic thinking.[132] Precision strike capabilities, which the United States developed in the 1970s and 1980s and which were wielded so spectacularly against Iraq in the First Gulf War, have proliferated throughout the world, often to competitors who wish to thwart US power projection. This is a critical trend that, until recently, has received insufficient top-level attention. As Deputy Secretary Robert Work notes, "While the United States fought two lengthy wars, the rest of the world did not sit idly by. They saw what our advantages were back in 1991's Desert

Storm, they studied them, and they set about devising ways to compete."[133] These capabilities, especially China's conventionally armed long-range anti-ship cruise and ballistic missiles, threaten the US Navy and its aircraft carriers, as well as runways and overseas bases in Korea, Japan, and even Guam. In so doing they directly undermine the backbone of American power projection capabilities, complicating the ability of the United States to operate in hot spots such as the East and South China Seas, the Taiwan Strait, and the Korean Peninsula. In addition to more conventional threats, advances in electronic, cyber, and space technologies can be used to undermine the software and information systems that support US warfighting.

To cope with this changing state of affairs, the United States must invest in new capabilities that can operate effectively in an increasingly contested Asian environment. Specifically, it will need longer-range assets that can be fielded from outside the "threat rings" created by an adversary's cruise and ballistic missiles, as well as underwater assets that can more safely operate within them. These assets would include a next-generation long-range bomber, long-range unmanned carrier-based strike aircraft, unmanned underwater vehicles (UUVs), guided missile submarines (SSGNs) and *Virginia*-class attack submarines with mission-enhancing payload modules, advanced mines, and high-speed strike weapons, among others.[134] While a focus on long-range and underwater platforms alleviates some of the threat posed by A2/AD technologies, the United States should not neglect passive defenses, including the dispersion of assets across multiple bases (as discussed in the previous section) and hardened facilities for aircraft and key infrastructure. In addition, continued investments in missile defense can provide some protection from precision strike capabilities. Finally, the United States should continue investing in a resilient cyberinfrastructure and should monitor and harness emerging technologies in hypersonics, electromagnetics, and directed energy.[135]

Many elements of the strategy outlined above have been adopted by the Pentagon, which has pursued a "third offset" program intended to maintain America's edge in military technology against emerging threats. The ultimate success of this effort will depend on an ability to surmount vested interests, confront bureaucratic obstacles, secure a consistent funding stream, and think creatively about the future.

Success will also require innovation in doctrine, as well as operational and tactical concepts. The Pentagon is already considering a variety of new operating concepts for maintaining access in the face of increasingly advanced denial technologies, including AirSea Battle and the more recent Joint Concept for Access and Maneuver in the Global Commons. Debates about the content and appropriateness of these various approaches will continue, but what remains clear is that they will need to emphasize "jointness" among the military services as well as coalition operations with allies. In that regard it may be useful for the United States to think more systematically not only about interoperability with US allies but also about interoperability between them. Relatedly, because US allies will be vulnerable to A2/AD technologies but crucial to US defense efforts, the United States will need to persuade them to set aside funds for costly but essential investments in their own defense capabilities. These should be capabilities that complement, rather than duplicate, US investments. This will likely prove especially challenging. Military mind-sets in Asia and even in the United States tend to be more traditional while the pace of military innovation and change remains transformational—a mismatch that will prove dangerous if it is not addressed.

In addition to modernizing its military forces, the United States will need to readjust its force posture now that ground wars in the Middle East and South Asia are winding down. Specifically it will need to shift its focus more toward expeditionary air and naval capabilities and somewhat away from ground forces. While ground forces will be useful on the Korean Peninsula, they are less relevant in other Asian contingencies, including the maritime threats in the East and South China Seas and in the Taiwan Strait. In addition, those drafting new operational concepts for conflict in the Pacific should continue to look for ways to incorporate land power, such as through army-operated antiship missile batteries and air-defense batteries.[136]

Finally, in addition to shifting resources among the services, the United States must also continue plans to shift resources across theaters. The navy is departing from its equal split between the Atlantic and Pacific Oceans and rebalancing 60 percent of its fleet toward the Pacific. Similarly, 60 percent of the air force's overseas-based services as well as a majority of its space and cybercapabilities will be allocated to the Asia-Pacific.[137] Although these efforts may come under pressure in the future, especially if conflicts in Europe and the Middle East intensify, they should continue in order to bring US force posture in line with the long-term strategic requirements of the twenty-first century.

Bolstering Presence: HADR and Military Diplomacy

From the dispatch of Teddy Roosevelt's "Great White Fleet" to the launch of Operation Unified Assistance following the 2004 Indian Ocean tsunami, demonstrations of presence—especially through HADR and military diplomacy—have been traditional missions for US forces in Asia. These missions reassure Asian states, signal the endurance of US commitments to the region, bolster partner capacity, and help save the thousands of lives endangered by the region's frequent natural disasters. One challenge to America's future force posture will be that many of the underwater and long-range capabilities ideally suited for a world where access is more difficult will be less effective for these kinds of tasks. As the United States modernizes its forces to prepare for these emerging conventional threats, it should also take care to retain and build upon capabilities that are useful for more traditional missions that demonstrate presence.

To date, US HADR capabilities in Asia are unmatched. The United States played a central role in most of the region's disasters, including the 2004 Indian Ocean tsunami, the 2011 tsunami and nuclear crisis in Japan, and Typhoon Haiyan, which struck the Philippines in 2013. Asia remains, however, the most crisis-prone region in the world. Its states sit astride overlapping tectonic plates (known as the "ring of fire") that cause earthquakes and tsunamis; additionally, the region is increasingly threatened by climate change because its dense populations are located near flood zones.[138] For these reasons the United States will need to strengthen its HADR capabilities within the region, which in turn requires fielding a consistent regional military presence that can respond flexibly and promptly when disaster strikes. To that end the United States needs more access agreements throughout the region so that it can better surge assistance into disaster zones. It should also have certain assets forward-deployed in the region at all times, and especially during typhoon seasons, such as hospital ships.[139] Similarly, pre-positioning supplies such as bottled water and medical equipment in disaster-prone regions will help expedite a US or local response. Finally, because successful HADR operations require close cooperation with regional governments and militaries, the United States should hold larger and more regular HADR exercises with regional countries. Some of these might be coordinated through regional multilateral organizations, such as ASEAN's first-ever multilateral HADR exercise in 2013. These exercises can facilitate the smoother integration of certain US capabilities that partners may lack with those capabilities that partner militaries already have. In these efforts the United States should also encourage more substantive participation from its allies and close partners, such as Japan, South Korea, Australia, India, and others, which will not only strengthen US alliances and the ties between allies but also broaden and multilateralize HADR operations throughout the wider region. While some of these states have worked with the United States before in HADR operations, much can still be done to harmonize resources, share information, time operations, and coordinate with civilian relief agencies.[140]

The United States should also strengthen military diplomacy within the region. Over the last several years, there has been a growing demand signal from countries in the region for greater opportunities to train, exercise, and interact with the US military for a broad range of potential missions. The United States should increase sponsorship of educational and professional exchanges, host or join more multilateral military exercises, disburse used equipment, and encourage joint planning and increased military aid. Relatedly, the United States should continue to engage in regular demonstrations of presence, such as port calls. Although some may see port calls of allied or partner ports as antiquated in an era when weaponry can reach out beyond the horizon, these simple operations can reassure allies, deter adversaries, and serve useful diplomatic and people-to-people purposes.

Promoting Democratic Values

From early attempts to build constitutional government in the Philippines to recent support for democracy in Burma, support for democracy has long been a core objective of US strategy in Asia, and it is one that has been reaffirmed by the Pivot to Asia. As we saw in the previous chapter, Asia is at a crossroads on the question of democratic governance, with so many of its states now in a transitional phase and making the consequential decision to move closer to or away from democracy. If those states are successful in their democratic transitions, then Asia could truly become a democratic pillar. This could have a transformative effect on the world's most dynamic region, providing support for a rules-based order, lubricating economic cooperation, fostering peace and stability, and enabling the construction of integrative international institutions.

The United States has long had an interest in supporting Asian states in their transition to democracy, but not all Asian governments agree it should pursue this goal. Lee Kuan Yew, former prime minister of Singapore, once argued that Asian values were different from liberal values and admonished the United States for trying to "foist [democracy] indiscriminately on societies in which it will not work."[141] While prudence and flexibility are always important in promoting liberal values, the simple fact is that democracy can no longer be seen as purely a Western system. Thriving democracies currently exist in India, Japan, Mongolia, South Korea, and Taiwan, while several other regional states like Indonesia and more recently Burma are working toward their own democratic consolidations. An important challenge for US policy will be to carefully and subtly encourage transitional states—often with proud postcolonial histories—down the path toward fuller democracy.

Assisting Transitional States

A hallmark of the Pivot to Asia has been reasonable success in transforming Burma from an unrepentant autocracy to a transitional state. The government has taken remarkable steps by releasing prisoners, implementing economic reforms, and tolerating greater press freedoms and the right to assembly, and it even held elections in 2015. Although problems remain, especially horrible violence against the country's Rohingya community, Burma's progress suggests the benefits of engagement over a policy of sometimes unproductive isolation.

Indeed, when one looks at the history of democracy in Asia, it becomes clear that engagement has often led to reform, and that the United States has historically used its military, economic, and diplomatic ties with allies and partners to encourage progress. For example, the United States leaned on South Korea, Taiwan, and the Philippines at critical and decisive moments, pushing them to soften or abandon repressive structures. Today a similar effort must be made with Thailand, a US ally that has strayed from the democratic path following a prolonged coup and drifted closer to China. Isolating Thailand internationally is not the solution and will only drive it further into China's arms; rather, as it has with so many of its allies and partners, the United States should encourage and induce reform through a mixture of stern counsel and carefully applied pressure.

As discussed in the previous chapter, Asia is home to relatively few entrenched autocracies, a good many robust democracies, and several transitional states that could yet emerge as successful democracies in their own right. Several of Asia's states are in the midst of political transition, drifting toward democracy or in isolated cases away from it, including Bangladesh, Burma, Cambodia, Malaysia, Singapore, and Thailand. By building partnerships and intense bilateral relationships with these states, the United States will have the ability to promote democratic values through a mixture of people-to-people ties, economic exchange, military diplomacy, and subtle arm-twisting.

Of course the promotion of democracy in these transitional countries cannot be one-sided and unilateral. The United States should make its views on human rights clear, but it should avoid isolating societies or attempting to transform them through force or coercion. These efforts often push states toward less values-driven powers and can also provoke backlash that can tarnish liberal values and harm American interests. For the most sensitive and challenging cases, the best approach is to focus on issues that matter most to people in the region no matter who is in power, such as education, poverty alleviation, and natural-disaster response—all of which can lay the foundation for both development and democracy—while keeping the lines of communication open between officials in both countries. This being the case, American policy must be flexible if it to be successful. In addition, it should also be long term, especially because distractions from Asian affairs can allow hard-fought gains to evaporate.

Challenges Old and New

Aside from Asia's transitional states, the region is also home to several entrenched autocracies. While the potential for long-term change is much more limited in these challenging cases, there is some cause for optimism. The budding security and economic relationship between Washington and Hanoi offers the United States a unique opportunity to persuade the country's leadership to consider a less autocratic and repressive course, and US officials often make clear that we could have a much closer strategic relationship with Vietnam if it were to undertake certain liberalizing steps domestically. In contrast, the United States lacks close ties to North Korea and Laos, which frustrates any democratic agenda.

With regard to China, prospects for progress are dim but hardly hopeless. Although prognostications that a democratic China is just around the corner have been disproven time and time again, the simple fact remains that China faces a unique challenge—its party requires growth to stay in power, and yet growth in turn requires education, innovation, and the creation of a middle class, factors that in the long run create demands for greater political expression. China's own sensitivity about its international image as well as its increasing prosperity together offer the possibility of modest successes on human rights and other matters.

Across the region, one of the most important and yet still poorly understood issues on which American policymakers will need to work is Internet freedom. Under Secretary Clinton, who gave a much-needed speech on Internet freedom in 2010, the United States made access to the global Internet a major policy priority.[142] While the United States may have been the birthplace of the Internet, Asia is its future. As we saw in chapter two, Asia's Internet population is already the world's largest, exceeding the combined Internet population of Europe and the Americas. Although there is a growing international consensus among Asian democracies on the importance of free speech and religion, the Internet is a relatively fresh phenomenon that confounds governments and to which access is not yet viewed as a universal right. For this reason Internet freedom is not an issue simply for autocracies like China but also one for democracies, such as India and Indonesia, that place occasional restrictions on Internet access. More ominously, excitement over the democratic potential of the Internet and social media has given way to some degree of apprehension as autocracies, notably China, use aggregation and big data to create Orwellian systems for monitoring their populace's every online—and offline—action.[143] As Asia's governments grapple with how to regulate and police the Internet, the United States has a unique role to play in beginning a conversation on Internet freedom, enshrining the norm that Internet access is an important and fundamental right, and helping other states manage the unique challenges it poses.

Strengthening People-to-People Ties

The preceding sections have discussed economic, diplomatic, military, and other instruments of statecraft that are fundamental to US efforts in Asia. The unique value-add of people-to-people ties to this mix, however, is that they can effectively humanize these sometimes abstract and impersonal pillars of American engagement. In that process, people-to-people exercises can break down barriers of misperception, create enduring personal connections, and build a wealth of area-specific expertise that can have profound consequences for US engagement in Asia. Importantly, people-to-people ties are a societal project, one that is most effective when it touches on social sectors as diverse as academia, science, arts and culture, sports, civil society, business, and professional groups. This in turn calls for an approach that is diversified and broad-based, one grounded in the simple notion that specialists in horticulture or civil engineering or basketball from vastly different cultural and professional backgrounds can teach each other important lessons.

The United States has a variety of people-to-people programs in place. Prominent examples include the Fulbright Program and the Peace Corps, but countless others have been implemented through the State Department's Bureau of Educational and Cultural Affairs as well as other agencies. Outside of government, nonprofit organizations like the Institute of International Education and the American Bar Association, among others, play important roles in building bridges across borders. Crucially, and outside these often programmatic and institutionalized approaches to building people-to-people ties, Asian American diaspora connections have organic and influential roles in building bridges between the United States and Asia that have not received sufficient policy focus.

In the period ahead, the United States needs to fundamentally elevate people-to-people ties in its statecraft and view them as critical elements of an integrated Asia-Pacific strategy.

First, the United States should increase the Asia-Pacific focus of its educational programs. Educational programs are unique because they target youth whose views about one another are as yet unformed and still rather malleable. A quintessential example of a successful effort to boost student exchanges is the 100,000 Strong Initiative launched by President Obama and Secretary Clinton in 2009. This initiative was intended to increase the number of Americans studying in China to 100,000 in five years, and succeeded in meeting that goal.[144] Similar efforts with other Asian countries could help round out US people-to-people diplomacy in the region. In addition, efforts modeled after this one would have clear metrics and benchmarks for progress, thereby providing continued momentum to bilateral ties. Existing programs that are already well regarded, especially the Fulbright Program and the Peace Corps, would benefit from expansion.

Second, an important part of people-to-people ties involves not only sending US citizens abroad but also actively working to increase the number of foreign citizens choosing to come to the United States. The difficulty of these efforts is perhaps best illustrated by Japan's dramatic withdrawal from study-abroad programs in the United States. In the mid-1990s Japan was the leading source of foreign students in the United States; today it is closer to eighth or ninth. This is a decline owing as much to a surge in foreign students from other countries as it is to a stunning decline in the absolute number of Japanese visiting the United States, which has dropped by half in roughly ten years.[145] What Japan's example suggests is that people-to-people ties require active efforts to attract visitors from other countries as well as efforts to send Americans abroad, and careful attention must be paid to trying to balance these relationships when possible. To that end the United States should establish more high-level people-to-people consultations with Asian states similar to the one it holds annually with China.

Third, unofficial people-to-people ties are likely to be an important part of US engagement with Asian states, especially through what some now term "diaspora diplomacy." Asian Americans are the fastest growing demographic in the United States as well as one of the wealthiest and most influential, and they now make up 6 percent of the population.[146] Asian Americans are finding success in politics, film, business, science, and countless other fields. Thriving Asian diaspora communities maintain their own version of people-to-people ties with family members in Asia that can provide ballast and domestic support for US Asia policy. For instance, Indian Americans played an important role in organizing an event at Madison Square Garden in 2014 for newly elected Indian prime minister Narendra Modi, drawing the attendance of several US senators and congressmen.[147] As Asian Americans grow in number and influence, the United States would benefit from facilitating and supporting these organic people-to-people ties. Asian diaspora communities have been ambassadors between the United States and the countries of the region for decades, facilitating commercial, cultural, and other linkages, but they have generally not received official attention commensurate with their importance and growing significance. That alone could encourage closer US people-to-people ties with Asians and produce new opportunities for supporting diaspora communities. In addition, the US government would benefit from incorporating diaspora communities into policies to develop people-to-people ties, and in so doing, can act to strengthen the natural links between American diversity and the country's Asian interests.

Involving European Partners

Writing on American engagement in Asia, Philip Zelikow remarked that one striking aspect has been "its growing loneliness." While external powers were once major players in Asia, in "a strategic sense, they are now mostly gone."[148] The United States should encourage its Western allies, especially those in Europe, to work with it more closely to secure Asian and broadly shared objectives. Indeed, nearly every consequential diplomatic endeavor undertaken by the United States on the global stage has been a joint venture with allies in Europe, and the Pivot should be no different.

Those who criticize the Pivot as an unwarranted diminution of US focus on European affairs often fail to realize that it is meant to be a Pivot to Asia with Europe, not a Pivot to Asia from Europe. Indeed, the only countries pivoting faster to Asia than the United States are found in Europe. While European nations share many American values and hold similar interests in Asia's future, the transatlantic partnership has not yet evolved to a point of routine coordination on efforts to achieve these common objectives. A closer US-European partnership on Asian affairs would provide a wider range of tools and resources that are often complementary. For example, while the United States can provide security in ways that exceed the capacities of Europe, Europe has the economic range and institutional experience to support large-scale development goals and multilateral forums that promote the rule of law. Through a combination of hard and soft power, a greater transatlantic partnership focused on Asia has an opportunity to achieve security and prosperity throughout the Asia Pacific region.[149]

First, coordination with Europe can prove beneficial on historical US objectives in Asia. The United States has long-standing interests in promoting Asian trade, and it can work with European states on encouraging higher standards through consultation and coordination on their respective trade agreements with Asian states. Similarly, transatlantic cooperation on issues in global economic governance will be important as emerging Asian economies become stakeholders in existing economic architecture. The United States has also had an enduring interest in promoting democracy in Asia, and can harness European support for human rights and the rule of law through shared approaches to transitional states and by undertaking joint programs, such as monitoring efforts, training activities, and legal exchanges. Coordinating US and European approaches in promoting liberal values is especially useful because it elevates what might otherwise appear to be ideological American criticisms to appeals to widely held international values.

Second, as Asia struggles to craft nascent institutions, the United States should pull Europe into the process when possible. Given Europe's unique experience in crafting institutional architecture that can bring historical enemies together in the spirit of cooperation, its states may be able to play an important role in helping build and institutionalize these Asian multilateral organizations. The European Union is a member of the ASEAN Regional Forum, established the Asia-Europe Meeting (ASEM), and has joined the Korean Peninsula Energy Development Organization (KEDO), but many additional organizations could benefit from European involvement.

Third, the United States and Europe can also work together on creating and bolstering norms governing the global commons. For example, shared support for freedom of navigation, especially given the disputes in the South and East China Seas, is essential and can send a powerful signal to China that objection to its policies in these waters is grounded in international principles and not great-power politics. In addition, transatlantic cooperation can help ensure that sound international norms and principles are put in place to manage emerging challenges in the global commons, especially related to cyber and space.

Fourth, with regard to security, the United States and Europe should pursue close partnerships with Asian states. This may in part require changes to NATO's bureaucratic structure, for example the opening of liaison offices in Asian capitals and the creation of an Office of Asian Affairs in the International Staff. In addition, NATO could cooperate with Asian partners on maritime security and missile defense and open NATO schools to Asian officers.[150]

Finally, as tightened budgets clash with growing responsibilities, transatlantic cooperation offers opportunities for integration, complementarity, and occasional burden sharing—allowing both the United States and Europe to do more at a time of resource strain. Europe's assistance budgets are substantial, and greater coordination with the United States in regional aid efforts is well warranted. The United States' Pivot to Asia cannot and should not be a solitary effort, and Europe can make important contributions in pursuit of shared interests and objectives to the benefit of Americans, Europeans, and Asians alike.

Conclusion

From the Open Door Policy of the late nineteenth century through to contemporary efforts to sustain Asia's operating system, the United States has long played an important and indispensable role in maintaining peace and prosperity across the Asia-Pacific. Today Asia's future is at a moment of transition that beckons for American engagement, attention, and strategic consideration. To that end this chapter discussed ten elements that should form the core components of a comprehensive and integrated strategy for the early years of the Asian Century. They are (1) clarifying the Pivot, (2) strengthening US alliances, (3) setting the contours for China's rise, (4) building new partnerships, (5) embracing economic statecraft, (6) joining regional institutions, (7) bolstering US forces, (8) promoting democratic values, (9) strengthening people-to-people ties, and (10) engaging European partners. This broad-based "plan for the Pivot" will be essential to American efforts to bend the arc of Asia's future toward peace and prosperity.

If this plan is to succeed, the United States will need to overcome serious domestic and foreign challenges to the Pivot's future. On the home front, the United States faces a fractured foreign policy consensus, a dysfunctional government, and public support for retrenchment rather than international engagement. At the same time, the United States has invested inadequately in long-term planning, human capital development, and military modernization. On the international stage, the looming risk of crisis in the Middle

East could pull scarce top-level attention away from Asia at a time when Asian states themselves appear to be increasingly frustrated with American hesitance and inattention. If these challenges to the Pivot go unaddressed, the Asian Century could slip beyond the influence of US policy. We turn now to consider these risks to the Pivot's promise.

CHAPTER SEVEN

Risks to the Pivot's Promise

Challenges to America's Asia Strategy

Although the chief elements and philosophy animating the Pivot have garnered broad support across Asia—and perhaps as importantly, across parts of the political aisle in the United States as well—the enterprise nevertheless faces sizable obstacles in both implementation and execution. Many of these are domestic, related to a fracturing foreign policy consensus, political gridlock, strained defense budgets, public fatigue, and bureaucratic difficulties in long-term planning and human capital investment and cultivation. Others are international, such as the lingering crises of the Middle East that draw attention away from the Pivot, as well as the growing risk that US absence, missteps, or hesitancy in Asia could irreparably diminish American credibility within the region.

The Pivot's success demands that the United States raise its game to confront and overcome most or all of these domestic and international difficulties. Amid shifting and increasingly complex regional dynamics in Asia, America will also have to learn to operate with greater nuance and subtlety (not always watchwords of US diplomacy). To the doubters of US fortitude, the United States has time and again across decades and crises too numerous to count risen to cope with new challenges, exhibiting a capacity for resilience and reinvention that has laid low those who bet against it. With focused political leadership committed to a well-conceived Asia policy, the United States can prevail over these obstacles and succeed in this critical Asian gambit. We turn now to consider each of the challenges to the Pivot respectively, with the belief that the first step in surmounting these obstacles lies in identifying and understanding them.

Fracturing Foreign Policy Consensus

For decades a bipartisan majority consensus in the United States has undergirded American activism on the international stage. That consensus was born during the early years of the Cold War, when Senator Arthur Vandenberg declared famously that "politics stops at the water's edge."[1] His memorable maxim was guided by the belief that during that time of grave international danger, American politicians could ill afford to play politics with the country's international interests and security. Respect for a degree of unity in foreign relations mostly held throughout the early Cold War period as politicians tried to put domestic differences aside on matters of international policy, affording the United States enough cohesion to confront the threat of nuclear-armed Communism with a degree of purpose and determination. The eventual overextension of American power in Vietnam, however, and the national trauma that accompanied it, fractured this unity and led to divisive disputes between Republicans and Democrats—and indeed to divisions within the two parties themselves. A new, albeit weaker, consensus reemerged between centrist Democrats and a solid Republican flank, thereby reestablishing a somewhat unstable majority in support of American internationalism. As a result the ensuing decades saw general support convened around a few central foreign policy tenets, including robust defense spending for a forward-deployed strategy, support for strong security ties with key international partners, and the active maintenance of an open trading system. Global prosperity and a strong American purpose abroad owe an enormous debt to this uneasy but still persistent coalition.

Today, however, that once-fragile bipartisan consensus has fractured. For one thing, the Cold War's conclusion deprived the United States of an overriding foreign adversary that had concentrated the minds of American politicians and strategists as well as focusing the efforts of the American military. Then the bitter, recriminatory politics and controversy of the ill-fated Iraq War weakened further what consensus had emerged after the devastating September 11 attacks.

These ideological divisions have hobbled bipartisan responses to Iraq, Afghanistan, Libya, Syria, the broader war on terror, and the recent return of conflict and tension in Europe. But it is not just the growing gap between the two parties that threatens the ability of the United States to face challenges on the international stage. As the divides between the Democratic and Republican parties have widened, so too have the divides within them.

The Democrats have a longer history of intraparty debates on international relations, many of which continue to this day, and broadly take place between the pragmatist and the idealist wings of the party.[2] The former include "globalists," who believe in the power of economic and technological globalization as well as international institutions, and "Truman Democrats" who support these same institutions but stress the importance of military power and US moral leadership in international politics. In contrast, what might be termed the "idealist" wing of the Democratic Party includes "come home Americans," who are distrustful of international trade and military intervention, and "American skeptics," who are suspicious of the application of US power and are concerned about how American intervention can affect local conditions. In broad terms, then, Democrats have long been divided between one wing that supports a muscular American role in international affairs and another that feels the United States should be less interventionist and engage more gingerly using nonmilitary means.[3]

The pragmatist wing favoring an engaged US policy was once able to align with a more unified Republican Party on foreign policy, but today the Republicans themselves are increasingly divided, with several forces pushing the party to fundamentally rethink its traditional commitment to internationalism. These forces include the return of nativist isolationism, the reemergence of fiscal conservatism, and the rise of the Tea Party.[4] Some figures, including Rand Paul (R-KY) and Mike Lee (R-UT), represent libertarian strains of conservatism that call for the United States to return to a more isolationist international position. They seem to hark back to the Republican Party's skepticism of internationalism in the 1930s, when the aftermath of World War I and the malaise of the Great Depression gave rise to "America first" senators like Gerald Nye and Robert A. Taft. Amid this isolationist resurgence, a growing number of fiscal conservatives have turned an increasingly skeptical eye toward the defense budget, slashing it and capping its growth through the 2011 Budget Control Act and subsequent sequester.

Those doubtful of a split in Republican attitudes to foreign policy often point out that libertarians have not performed well in Republican elections and that foreign policy remains a top concern for GOP voters. That may be, but a nativist and populist skepticism of international engagement and of global institutions has since jumped the loose boundaries of the libertarian wing and become much more mainstream within the Republican Party. Indeed, these views have been adopted by even nonlibertarian politicians, including Donald Trump, who during the 2016 GOP primaries routinely inveighed against US alliances and trade agreements and even welcomed a Russian presence in Syria, and Senator Ted Cruz (R-TX), who proclaimed support for an "America first" foreign policy.[5] This lies in stark contrast to the more activist position of the once-dominant neoconservative wing and the party's historically robust support for free trade. Even if the high tide of Republican skepticism and isolationism begins to recede, what remains clear is that the internationalist consensus of the Republican Party has now fractured and can no longer be taken for granted. Even internationalist members of the Republican Party can find themselves criticized by an increasingly restive base for cooperating with Democrats on matters of foreign policy. With both parties and also the electorate now starkly divided, the foreign policy consensus is under profound duress.

Despite these strains, Asia policy remains an area of surprising consensus that is far less partisan than policy for other regions, such as the Middle East. This is in part because a smaller cohort of people is involved in Asian affairs, and the fundamental issues at stake—strong alliances, free trade, and a forward-deployed presence—are supported by internationalists in both the Democratic and Republican Parties. Even the historic US opening to China in the Nixon and Carter administrations involved key players in both the Republican and Democratic parties. In contrast, there is scarce middle ground or consensus over Middle East policy on issues ranging from Syria to the Iran nuclear agreement to Afghanistan.

Deadlock and Dysfunction

With threats and challenges multiplying across the globe, but disagreement and division festering at home, the United States is now struggling to field an effective government that can fulfill even basic functions, such as passing a budget or remaining open for business. The growing stridency and partisanship of American politics is leading to acute political polarization and dysfunction. Congress today is more polarized than at any time in recent decades. In the 1980s, 80 percent of the members of the House of

Representatives could be found in the political middle—that is, between the most liberal Republican and most conservative Democrat. Today it is less than 1 percent.[6] Commentators in the *New York Times* wryly remarked that the only silver lining to these dark clouds is that "it is mathematically impossible for Congress to get much more polarized."[7] This desertion of the political center is not only an elite phenomenon but also a popular one, and it is increasingly widespread within the electorate.[8]

Partisan gridlock at first blush may not seem to have much of an effect on foreign policy, where the president often has a degree of autonomy from congressional strictures. As the late James Q. Wilson argued, however, political polarization "encourages our enemies, disheartens our allies, and saps our resolve."[9] American dysfunction—including the resulting budget deadlocks and policy stagnation—siphons top-level attention away from foreign policy, raises concerns about US staying power, and prevents the United States from effectively adapting to shifting global circumstances.

Domestic deadlock has already had repercussions for US standing in Asia. In 2011 congressional wrangling over the debt ceiling reached dangerous heights when Republicans demanded large budget concessions in exchange for a debt ceiling increase. Absent such an increase, the United States would not be able to pay its bills and would—for the first time in history—default on its debt. Since US treasuries and the dollar are at the heart of the global financial system, a default would not only seriously tarnish the full faith and credit of the United States but also open up the possibility of a serious global economic crisis as investors grew to doubt the value of US debt. That one side in the United States was willing to risk deep self-inflicted wounds by playing politics with US credit and the health of the global economy was mystifying to most international audiences. Traveling to Hong Kong with Secretary Clinton in 2011 at the height of the crisis, I argued that the classic American speech—one that emphasized economic reforms and market opening—was not what Asian leaders wanted to hear. For them the unrecognizable dysfunction in Washington was more pressing and concerning than the bilateral economic agenda. They needed reassurance that the United States would not ruin itself and the global financial system it had helped build over generations by defaulting. Secretary Clinton's speech skillfully acknowledged these concerns. "As I have traveled around the region, a lot of people have asked me about how the United States is going to resolve our debt ceiling challenge," she stated. "Let me assure you we understand the stakes. We know how important this is for us and how important it is for you."[10] Secretary Clinton also made clear that the United States role in Asia would endure. Together these reassurances helped placate Asian anxieties, but the fact that they needed to be made at all led to ripples of anxiety and concern that even today continue to buffet Asia's shores.

The haunting image of a superpower threatening to grievously injure itself in a fit of partisan dysfunction would remain difficult to shake, not least because two years later another debt crisis occurred. This time it forced President Obama to cancel a long-planned trip to the region, including his attendance at two important Asian summits, so that he could attend to the political situation at home. The president's trip had been planned as a demonstration of American leadership in the region and its cancellation constituted a considerable setback, again fueling a sense of concern and unease on the part of regional leaders. While missing a meeting or two may seem a relatively minor slight, one of the most underestimated aspects of foreign policy in Asia is the so-called Woody Allen rule for effective stewardship—that is, the simple importance of "showing up," which we discuss in greater detail in the following chapter. Asian interlocutors keep careful track of when and where American presidents visit as a proxy measure of US commitment, and the fact that many presidents throughout recent US history have canceled trips to the region because of pressing domestic concerns is not lost on Asian audiences. China, in particular, benefited from and reveled in President Obama's absence, using the East Asia Summit to push forward its alternative to the TPP, the Regional Comprehensive Economic Partnership (RCEP).[11] Its actions demonstrated clearly that other countries are poised to fill a potential leadership vacuum, and not in ways favorable to the United States, should Washington fail to fulfill its traditional role. This is the definition of a self-inflicted diplomatic wound.

The perception that the United States cannot get its own house in order on basic priorities raises concurrent doubts about US staying power in Asia. Overcoming the problems associated with internal political strife will depend in the short term upon the firm and steady resolve of American officials to commit to foreign policy priorities. It will also require routinely underscoring our firm and unwavering commitment to the Asia-Pacific region through both words and deeds. Above all, some reconstituted elements of an alignment between internationalist Democrats and Republicans will be paramount to maintaining an active and successful foreign policy. To this end a concerted effort to rediscover some common ground on foreign policy between and within the two political parties may be one of the most important ingredients for building a successful and lasting policy toward the Asia-Pacific region.

Inadequate Defense Spending

Over the last five years, defense spending has seen significant cuts. The origin of these cuts is a story of political failure rather than one of considered national security prioritization. When Republicans and Democrats were unable to reach an agreement to raise the debt ceiling in 2011, putting the country at risk of defaulting on its debt, both sides agreed to cap defense and nondefense spending and then to create a congressional supercommittee to negotiate the next round of cuts. To incentivize each side to find an agreement, they created an enforcement mechanism believed to be unpalatable to all sides—automatic cuts to defense and nondefense spending (i.e., the sequester) that would begin in 2013 if no agreement was reached. The defense cuts were not policy but meant as a price for failure, one that was thought high enough to persuade Republicans to compromise. With the rise of the Tea Party, isolationists, and fiscal conservatives, the supposedly unpalatable defense cuts were swallowed at the expense of US national security.

The sequester of defense spending began in 2013 and almost immediately spurred vocal objections from top officials. Former secretary of defense Chuck Hagel used his first major policy address to warn against the nearly $1 trillion in coming cuts, and Secretary of Defense Ash Carter declared to Congress that the cuts would make the United States "less secure."[12] Deputy Secretary of Defense Bob Work called sequestration "an utterly stupid and irresponsible way to cut budgets" because it required all line items to be cut equally without discrimination.[13] Although a 2015 agreement spares the Defense Department from much of the sequester's impact for the next two years, that relief is temporary, and the prospect of more automatic cuts still looms on the horizon, complicating long-term planning. Even after this reprieve from cuts, defense spending still sits at roughly $100 billion below what it was at the height of the wars in Iraq and Afghanistan and, as a percentage of the federal budget, remains at a near-historic low.[14]

This top-down budget austerity has been met with bottom-up cost pressures, as rapidly expanding personnel costs, excess base infrastructure, and administrative bloat siphon funds that might otherwise flow to defense modernization. The fact that much of the defense budget consists of inflexible accounts sometimes held captive by bureaucratic or external interests amplifies the problem by limiting the scope for reprioritization. At times this can result in needlessly cutting important capabilities that lack sufficient political support.

The challenges posed by falling defense budgets, rising personnel costs, and inflexible defense accounts are serious, especially since *now* is the time for the US military to engage in fresh thinking about the future. As Secretary Carter notes, "After years of war, which required the deferral of longer-term modernization investments," we need "renewed emphasis on preparing for future threats, especially threats that challenge our military's power projection capabilities."[15] This effort is complicated by the fact that the defense budget is used as a football in budget politics and that planners have no sense of the shape of tomorrow's funding environment. It is especially difficult without some kind of bipartisan political consensus on the importance of reform, especially since a refocus in strategic priorities is likely to incur opposition from several groups.

One particular reprioritization that is long overdue and also particularly likely to garner opposition is a renaissance for maritime strategy and procurement. Over the last fifteen years of war in the Middle East and South Asia, the United States has invested disproportionately in ground forces and special operations; now the maintenance of US commitments in the Asia-Pacific will call for greater reinvestment in air and naval power projection capabilities, similar to the maritime strategy implemented by Secretary of the Navy John Lehman in the 1980s. This refocus on the maritime theater and on power projection capabilities will be both costly and politically challenging, especially if bases must be closed, funding redirected, and coveted platforms shuttered. Indeed, the return of conflict in Europe and the possibility of another land war in the Middle East may put pressure on maritime strategy, which has at times been shortchanged by interservice rivalry. During the Truman administration, for example, the carrier aviation capabilities that now form the backbone of US power projection were almost destroyed by an army and air force push for resources at a time of postwar budget rationing.[16]

Similarly, with the proliferation of anti-access/area-denial technologies around the world, the United States will have to think anew about how to maintain access in contested environments, which will require serious changes in force structure and posture. As the previous chapter made clear, investments in long-range and undersea assets will be useful but costly, both politically and economically.

The success or failure of necessary reforms and restructuring bears directly on the credibility of US alliance commitments in Asia and is therefore critical to the Pivot's eventual success, with many analysts arguing that defense cuts and a failure to reprioritize defense spending will have "a particularly negative impact on America's ability to stabilize and influence Asia."[17] Likewise, allies in the region frequently (although most often in private) express deep concerns about the knock-on effects of these trends on the US military presence in Asia, particularly in the context of large and growing defense budgets in China and elsewhere.

These concerns are not without merit. Nevertheless, with continued vision and leadership, the military elements of the Pivot can and should continue. In fact, this is precisely the direction the White House and Pentagon are pursuing in concert today, with the support of key senators and House members, including John McCain and Randy Forbes, among others.

A few key facts should be kept in mind as skeptics question America's ability to continue serving as a force for peace and stability in Asia. When adjusted for inflation and shown in real dollar amounts, the US defense budget will remain higher than at any point during the Cold War, even under the largest estimates of possible reductions.[18] Similarly, the US defense budget continues to dwarf those of its allies and potential adversaries. Admittedly, overall levels of defense spending can be deceiving, as the United States must maintain a global defense posture, in contrast to countries in Asia that concentrate their forces in the region. In addition, US defense budgets often appear inflated relative to those of other countries because of the higher cost of labor and employee benefits in the United States. That being said, as Chuck Hagel reiterated at the Shangri-La Dialogue in May 2014, the United States remains "committed to ensuring that any reductions in US defense spending do not come—*do not come*—at the expense of America's commitments in the Asia-Pacific."[19] The Defense Department is making good on this promise. The navy and air force are both on schedule to fulfill commitments to increase the percentage of their forces in the Asia-Pacific to 60 percent by 2020, and PACOM is regaining units and equipment returning from Afghanistan.

US forces in Asia will also be receiving the best and latest equipment, including the F-35 Joint Strike Fighter. More advanced US air defense and missile defense combatants, as well as improved radar capabilities, are also entering the region. The new P-8 maritime patrol aircraft will first deploy in the Pacific, as will new longer-range missiles. In addition, high-altitude long endurance (HALE) UAVs such as the Global Hawk and Triton will be operated by the United States and key allies including Japan and Australia. This hardware will be supplemented by novel approaches to maintaining and enhancing the US military's forward presence, including the employment of more rotational forces and more frequent demonstrations of American power.[20] Not to be underestimated, the Pivot is further supplementing American military might by strengthening US alliances, building capacity among US partners, and increasing the pace of US multilateral exercises in Asia. Finally, in addition to improving its hardware, the United States is designing new plans and strategies to respond to emergent challenges at both ends of the escalatory spectrum, including China's anti-access capabilities and its aggressive use of paramilitary forces below the military threshold in territorial disputes, as well as piracy on the high seas and humanitarian crises.

Of course, perceptions of American decline and concerns about US staying power are real, and the strategic challenges in Asia will not soon abate. This only underscores the need for the United States to keep top-level focus on the maintenance of security capabilities in Asia. Ending sequestration and reorienting the US military budget remain an important task for America's current and future leaders.

Retrenchment in the United States

Any effort to marshal the political will and resources necessary to execute a successful pivot to Asia will also have to contend with a growing sense of exhaustion among the American people. The pressure to "come home" is motivated by a general sense of discomfort and anxiety triggered not by Asian developments but in large part by disappointment in the Middle East. More than a decade of war, expensive in terms of both blood and treasure, has produced little tangible progress. A low point for many Americans came in 2015 when ISIS forces took Ramadi, a city Americans had fought hard to pacify during the 2007 troop surge and Sunni Awakening, revealing the Sisyphean quality of American efforts in the region. The seeming absence of progress in Iraq and Afghanistan, combined with the trauma of the financial crisis, have eroded the postwar consensus for international engagement. A recent Pew Research poll found that a majority of Americans—more than at any other time in the survey's fifty-year history—favored pulling back in order to "let other countries get along the best they can on their own."[21] President Obama reflected these sentiments when he announced in 2011 that it was "time to focus on nation building at home."[22]

Although these views animate much of contemporary public opinion on foreign policy, the rise of ISIS and a wave of terrorist attacks in Europe and the United States have contorted them in certain respects. While the American people seem to generally favor withdrawal and retrenchment, in select cases they want to lash out at enemies in the Middle East with indiscriminate and punishing attacks and air strikes. The desire to bomb groups in Iraq or Syria, however, does not translate into a larger policy of engagement and internationalism and is of limited relevance to Asia policy. With some exceptions, the shadow of retrenchment still lingers over the American consciousness.

The prevailing frustration with international engagement is rooted in the legacies of the past. In the wake of every modern conflict, the American public has consistently called upon politicians and officials to return their focus to domestic issues. As Stephen Sestanovich has written, the oscillation between periods of maximalist foreign policy and periods of retrenchment is clear throughout much of American history. A sharp crisis—such as North Korea's attack on the South in 1950 or the September 11 attacks in 2001—has often precipitated maximalist responses and overcommitment. "When the maximalist [president] overreaches," he argues, "the retrencher comes in to pick up the pieces. Then when retrenchment fails to rebuild American power, meet new challenges, or compete effectively, the maximalist reappears, ready with ambitious formulas for doing so."[23] The past fifteen years of unrelenting conflict in the Middle East and South Asia constitute a maximalist period, one that has once again triggered an instinctive insularity in the American people, leading to calls for foreign policy retrenchment.

At the same time, Americans are increasingly skeptical of global economic engagement. The overhang from the financial crisis has led a sizable number of Americans to lose confidence in the link between globalization and domestic growth and employment. Fears are mounting that deeper engagement with the global economy and with Asia in particular could bring fierce competition that would threaten US jobs, leading some Americans to oppose the TPP and other trade agreements.

It is no surprise that Americans appear overwhelmed by the complexity of challenges and disorder in the international system. Another foe now rises in Iraq to threaten a third Gulf War in as many decades, Syria is ever deeply mired in chaos and civil war, and in the West, Russia is assuming an increasingly antagonistic stance toward the United States. Unfortunately, the list goes on. Nevertheless, as the title of Robert Kagan's thoughtful essay in the *New Republic* states, "superpowers don't get to retire."[24] With global order seemingly deteriorating, the United States can ill afford to withdraw from the world. It is the maintenance of that global order that has allowed the United States and American ideals to prosper and flourish for the last seventy years.

In this environment, building public support for Asia policy will be a complicated task. Even though the present malaise originates in Middle East disappointment and domestic economic anxieties, it nonetheless affects foreign policy more or less indiscriminately. Although internationalist and strong-defense strains still exist in US politics, there are subtle—and not so subtle—signs in Congress that the United States may be entering a new era in which US engagement in Asia will be a tougher sell. Together these public and political constraints will only make a hard job even harder: when it comes to Asia, the to-do list is long. The Pivot therefore faces a challenge of determination and resolve, as well as questions on the quality and comprehensiveness of its implementation.

The case for refocused attention faces another unique challenge: it does not come in the context of a clear and present threat to American interests. The history of American engagement with the world has frequently been driven by direct challenges to America's security or way of life, be they from fascism, totalitarianism, Communism, or Islamic extremism. These adversarial forces created a prevalent view in Washington and among the

American people that the world could be split between those who were with us and those who were against us.[25] Based on clear goals and objectives, US foreign policy was relatively easy to understand and support.

This type of stark worldview does not apply to modern Asia (although aspects of China's rise in power and recent muscle flexing are subjects of mounting concern). For that reason the Pivot is predicated not on a reaction to a clear-cut and unambiguous threat, but more on the recognition that the Asia-Pacific will become an increasingly key driver of global politics and economics in the twenty-first century.[26] Among other things, this will call for a more complex strategic approach in which, for instance, competitors will have to be engaged and allies sometimes coaxed.

Absent a clear spur to action, and an articulated strategy to back it up, it will be difficult to rouse a conflict-weary country tired of ambiguous results and fearful of economic competition to take the steps necessary to Pivot to Asia. Nevertheless, a compelling narrative is readily available: Asia is the world's fastest-growing region, boasts the world's largest middle class, and is home to many allies and countries favorable to US involvement. Deeper economic engagement with Asia will not lead to job losses but will instead boost American exports and increase American wages by leveling the playing field with competitors—as a 2016 report on the TPP by the Peterson Institute makes clear.[27] In sum, US prosperity is linked more to Asia than to any other region, and its bounty and dynamism should be harnessed to power American revitalization and restoration.[28]

More needs to be done to communicate these benefits directly to the American people. While President Obama has given two major speeches describing and explaining the Pivot, both have been in Asia and designed for Asian consumption. A speech aimed at the domestic audience underscoring our overall approach is probably much needed if not long overdue. Although Presidents Bush and Obama have given such speeches on Middle East policy, nothing comparable has been done on Asia policy. Moreover, the case for Asia need not be made exclusively at the federal level, especially since local and state officials are some of the first to see the direct benefits of the Asia opportunity through people-to-people exchanges, commerce, or exports.

Americans may be far more receptive to such arguments than some skeptics fear. Even in a climate where Americans remain wary of foreign involvements, roughly 60 percent of the country supports the Pivot to Asia.[29]

Support in the abstract for the Pivot does not mean that Americans fully grasp the costs, benefits, and trade-offs of a more robust Asia policy, but it does suggest that there is room for persuasion. It is now time for American leaders—including the president, cabinet secretaries, and congressional leaders—to make the pitch.

Continuing Challenges in the Middle East

The unrelenting and often unrewarding foreign policy crises of the Middle East present a challenge to US policy in Asia. The brutal conflict in Syria has claimed nearly 250,000 lives and displaced eleven million people while evolving into a larger war involving regional and global powers, such as the United States, France, and Russia. ISIS, which now controls a state that stretches from Iraq into Syria, has launched terrorist attacks in France, bombed a civilian Russian jetliner, and inspired radicals abroad while subjecting the population under its control to medieval barbarisms. Egypt, the most populous Arab state, is now under military dictatorship after a brief flirtation with democracy. Afghanistan and Libya are still racked by instability. Meanwhile, Saudi Arabia and other Gulf states have cut off ties to Iran.

These crises all demand enormous, ongoing attention, siphoning away resources and scarce top-level attention from other diplomatic efforts. Even as the Obama administration has sought to turn its attention elsewhere, the Middle East continues drawing the United States back in, leading some commentators to suggest cheekily that the real Obama Pivot is one *back* to the Middle East.[30] Unfortunately, such a refocus is not at all unprecedented. The specter of conflict in this challenging region has haunted the foreign policies of the last several administrations. Nowhere is this clearer than in the tragic reality that, for the past twenty-five years, every US president from George H. W. Bush to Barack Obama has gone on national television to announce that the United States would commence military operations in Iraq.[31]

Continuing and deep US involvement in the Middle East is virtually assured in the years ahead, which raises questions about whether the United States will have the bandwidth to successfully rebalance toward Asia. The answer is complicated. Although foreign policy priorities are not strictly zero-sum games, there is unquestionably some tension between US policy in these two regions. During the Bush administration, top-level officials including Secretary of State Condoleezza Rice felt "ridiculous heading to Southeast

Asia while trying to negotiate an end to war in the Middle East," and diplomats throughout the region saw clearly how US inattentiveness contrasted
unfavorably with Chinese activism.[32] US foreign policy is out of balance,
and policymakers have a tendency to elevate the intransigent problems of the
Middle East over the more patient game of strategy that awaits us in Asia.
All too often policymakers make the imprudent and sometimes dangerous
choice to take Asia's peace and prosperity for granted, overlooking the fact
that Asia offers four treacherous paths to great-power war: the Korean Peninsula, the Taiwan Strait, and the South and East China Seas. What is needed
is a nuanced and steady refocus in US attention eastward. It should take
place gradually, over many years, as the US government expands its understanding of US interests to include both the peril and promise of Asia, and
resolves, as best it can, to present challenges in the Middle East.

Restructuring US foreign policy to give more attention to Asia does not
entail an abrupt departure from the Middle East. In fact there are more syn-
ergies between a sustained US role in the Middle East and the Pivot to Asia
than immediately meet the eye.

First, as Asian states rise in wealth and influence, they have the capability
to assist in other parts of the world. The Pivot is therefore not simply a rebalance of American resources toward Asia, but also an effort to build greater
cooperation with an ascending region that is critical to addressing challenges including climate change, nuclear proliferation—and, yes, instability
in the Middle East and South Asia. Encouraged by the United States over
the last decade, Asian states have quietly and gradually joined the United
States to become substantial stakeholders in these two troublesome regions.
Asia consumes some thirty million barrels of oil every day, more than twice
the amount of the European Union, and an overwhelming share of those
imports will come from the Middle East. Regional leaders understand that
a hasty US retreat from the Middle East would carry with it unacceptable
risks to their countries' energy security and economic growth. For these reasons Asian countries have begun to develop "out of area" perspectives, looking beyond their immediate backyard for the first time to regions critical to
global stability. Australia, Indonesia, Japan, Malaysia, New Zealand, South
Korea, and Thailand have all contributed combinations of diplomatic, economic, and in some cases even military support in the Middle East. They
have funded schools and civil society, trained judges and doctors, and spon-

sored new programs in agriculture and education. China has become a major regional investor, a contributor to antipiracy operations, and an active participant in the behind-the-scenes diplomatic initiatives aimed at constraining Iran's nuclear ambitions and at securing an Afghan peace. These efforts by Asian states have not been risk-free and are sometimes unpopular on Asian home fronts—even more so if they were perceived to have ended badly. And yet Asian nations have continued investing substantial political capital, financial support, and military forces in the region—they see enduring linkages between policy in Asia and the complex realities of the Middle East.

Second, the linkages between commitments made in different regions apply not only to resource flows but also to perceptions of American credibility. Indeed, a fundamental reality well appreciated by both Middle Eastern and Asian interlocutors, but sometimes ill understood by critics of the Pivot, is that credibility has transference qualities across regions. A failure of the United States to stand by its commitments in the Middle East can ripple dangerously into Asian or Eastern European politics, raising questions about the credibility of American obligations to its treaty allies or to principles such as freedom of navigation. Similarly, US hesitancy or absence in Asia can influence perceptions of American power and prestige in the Middle East, inducing partners in the region to set out on more independent and perhaps destabilizing foreign and security policies. The Pivot is not an abrogation of US responsibilities in one region in favor of their maintenance in another, but rather a call to ensure that Asia—a region that has often been a secondary theater—is afforded the resources and attention needed to maintain the credibility of US commitments worldwide.

The Pivot does not demand a dramatic reduction in American attention to the Middle East but a gradual rebalancing of our foreign policy priorities to take seriously Asia's challenges and opportunities. In essence, global demands—in several regions—for engaged and creative American diplomacy are growing, not declining. As a consequence the United States can ill afford to fundamentally retire or withdraw from one region in favor of another. At the same time, it cannot allow the problems and paradoxes of one region to override fundamental strategic questions in other vital regions. Put simply, no part of the Pivot to Asia calls upon the United States to forfeit its role as a global power; on the contrary, it calls upon the United States to more faithfully embrace that role in a balanced and sustained way.

Longer-Term Planning

David Shambaugh writes that the history of US diplomacy in Asia has often been "highly episodic, sometimes neglectful, and not always deeply engaged."[33] The Pivot's success rests partly on whether the United States can extricate itself from this unfortunate historical pattern, which will require not only a sustained US commitment to the region, but also a change in mind-set and culture in Washington. Specifically, a successful policy in Asia will call for making long-term, strategic planning a more central feature in the formulation of US foreign policy. Asia in particular is in need of such an approach, with long-standing shifts in the region's balance of power, economic relationships, and military technologies carrying serious implications for the region's prosperity and the American position there. In short, the endurance of US influence calls for a policy that anticipates and adapts to these and other changing circumstances.

There have been times when such foresight proved advantageous. In the period between the First and Second World Wars, the United States Army and Navy developed a series of plans known as War Plan Orange for a possible conflict with Japan, and these efforts partly anticipated the island-hopping campaign eventually used when conflict later erupted in the Pacific.[34] In the 1950s, Dwight Eisenhower launched Project Solarium—one of the most distinctive strategic planning exercises ever undertaken in the United States government—with the aim of crafting an elite consensus from divergent views on Soviet policy. It pulled together experts from inside and outside the government and forced policymakers to think through their assumptions about long-term US objectives, the various drivers of Soviet policy, and the implications of different policy options on US interests and global stability—concluding ultimately in the drafting of the Basic National Security Policy (NSC 162/2). More recently, as the Cold War came to a close, Joseph Nye led a strategic review of US policy in the Asia-Pacific that culminated in the Nye Initiative, which thought ahead to the maintenance of the US-Japan alliance, the rise of China, and North Korea's nuclear weapons program. As these examples suggest, the United States has a proud—though inconsistent—history of long-term strategic planning.

In contrast to that earlier era, the present inability of the US government to focus on long-term policy is troubling and detrimental to US interests. Writing in 2006, Michèle Flournoy and Shawn Brimley noted that for "a country that continues to enjoy an unrivaled global position, it is both remarkable and disturbing that the United States has no truly effective strategic planning process."[35] Even the onset of the global war on terrorism failed to produce a cohesive grand strategy that would coordinate and guide America's military, economic, and diplomatic instruments in pursuit of US objectives and interests. For the most part, the years following the Cold War have seen a US policy that is reactive rather than affirmative and ad hoc instead of systematic.

American difficulties with long-term planning stem in part from the Cold War's conclusion, which marked the end of a grand strategy that had generally united American political parties on foreign policy and helped define the country's objectives and place in the world for nearly half a century. In most cases long-term planning in the US foreign policy apparatus is too detached from both policymaking and resource allocation, and most agencies struggle to develop their own strategies. The State Department's policy planning staff (S/P), for instance, is not well integrated into the decision-making loop of the wider State Department, with a separation existing between policy planning thinkers and policymaking doers.[36] Dennis Ross, a storied diplomat and former S/P director, noted that the office is treated by others in the building "as if you are an organ transplant and they are there to reject you."[37] The Defense Department faces similar challenges in thinking about the long term, and these are amplified by the reality that investments in future military capabilities often require both considerable funds, support from the services, and firm congressional backing. With respect to long-term economic policy, the US government struggles to integrate economics and strategy into economic statecraft—partly because economic issues are spread among so many different US agencies. Formulating a national grand strategy through a complicated interagency process, especially when individual agencies struggle to produce their own parochial strategies, is like trying to assemble a jigsaw puzzle with incomplete or missing pieces.

To these serious challenges must be added the tendency to favor short-term perspectives and results over broad vision and long-term strategy—a characteristic of government endeavors in the twenty-first century. This is in part the result of a political system where twenty-four-hour news cycles and long campaign windows have engendered a feeling of constant electioneering and the need for achieving immediate gains rather than making longer-term investments. In this environment the long-term agenda of policymakers has been defined as anything longer than a week.[38] As former national security advisor Thomas Donilon noted, "in every Administration, one of the great challenges in the implementation and execution of foreign policy is to prevent daily challenges and cascading crises from crowding out the development of broader strategies in pursuit of long-term interests."[39] These difficulties are then complicated by the rise in partisan polarization, uncertain budgets (especially for the Defense Department), and the increasing complexity of an international arena in which nonstate actors, cyberterrorism, autonomous technologies, economic interdependence, and a host of other unanticipated and ill-understood challenges proliferate.

Long-term planning is a difficult task and one not very well practiced in Washington. In its absence the United States has defaulted to a "short-termism" that is reactive and ill suited for adapting to the future or shaping global trends. The announcement of the Pivot to Asia united many across the foreign policy apparatus in a recognition that Asia needs to be elevated in the counsels of American foreign policy and requires a rebalancing of long-term economic, military, and diplomatic initiatives. The next stage will require Washington to fully embrace a long-term strategy for Asia, perhaps through a twenty-first-century Project Solarium for the region that creates high-level consensus on the changing strategic landscape. Only with some measure of high-level consensus will the United States be able to formulate a plan that is integrated across diplomatic, economic, and military instruments of policy in service of considered long-term US objectives in this rising region.

Developing Human Capital

The importance and abstraction of foreign policy can sometimes overshadow the fact that, beneath the rhetoric and strategizing, all policy is fundamentally conceived of and implemented by people. Their initiative, experience, and talents are vital—and sometimes decisive—ingredients in the success of US efforts. It is therefore all the more troubling that the United States currently faces a shortage of the necessary human capital with which to successfully lead a sustained and nuanced Pivot to Asia. After more than a decade of war and counterinsurgency in the Middle East and Southeast Asia, the United

States has trained and promoted an entire generation of soldiers, diplomats, and intelligence specialists fluent in the arcana of sectarian rivalry, tribal affiliations, and post-conflict reconstruction strategies. So far Washington has not made any comparable effort to develop a significant cadre of Asian experts across the US government. Indeed, this generation has produced famous and accomplished leaders—such as Generals Schwarzkopf, Petraeus, McCrystal, and Allen—who cut their teeth on Middle Eastern conflicts. However, it has yet to produce comparable military leaders who evoke the legacy of Asianists like Admiral Chester Nimitz and General MacArthur. On the contrary, a surprising number of senior government officials—including cabinet officials—make their first official visits to the region only once they have reached high-level positions near the end of their careers.

This lack of human capital with firsthand knowledge of Asia is a clear and genuine weakness in the US foreign policy establishment. Even the most accomplished public servant will find it difficult to navigate Asia's complexities without prior experience in the region. The complex legacy of history, the challenges of cultural differences, and the intricacy of the region's internal politics all conspire to make short work of diplomatic novices less familiar with Asia. In addition, Asian interlocutors are finely attuned to false steps and mistakes by the United States. For instance, the failure of President Obama to follow through on his redline commitment to respond to Syria's use of chemical weapons continues to reverberate through Asian policy councils. In order to build stronger political, diplomatic, economic, and military bridges across the Pacific, we must be able to talk to one another, understand each other, and work together. The need for such knowledge and expertise is urgent—and growing.

The Pivot to Asia will therefore have to include attention to personnel budgets in civilian government agencies—as well as at the Pentagon—as the United States invests more in ensuring that US diplomats, aid workers, trade negotiators, and intelligence professionals have the necessary language skills and exposure to Asia they need to do their jobs well. Arguably, changes in personnel policy have already been an important part of the Pivot. The State Department, for example, created seventy new positions for specialists on East Asia and the Pacific.[40] Other agencies, as well as the military services, are likewise investing in a cadre of Asia experts for the twenty-first century.

An important part of human capital development takes place outside the government, and well before its employees even enter government service. Today's students are tomorrow's doctors, lawyers, businessmen—and, yes, even diplomats. Educational initiatives that embed Americans within the languages and cultures of Asia are vital to preparing the United States for the Asian Century. These experiences can have an indelible impact on the career of US students, who, once bitten by the "Asia bug," may find working in the region through government agencies or multinational companies to be their calling. The exchanges also help build bridges between the United States and Asia that are enduring and deeply personal, changing perceptions of the United States held abroad one person at a time. There are many programs designed to increase capacity and understanding, and I am proud to have been involved with one major US initiative in particular intended to help build a reservoir of American expertise on Asia. The 100,000 Strong Initiative, launched by President Obama and Secretary Clinton in 2009, is intended to increase the number of Americans studying in China. Its goal was to send one hundred thousand American students to study in China within five years and, by July 2014, that ambitious goal had been achieved.[41] The new goal is to increase to one million the number of US students studying Mandarin. If even a fraction of those students choose to enter the government and work on Asia policy, they will be a testament to the value and long-term benefit of this program and a sorely needed addition to the human capital stock of the US government.

Mutual Frustrations and Decoupling

The United States and Asia, drawn together by a shared history for decades, could soon face the possibility of mutual estrangement. The root cause of a potential separation would be a crisis of faith and a surge in mutual frustrations: Asians may grow less confident about the reliability of the United States and Americans may grow more uncertain about whether Asia contributes to or undermines American prosperity.

Asian patience with a partner that has often viewed the region as a secondary theater is not inexhaustible, and once it is depleted, Asians could reverse their historical desire for closer relations with Washington. Americans sometimes forget that one of the keys to US influence in Asia is that allies, partners, and friendly states throughout the region all welcome a robust American role in Asia's affairs. They invite the United States to access local military facilities, engage in regional exercises, participate in multilateral forums, and assist in disaster relief. On some of the more sensitive issues in the region, including the situation in the South China Sea or the trouble on the Korean Peninsula, Asian states consult with Washington about their own positions and actions. It would be much more difficult for Washington to advance its interests or fulfill its historical role in Asia without this inviting and accommodating attitude—and Washington takes it for granted at its own peril.

Americans, for their part, may not only take their influence in Asia for granted but actively begin to question its value. Many Americans are increasingly frustrated with traditional arguments for international engagement and globalization. Those who see the American economic recovery as unequal or inadequate may already be drifting toward a darker worldview, one in which Asia would be viewed not as a land of prosperity and plenty but as a source of threats, both to American workers in the form of cheap imports and to American security in the form of unrewarding conflict. As the United States finds its foreign policy consensus and defense budgets under pressure, its public opinion turning against internationalism, and its attention drawn toward continuing challenges in the Middle East, the quality and consistency of US policy in Asia could suffer as Americans forget why Asia policy matters.

These mutual anxieties and frustrations could well prompt a subtle or even sharp decoupling if not handled correctly, especially if they arise in the near term. The need for nimble and flexible American involvement in Asia will continue to grow, but paradoxically, so too will the risk that brief bouts of American inattentiveness, absence, or hesitance could lead Asian states to be far less accommodating or patient. For example, a failure to complete the TPP or address Chinese provocations, or perhaps an intractable budget crisis that results in a default on US debt or a slashing of the defense budget, could unintentionally but irreversibly erode American credibility as an Asian player, with powerful implications for the country's regional—if not global—leadership. The present political gridlock, foreign policy indecision, and absence of critical legislation could come to be seen by many Asian states as accents on the portrait of American decline.

In practical terms this means that the Pivot to Asia may be bounded by a window. If the United States waits too long to reaffirm its essential commitments to the region, or if its leaders wait too long to explain the important link between Asia and American prosperity, then the window could close. Should that happen, the legitimacy of American leadership will be tarnished as the region's states come to doubt the credibility and endurance of US promises and assurances. Such an outcome is certainly avoidable. With determined diplomacy and strong political leadership—even in the face of crises and constraints elsewhere—the United States can still persuade and reassure its citizens of Asia's promise and its allies and partners of American dependability.

Conclusion

The Pivot to Asia faces a number of obstacles. A fracturing foreign policy consensus, chronic political dysfunction, and growing public weariness together challenge America's capacity for internationalist policy. Scarce and inflexible defense funding jeopardizes the forward-deployed presence in Asia, while the larger foreign policy bureaucracy struggles with long-term planning and with training new Asia hands. The Middle East, meanwhile, draws resources and top-level US attention away from Asian efforts. The total effect of all of these challenges is that American policy in Asia has been at times unfocused and inattentive, and the region's states are themselves increasingly frustrated with Washington's occasional tendency to drift.

These challenges are daunting but they are not insurmountable. Many are crises of will, less so questions of capability. What is needed ultimately is a bipartisan consensus around the idea that history of the twenty-first century will be written in Asia, a region that will be central to American prosperity for the foreseeable future. A positive vision, one of a bountiful region whose growth and dynamism can be harnessed to the benefit of the American people, can build modest public support for US internationalism in Asia. Together these efforts can—at least as far as Asia policy is concerned—address some of the political gridlock, inflexible defense cuts, and public fatigue that together burden US Asia policy. Beyond these changes, the United States will need to think anew about its force posture in an anti-access world; to restructure a national security apparatus geared to day-to-day challenges; and to reform personnel policy to build expertise for the Asian Century. Crucially, policymakers will also need to think seriously about whether a foreign policy that remains overweighted in the Middle East is truly in America's best strategic interests.

A successful Pivot to Asia will require acknowledging and addressing these and other challenges. At the core, the Pivot is not simply a policy proposal but a choice—one that requires the United States to embrace, for its own sake, a vital region home to both the most consequential challenges and the most breathtaking opportunities of the next century.

CHAPTER EIGHT

Implementing the Pivot

The Lessons of Modern Diplomacy

The previous chapters have been largely about the construction of strategy and the importance of an overarching framework for advancing US policies and priorities across Asia. This part of the book is something different, a more personal approach to the practice of diplomacy. Think of the previous chapters as more about the machinery of Asian interactions while this chapter focuses on the hydraulics of diplomacy or, simply put, the human dimension of the equation. It is about what the experience has been like for me to cross a diplomatic high-wire strung across Asia, all the while keeping attention firmly focused on the path ahead and the future, rather than on being overly focused on the risks lurking below. This account touches on some of the things I have learned from twenty-five years of service and observation, hundreds of trips to the region, and thousands of diverse diplomatic encounters and engagements. This is by no means intended to be an exhaustive list of how to be an effective diplomat in Asia; it is more about some of those things that are not found in academic texts, college classrooms, or diplomatic histories. These are the kinds of things that can only be learned in the aftermath of long jet-lagged flights, sleepless nights marked by existential questions, and sometimes groggy diplomatic encounters over exotic Asian meals.

Twenty-first Century Diplomacy

The Situation Room, from which much of US global strategy and policy emanates—at least in theory if not always in practice—is a small, uncomfortable, low-ceilinged, windowless bunker in the White House basement. At virtually every hour of the day, participants from relevant Washington agencies around town file into this room with assigned seats for a meeting presided over by one of the president's senior advisors from the National Security Council. Since the National Security Act of 1947 and the creation of the National Security Council in the Office of the President, the NSC has steadily gained political power and bureaucratic sway along Washington's corridors of power. In the past, soft drinks and M&Ms were provided to the lucky meeting-goers, but in recent years those perks have disappeared and participants are expected to get through long meetings without even a sip of water. It's basically as if Bear Bryant, the famously stern football college coach of Alabama, were running a government meeting. Working in the White House and surrounded by the accoutrements of American power— the technology, motorcades, presidential cufflinks, official airplanes, helicopters, and Secret Service agents—it is sometimes easy to forget that real diplomacy is practiced out in the field rather than in the confines of these cloistered spaces.

Modern technology has rendered outmoded some past practices of tactical decision-making and seat-of-the-pants best diplomatic judgments, and this has led to much more centralization in the White House and less delegation of control across many government endeavors. For instance, no longer can naval commanders or contemporary diplomats claim that the voice on the other end of the encrypted device is "breaking up" and respond that "I need to take this one on my own" like in those old black-and-white war movies. Increasingly, forward-deployed military officers and diplomats set out attached to a long and sometimes constricting technological leash, expected to report back and take directions on even the most seemingly inconsequential matters. Even seasoned and acclaimed diplomats like Richard Holbrooke, Christopher Hill, William Burns, and John Kerry occasionally chafe at the imposition of these constraints. They all understood on some level and demonstrated through their own intrepid actions that diplomacy by Situation Room is essentially not what modern diplomacy is all about. It is a time-honored necessity that understanding the intricacies of the local setting, reacting to the regional context, and reading the reactions of the counterparts sitting across the table are critical parts of any effective diplomatic encounter. Top-level guidance is, of course, required, but smothering control can often be counterproductive. Effective diplomacy requires a degree of improvisation and trust placed in the hands of the diplomat, and sometimes it is just not possible to phone home in the heat of a tense and rapidly moving engagement.

Much of this approach runs counter to the instincts of an increasingly empowered National Security Council that seeks tight control over most aspects of America's strategy formulations and diplomacy. A senior official at the NSC once described diplomats and others as merely "implementers" of policies developed in the White House, but the reality is actually quite different. There is inevitable innovation in any effective effort to implement. To really be effective as an advocate or negotiator on the global stage requires being out there, surveying the scene, sitting down with international partners, and exerting best judgments, having been provided the general parameters for the overall mission. The neatly summarized findings and "do outs" from NSC meetings are all well and good, but the realities of the world of diplomatic prowess and decision-making require getting out in the field. Improvisation, creativity, and even audacity are sometimes the essential ingredients in a successful international deliberation. Many of the new generation of ambitious American foreign policy practitioners seek assignments in the sun-deprived confines of the NSC, partly because they see the trend toward the accumulation of power and decision-making at the center. Although these vitamin D–deficient bureaucrats play an essential role, give me the visceral and real-life rigors of being at the end of the proverbial technological communication line every time, out in the field trying to make out those garbled instructions coming from Washington.

The Balance of Power versus the Power of Balance

Sometimes, the most powerful insights arrive inadvertently. For me, one of the most thought-provoking encounters occurred during the visit of a Japanese defense strategist and his interpreter to my office in the Pentagon during the 1990s. Both were anxious about visiting the center of American global military power and operations, and they settled nervously into a discussion with me around the future of the US role in Asia. As the conversation began, the interpreter fidgeted uncertainly on the edge of his seat, increasingly worried about word choices for appropriate translations during our back-and-forths, and looking as if his bulging neck was about to burst his tight white shirt. The visiting Japanese academic went on at some length about the complexities of the Asian balance of power. Somehow the nervous interpreter, with sweat now in his eyes and clutching his notepad, kept inverting the words in this sequence. Instead of balance of power, he kept talking about Asia's power of balance, over and over. The academic was unaware of this dyslexic interpretation and left my office after a half hour of polite discussion around the changing politics of Asia. However, that brief encounter has stayed with me ever since.

American strategy has been a near constant search over the decades for an effective balance of power in Asia and for the necessary steps to prevent the region from coming under the domination of any state. However, it is also the case that effective US strategy requires that we seek the power of balance, aligning all the tools of our diplomacy—high-level political engagement and consultations, military options, trade promotion or sanctions, and human rights demarches—in a harmonious way that together hopefully amplifies and reinforces national objectives. When the US approach places one element of our strategy out of balance with the others, the equilibrium and effectiveness of the overall strategy suffers. The notion of balance applies in other circumstances as well. The United States must balance between clear demonstrations of positive engagement with Beijing where possible and firm displays of preparation and vigilance when necessary. In addition, Washington should seek to balance traditional approaches to national security concerns of territorial sovereignty and provocation with emerging transnational challenges such as climate change and piracy. As such, as the United States seeks greater engagement in the region across the board, it is imperative that America do so in a manner that favors balance. Indeed, in contemporary Asia, the power of balance is an essential feature in the actual maintenance of the balance of power.

The Only Americans We Have

The challenges of Asian diplomacy are increasingly attracting a larger cohort of American strategists and practitioners, many of whom cut their teeth on the Cold War politics of Europe or the recent martial challenges in the Middle East. They come to Asia armed with European metaphors and historical comparisons and seek to apply these earlier experiences to a very different set of challenges in the Asia-Pacific region. A little secret of Asian diplomacy is that often even polite interlocutors sitting across the table will tune out

American visitors who drone on about the lessons of Europe or the implications of recent setbacks in the Middle East.

Still, my favorite anecdote to help understand the modern conception of the United States in Asia (beyond the many useful scenes found in the contemporary movie *Jerry McGuire*) is the modern story surrounding the early 1980s encounter between the then secretary general of NATO Lord Peter Carington and a group of European interlocutors at NATO headquarters in Brussels. Lord Carington, one of Margaret Thatcher's closest aides who had been selected for situations such as these, listened patiently to a group of European diplomats and military officials react to the most recent policy proclamation from the Reagan administration. With growing ire and disdain, the Europeans went beyond the narrow specifics of the actual policy initiative emanating from Washington and started describing Americans as ignorant and arrogant, without a conception of history or knowledge of their respective national politics, and lacking in all diplomatic grace—and cuisine. As the conversation became more heated, Lord Carington listened thoughtfully, but intervened finally with: "Ah, but alas—they are the only Americans we have." This left his European colleagues without a response.

While this is a somewhat stark rendition of an enduring American role, the fact remains that the stabilizing circumstance described by Lord Carington is as true in Asia today as it was in Europe yesterday. The American role persists. Asian nations and leaders have a deep, abiding, and fundamental distrust of many of their nearby neighbors and look to the distant and generally benevolent role of the United States as a stabilizing presence. If anything, this factor has grown in the calculus of Asian strategists and commentators in recent years with serial North Korean provocations, rising maritime territorial tensions, and mounting defense budgets and armaments. Even as the region develops more serviceable multilateral institutions and robust regional cooperation, a leading American role will be an essential feature of the security, commercial, and political infrastructure of Asia going forward. It is in the US interest to help sustain this essential logic and the associated American role into the future. Indeed, the Americans are the only Americans that Asia has.

Working in the Garden

Asian policy has long been animated by the search for the perfect metaphor to represent American exertions in the region over the generations to promote peace and stability. We have served as an off-shore balancer to ensure regional harmony, but the mental image of a man with a long pole balancing on a dangerous tightrope being buffeted by high winds and the elements does not effectively capture the nature of the challenge. Likewise, our quest to sell a million shirts or save a billion souls suggests the contrasting approaches of a salesman or a preacher. Such representations are indeed part of America's Asian legacy, but each image represents an incomplete picture of our overall endeavors in the region over long years of exertion.

Perhaps the most enduring and useful image of the American mission in Asia comes from George Shultz, the venerable former secretary of state. He described the tasks as akin to gardening:

> If you plant a garden and you go away for six months and you come back, what have you got? Weeds. And you can't get them out without getting all the flowers and the vegetables or whatever you planted there out. Same thing is true in diplomacy. If all you do is go to people when there's some sort of a crisis, well, your garden is full of weeds. So you've got to have, particularly with major countries, some sort of process of gardening, of going there, talking, sorting out issues, setting up some kind of agenda...and then when something comes up that's a big problem, you've laid the groundwork of understanding and some ability to talk in reasonably candid terms.[1]

However, as appreciated and long-standing as Shultz's gardening metaphor remains, it does have some limitations of use in contemporary circumstances. The notion of gardening suggests a serene and passive pastime that is somewhat reactive and defensive in nature, requiring less creativity but more patience. These qualities are still important, but conveying a more activist and involved role would be invaluable.

My nomination for a complementary metaphor for the contemporary challenges of Asia is the orchestra conductor. Each member or section of an orchestra represents an independent source of melody, harmony, or percussion. However, when harnessed as a group, they undeniably transcend their individual contributions to the musical score. The role of the conductor is to choose the most appropriate music and to coax the best from the orchestra's many and diverse members, taking care that, for instance, the horns do not drown out the strings and insisting all the while that there be strict adherence to the established tempo. A good conductor understands his (or her) role and recognizes that many eyes are always on him. There is an undeniable dimension of performance art involved. There are times that require drama, with expressive arms waving in synchronization with the music, and other points during a performance that necessitate subtlety and virtually disappearing from the scene. All in all, the conductor allows the orchestra's strings, woodwinds, horns, flutes, and percussion sections to stay together and to meet their fullest potential. The conductor coaxes the best performance from all but sets equally high expectations for his own contributions to the endeavor. The conductor is at once part of the orchestra and apart. He understands that without him standing in front of the assembled group there is no one to lead. Even the principal first violin with all his skill and dexterity cannot lead the diverse group of musicians around him. At the end of any performance, it is the musicians who receive the lion's share of the credit and applause, and it is the conductor who selflessly recognizes the individual contributions, but each and every member of the orchestra understands it is only through the actions of the conductor that their fullest potential has been reached.

Making Maximum Efforts

A critical element in the successful practice of Asian diplomacy is the demonstration of strength and endurance in the face of personal exhaustion. The Japanese have a phrase for this trial by tiredness: make maximum efforts. In many respects, effective Asian diplomacy requires mastering the often debilitating rhythms and exertions of jet lag and the sleepless nights in nameless hotel rooms, followed by the unrelenting demands of diplomacy. When almost every effort to negotiate a joint statement, trade agreement, or communiqué requires lengthy, intense discussions and last-minute deal-making, by the last stages of any diplomatic encounter both sides are thoroughly exhausted. However, it is generally then and only then that agreements can be cut and delivered. The White House would sometimes provide guidance to conclude the joint statement or joint fact sheet long before US and Chinese leaders would sit down to meet, and invariably, the finishing touches of any document were being frantically concluded and then photocopied only just as the Chinese leader was getting ready for the twenty-one-gun salute on the White House lawn, rarely if ever before.

The point of this is that Asian interlocutors expect to see the fullest possible effort, and it is through that personal fortitude—as important in some ways as personal trust—that Asians make judgments about when it is time to find common ground. It means that any American diplomat must be prepared to work without sleep for days on end and develop strategies to fend off sleep in meetings during painfully long presentations from counterparts.

Japanese culture has somehow developed an understanding that when their leaders sleep in meetings with outsiders they are really just listening intently, and this diplomatic fiction is widely accepted. However, no such slack is cut for American diplomats, and as such, staying awake is essential. I remember once at the end of a long day of flights from the United States and endless meetings at a multilateral forum on the Pacific islands in Cairns, Australia, I settled into a couch for a meeting with then prime minister Kevin Rudd in his ornate hotel room overlooking the Great Barrier Reef. It is a rare honor for an assistant secretary to meet with a prime minister, and even though I had known Kevin for many years before, I very much looked forward to the opportunity. However, there was just one problem: I was tired beyond belief. I remember the start of the meeting, when the prime minister and his team welcomed me to Australia, but somehow, during the encounter, I must have dozed off. I woke up several hours later, still sitting in my suit on the couch, with all the lights turned off and every member of the Australian delegation long gone. Since then, I learned from Secretary Clinton to carry a small tin of chili peppers with me whenever I travel. Just a little dab between your cheek and gums can keep you awake through even the most interminable presentation. It can have other positive impacts as well. I remember one Asian interlocutor being particularly touched by my apparent tears after his impassioned presentation on his country's position regarding the South China Sea.

So in short, diplomatic success often requires a degree of exhaustion to really set things in motion, and many times it is only when personal resources, fortitude, and perseverance are low that the greatest progress can actually be made. This suggests the importance of working in shifts and knowing that any outcomes must be carefully checked for oversights or mistakes. Patience is key, but so too is endurance. It also suggests that comfortable chairs, suitable for listening intently, are a plus.

Showing Up

An inordinate amount of time and attention in every aspect of government is consumed by an effort to find a new policy framework, presidential doctrine, or innovative program. In this respect, the imposing shadows of the past loom large, such as George Kennan's "X Article" articulating the containment strategy toward the Soviet Union; the enunciation of the Marshall Plan, which called for the rebuilding of war-torn Europe; or President Reagan's speech calling for Soviet leader Mikhail Gorbachev to tear down the Berlin Wall.

However, despite this heady stuff, American policy is often judged by more mundane matters in Asia. The vast distances involved, the competing demands, and the scheduling necessary for on-the-ground stops require the commitment of that scarcest commodity in the government: the time and attention of senior-most officials. For an Asian policymaker or staffer in the US government, the most frightening period is always the weeks before any major sojourn to the region by the secretary of state or the president of the United States. I can remember many a meeting in the West Wing when a domestic policy advisor would chime in to a trip-planning session for the president about why this particular upcoming trip to Asia was "off message" and "not a good use of time." In fact, I can't remember a trip-planning session that ever went off smoothly, without someone asking the question about why in fact we were going. In some cases and under certain circumstances, leaders and statesmen cancelled their trips. There are no hard and fast figures on this, but I suspect that this is truer of Asian travel than travel to any other region. There is a sense that either pressing domestic issues or other regional challenges are more important, it's hard to be away from Washington for such a long period, or perhaps maybe that a visit to the region creates discordant images, such as concerns about job losses and unfair commercial competition during periods of suboptimal economic performance at home.

Still, the personal dimension of American diplomacy is probably the least understood and most important facet of American power in Asia. This is why the most insightful strategic doctrine to be articulated about Asia actually comes from, of all people, Woody Allen: his oft-quoted notion that 80 percent of success in life involves just showing up is deeply relevant for Asian circumstances. Many times, Asian interlocutors are not seeking an innovative new policy formulation or creative approaches to an intractable diplomatic problem from the senior US representative, but instead a steady-ing presence rather than an empty chair at the Asian table without an Ameri-can participant. Asian interlocutors are most reassured when they can look over to see that exhausted American representative fighting back jet lag and occasionally boredom but nevertheless providing steady reassurance, just by showing up.

"China Is a Big Country"

Knowledge in Asia often follows a kind of sine curve, with understanding and insight oscillating between simplicity and complexity. A novice will ren-der a very basic finding after initial exposure. Seasoned analysts describe current circumstances in extensive detail with the benefit of deep historical background, while a Mandarin bureaucrat might cut to the insightful core of an issue with a simple sentence. Simplicity leads to complexity, which finally arrives back at simplicity.

Once, many years ago, while visiting US Pacific Command (PACOM) in Hawaii, I traveled with a group of Washington diplomats dressed uncom-fortably in dark suits and ties while the island-based officials wore khakis, floral aloha shirts, and wrap-around sunglasses. We were ushered in to meet with the recently appointed admiral who had just taken command of PACOM. This was during the period when combatant commanders had outsize roles in policy formulation and actions in their respective theaters of operations. The admiral had spent most of his earlier career focusing on other military and administrative matters in distant regions and had only recently focused on Asia with this new assignment. He had not traveled in Asia yet, but that did not dissuade him from offering his insights about the complexities of the region with a confidence and sureness that only comes with being in command and wearing four stars. He sat back in his enormous leather chair and opined about the modern wonders of China, a place that many of us had visited dozens of times and worked on for a generation. He had just started to receive classified briefings about the inner workings and ambitions of China from his J-2 team beavering away in the bowels of a Pearl Harbor bunker so was able to proclaim with a certain sureness: "You know, China is a big country."

A few weeks later, I was attending an academic conference on China when I happened to hear a fascinating lecture by an up-and-coming university professor who had spent several years studying and conducting field research in rural China. She talked knowledgeably—and in great detail and at length— about the legacy of 1970s-era local agricultural policies on modern Chinese food production and how these policies in turn had shaped the trajectory of modern China. She described how decisions on production quotas and state-delivered supplies, like fertilizer and water, were taken by bureaucrats and what impact these decisions had on China's food system. The presentation was rigorous with historical context and complex bureaucratic insights.

At the conclusion of the conference, I had an opportunity to stop by and visit with Robert A. Scalapino, the revered University of California, Berkeley, professor who provided generations of students, scholars, and practitioners with profound insights into how China's role on the international stage was evolving and why its policies were shaped by thousands of years of history along with the country's unique culture. He was elderly by that time, in the winter of his life, but still the mere mention of Asia caused him to perk up, and as the discussion turned to China, it brought a spark to his eyes. When asked about an apparent contradiction in Chinese diplomacy, as Beijing inexorably sought to improve relations with neighbors but take a tougher line simultaneously, Bob looked off in the distance and smiled with a lifetime's sum total of training, temperament, and reflection, and simply offered: "You know, China is a big country."

The Two-level Game Theory

It is often said that the gap between government service and the pursuits of modern academia is growing wider with each semester. Contemporary academics at elite universities are often discouraged from regional studies and instead focus on arcane matters of statistical interpretation and post-feminist perception. Their counterparts in government are also increasingly alienated from academic enterprises that seem irrelevant to the everyday challenges that government service provides. Nevertheless, there are powerful academic areas of study and scholarship that provide essential insights for practitioners, and indeed much of this work goes beyond the simple analysis of complex regional dynamics or area studies, pursuits that have largely fallen out of favor on university campuses.

One example of a highly relevant and illuminating academic pursuit is Robert Putnam's excellent treatise on the "two-level game theory."[2] His powerful observations are about how any international diplomacy invariably carries with it a parallel and similar domestic set of negotiations, and effective diplomatic undertakings must understand and anticipate the interplay between the two levels. Doing so can mean the difference between success and failure. Indeed, these internal interactions and their relationship with international diplomacy are some of the most complex aspects of any set-piece diplomatic engagement.

My most powerful experience of the two-level game theory in action was around the complexities of the situation surrounding US forward military bases in Okinawa. Ever since the tragic rape of a young local girl on the way home from school in 1995, the United States and Japan have conducted a sometimes tense, exceedingly difficult, and increasingly high stakes diplomacy about how to sustain and appropriately adjust the US Marine presence in Okinawa to reduce burdens on local communities but preserve capabilities to support peace and stability. US and Japanese diplomats have been in charge of this process for twenty years, but each side must deal with the challenging internal politics associated with the effort. From the Japanese government's perspective, they must always take careful account of the deep sense of aggrievement felt by the Okinawan representatives and people, who often have uncompromising positions with regard to any diplomacy over the destiny of US military bases on the island. For the United States, US Marines manifest an overriding sense of responsibility for any discussion that would have an impact on deployment philosophies and training options on an island that serves as the US foothold in the Asia-Pacific. As such, the high-profile diplomatic encounters between the United States and Japan garner the most public attention, with the appearance of diplomats sitting across from each other at a long table hashing out mutually acceptable adjustments. In reality, it is in the backroom discussions and the meetings in advance of this high-profile diplomacy where the dug-in internal stakeholders at the other end of the two-level game hammer out outcomes and where the ultimate parameters of negotiations are fundamentally shaped and decided.

In this respect, the role of the diplomat is to conduct both the internal and external dimensions of diplomacy in such a way that trust is not broken in either set of relationships—often an exceedingly difficult task. Further complicating the situation is the fact that key domestic actors in one country often work around their own official representatives and seek to make appeals directly to diplomats on the other side, so US Marines will seek to directly influence Japanese diplomats, just as Okinawan local politicians seek out opportunities for interactions with American diplomats.

The point of recounting this rather arcane political science article is that there is actually much of relevance from the modern academy that has a bearing on the formulation and execution of American statecraft. Insights such as those found in the two-level game theory analysis can help advance complex understanding of circumstances and provide diplomats with essential insights. Other examples of powerful frameworks of academic analysis include Joe Nye's concept of "soft power" and John Ikenberry's observations about the nature of the liberal international order. These academic treatments likewise can help illuminate the world where diplomats operate, far from the ivory tower.

Closing the Anecdote Gap

In Asian diplomacy, it always seems as if your counterparts have the advantage when it comes to useful anecdotes or colorful historical allusions. Someone is always killing the chicken to scare the monkey or crossing the river by feeling the stones. In fact, the sayings of Mao Zedong, Zhou Enlai, the famed World War II Japanese admiral Isoroku Yamamoto ("We have awakened a sleeping giant."), and Sun Tzu are all so good that Western interlocutors will often quote memorable lines back to Asian counterparts. I once heard a distinguished Asian diplomat confess that if another Western guest recommended letting a thousand flowers bloom, he would be physically ill. Some sophisticated Western interlocutors are able to use Greek mythology when underscoring their points. For instance, Bob Kagan began a remarkable column on the current predicaments of the Republican party with a learned rendition of a story from Greek tragedy: "When the plague descended on Thebes, Oedipus sent his brother-in-law to the Delphic oracle to discover the cause. Little did he realize that the crime for which Thebes was being punished was his own." Others employ the mythical Sisyphus to describe toiling away at seemingly endless or hopeless tasks or Medusa for someone confronting an uncomfortable or unsightly truth.

My preference for historical analogy is popular American culture, particularly movies. I find that there are several recent films that convey timeless verities that can be extraordinarily useful in an Asian context, even if your counterpart has never seen that particular film. For instance, Richard Gere in *An Officer and a Gentleman* is urged to quit by the tough drill instructor played by Louis Gossett Jr., who uses a water hose in his face to try to get him to renounce his officer candidacy. Instead, Gere perseveres and, under some emotional duress, exclaims, "I got nowhere else to go. . . . I got nowhere else to go." This is a useful way to convey to an Asian interlocutor that, although they are perhaps frustrated with the United States, Washington is their best—or indeed only—option. Another useful film reference comes when Jerry McGuire in the movie of the same name pleads with Cuba Gooding Jr.'s character to "help me help you." This sequence is valuable in circumstances when an Asian partner is making it difficult for the United States to assist in some complex task.

Then, of course, the real mother lode of cinema snippets that can be mined for gold is found in *The Godfather*, in which there are innumerable classic dialogue interactions with myriad possibilities. Tessio, the capo lieutenant in the Corleone crime family, indicates, "It's not personal; it was only business." Marlon Brando, as the Godfather, instructs Sonny to "never tell anyone outside the Family what you are thinking again." And Michael Corleone underscores that he'll "make [his counterpart] an offer he can't refuse." *The Godfather* is a font of diplomatic wisdom, and essentially every negotiation gambit can be found somewhere in the film. The movie also offers an example of the truest maxim for a diplomat: Do all the small favors requested because someday you'll need to call in a large one—like taking care of Sonny's bullet-riddled body. So while the learned refer to the lessons of Aristotle or the wisdom and tragedy of the Greek gods, and Asian interlocutors use the wisdom of the aforementioned leaders and military strategists, I will stick with American film lore for my reference points.

Strategic Dialogue

Richard Nixon and Henry Kissinger were deeply engaged in US diplomacy in Asia during their time, including orchestrating the opening to China, overseeing the conduct of war in Vietnam, enunciating the Guam Doctrine, and conducting the secret bombing campaign in Cambodia, but one of the most indelible legacies of their time in office is the advent of strategic dialogue with China. Even a fleeting review of their encounters with Zhou Enlai and Mao Zedong around the time of the opening to China reveals the most fascinating exercises in modern strategic dialogue. Several utterances from Chinese leaders have passed into antiquity, such as the assessment of the meaning of the French Revolution ("It's too early to judge.") or the meaning of diplomacy ("All diplomacy is a continuation of war by other means."). These conversations were generally unscripted and wide-ranging and set the contours for the most complex bilateral relationship of modern times.

In the period since, there has been a general yearning to recreate the quality of these strategic interactions between the US and Chinese interlocutors, whereby both sides are able to offer deep philosophical and strategic insights into how they see their respective worlds. However, much has changed since the time of Nixon, Kissinger, Zhou, and Mao. There are bureaucratic constraints on both sides and a longer record of foreign policy precedence to take into account. I have had a seat at many a strategic dialogue between the highest levels in recent years, and most of them on some level have been disappointing. President Obama would often try to draw his Chinese interlocutors out into a discussion around intellectual property, nuclear proliferation, or climate change, hoping for a high-level exchange of views. However, modern Chinese leaders are much more likely to demur from such musings and instead tend to follow the text prepared for them by faceless bureaucrats in either the foreign ministry, State Council, or from one of the economic organs. Chinese leaders in turn would seek to elicit American fidelity to the newest concept of great power relations or bilateral coexistence and would invariably be disappointed when President Obama failed to recite the exact wording that they sought.

In a sense, strategic dialogue has become another set piece of diplomatic interaction, an exercise to see how quickly the leaders can get to the section of the binder where the best answer to the approximate question of your interlocutors can be addressed. In this respect, strategic dialogue resembles not so much a conversation but an exchange of official positions. I can remember watching one of the encounters between President Obama and then Chinese president Hu Jintao, in which Hu skillfully parried Obama's questions, turning to the appropriate section in his official binder with a nimbleness that belied his advanced age. But it was also clear that he had practiced this exercise. There was a discernable residue of oil on each page tab where it had been turned literally dozens and dozens of times in preparation for the "strategic dialogue."

However, even though these often staged encounters can seem less than advertised and a far cry from Nixon and Mao—probably to both sides—it does not mean that strategic dialogue is absent in the US-China relationship. It has simply taken other forms. Now, real strategic interaction takes place at lower levels on late nights between the two sides as they work together on shared tasks, such as hammering out the official joint statement. My experience with negotiation over the joint statement came when US and Chinese interlocutors met at the State Department, spending days trying to develop and ratify a consensual view of the future in advance of the arrival of Hu Jintao to Washington, D.C. This was not an overt strategic dialogue, but an encounter in which preferences and bottom lines emerged in full view only over time. In this joint statement, the United States sought to create an essential equivalence and linkage between fundamental objectives in Washington and Beijing. Beijing sought deep assurances that the United States welcomed China's arrival on the international scene and would not take steps to block its ascendance in any way. The United States in turn sought a subtle concession from China: that it continue to welcome an American role in Asia and the two would work well together to help preserve peace and stability. While the United States was prepared to offer strong reassurance about China's growing role in Asia and its import for global politics, try as we might, it proved difficult to get a corresponding acknowledgment that a continuing US role in Asia was positive from Beijing's perspective. This suggests the ambivalence that China exhibits with respect to the continuing American role in Asia. However, this point would never be ostentatiously delivered by Chinese interlocutors to the American team sitting across from them at a long table, but instead only reveals itself in subtle ways during intense negotiations around that most thankless of tasks, the negotiation of the joint statement.

Nothing is more burdensome and less welcome in government than being assigned the task of negotiating the official joint statement. It means brutal debates and long hours toward forging a joint document that can be presented successfully as a vision acceptable to both sides. However, no exercise is more important when seeking clarity about what really matters to the people across the table. It is the very essence of strategic dialogue.

Thank You for Your Service

It is almost impossible for a modern American military man or woman walking down a street in uniform to avoid a virtual stampede of his fellow countrymen, stopping and thanking him for his service to the nation. These protestations are a form of patriotism and war guilt, a leftover from the sad homecoming given an earlier generation of Vietnam-era soldiers returning stateside to ignominy and hostility after brutal fighting in the jungles of Southeast Asia, and a current recognition that a tiny 1 percent of the US population has undertaken 100 percent of the fighting in Afghanistan and Iraq.

This very public if complex appreciation is nothing remotely similar to the everyday experience of America's other army deployed abroad, its foreign service officers and civil servants that inhabit America's embassies and diplomatic compounds across the globe. Often distrusted by presidents (see, for instance, Richard Nixon, Franklin Delano Roosevelt, and George W. Bush), unfairly caricatured in popular culture as either weak or sinister paper pushers (see for instance movies such as *Rules of Engagement* or dark depictions of American diplomats in the Bourne series), or castigated in congressional testimony as wasteful and incompetent (see the regular diatribes of Darrell Issa or virtually any other House Tea Party member—not to mention claims of widespread treason by the notorious Joseph McCarthy in the 1950s), the foreign service is subjected to popular and political disdain that is often disheartening to the highly skilled civilian diplomats that seek to promote American interests and values through means other than war.

I served with them as assistant secretary of state for Asia in Foggy Bottom and would regularly receive letters or notes from Americans traveling abroad who were assisted in big ways and small by foreign service officers. These missives invariably had a hint of surprise: Oh my gosh! This person went beyond the call of duty to help me! Imagine my surprise!

There have been literally hundreds of books written in recent years about the dark contours of conflict in the Middle East, examining the lives and sacrifices of the khaki-clad warriors fighting on unforgiving battlegrounds. In contrast, almost nothing has been written about their civilian counterparts, and the role they have played in the Middle East campaigns and elsewhere (save for the somewhat unflattering depiction in Rajiv Chandrasekaran's *Imperial Life in the Emerald City*). Further, there is even less written about the exploits in Asia of the forward-deployed diplomats, save for a few excellent accounts of the recent record of dead-end diplomacy with North Korea. It has been said that the military is the one instrument of the US government on steroids while the rest of the bureaucracy—most particularly the State Department—struggles on life support. You would not know it from the determination and tenacity of the contemporary State Department officers I witnessed executing their myriad missions across Asia.

After four arduous years at State surrounded by some of the finest Americans I have ever been privileged to serve with, I would offer a simple, heartfelt ode to each of them: thank you for your service.

Conclusion

Air Force One settled softly onto the main runway of Yangon's international airport on a bright, clear Southeast Asian day in December 2012. The sky blue 747 with the distinctive President of the United States seal made of arrows and olive branches—really the most powerful weapon in the arsenal of American soft power—taxied along the dilapidated apron and came to a stop beside an excited crowd of well-wishers. China might be able to offer their bridges, dams, towers, and other massive infrastructure projects to acquisitive Asian neighbors, but we still had the baddest plane on the planet. On board that day waiting to deplane were President Obama and his traveling party, including Secretary of State Clinton and a few others from our State Department team. This would be the first visit of a president to Burma in history and everyone inside the plane and those waiting outside on the humid asphalt for the official arrival ceremonies understood the significance. In many ways this was the final step in the first phase of the opening to the cloistered country, orchestrated largely by Secretary Clinton through very public and risky efforts of direct, high-stakes diplomacy over the preceding three years and quiet behind-the-scenes cajoling and reassurance that had brought us to this day. She had skillfully managed to gain the trust of the military henchmen who had run the country for several brutal decades and the confidence of the recently released prisoner of conscience who served as the flickering hope of a nation from her long house arrest, Aung San Suu Kyi. It always made me angry—and struck at my own sense of purpose and pride—when I heard critics say that Clinton had really had no big diplomatic achievements from her time at Foggy Bottom. Really? Had they not been paying attention? One of the world's most isolated, tragic, and magical lands had finally opened to the world because of intrepid American diplomacy, perhaps fundamentally changing the trajectory of Asia.

Secretary Clinton's accomplishments did not end with the Burma opening. She helped advocate for and paved the way for the United States to join the East Asia Summit. She declared at the ASEAN Regional Forum in Hanoi in 2010 that the United States had a vital strategic interest in preserving freedom of navigation through the South China Sea. Clinton conducted extensive and challenging diplomacy with Chinese interlocutors on imposing Iranian sanctions, addressing North Korean provocations, and determining the fate of a blind dissident. She helped design and implement the US humanitarian response to the nuclear calamity in Japan, and supported disaster relief in the Philippines and Thailand. Clinton helped break the diplomatic stalemate between the United States and New Zealand, restoring strong official relations after twenty-five years of strategic neglect. She strengthened each of our bilateral security ties, from Japan and South Korea to Australia, the Philippines, and Thailand. Perhaps most important, Secretary Clinton was an indefatigable presence in Asia, the only secretary of state to visit every Asian country and many in the Pacific, several on numerous occasions. And the Burma opening was the crowning achievement of her tenure at State, demonstrating all her considerable powers of persuasion and perseverance.

Yet despite the quiet satisfaction she felt about the improving prospects in Burma, Clinton understood fundamentally that this was the president's day and his mission, and she would be careful to always slip unobtrusively behind him at every festivity and official event during our short sojourn in this exotic place of gold temples and orange-cloaked monks. She would whisper to him out of sight with insights about key interlocutors he was meeting and provide details about the places he was seeing that simultaneously were both alien and familiar to him, but she always knew her place. She also understood fully that the message of two Democratic aspirants for president of the United States now working closely and loyally together after the bitterest of campaigns sent a powerful signal of purposeful unity to a country divided by military uniforms, ethnic identity, and wealth inequality.

Every time that we traveled with the president in Asia, it was always striking to see how much nostalgia and his early adolescent experiences shaped his view of the region. Obama has been described as our first Pacific president—even though Nixon and Reagan both lived in California and Teddy Roosevelt was consumed with the promise of the Orient East—but there is something unique to him about this particular moniker. His early experience as a self-described alienated black youth traveling around the region with a white mother, staying in hostels and trying new cuisines in street markets, gave him an altogether different perspective. The memory of these tastes and images would come flooding back to him suddenly and sometimes reverentially on these trips, and for a few moments he would either be lost in thought or instead regaling us with some mischief he had got up to with misbehaving kids along some back alley of an Asian city while his mother was busy bringing American development idealism to their parents in another part of the city. Secretary Clinton and President Obama often bonded over some of these stories and I wondered whether the president's do-gooder mother, inspired to service by the launching of the Peace Corps and the Alliance for Progress in her youth, struck a generational chord with Clinton.

On these trips, they made a formidable pair. Even in large groups of leaders from across a diverse region they were instantly recognizable, like two keenly observant political velociraptors surveying the scene from the pinnacle of the political food chain. They both understood that this trip presented them with substantial upsides but also some risks. The political situation was exceedingly delicate, especially given lingering distrust between opposition groups and the dominant military as well as worries over ethnic violence and disenfranchisement. It was to be Clinton's last trip with Obama as secretary and a kind of swan song, but in truth there really are no victory laps in diplomacy. The race never stops and the game continues. Still, Secretary Clinton had run a strong leg and there was a widely held view of her able stewardship of the department. For the president, this was modest vindication for his open-hand rather than clenched-fist approach to regime outliers on the global stage, and the Burma touchdown of Air Force One was all the more significant given that this was before the opening to Cuba and the nuclear accord with Iran. So this was the larger setting for our visit, with both high stakes and clear rewards in play.

My day had started out well at least. The president and his massive traveling armada had just finished a day of visits in Bangkok, and we were to leave the following morning bright and early for the airport to make the short flight to Yangon. The visit to Thailand carried its own complexities as the country lurched again toward a military coup, but now it was time to take the show to Burma. There is a bizarre ritual in official government travel that you must pack your bag up the night before and leave it outside the hotel door for the Secret Service to scan, inspect, and then load on the plane. It's called the bag drag and you must take extra care that you have kept your essentials with you for getting dressed in the morning while the rest of your travel belongings are long gone. I had trouble sleeping that night after learning that I had been included with Secretary Clinton in the president's party for the Burma stop. I woke up every few hours to make sure I had all my necessary items. Suit, check, white shirt, check. Favorite good luck blue tie, check. Socks, check. Finally, it was time to wake up, and I scrambled to get ready and make my way to the gathering place for the security check and transport to Air Force One. In presidential travel, you muster in inverse relation to your status, with the president arriving only at the last minute. It was probably four hours before the president would climb on board Air Force One with the turbines just beginning to whine when I arrived at my assigned time to a virtually vacant lobby, but no matter—I was going to Burma with President Obama.

There is always a great unspoken fear when making your way onto the president's plane as a guest that there has been a terrible mistake with the seating manifest and in fact there is no place for you. I was instantly relieved when I saw the blue presidential name tag on the cushion of the seat with a simple "Campbell" typed across it. I settled in for takeoff and reviewed for the umpteenth time the briefing binder and talking points to be used by the president. Once airborne for the short plane ride over from Bangkok, Secretary Clinton strolled back to Jake Sullivan, her ablest staffer, and me sitting in the rear of the plane, greeted us warmly, and told us that the president wanted to be briefed. She wore the lovely silver necklace given to her by Aung San Suu Kyi on a previous visit to Burma as the two bonded over politics and personal destiny. She paused ever so slightly to thank us both for the hard work that helped get us to this moment. That was one thing about Secretary Clinton, she always took care of her staff and that bred a loyalty in many of us that transcends the years. Together, we went forward to the office in the front of the plane where the president was sitting with his leg casually draped over a nearby chair, sharing a restrained laugh with his key staff. Ben Rhodes, who had developed a passion of his own for the Pivot to Asia and worked hard and smart to make the Burma opening a reality, was standing next to the president and nodded to us as we arrived, a subtle acknowledgment of shared purpose. The president was his usual self, cool as the other side of the pillow, and I was going to try to avoid some discordant display of exuberance that would mark me as not among the no-drama Obama crowd. The briefing went well and the State Department team was able to answer all the president's probing and incisive questions about what we would encounter on the ground.

This is where things started to go wrong for me. As I made the way back to my seat aft, it dawned on me that this would likely be my last chance to ride on Air Force One. Certainly I deserved a few mementos from this historic trip to share with my daughters back home? Maybe I'd just pick up a few things lying around. I imprudently started to collect everything that was not bolted down that bore a presidential seal—cards, napkins, candy, stationery, an ashtray, and I think maybe a flashlight. I shoved them all into my jacket pockets, looking like a stuffed cornfield scarecrow rather than a pinstriped diplomat when I was done. I nervously sat back down and waited for landing. You are assigned a vehicle for the presidential motorcade and in these instances your car number accords directly with your rank. I think I was in car forty-five at the very end of the long procession, and this would mean running to reach the vehicle at the very back before the president left in his airlifted armored car for the ride into town. In presidential travel, the very worst thing that can happen to you is missing the motorcade. There were apocryphal stories of a young press aide missing the motorcade in London a few months back. He finally caught back up to the traveling team in Brussels, two days later. So I would have to hustle.

As the plane finally came to a stop in front of the viewing stand, the president and the secretary waited near the forward door for the formal welcoming ceremonies. Normally the president walks down the steps slowly and alone, but today he had asked Secretary Clinton to walk with him, an unspoken tribute to her role in the Burma opening. I looked out the plane window and saw my old friend Derek Mitchell, our new ambassador, waiting below, and felt a pang of gratitude. I had worked on this opening for three years—spanning secret meetings with the junta leaders, long negotiating sessions with Aung San Suu Kyi about the conditions for her release, difficult encounters with Capitol Hill skeptics and interagency doubters, diplomacy with European and other Asian states about the appropriate speed of engagement and sanctions lifting, and endless hours of strategizing with trusted staff—and we were finally here. I wanted to stop for a moment to pause and reflect but instead had to descend down the back steps of the plane and run full speed in the South East Asian humidity to my assigned car, about half a mile away, at the tail end of a very long line of idling black vehicles.

As staffers and aides moved quickly toward to their assigned vehicles in the motorcade, I rushed to get to mine before the entire caravan set off for the city center. I noticed that I was being followed by two Secret Service agents as I made my way to the car in the distance, like a shimmering mirage in the steamy heat. I picked up my pace and looked back to see that they were closing the gap. I was certain that they were coming to get me for the Air Force One chintz I had pilfered from the plane. I picked up my speed. Pretty soon we were all sprinting down the runway, but it was no use, they were catching up and calling out for me to stop. I turned around to turn myself in, but before I could confess, one of the agents, who was surprisingly out of breath, wheezed, "Mr. Campbell, the president wants you to ride with him into the city in the presidential limo." I immediately stopping removing the lifted loot from my suit pockets and tried to gather myself. I tried to rearrange the ill-gotten contents of my bulging suit pockets, now sweat stained, and quickly picked up those things that had fallen out during the sprint. Now we were all running full speed in the other direction toward the president's waiting black limo.

By the time I arrived at the side of the shiny sleek black sedan, I was completely covered in perspiration. It looked like I had just gone swimming in a steaming hot bath in my suit. My drenched white shirt looked like cellophane stretched tight over a plate of potato salad. I climbed in the president's battle wagon and wedged myself into the jump seat facing the president. I had always wondered about the feel of two things: what was the drive like in the president's armored car and how does the outfield grass at Fenway Park feel underfoot? Is there a springy cushion in the grass turf or is the sod firm? I can now report on the former. The car was enormous and ungainly and the Secret Service agent in the driver's seat was clenching a custom steering wheel that was cartoonishly small, barely eight inches in diameter.

Once I was seated, we immediately set off. As we left the airport and made our way into downtown Yangon, it became immediately apparent that there were hundreds of thousands of people lining the way—literally ten people deep on each side of the road for miles—to greet the American president. President Obama was flanked by Secretary Clinton and his Secret Service detail in the back seat and he waved offhandedly to the excited crowds. Just about the time when I had finally caught my breath and stopped noticeably heaving, the president turned to me and said simply, "Tell me about Burma," and locked his gaze on me intently. I tried to gather myself to tell the abbreviated history of this most enchanting, vexed place. I told the president about the beauty of the vast country around us with its still pristine hardwood forests, raging rivers, and native tigers; the controversy over the country's name (Myanmar vice Burma); its many contending and distrustful ethnic groups; its harrowing role during World War II and the famous "Burma Road" to China; the following years of brutal, unrelenting military rule; and its current contested domestic politics and fledgling opening and outreach to the US. I did what you are never supposed to do when briefing the president: I pretty much lost myself in the story. As we finally approached the city and the necessary end of my monologue, I turned to see on the horizon the soaring gold tower of Shwedagon Pagoda dominating the skyline, one of the true splendors of Asia. Without really thinking, after telling the president about its gilded gold exterior, its ninety-nine-meter height, and its sacred place in Buddhism, I blurted out, "No visit to Burma is complete really without a visit to Shwedagon." The president whirled immediately to his head of security detail and demanded, "If it's so amazing, why aren't we going, then?"

I had inadvertently stumbled into a recurring White House drama: the president wanting to loosen the constraints on his ability to explore and the Secret Service insistence on security. Apparently, the Shwedagon grounds were difficult to lock down, and the security detail was uncomfortable having to remove their shoes—it's harder to shoot stuff in stocking feet. Anyway, the president finally overcame their reservations and ended up having a terrific off-the-record sojourn to Shwedagon, and indeed the entire trip was a resounding success. The visit was messaged as a kind of presidential progress report, a clear show of support and intent to shape the political surroundings in ways to reinforce relations with the outside world. The opening to Burma was real and the geopolitics of Asia were subtly shifting, and the president's trip helped secure this foothold for progress in a long closed country. I enjoyed every minute of the visit, except for the hostile looks from the

Secret Service detachment who glared at me on every stop during that day in Yangon. As we climbed aboard Air Force One for the flight onward at the end of an emotionally overwhelming day, the president stopped for a minute by my seat before heading back to his cabin and turning his attention to other pressing matters. He shook my hand and simply said, "That was a big day, Kurt, and some good work. Thank you." And then he was gone. I had no idea that the president actually knew my name.

That was essentially my last big trip as assistant secretary of state for Asia. I would leave government service a few months later after nearly four years, seventy-nine trips abroad, thousands of diplomatic engagements, and more adventures than I could count. The Pivot I helped launch was part of a larger recognition that the United States must accord the region a greater degree of strategic regard. The entire experience left me with an enduring view that Asia was where it's at, and the overall time in service serves as the real inspiration for the message and meaning behind this exploration of the future of American statecraft in Asia.

This book began with a simple and unrelenting truth: The lion's share of the history of the twenty-first century will be written in Asia, a region that encompasses half the world's population and will contain three of the world's four largest economies by 2030. As we saw in chapter two, the stakes and dimensions of this rising region are enormous. The arc from Japan and China to India is the most dynamic in the world, home to the world's fastest-growing economies, its largest middle class, and some of its most dangerous security hotspots. Asia's size and prosperity make it crucial to the formulation and execution of virtually every major US policy priority. The prosperity and stability of the American-led order rests in part on how Washington manages Asia's intensifying security competition and China's historic rise. The path to halting climate change runs through Asia, already the producer of more carbon emissions than any other region. In the struggle with radical Islam, Asia's moderate and prosperous Muslim democracies—like Indonesia—offer a powerful reply to those who harken back to medieval Islamic traditions in Iraq and Syria. Asia is also a region of hope, as the previous story of presidential engagement in Burma attests. And, in the effort to renew the wellsprings of American power and boost American employment, Asia is the indispensable market, supplier, and partner. The prosperity of every American worker is already intimately intertwined with developments there and effective trade statecraft and subsequent enforcement can benefit US businesses and work-ers alike. On countless issues, Asia is at the center.

The history of American engagement in Asia, explored in detail in chap-ters three and four, reveals that US policy in this region has a long and com-plicated legacy, with several recurring themes and tendencies shaping the historical evolution of American strategy. The goals of selling shirts, sav-ing souls, spreading democracy, and protecting territory have been enduring and constant ends of American strategy and policy, and the United States has sought to achieve them by safeguarding the region from hegemony and restricting the imperial ambitions of Britain, Japan, and the Soviet Union in Asia. All too often, though, costly periods of withdrawal and neglect usu-ally followed soaring military or diplomatic successes. This cycle of intense focus and relative strategic neglect has blighted American efforts in Asia for decades. This tendency stemmed in part from the tyranny of the geographic and cultural distance between the United States and Asia, which compli-cated sustained US engagement and produced myths and misperceptions about Asia that sometimes overrode larger strategic imperatives. In addition, the exigencies of communist advance in Europe and punishing conflict in the Middle East all too often left Asia a "secondary theater" and the US Asia policy apparatus short-staffed, jeopardizing US interests. Today, as the United States sets out to construct a strategy suitable for the challenges of the twenty-first century, it will need to break the habit of occasional absence, hesitancy, and inattentiveness in this consequential region.

The necessity of a new strategy, one that builds on the rudiments of pre-vious strategy but goes further, is manifest. If the United States is to achieve long-standing interests in Asia, it will need not only to prevent the emergence of an Asian hegemon, the main focus of past efforts, but also to strengthen Asia's operating system—that is, the complex legal, security, and practical arrangements that have underscored four decades of Asian prosperity and security and provide the scaffolding for common efforts to solve transna-tional challenges. This operating system, which rests on principles like free-dom of navigation, free trade, regional transparency, and peaceful resolution of disputes, is at the core of Asia's future and American interests. The most promising Asia strategy—and one that is at the center of the Pivot—blends several competing approaches. It focuses not only on allies but also on part-ners; it looks to solve transnational problems but does not ignore traditional security concerns; and it seeks to manage both cooperation and competition in ties with China. This book articulates a clear view that just as China has risen, elements of US strategy must also evolve, and this process of renovation is essential to the overall viability of the Pivot. The strategy and attitudes that animated the effort to lure China out of its self-imposed internal exile when it was poor and underdeveloped forty years ago are very different from the policies necessary today to shape the choices of the fastest arriving power on the international scene in history. The necessity for an integrated approach requires the United States to move beyond serving as a "gardener" for Asia, in the metaphor of former secretary of state George Schultz, who used the term to describe dutifully tending to the disputes and controversies that surface time and again in US bilateral ties and in the surrounding region. In the twenty-first century, the United States must now evolve to become a more broadly focused "orchestra conductor," one that coordinates the increasingly independent efforts of Asian states and multilateral institutions in common cause to shape Asia's future.

This is the time for implementing such a comprehensive American strategy for Asia. As chapter five made clear, after decades of rapid growth and heightening tensions, Asia is now facing a profoundly important period of uncertainty, flux, and transition that will define its future and require resolute American action and presence. Asia is being pulled between hegemony and a regional balance of power. Its operating system is drawn between twenty-first-century and nineteenth-century rules of the road. Its established and emerging powers are deciding whether to become stakeholders or spoilers. Its militaries are drifting between conflict and peaceful coexistence. Its transitional states are deciding whether to embrace democracy or fall back on authoritarian ways and domestic repression. And its economic structure and trade relations are being pulled between high standards and soft protectionism. Because Asia will in many circumstances end up living somewhere on the spectrum in between these sets of two stark choices, a crucial and enduring component of the Pivot will be to bend the arc of the Asian Century more toward the imperatives of Asian peace and prosperity and long-standing American interests.

To that end, this book offers a detailed and lengthy ten-point plan for accomplishing this task in chapter six. First, the United States needs to *clarify the Pivot and mobilize public support* for it through an annual strategy document articulating its purpose and promise, as well as through direct presidential communication to the broader public on the importance of US Asia strategy. Second, the United States must *bolster its alliances* by adding a "tire" to the familiar "hub and spokes" alliance structure, thereby joining each and every allied spoke to the others while strengthening the ties of all spokes to the US hub. Third, the United States should endeavor to *shape the contours of China's rise.* In Secretary Clinton's words, the United States will have to learn "how to find common ground and how to stand our ground" in relations with China. This will call for understanding the drivers behind a more assertive Chinese foreign policy in the era of President Xi Jinping, as well as a thorough work plan for managing China's assertiveness, to be sure, but also for seeking increased opportunities to foster cooperation.[1] Fourth, the United States will need to *deepen regional partnerships* by broadening the hub and spokes system beyond allies to incorporate other regional partners, such as India, New Zealand, Taiwan, Southeast Asian states, and Pacific island states. Fifth, the United States will benefit from *pursuing economic statecraft,* including through the TPP and other agreements, in order to create a long-term trading system in Asia that is high-standard, resistant to protectionism, and capable of institutionalizing America's economic principles and presence. Sixth, the United States must *commit to multilateralism.* It should engage directly and actively as a multilateral institutional player in its own right but also encourage Asian states to become *more* committed stakeholders in global institutions. A key feature of American statecraft must be to actively support Asia's nascent but promising multilateral organizations, both to shape their evolution and to ensure the United States a seat at the tables where Asia's future is discussed. Asia's institutional framework should trend toward trans-Pacific groupings rather than Pan-Asian efforts. Seventh, the United States must *strengthen and diversify its military capabilities* by ensuring it receives ample, consistent, and flexible funding. Only then can it effectively cope with A2/AD technologies, diversify its posture southward, and increase presence through exercises, port calls, and humanitarian assistance and disaster relief. Eighth, the United States should prudently and flexibly *promote its values,* making special efforts to help Asia's transitional states consolidate their democracies and strengthen domestic institutions and civil society. Ninth, the United States can humanize the otherwise abstract and impersonal pillars of American engagement by *strengthening people-to-people ties,* not only through US government programs, but also through nongovernmental organizations and the Asian American community. Tenth, the United States should *involve European partners* more directly in the conversation about Asia's destiny and our respective roles in it. Nearly every consequential diplomatic endeavor undertaken by the United States has been done with allies in Europe, and the Pivot should be no different.

The ten principles that comprise the plan for the Pivot will undoubtedly face challenges in the period ahead, as chapter seven discussed in detail. Many are domestic, as the foreign policy consensus frays, deadlock blocks critical legislation, defense and civilian diplomacy budgets face pressure, the public turns inward, and the US bureaucracy struggles both to formulate long-term policy and to cultivate experienced and able Asia hands. These challenges are daunting but they are not insurmountable, and they are more akin to tests of will than questions of capability. What is needed is ultimately a bipartisan consensus around the idea that the future of the twenty-first century will largely play out in Asia, as well as modest public support for the notion that Asia's dynamism should be harnessed to the benefit of all Americans. None among a procession of US presidents has yet to give a speech outlining these arguments to the American public, in contrast with numerous high-level proclamations around combat operations in the Middle East, and a public campaign for Asia policy is long overdue. The United States and Asia, drawn together by a shared history of sacrifice and mutual endeavor for decades, may well face the possibility of decoupling and mutual estrangement as Asians grow less confident about the reliability of the United States or, conversely, Americans grow more uncertain of whether Asia contributes to or undermines American prosperity. In practical terms, this means that the Pivot to Asia may be bounded by a window. If the United States waits too long to reaffirm its essential commitments to the region, or if its leaders wait too long to explain the important link between Asia and American prosperity, then the prospects for an enduring and stable American role in the Asian century ahead will dim considerably.

Through the pages of this book, it has been argued that a particularly enduring challenge to the Pivot emerges from the dark contours of the largely unrewarding and unrelenting conflict in the Middle East, which threaten to siphon scarce top-level attention and resources away from this Asian endeavor. The US experience in this troublesome region is perhaps best summed up by the overacting of Al Pacino as Michael Corleone in the *Godfather* trilogy: "Just when I thought I was out," he famously laments, "they pull me back in." Even after the conclusion of the wars in Iraq and Afghanistan, the rise of ISIS, the civil war in Syria, Iranian machinations, and near anarchy in Libya and Yemen together cry out for American attention. No one is advocating an American withdrawal from the region, but it cannot be in US interests to field a foreign policy so imbalanced that it allows for the concerns of one region to completely override our vital interests in others. While the Middle East will always command top-level attention, US foreign policy pursuits must be about more than the Middle East. This book has argued that it is time for a necessary course correction in American diplomacy, including an elevation of Asia in the councils of American policymaking and a gradual reorientation of strategic time and attention away from the intractable crises of the Middle East to the longer and more patient game of strategy that awaits in Asia.

The Pivot, both this book and the policy that it describes, has argued for precisely such a reorientation. The United States has an irrefutable interest in Asia and the course it will take in the years and decades ahead. The Pivot to Asia recognizes this fundamental reality and is based on the belief that Asia's dizzying scale and stunning ascent, combined with its unique receptiveness to American leadership, will reward US engagement with a substantial positive return on political, economic, and military investments. With determined American action, the United States will be uniquely poised to capture the promise and overcome the pitfalls of the coming Asian Century. Indeed, as it plays host to the twenty-first century, Asia will extend or curtail the legacy left by the United States in the twentieth, and in so doing, hold American hopes for a new century that is less bloody, more cooperative, and more just than the last. The United States has helped fashion a remarkably durable and beneficent operating system for the entire region that sets a foundation for future activity, and sustaining and adapting this system must be a prime directive for strategy in the time ahead. For the United States, marked by an indelible and enduring sense of mission to shape tomorrow's world, the Pivot to Asia offers this country the best chance to sustain its power, interests, and well-being in the dynamic period rising on the horizon.

Notes

Introduction

1. Barack Obama, "Remarks by President Obama and Prime Minister Shinawatra in a Joint Press Conference," Bangkok, October 18, 2012. https://www.whitehouse .gov/the-press-office/2012/11/18/remarks-president-obama-and-prime-minister -shinawatra-joint-press-confer

2. James Steinberg and Michael E. O'Hanlon, *Strategic Reassurance and Resolve: US–China Relations in the Twenty-First Century* (Princeton: Princeton University Press, 2014), 11.

3. Asian Development Bank, *Asia 2050: Realizing the Asian Century. Executive Summary* (Manila: Asian Development Bank, 2011).

4. Tazeem Pasha and Rachel Crabtree, "Foreign Direct Investment in the United States: Drivers of US Economic Competitiveness," (Department of Commerce, International Trade Administration, December 31, 2013).

5. Richard Wike, Bruce Stokes, and Jacob Poushter, "Global Publics Back U.S. on Fighting ISIS, but Are Critical of Post-9/11 Torture" (Pew Research Center, June 23, 2015), 13.

6. See "Remarks by National Security Advisor Tom Donilon on President Obama's Asia Policy and Upcoming Trip to Asia," November 15, 2013. http://www.white house.gov/the-press-office/2012/11/15/remarks-national-security-advisor-tom -donilon-prepared-delivery

Chapter One: The Pivot Defined

1. Hillary Clinton, "America's Pacific Century," *Foreign Policy*, November 2011.

2. Hillary Clinton, *Hard Choices* (New York: Simon & Schuster, 2014), 45–46.

3. President Obama referred to the Pivot in his 2012 debate with Mitt Romney and more recently in a 2014 press conference with President Xi Jinping.

4. Clinton, "America's Pacific Century."

5. Kim Ghattas, "Why Obama Is Making Time for Asia," *BBC News*, November 11, 2013.

6. "Editorial: A Proper Pivot Towards Asia," *Washington Post*, July 14, 2012.

7. Haass objects to certain aspects of its implementation and prefers the term *rebalance*. Richard Haass, "The Irony of American Strategy," *Foreign Affairs* 92, no. 3 (2013). Haass is quoted in "Richard Haass: Obama Has Made Middle East 'Much Worse,'" *Washington Free Beacon*, October 27, 2014. http://freebeacon.com/national-security/ richard-haas-obama-has-made-middle-east-much-worse-damaged-american-reliability/

8. Peter Ennis, "Mike Green: 'The Asia Pivot Is Both Political, and Good Policy,'" *Dispatch Japan*, February 20, 2012. http://www.dispatchjapan.com/blog/2012/02/mike-green-the-asia-pivot-is-both-political-and-good-policy.html

9. Leon Panetta, "The US Rebalance Towards the Asia-Pacific," Speech before the Shangri-La Dialogue, Singapore, June 2, 2012.

10. Robert Sutter, *The United States and Asia: Regional Dynamics and Twenty-First Century Relations* (New York: Rowman & Littlefield, 2015), 80–82.

11. Jackie Calmes, "Trans-Pacific Partnership Is Reached, but Faces Scrutiny in Congress," *New York Times*, October 6, 2015.

12. Sutter, *The United States and Asia: Regional Dynamics and Twenty-First Century Relations*, 83.

13. Shawn Brimley and Ely Ratner, "Smart Shift," *Foreign Affairs* 92, no. 1 (2013): 180.

14. Lee Hsien Loong and Fareed Zakaria, "Interview with Lee Hsien Loong," *Fareed Zakaria GPS*, CNN, aired February 5, 2012. http://transcripts.cnn.com/TRANSCRIPTS/1202/05/fzgps.01.html

15. Sutter, *The United States and Asia: Regional Dynamics and Twenty-First Century Relations*, 89.

16. Michael J. Green and Nicholas Szechenyi, *Power and Order in Asia: A Survey of Regional Expectations* (Washington, D.C.: Rowman & Littlefield, 2014), 9.

17. Wike, Stokes, and Poushter, "Global Publics Back U.S. on Fighting ISIS, but Are Critical of Post-9/11 Torture," 33.

18. Thomas Christensen, *The China Challenge: Shaping the Choices of a Rising Power* (New York: W. W. Norton, 2015), 248.

19. Ralph Cossa and Brad Glosserman, "Return to Asia: It's Not (All) About China," *PacNet*, no. 7 (January 30, 2012).

20. Daniel Blumenthal, "Pivoting to Asia: The Good, the Bad, and the Ugly," *Foreign Policy*, July 3, 2012. http://foreignpolicy.com/2012/07/03/pivoting-and-rebalancing-the-good-the-bad-and-the-ugly/

21. Ashley J. Tellis, *Pivot or Pirouette: The U.S. Rebalance to Asia* (Bangalore: National Institute of Advanced Studies, 2014), 2, 7.

22. Michael J. Green, "The United States and Asia after Bush," *The Pacific Review* 21, no. 5 (December 2008): 586.

23. John Burton and Roel Landingin, "Asia Questions US Regional Influence," *Financial Times*, July 31, 2007.

24. Condoleezza Rice, *No Higher Honor* (New York: Simon & Schuster, 2011), 485.

25. For a transcript of these remarks, see Hillary Rodham Clinton and Surin Pitsuwan, "Beginning a New Era of Diplomacy in Asia: Remarks with ASEAN Secretary General Dr. Surin Pitsuwan," U.S. Department of State website, February 18, 2009. http://www.state.gov/secretary/20092013clinton/rm/2009a/02/119422.htm

26. Amitai Etzioni, "The United States' Premature Pivot to Asia," *Society* 49, no. 5 (2012): 395.

27. Robert Kagan, "U.S. Can't Ignore the Middle East," *Washington Post*, November 20, 2012.

28. Clinton, *Hard Choices*, 45–46.

29. For a transcript of some of these remarks, see Ali Wyne, "Tom Pickering Interviews Henry Kissinger on America's Rebalancing Towards the Asia-Pacific," *Huffington*

Post, December 11, 2013. http://www.huffingtonpost.com/ali-wyne/tom-pickering-interviews-_b_4426774.html

30. Herman Van Rompuy, "Europe's Political and Economic Challenges in a Changing World," Winston Churchill Lecture, Zurich, November 9, 2011). http://eeas.europa.eu/delegations/switzerland/documents/more_info/speeches/2011-11-09_van_rompuy_churchill_lecture.pdf

31. Kurt Campbell and Ely Ratner, "Far Eastern Promises," *Foreign Affairs* 93, no. 3 (2014).

32. Sutter, *The United States and Asia: Regional Dynamics and Twenty-First Century Relations*, 77.

33. Barack Obama, "Remarks by President Obama and President Xi Jinping in Joint Press Conference," November 12, 2014. https://www.whitehouse.gov/the-press-office/2014/11/12/remarks-president-obama-and-president-xi-jinping-joint-press-conference

34. Sutter, *The United States and Asia: Regional Dynamics and Twenty-First Century Relations*, 71.

35. Campbell and Ratner, "Far Eastern Promises."

36. Robert Ross, "The Problem with the Pivot," *Foreign Affairs* 91, no. 6 (2012).

37. Michael Chase and Benjamin S. Purser, "Pivot and Parry: China's Response to America's New Defense Strategy," *China Brief* 12, no. 6 (2012).

38. Ross, "The Problem with the Pivot."

39. Ibid.

40. Wike, Stokes, and Poushter, "Global Publics Back U.S. on Fighting ISIS, but Are Critical of Post-9/11 Torture," 13.

41. Michael D. Swaine, "Chinese Leadership and Elite Responses to the U.S. Pacific Pivot," *China Leadership Monitor* 38, no. 3 (2012): 4–5.

42. Chase and Purser, "Pivot and Parry: China's Response to America's New Defense Strategy."

43. Michael J. Green and Daniel Twining, "Dizzy Yet? The Pros and Cons of the Asia 'Pivot,'" *Foreign Policy*, November 21, 2013.

44. Aaron L. Friedberg, "The Sources of Chinese Conduct: Explaining Beijing's Assertiveness," *The Washington Quarterly* 37, no. 4 (2015): 145.

45. Michael J. Green and Zack Cooper, "Revitalizing the Rebalance: How to Keep U.S. Focus on Asia," *The Washington Quarterly* 37, no. 3 (2014): 26.

46. Dina S. Smeltz and Craig Kafura, "Americans Affirm Ties to Allies in Asia" (The Chicago Council on Global Affairs, October 28, 2014).

47. "New Poll Shows Vast Majority of Americans Support Trade Agreements," *Business Roundtable*, March 11, 2014. http://businessroundtable.org/media/news-releases/new-poll-shows-vast-majority-americans-support-trade-agreements

48. Richard Haass, *Foreign Policy Begins at Home: The Case for Putting America's House in Order* (New York: Basic Books, 2013), 106.

Chapter Two: The Stage for the Pivot

1. "ISAPS International Survey on Aesthetic/Cosmetic Procedures Performed in 2011" (The International Society of Aesthetic Plastic Surgeons, 2011), 10.

2. Jason Chow, "China Is Now World's Biggest Consumer of Red Wine," *Wall Street*

Journal, January 29, 2014. blogs.wsj.com/scene/2014/01/29/china-is-now-worlds
-biggest-consumer-of-red-wine/

3. While this figure measures by volume, soju, the most popular drink in South Korea, contains only half the amount of alcohol of vodka, the drink of choice in Russia. Robert Ferdman and Ritchie King, "South Koreans Drink Twice as Much Liquor as Russians and More than Four Times as Much as Americans," *Quartz*, February 2, 2014. http://qz.com/171191/south-koreans-drink-twice-as-much-liquor-as-russians -and-more-than-four-times-as-much-as-americans/

4. Lant Pritchett and Larry Summers, "Asiaphoria Meets Regression to the Mean," M-RCBG Faculty Working Paper Series, November 6, 2013.

5. Barack Obama, "Remarks by President Barack Obama at Suntory Hall," Suntory Hall, Tokyo, Japan, White House Press Office, November 14, 2009. http://www .whitehouse.gov/the-press-office/remarks-president-barack-obama-suntory-hall

6. Michael Shermer, "Why Our Brains Do Not Intuitively Grasp Probabilities," *Scientific American*, September 2008.

7. These are China, Japan, India, Australia, and South Korea.

8. East-West Center Research Program, *The Future of Population in Asia* (Honolulu: East-West Center, 2002), 5.

9. For more on this campaign, see Judith Rae Shapiro, *Mao's War Against Nature: Politics and the Environment in Revolutionary China* (Cambridge University Press, 2001).

10. See statistics compiled in Angus Maddison, *Contours of the World Economy 1–2030 AD: Essays in Macro-Economic History* (Oxford: Oxford University Press, 2007).

11. Homi Kharas and Geoffrey Gertz, "The New Global Middle Class: A Cross-Over from West to East" (Washington, D.C.: Brookings Institution, Wolfensohn Center for Development, 2010), 5–6.

12. Adapted from Thomas P. M. Barnett's thought experiment in James Fallows, *China Airborne: The Test of China's Future* (New York: Vintage Books, 2012), 9.

13. Damien Ma and William Adams, *In Line Behind a Billion People: How Scarcity Will Define China's Ascent in the Next Decade* (Saddle River: FT Press, 2012).

14. Fallows, *China Airborne: The Test of China's Future*, 10.

15. William T. Wilson, "Asia's Economic Miracle Has Peaked," *The National Interest*, November 10, 2014. http://nationalinterest.org/feature/asia%E2%80%99s-economic -miracle-has-peaked-11636

16. "Statistical Yearbook for Asia and the Pacific 2013" (United Nations Economic and Social Commission for Asia and the Pacific, 2013), 1–25.

17. These statistics can be found in *The CIA World Factbook 2015* (New York: Skyhorse Publishing, 2015).

18. "World Population to 2300" (United Nations Department of Economic and Social Affairs, Population Division, 2004), 236–240.

19. "Wasting Time: India's Demographic Challenge," *Economist*, May 11, 2013.

20. "World Population to 2300," 236–240.

21. "Millennium Development Goals Fact Sheet," in *United Nations Summit, High-Level Plenary Meeting of the General Assembly*, 2010. http://www.un.org/millenni umgoals/pdf/MDG_FS_1_EN.pdf

22. "Millennium Development Goals: India Country Report 2014" (Government of India, Ministry of Statistics and Programme Implementation, 2014); "The Millen-

nium Development Goals Report 2014" (United Nations, 2014), 8; World Bank, *2013 Atlas of Global Development* (Glasgow: Collins Bartholomew, 2013), 31.

23. Saritha Rai, "Living Like the Other Half," *New York Times, India Ink: Notes on the World's Largest Democracy,* October 20, 2011. http://india.blogs.nytimes .com/2011/10/20/living-like-the-other-half/

24. "Poverty in Asia," *Economist,* August 30, 2014.

25. Rai, "Living Like the Other Half."

26. OECD/World Health Organization, *Health at a Glance: Asia/Pacific 2014: Measuring Progress towards Universal Health Coverage* (Paris: OECD Publishing, 2014), 18–20.

27. Historical data on life expectancy in Asia can be found in OECD/World Health Organization, *Health at a Glance: Asia/Pacific 2012: Measuring Progress towards Universal Health Coverage* (OECD Publishing, 2012), 12–13.

28. Simeon Bennett and Kanoko Matsuyama, "Asia's Cancer Rate May Jump by Almost 60% by 2020," *New York Times,* April 23, 2007.

29. "The Global Anti-Tobacco Survey Atlas" (Center for Disease Control Foundation, 2015), 30, 102–103.

30. "The Millennium Development Goals Report 2014," 16.

31. Data extracted from "UNESCO eAtlas of World Literacy" (UNESCO Institute for Statistics, 2015).

32. *Higher Education in Asia: Expanding Up, Expanding Out* (Montreal, Canada: UNESCO Institute for Statistics, 2014), 18.

33. Yojana Sharma, "What Do You Do with Millions of Extra Graduates?" *BBC News,* July 1, 2014.

34. Geeta Anand, "India Graduates Millions, but Too Few Are Fit to Hire," *Wall Street Journal,* April 5, 2011; *Higher Education Across Asia: An Overview of Issues and Strategies* (Manila: Asia Development Bank, 2011).

35. World Bank, *2013 Atlas of Global Development,* 104; *State of the World's Cities 2012/2013: Prosperity of Cities* (Nairobi: United Nations Settlements Program, 2012), 126.

36. "Statistical Yearbook for Asia and the Pacific 2013," 11–17.

37. Te-Ping Chen, "Introducing China's Future Megalopolis: The Jing-Jin-Ji," *Wall Street Journal,* April 4, 2014.

38. Defined as buildings taller than 400 feet.

39. United Nations, "The World Urbanization Prospects: 2014 Revision Highlights" (United Nations Economic and Social Affairs, 2014), 26.

40. "Urban World: Mapping the Economic Power of Cities" (McKinsey Global Institute, March 2011).

41. "Global Power City Index 2014" (Institute for Urban Studies, Mori Memorial Foundation, 2014), 24.

42. "2014 Global Cities Index and Emerging Cities Outlook" (A.T. Kearney, 2014).

43. Gardiner Harris, "Poor Sanitation in India May Afflict Well-fed Children with Malnutrition," *New York Times,* July 13, 2014.

44. *State of the World's Cities 2012/2013: Prosperity of Cities,* 127.

45. World Bank, *2013 Atlas of Global Development,* 105.

46. "The Final Frontier: Sanitation in India," *Economist,* July 19, 2014.

47. Kartikay Mehrotra, "India's Toilet Race Failing as Villages Don't Use Them," *Bloomberg News*, August 4, 2014.

48. "The Final Frontier: Sanitation in India."

49. Edward Wong, "Air Pollution Linked to 1.2 Million Premature Deaths in China," *New York Times*, April 1, 2013.

50. Edward Wong, "On Scale of 0 to 500, Beijing's Air Quality Tops 'Crazy Bad' at 755," *New York Times*, January 12, 2013.

51. This data is available at "Ambient (Outdoor) Air Pollution in Cities Database 2014," World Health Organization, 2014. http://www.who.int/entity/quantifying_ehim pacts/national/countryprofile/aap_pm_database_may2014.xls?ua=1

52. International Monetary Fund, *World Economic Outlook 2014: Legacies, Clouds, Uncertainties* (Washington, D.C.: International Monetary Fund, 2014).

53. Projections are available using data from International Monetary Fund, *World Economic Outlook 2015: Uneven Growth: Short-Term and Long-Term Factors* (Washington, D.C.: International Monetary Fund, 2015).

54. *Purchasing Power Parities and the Real Size of World Economies: A Comprehensive Report of the 2011 International Comparison Program* (Washington, D.C.: World Bank, 2015), 17.

55. Richard Dobbs, Jaana Remes, and James Manyika, "Urban World: Cities and the Rise of the Consuming Class" (McKinsey Global Institute, June 2012).

56. International Monetary Fund, *World Economic Outlook 2015: Uneven Growth: Short-Term and Long-Term Factors* (Washington, D.C.: International Monetary Fund, 2015).

57. These data are routinely updated at "Country Comparison: Real GDP Growth Rate," *CIA: The World Factbook*, 2015. https://www.cia.gov/library/publications/the-world-factbook/rankorder/2003rank.html

58. Homi Kharas and Geoffrey Gertz, "The New Global Middle Class: A Crossover from West to East," in *China's Emerging Middle Class: Beyond Economic Transformation* (Washington, D.C.: Brookings Institution Press, 2010), 38.

59. "Statistical Yearbook for Asia and the Pacific 2014" (United Nations Economic and Social Commission for Asia and the Pacific, 2014), 26.

60. World Bank, *2013 Atlas of Global Development*, 78.

61. *Doing Business 2015: Going Beyond Efficiency* (Washington, D.C.: World Bank, 2014), 4.

62. Transparency International, "Corruption Perceptions Index 2014" (Transparency International, 2015), 7.

63. Francis Fukuyama, *Trust: The Social Virtues and the Creation of Prosperity* (New York: Free Press, 1995).

64. David Barboza, "In China, Projects to Make the Great Wall Feel Small," *New York Times*, January 12, 2015.

65. "Aerotropolitan Ambitions," *Economist*, March 14, 2015.

66. "Road-Building Rage to Leave U.S. in Dust," *Wall Street Journal: China Realtime*, January 18, 2011. http://blogs.wsj.com/chinarealtime/2011/01/18/road-building-rage-to-leave-us-in-dust/

67. James T. Areddy, "China's Building Push Goes Underground," *Wall Street Journal*, November 10, 2013.

68. Shibani Mahtani, "Singapore Tops Survey with World's Best Infrastructure," *Wall Street Journal: Indonesia Realtime*, December 5, 2012. http://blogs.wsj.com/indonesiarealtime/2012/12/05/singapore-tops-survey-with-worlds-best-infrastructure/

69. *The Global Competitiveness Index 2014–2015* (Switzerland: World Economic Forum, 2014), 16–17.

70. These and other useful statistics can be found in the transportation (运输) section of *China Statistical Yearbook 2015 [中国统计年鉴]* (Beijing: China Statistical Press [中国统计出版社], 2015). Information on India's expressways can be found in Craphts Consultants, "Formulation of Master Plan for Indian National Expressway Network: Final Project Report" (Indian Ministry of Road Transport and Highways, 2009). http://morth.nic.in/writereaddata/linkimages/SL_Final_Report_Part13901147970.pdf

71. *China Statistical Yearbook 2015 [中国统计年鉴]*; Manoj Kumar, "India to Seek Foreign Investment in Giant, Creaking Rail Network," Reuters, January 9, 2014. http://www.reuters.com/article/2014/01/09/india-railways-idUSL3N0KJ21D20140109

72. Nauzer Bharucha, "India Needs to Build 30k Units Daily for 8 Years to Meet Housing Needs," *Times of India*, August 20, 2014.

73. "Bad Policy as Much as Bad Infrastructure Is Holding Indonesia Back," *Economist*, May 9, 2014.

74. "Statistical Yearbook for Asia and the Pacific 2013," xiv.

75. Ibid., 281.

76. Ibid., 282.

77. Regional data on telecommunications and Internet usage from 2005 to 2015 can be found in "World Telecommunication/ICT Indicators Database," International Telecommunication Union, 2015. http://www.itu.int/en/ITU-D/Statistics/Pages/stat/default.aspx

78. Ibid.

79. Ibid.

80. "State of the Internet, Q4 2014" (Akamai Technologies, 2015).

81. Simon Mundy, "South Korea Targets 5G Global Supremacy," *Financial Times*, November 25, 2014.

82. *Asian Development Outlook 2013: Asia's Energy Challenge* (Manila: Asia Development Bank, 2013), 53.

83. This data is available through the U.S. Energy Information Administration database. "International Energy Statistics," U.S. Energy Information Administration, 2015. http://www.eia.gov/cfapps/ipdbproject/IEDIndex3.cfm

84. World Bank, *2013 Atlas of Global Development*, 124; "International Energy Statistics," U.S. Energy Information Administration, 2015. http://www.eia.gov/cfapps/ipdbproject/IEDIndex3.cfm

85. *Asian Development Outlook 2013: Asia's Energy Challenge*, 56.

86. *World Energy Outlook 2014* (Paris: OECD/International Energy Agency, 2014), 80–82.

87. Ibid., 74.

88. Ibid., 235; *Southeast Asia Energy Outlook* (Paris: OECD/International Energy Agency, 2013), 45.

89. *World Energy Outlook 2014*, 191, 197; Brad Plumer, "The Big Climate Question: Will the World Build 1,200 New Coal Plants?" *Washington Post: Wonkblog*, November 20, 2012. http://www.washingtonpost.com/blogs/wonkblog/wp/2012/11/20/1200-coal-are-plants-being-planned-worldwide-what-happens-if-they-all-get-built/; Ailun Yang and Yiyun Cui, "Global Coal Risk Assessment: Data Analysis and

Market Research" (World Resource Institute, November 2012). http://www.wri.org/publication/global-coal-risk-assessment

90. *World Energy Outlook 2014*, 246; "Who's Winning the Clean Energy Race? 2013" (Pew Charitable Trusts, April 3, 2014).

91. *World Energy Outlook 2014*, 233–236.

92. Chisaki Watanabe, "Japan Solar Capacity Forecast at 100GW in FY2030 by Lobby Group," *Bloomberg News*, August 8, 2014; Feifei Shen, "China Solar Project Delays Mean Japan Could Be Largest Market," *Bloomberg News*, November 27, 2014.

93. Chisaki Watanabe, "Floating Solar Power Hits Land-Squeezed Japan Under Kyocera Plan," *Bloomberg News*, August 19, 2014.

94. "Here Comes the Sun: Bringing Solar Energy Out of the Dark," *New Delhi Times*, August 16, 2014; "Gujarat Solar Park: Asia's Largest Solar Power Park Opens," *Economic Times*, April 19, 2012.

95. *Southeast Asia Energy Outlook*, 45.

96. Tim McLaughlin and Sithu Lwin, "US Firm's Investment to Tackle MDY Power Woes," *Myanmar Times*, August 30, 2014.

97. *World Energy Outlook 2014*, 235; *Southeast Asia Energy Outlook*, 45.

98. "Statistical Yearbook for Asia and the Pacific 2012" (United Nations Economic and Social Commission for Asia and the Pacific, 2012), ix.

99. Ibid.

100. *World Energy Outlook 2014*, 99.

101. Justin Gillis, "Climate Panel Cites Near Certainty on Warming," *New York Times*, August 19, 2013.

102. Gardiner Harris, "Borrowed Time on Disappearing Land," *New York Times*, March 28, 2014.

103. Ibid.

104. Robin McKie, "Global Warming to Hit Asia Hardest, Warns New Report on Climate Change," *Guardian*, March 22, 2014.

105. "Economic Costs of Rising Sea Levels in Asia and the Pacific," Asia Development Bank, January 3, 2014. http://www.adb.org/features/economic-costs-rising-sea-levels-asia-and-pacific

106. "From Copenhagen Accord to Climate Action: Tracking National Commitments to Curb Global Warming," Natural Resources Defense Council, n.d. http://www.nrdc.org/international/copenhagenaccords/

107. "Smoggy Beijing to Ban Coal Use," *Xinhua*, August 24, 2014.

108. Jeffrey Goldberg, "Drowning Kiribati," *Bloomberg Businessweek*, November 21, 2013.

109. "The Asia Pacific Disaster Report, 2010: Protecting Development Gains" (UNESCAP and UN International Strategy for Disaster Reduction, 2010), 2.

110. Ibid., xii.

111. Debarati Guha-Sapir, Philippe Hoyois, and Regina Below, "Annual Disaster Statistical Review 2012" (Centre for Research on the Epidemiology of Disasters, Université Catholique de Louvain, 2012), 29.

112. Cris Larano, "Death Toll in Philippines from Typhoon Haiyan Tops 6,000," *Wall Street Journal*, December 13, 2013.

113. Megha Rajagopalan, "China's Meager Aid to the Philippines Could Dent Its Image," Reuters, November 12, 2013.

114. "The Asia Pacific Disaster Report, 2012: Reducing Vulnerability and Exposure to Disasters" (UNESCAP and UN International Strategy for Disaster Reduction, 2012).

115. Shanshan Wang and Eric Pfanner, "China's One-Day Shopping Spree Sets Record in Online Sales," *New York Times*, November 11, 2013.

116. "International Shipping Facts and Figures—Information Resources on Trade, Safety, Security, Environment" (International Maritime Organization, March 6, 2012).

117. "The Humble Hero," *Economist*, May 18, 2013.

118. Rose George, *Ninety Percent of Everything: Inside Shipping, the Invisible Industry That Puts Clothes on Your Back, Gas in Your Car, and Food on Your Plate* (New York: Metropolitan Books, 2013), 4.

119. Ibid., 3–4.

120. United Nations Conference on Trade and Development, *Review of Maritime Transport: 2014* (New York: United Nations, 2014), 7–10.

121. "U.S. Seaborne Trade by World Region, 2012–2013," American Association of Port Authorities, 2013.

122. "Top 50 World Container Ports," World Shipping Council, 2014. http://www.worldshipping.org/about-the-industry/global-trade/top-50-world-container-ports

123. Naomi Christie, "Shipping Measure Collapses to Record Amid Lack of Coal to China," *Bloomberg*, February 11, 2015.

124. Eoghan Macguire, "Maersk 'Triple E': Introducing the World's Biggest Ship," *CNN: The Gateway*, June 26, 2013. http://edition.cnn.com/2013/06/26/business/maersk-triple-e-biggest-ship/

125. David Shukman, "The Largest Vessel the World Has Never Seen," *BBC News*, December 16, 2014.

126. These statistics can be found in Shipping and Trade products issued by Clarkson Research Service. http://english.donga.com/srv/service.php3?bicode=020000&biid=2015040687128

127. Andrew Erickson and Austin Strange, "China and International Antipiracy Effort," *Diplomat*, November 1, 2013.

128. "Piracy and Armed Robbery Against Ships" (ICC International Maritime Bureau, January 2014).

129. "South China Sea" (U.S. Energy Information Administration, February 7, 2013). https://www.eia.gov/beta/international/analysis_includes/regions_of_interest/South_China_Sea/south_china_sea.pdf

130. Myra MacDonald, "Asia's Defense Spending Overtakes Europe's: IISS," Reuters, March 14, 2013.

131. Sam Perlo-Freeman and Carina Solmirano, "Trends in World Military Expenditure, 2013" (Stockholm International Peace Research Institute, April 2014).

132. Jeremy Page, "China Raises Defense Spending 12.2% for 2014," *Wall Street Journal*, March 5, 2014.

133. Daniel R. Russel, "Maritime Disputes in East Asia," Testimony before the House Committee on Foreign Affairs Subcommittee on Asia and the Pacific, February 5, 2014. http://www.state.gov/p/eap/rls/rm/2014/02/221293.htm

134. "Forecast International Expects Defense Spending to Project Upward Across Asia-Pacific Region." *NASDAQ OMX Globe Newswire*, October 21, 2013.

135. Greg Torode, "Vietnam Building Deterrent against China in Disputed Seas with Submarines," Reuters, September 7, 2014.

136. "Military and Security Developments Involving the People's Republic of China" (Office of the Secretary of Defense, 2014).

137. "Full Text: China's Military Strategy," *Renmin Wang [人民网]*, May 25, 2015. http://en.people.cn/n/2015/0526/c90785-8897779.html

138. This data can be found in the Historical Tables files posted on the Office of Management and Budget website. "Table 14.5: Total Government Expenditures by Major Category of Expenditure as Percentages of GDP: 1948–2014" (Office of Management and Budget: Historical Tables, 2015). https://www.whitehouse.gov/omb/budget/Historicals

139. Juliette Garside, "Apple Overtakes Samsung as the World's Biggest Smartphone Maker," *Guardian*, March 4, 2015; George Chen, "China to Replace US as World's Top Consumer Tech Market, Says CES Chief," *South China Morning Post*, May 25, 2015; Bruce Einhorn, "Chinese TV Maker Hisense Takes Aim at Sony," *Bloomberg*, July 31, 2014; Sam Grobart, "Samsung Wants to Be the World's Biggest Appliance Maker by 2015," January 9, 2014.

140. Charles Duhigg and Keith Bradsher, "How the U.S. Lost Out on iPhone Work," *New York Times*, January 21, 2012.

141. Ibid.

142. Ibid.

143. Ibid.

144. Malcolm Moore, "Mass Suicide Protest at Apple Manufacturer Foxconn Factory," *Telegraph*, January 11, 2012.

145. "Tata Nano: World's Cheapest Car Gets an Image Makeover," *BBC News*, August 22, 2013.

146. Andy Sharman, "Hydrogen and Electric Vehicles Battle for Supremacy," *Financial Times*, November 20, 2014.

147. "What Happened to Japan's Electronic Giants?" *BBC News*, April 2, 2013. http://www.bbc.com/news/world-asia-21992700

148. "Theatrical Market Statistics 2014" (Motion Picture Association of America, 2014), 5.

149. Peter Ford, "Chinese Roll Their Eyes at Local Footage Added to *Iron Man 3*," *Christian Science Monitor*, May 10, 2013.

150. Ibid.

151. "Theatrical Market Statistics 2014," 5.

152. Martin Chilton, "China's *Iron Man 3* Milks Its Product Placement," *Telegraph*, n.d.

153. Ben Fritz and John Hom, "Reel China: Hollywood Tries to Stay on China's Good Side," *Los Angeles Times*, March 16, 2011.

154. James Daniel, " 'Iron Man 2' Execs 'Changed Film for Chinese Audience' by Adding Four Minutes to the Film with Chinese Actors," *Daily Mail*, 13 May 2013.

155. Tom Shone, "Hollywood Transformed: How China Is Changing the DNA of American Blockbuster Movies," *Financial Times*, July 25, 2014.

156. Quoted in Evan Osnos, "Hollywood and China: Revenue and Responsibility," *New Yorker*, February 20, 2013.

157. Tim Walker, "Hollywood Targets Asian Audiences as US Films Enjoy Record-Breaking Run at Chinese Box Office," *Independent*, June 9, 2014.

158. Patrick Frater, "How China's Homegrown Biz Is Threatening Hollywood's Payday," *Variety*, September 12, 2013.

159. Ibid.

160. Patrick Frater, "Chinese Movies Top Global Box Office Chart," *Variety*, February 15, 2016.

161. Rob Cain, "It's a Bollywood-Hollywood David vs. Goliath Showdown at China's Cinemas," *Forbes*, June 7, 2015.

162. Niall McCarthy, "Bollywood: India's Film Industry by the Numbers," *Forbes*, September 3, 2014.

163. Anjani Trivedi, "Christie's: Evolution of an Asian Art Market," *CNN Style*, November 26, 2013. http://www.cnn.com/2012/11/30/business/asian-art-market-curiel/

164. Adam Georgina, "Where Next for Hong Kong, Asia's Art Hub?" *Art Newspaper*, May 22, 2013.

165. Susan Moore, "Sotheby's Hong Kong Art Sales: A Record-Smashing Good Time," *Financial Times*, October 11, 2013.

166. Frederik Balfour, "Billion-Dollar Art Basel Hong Kong Woos Chinese Buyers," *Bloomberg*, May 19, 2014.

167. Scott Reyburn, "East Meets West at Hong Kong Art Fair, but Who Is Buying?" *New York Times*, May 15, 2014.

168. "The Art Market in 2014" (ArtPrice, 2015), 13.

169. "The Art Market in 2013" (ArtPrice, 2014), 20.

170. Reyburn, "East Meets West at Hong Kong Art Fair, but Who Is Buying?"

171. "Contemporary Art Market 2014: The ArtPrice Annual Report" (ArtPrice, 2014); Georgina, "Where Next for Hong Kong, Asia's Art Hub?"

172. Trivedi, "Christie's: Evolution of an Asian Art Market."

173. "Ai Weiwei," *ArtReview: Power 100*, 2015. http://artreview.com/power_100/ai_weiwei/

174. David Barboza, Graham Bowley, and Amanda Cox, "Forging an Art Market in China," *New York Times*, October 28, 2013.

175. Shanoor Seervai, "At Christie's Second India Auction, Signs of a Maturing Art Market," *Wall Street Journal*, December 12, 2014.

176. John Krich, "Malaysia's Art Scene Is Changing with New Auction Houses," *Wall Street Journal*, October 16, 2014.

177. "Contemporary Art Market 2014: The ArtPrice Annual Report."

178. Holland Cotter, "Acquired Tastes of Asian Art," *New York Times*, February 21, 2013.

179. Jemma Galvin, "The Art of Investing," *Focus ASEAN*, August 8, 2014.

180. Ibid.

181. "A Record Is Shattered: Asia Week New York Sales Hit $200 Million," *Asia Week New York*, March 2014. http://asiaweekny.com/press-release/record-shattered-asia-week-new-york-sales-hit-200-million/

Chapter Three: Patterns Preceding the Pivot

1. Michael Crichton, *Timeline* (New York: Alfred A. Knopf, 1999), 85.

2. For a good summary of the significance of American geography, see Robert Kaplan, *The Revenge of Geography: What the Map Tells Us about Coming Conflicts and the Battle against Fate* (New York: Random House, 2012).

3. Trevor Eischen, "Barack Obama's Name for David Cameron: 'Bro,'" *Politico*, January 5, 2015.

4. One of the most-cited works on these ships is Arthur Hamilton Clark, *The Clipper Ship Era: An Epitome of Famous American and British Clipper Ships, Their Owners, Builders, Commanders, and Crews* (New York: G. P. Putnam and Sons, 1910), 45–46.

5. Ibid., 97.

6. James Bradley, *The Imperial Cruise: A Secret History of Empire and War* (New York: Little, Brown, and Company, 2009), 5.

7. Figure adapted from those in Bradley, *The Imperial Cruise*.

8. "Relaxed, All-Day Dining with an Asian-Inspired Twist," *Muze | Mandarin Oriental Hotel*, 2015. http://www.mandarinoriental.com/washington/fine-dining/muze/

9. "Business Profile," Mandarin Oriental Hotel Group. http://photos.mandarinoriental .com/is/content/MandarinOriental/corporate-business-profile

10. Sheridan Prasso, *The Asian Mystique: Dragon Ladies, Geisha Girls, and Our Fantasies of the Exotic Orient* (New York: PublicAffairs, 2005), 389.

11. "Annual Report 2014," Mandarin Oriental International Limited. http://photos .mandarinoriental.com/is/content/MandarinOriental/corporate-14arMOIL-1

12. "Singapore Girl," 2015. http://www.singaporeair.com/en_UK/flying-with-us/singa poregirl/

13. Prasso, *The Asian Mystique*, 391.

14. Ibid., 11.

15. Amy Chua, *Battle Hymn of the Tiger Mother* (New York: Penguin Books, 2011).

16. Prasso, *The Asian Mystique*, 146.

17. Ibid., 11.

18. Ibid.

19. Jeffrey Record, *Japan's Decision for War in 1941: Some Enduring Lessons* (Carlisle, PA: The Strategic Studies Institute, 2009), 8, 53.

20. Abby Phillip, "Was Margaret Cho's North Korea Act Biting Comedy or Just Racist?" *Washington Post*, January 12, 2015.

21. Kevin Wong, "As an Asian-American, Here's Why Bruce Lee Still Matters," *Complex*, June 18, 2014.

22. Liza Mundy, "Cracking the Bamboo Ceiling," *Atlantic*, November 2014.

23. John Soennichsen, *The Chinese Exclusion Act of 1882* (Santa Barbara, California: Greenwood, 2011), 116.

24. Warren Cohen, *America's Response to China: A History of Sino-American Relations* (New York: John Wiley & Sons, 1971), 33.

25. Ibid.

26. "Milestones 1921–1936: The Immigration Act of 1924 (The Johnson-Reed Act)," Office of the Historian, United States Department of State, November 1, 2013. http://history.state.gov/milestones/1921-1936/immigration-act

27. Quoted in ibid., 47.

28. Ibid., 35.

29. Christopher Frayling, *The Yellow Peril: Dr. Fu Manchu and the Rise of Chinaphobia* (London: Thames & Hudson, 2014).

30. Tina Chen, *Double Agency: Acts of Impersonation in Asian American Literature and Culture* (Redwood City, California: Stanford University Press, 2005), 200.

31. Gregory Mank, *Hollywood Cauldron: Thirteen Horror Films from the Genre's Golden Age* (Jefferson, North Carolina: McFarland & Company, 1994), 84.

32. Naoko Shibusawa, *America's Geisha Ally: Reimagining the Japanese Enemy* (Cambridge, Massachusetts: Harvard University Press, 2006), 1; "Japan's Mark Is Taboo," *Washington Post*, December 11, 1941, 8; "Cleveland May Drop Japan Street," *New York Times*, December 31, 1941, 19.

33. Gary Okihiro, *The Columbia Guide to Asian American History* (New York: Columbia University Press, 2001), 104.

34. Ibid., 2.

35. G. Edward White, *Earl Warren: A Public Life* (New York: Oxford University Press, 1982), 69.

36. Shibusawa, *America's Geisha Ally*, 2.

37. Ibid., 292.

38. Marie Thorsten, *Superhuman Japan: Knowledge, Nation and Culture in US-Japan Relations* (Abingdon, Oxon: Routledge, 2012); Ezra Vogel, *Japan as Number One: Lessons for America* (Lincoln, Nebraska: iUniverse, 1999).

39. Karl Taro Greenfield, "Return of the Yellow Peril," *Nation*, May 11, 1992.

40. Edward Said, *Orientalism* (New York: Vintage Books, 1979).

41. "The Rise of Asian Americans" (Pew Research Center, June 19, 2012).

42. John King Fairbank, *China: The People's Middle Kingdom and the U.S.A.* (Cambridge, Massachusetts: Harvard University Press, 1967), 60–61.

43. Jacques Downs, *The Golden Ghetto: The American Commercial Community at Canton and the Shaping of American China Policy, 1784–1844* (Plainsboro, New Jersey: Associated University Presses, 1997), 72.

44. Arthur Power Dudden, *The American Pacific: From the Old China Trade to the Present* (New York: Oxford University Press, 1992), 5–6.

45. Charles Holcombe, *A History of East Asia: From the Origins of Civilization to the Twenty-First Century* (New York: Cambridge University Press, 2011), 195.

46. David T. Courtwright, *Dark Paradise: A History of Opiate Addiction in America* (Cambridge: Harvard University Press, 2001), 65.

47. Holcombe, *A History of East Asia*, 196.

48. See Peter C. Perdue, "The First Opium War: The Anglo-Chinese War of 1839–1842," MIT: *Visualizing Cultures*, 2011. http://ocw.mit.edu/ans7870/21f/21f.027/opium_wars_01/ow1_essay03.html

49. Downs, *The Golden Ghetto*, 299.

50. Quoted in Mike Green, *The Problem of Asia*, forthcoming.

51. For more on this see W. G. Beasley, *The Perry Mission to Japan, 1853–1854*, (Richmond, Surrey: Japan Library, 2002); William McOmie, *The Opening of Japan, 1853–1855: A Comparative Study of the American, British, Dutch, and Russian Naval Expeditions to Compel the Tokugawa Shogunate to Conclude Treaties and Open Ports to their Ships* (Folkestone: Global Oriental, 2006).

52. Thomas Bender, *A Nation among Nations: America's Place in World History* (New York: Hill and Wang, 2006), 238.

53. Cohen, "The United States as a Power in East Asia," *America's Response to China*, 46.

54. For more on this see Robert Bickers, *The Scramble for China: Foreign Devils in the Qing Empire, 1832–1914* (London: Allen Lane, 2011).

55. Yoneyuki Sugita, "The Rise of an American Principle in China: A Reinterpretation of the First Open Door Notes towards China," in Richard Jensen, Jon Davidann, and Yoneyuki Sugita (eds), *Trans-Pacific Relations: America, Europe, and Asia in the Twentieth Century* (Westport: Praeger, 2003), 3.

56. See Steven J. Ericson and Allen Hockley, *The Treaty of Portsmouth and its Legacies* (Hanover: Dartmouth College Press, 2008).

57. Philip Zelikow, "American Engagement in Asia," in Robert D. Blackwill and Paul Dibb (eds), *America's Asian Alliances* (Cambridge: MIT Press, 2000), 20.

58. "GDP, 2013" World Bank, 2016, http://data.worldbank.org/indicator/NY.GDP .MKTP.KD?order=wbapi_data_value_2013+wbapi_data_value+wbapi_data_value -last&sort=desc

59. Geoff Dyer, *The Contest of the Century: The New Era of Competition with China— and How America Can Win* (New York: Deckle Edge, 2014), 22.

60. George B. Stevens and W. Fisher Markwick, *The Life, Letters, and Journals of the Rev. and Hon. Peter Parker, M.D.* (Boston: Congregational Sunday School and Publishing Society, 1896), 128.

61. For more see Barry Hankins, *The Second Great Awakening and the Transcendentalists* (Westport, Connecticut: Greenwood Press, 2004).

62. Quoted in Green, *The Problem of Asia* (chapter 1, p. 35).

63. John Rogers Haddad, *The Romance of China: Excursions to China in U.S. Culture, 1776–1876* (New York: Columbia University Press, 2008), 160.

64. Ibid., 164.

65. Cohen, *America's Response to China*, 51.

66. Robert G. Sutter, *The United States in Asia* (Plymouth: Rowman and Littlefield, 2009), 5.

67. Ibid., 9.

68. See Dorothy Jealous Scudder, *A Thousand Years in Thy Sight: The Story of the Scudders of India* (New York: D.J. Scudder, 1970).

69. "India's Best Medical Colleges 2014," *India Today*. http://indiatoday.intoday.in/ bestcolleges/2014/ranks.jsp?ST=Medicine&LMT=1&Y=2014, 2014

70. See Arthur Lewis Rosenbaum, "Yenching University and Sino-American Interactions, 1919–1952," *Journal of American-East Asian Relations* 14 (2007): 11–60.

71. Quoted in ibid., 11.

72. In the words of Madame Chiang Kai-shek, "No words which we could speak could sufficiently express our debt of gratitude to the missionary body all over China who have been a help to the distressed and the best of friends to the hundreds of thousands of refugees." See John W. Masland, "Missionary Influence upon American Far East Policy," *The Pacific Historical Review* 10, no. 3, (September 1941): 287. See also Laura Tyson Li, *Madame Chiang Kai-shek: China's Eternal First Lady* (New York: Atlantic Monthly Press, 2006), 142. See also Lawrence D. Kessler, *The Jiangyin Mission Station: An American Missionary Community in China, 1895–1951* (Chapel Hill: The University of North Carolina Press, 1996), 90.

73. Quoted in Shuhua Fan, "The End of an American Enterprise in China: The Harvard-Yenching Institute, 1949–1951," in Arthur Lewis Rosenbaum (ed) *New Perspectives on Yenching University, 1916–1952: A Liberal Education for a New China* (Chicago: Imprint Publications, 2012), 175.

74. See Christine Louise Lin, "The Presbyterian Church in Taiwan and the Advocacy of Local Autonomy," *Sino-Platonic Papers* no. 92 (January 1999).

75. "Text of Fr. Lombardi Interview with Vatican Radio," *Zenit*, December 30, 2014. http://www.zenit.org/en/articles/text-of-fr-lombardi-interview-with-vatican-radio

76. Prashanth Parameswaran, "The Pope's Pivot to Asia," *Diplomat*, January 6, 2015. http://thediplomat.com/2015/01/the-popes-pivot-to-asia/

77. "Christian Missionaries 'Forced Out' in Droves as China Cracks Down on North Korea Border City," *South China Morning Post*, August 12, 2014.

78. Quoted in David Halberstam, *The Coldest Winter: America and the Korean War* (New York: Hachette Books, 2008), 109.

79. Quoted in Halberstam, *The Coldest Winter*, 109.

80. Ibid.

81. Quoted in Michael H. Hunt and Steven I. Levine, *Arc of Empire: America's Wars in Asia from the Philippines to Vietnam* (Chapel Hill: The University of North Carolina Press, 2014), 15.

82. Hannah Fischer, "A Guide to U.S. Military Casualty Statistics: Operation Inherent Resolve, Operation New Dawn, Operation Iraqi Freedom, and Operation Enduring Freedom," Congressional Research Service, November 20, 2014. https://www.fas.org/sgp/crs/natsec/RS22452.pdf

83. Karl Hack and Tobias Rettig, *Colonial Armies in Southeast Asia* (New York: Routledge, 2006), 172; Emil Guillermo, "A First Taste of Empire," *Milwaukee Journal Sentinel*, February 8, 2004; Ray L. Burdeos, *Filipinos in the U.S. Navy and Coast Guard During the Vietnam War* (AuthorHouse: Bloomington, 2008), 14.

84. Guillermo, "A First Taste of Empire"; Hunt and Levine, *Arc of Empire*, 58.

85. Mark Twain, "The Greatest American Humorist, Returning Home," *New York World*, October 6, 1900.

86. Bradley, *The Imperial Cruise: A Secret History of Empire and War*, 1.

87. Glenn Hubbard and Tim Kane, *Balance: The Economics of Great Powers from Ancient Rome to Modern America* (New York: Simon and Schuster, 2013), 165.

88. Hunt and Levine, *Arc of Empire*, 60.

89. Ibid., 60–61.

90. "Navy of the United States," in *Nelson's Encyclopedia* (London: Thomas Nelson, 1907), 425.

91. Zelikow, "American Engagement in Asia," 21.

92. Quoted in Robert J. McMahon and Thomas W. Zeiler, *Guide to U.S. Foreign Diplomacy: A Diplomatic History* (Washington, D.C.: CQ, 2013), 162.

93. Ibid., 163.

94. Kichisaburo Nomura, "Japan's Demand for Naval Equality," *Foreign Affairs* 13(2) (1935): 196–203.

95. Hunt and Levine, *Arc of Empire*, 65.

96. Zelikow, "American Engagement in Asia," 21.

97. Walter LaFeber, *The Clash: U.S.-Japanese Relations throughout History* (New York: W. W. Norton, 1998), 170.

98. LaFaber, *The Clash*, 200; Roland H. Worth Jr., *No Choice but War: The United States Embargo against Japan and the Eruption of War in the Pacific* (Jefferson, North Carolina: McFarland and Company, 1995), 115–117.

99. Memo by Cordell Hull, October 8, 1940.

100. Quoted in Eric Larrabee, *Commander in Chief: Franklin Delano Roosevelt, His Lieutenants, and Their War* (New York: Harper & Row, 1987), 46.

101. Joseph C. Grew, *Turbulent Era: A Diplomatic Record of Forty Years, 1904–1945* (Boston: Houghton Mifflin, 1952), 1167n–1168n.

102. Joseph C. Grew, *Ten Years in Japan: A Contemporary Record Drawn from the Diaries and Private and Official Papers of Joseph C. Grew* (New York: Simon and Schuster, 1944), 469.

103. Joel Ira Holwitt, *"Execute against Japan": The U.S. Decision to Conduct Unrestricted Submarine Warfare* (College Station: Texas A&M University Press, 2009), 65; Harry Gailey, *War in the Pacific: From Pearl Harbor to Tokyo Bay* (Novato: Presidio, 1997).

104. Quoted in LaFeber, *The Clash*, 207.

105. Quoted in Sadao Asada, *From Mahan to Pearl Harbor: The Imperial Japanese Navy and the United States*, (Annapolis: Naval Institute Press, 2006), 267.

106. Walter Lippmann, "The Mystery of Our China Policy," quoted in Gordon, 52.

107. Rob Reiner (director), *The Princess Bride*, Act 111 Communications, 1987. Film.

108. Merle Miller, *Plain Speaking: An Oral Biography of Harry S. Truman* (New York: G. P. Putnam's Sons, 1974).

109. Stanley Weintraub, *MacArthur's War: Korea and the Undoing of an American Hero* (New York: Free Press, 2008).

110. David Halberstam, "MacArthur's Grand Delusion," *Vanity Fair*, October 2007.

111. Halberstam, *The Coldest Winter*, 624.

112. David H. Petraeus, "Korea, the Never-Again Club, and Indochina," *Parameters* 17 (December 1987): 61.

113. Shen Zhihua, "China and the Dispatch of the Soviet Air Force: The Formation of the Chinese-Soviet-Korean Alliance in the Early Stage of the Korean War," *Journal of Strategic Studies* 33(2), (2010): 211–230; Shu Guang Zhang, *Mao's Military Romanticism: China and the Korean War, 1950–1953* (Lawrence, Kansas: University Press of Kansas, 1995), 257.

114. Anne Leland and Mari-Jana "MJ" Oboroceanu, "American War and Military Operations Casualties: Lists and Statistics," Congressional Research Service, February 26, 2010. http://fpc.state.gov/documents/organization/139347.pdf, 10.

115. Petraeus, 67.

116. Hunt and Levine, *Arc of Empire* 180; Petraeus, 59–70.

117. For an explanation of Chinese behavior and a useful summary of the crisis, see Thomas Christensen, *Useful Adversaries: Grand Strategy, Domestic Mobilization, and Sino-American Conflict 1947–1958*, (Princeton: Princeton University Press, 1994), 194–198.

118. Howard Jones, *Crucible of Power: A History of American Foreign Relations from 1945* (Lanham: Rowman and Littlefield, 2009), 141.

119. Marvin L. Kalb and Deborah Kalb, *Haunting Legacy: Vietnam and the American Presidency from Ford to Obama* (Washington: Brookings Institution Press, 2011), 304.

120. Leland and Oboroceanu, "American War and Military Operations Casualties," 12.

121. Quoted in Kalb and Kalb, *Haunting Legacy*, 29.

122. See ibid.

123. Fredrik Logevall and Gordon M. Goldstein, "Will Syria Be Obama's Vietnam?" *New York Times*, October 7, 2014. http://www.nytimes.com/2014/10/08/opinion/will

-syria-be-obamas-vietnam.html?_r=0; John Barry, "Could Afghanistan Be Obama's Vietnam?" *Newsweek*, January 30, 2009. http://www.newsweek.com/could-afghanistan-be-obamas-vietnam-77749; James Mann, "How Obama's Foreign Policy Team Relates to the Vietnam War—Or Doesn't," *Washington Post*, June 22, 2012. http://www.washingtonpost.com/opinions/james-mann-how-obamas-foreign-policy-team-relates-to-the-vietnam-war--or-doesnt/2012/06/22/gJQAkVWKvV_story.html; Steven Portnoy, "John McCain Says Obama's ISIS Strategy Reminds Him of Vietnam," *ABC News*, November 12, 2014. http://abcnews.go.com/Politics/john-mccain-obamas-isis-strategy-reminds-vietnam/story?id=26857963

124. Quoted in Barbara W. Tuchman, *Stilwel and the American Experience in China, 1911–1945* (New York: Grove Press, 2001), 34.

125. See for example ibid.; Cole C. Kingseed, "The Pacific War: The U.S. Army's Forgotten Theater of World War II," *Army Magazine* 63(4) (2013).

126. Quoted in LaFeber, *The Clash*, 66.

127. Gailey, *War in the Pacific*, 43.

128. Ibid., 44.

129. Ibid., 44.

130. Hunt and Levine, *Arc of Empire*, 126.

131. Zelikow, "American Engagement in Asia," 23.

132. Hunt and Levine, *Arc of Empire*, 179.

133. Gary R. Hess, *Presidential Decisions for War: Korea, Vietnam, and the Persian Gulf* (Baltimore: Johns Hopkins University Press, 2001), 10; Hunt and Levine, *Arc of Empire*, 128.

134. Dean Acheson, "Speech on the Far East," January 12, 1950.

135. Philip Zelikow, "American Engagement in Asia," in Robert D. Blackwill and Paul Dibb (eds), *America's Asian Alliances* (Cambridge: MIT Press, 2000), 24.

136. Halberstam, *The Coldest Winter*, 102.

137. Zelikow, "American Engagement in Asia," 24.

138. For a discussion of the "Vietnam Syndrome" and its later manifestations, see Marvin Kalb, "It's Called the Vietnam Syndrome, and It's Back," Brookings, January 22, 2013. http://www.brookings.edu/blogs/up-front/posts/2013/01/22-obama-foreign-policy-kalb

139. *Public Papers of the Presidents: Nixon, 1969* (Washington, D.C.: Government Printing Office, 1970), 544–56.

140. Chalmers M. Roberts, "How Nixon Doctrine Works," *Washington Post*, July 12, 1970.

141. See Thomas J. Christensen and Michael A. Glosny, "China: Sources of Stability in US-China Security Relations," in Richard J. Ellings and Aaron L. Friedberg (eds), *Fragility and Crisis* (Seattle: National Bureau of Asian Research, 2003), 53–79; David M. Lampton, "The Stealth Normalization of Us-China Relations," *National Interest* 73 (Fall 2003): 37–48.

142. Quoted in Bill Sloan, *The Darkest Summer: Pusan and Inchon 1950: The Battles That Saved South Korea—And the Marines—From Extinction* (New York: Simon & Schuster, 2009), 28.

143. T. R. Fehrenbach, *This Kind of War: The Classic Korean War History* (Washington, D.C.: Brassey's, 2000), 67.

144. Ibid., 71

145. Ibid., 69.
146. Max Hastings, *The Korean War* (New York: Simon and Schuster, 1987), 18.
147. Bevin Alexander, *Korea: The First War We Lost* (New York: Hippocrene Books, 2004), 2.
148. Halberstam, *The Coldest Winter*, 138.
149. Ridgway, quoted in Stephen Sestanovich, *Maximalist: America in the World from Truman to Obama* (New York: Knopf, 2014), 41.
150. Halberstam, *The Coldest Winter*, 138.
151. Ibid., 150.
152. Mao Zedong, "The May 4th Movement," May 1939. https://www.marxists.org/reference/archive/mao/selected-works/volume-2/mswv2_13.htm; Fu Ying, "The Past of a Foreign Country Is an Unfamiliar World," *Financial Times*, August 25, 2014. http://www.ft.com/intl/cms/s/0/f43b47d6-2a06-11e4-8139-00144feabdc0.html #axzz3DPQitzhq
153. For more on casualty estimates during the Chinese Civil War see Michael J. Lynch, *The Chinese Civil War, 1945–1949* (Oxford: Osprey, 2010), 9.
154. David M. Oshinsky, *A Conspiracy So Immense: The World of Joe McCarthy* (New York: Oxford University Press, 2005), 109.
155. Quoted in Edgar A. Porter, *The People's Doctor: George Hatem and China's Revolution* (Honolulu: University of Hawai'i Press, 1997), 208.
156. Nancy Bernkopf Tucker, "The Evolution of U.S.-China Relations," David Shambaugh (ed), *Tangled Titans: The United States and China* (Lanham: Rowman & Littlefield Publishers, 2012), 34.
157. See Alexander, *Korea*, 17.
158. Tucker, "The Evolution of U.S.-China Relations," 34.
159. Ibid., 34.
160. Fehrenbach, 187.
161. Quoted in Alexander, *Korea*, 230–231.
162. Alexander, *Korea*, 17.
163. Fehrenbach, 188–189.
164. James Traub, *The Freedom Agenda: Why America Must Spread Democracy (Just Not the Way George Bush Did)* (New York: Farrar, Straus and Giroux, 2008), 13.
165. Wilson quoted in ibid., 13–14.
166. Lloyd Wheaton quoted in ibid., 15.
167. See ibid., 15.
168. Wong Kwok Chu, "The Jones Bills 1912–16: A Reappraisal of Filipino Views on Independence," *Journal of Southeast Asian Studies* 13(2) (1982): 252–269.
169. See Clifton Sherrill, "Promoting Democracy: Results of Democratization Efforts in the Philippines," *Asian Affairs* 32(4) (2006): 211–230.
170. John W. Dower, *Embracing Defeat: Japan in the Wake of World War II* (New York: W. W. Norton & Company, 2000); Alan Thomas Wood, *Asian Democracy in World History* (New York: Routledge, 2004), 40.
171. Shibusawa, *America's Geisha Ally*, 3.
172. Tracy Williams, "Rhetoric, Reality, and Responsibility: The United States' Role in South Korean Democratization," *Stanford Journal of East Asian Affairs* 4(1) (2004): 62–63.
173. David C. Cole and Princeton N. Lyman, *Korean Development: The Interplay of Politics and Economics* (Cambridge: Harvard University Press, 1971), 62.

174. William Gleysteen and Alan D. Romberg, "Korea: Asian Paradox," *Foreign Affairs* 65 (1987): 1052.

175. Selig S. Harrison, *The South Korean Political Crisis and American Policy Options* (Washington, D.C.: Washington Institute Press, 1987), 3.

176. Halberstam, *The Coldest Winter*, 640–641.

177. Samuel P. Huntington, *The Third Wave: Democratization in the Late Twentieth Century* (Norman: University of Oklahoma Press, 1993).

Chapter Four: The Pivot's Antecedents

1. Henry A. Kissinger, *World Order* (New York: Penguin Books, 2014), 233.

2. John Paton Davies Jr., "America and East Asia," *Foreign Affairs* 55, no. 2 (January 1977): 370.

3. Ibid., 374.

4. See chapters three and four of Michael Green's forthcoming book on the history of US strategy in Asia.

5. Ibid.

6. Mike McKinley, "Cruise of the Great White Fleet," Naval History & Heritage Command, April 1, 2015, http://www.history.navy.mil/research/library/online-reading-room/title-list-alphabetically/c/cruise-great-white-fleet-mckinley.html

7. Gailey, *War in the Pacific*, 43–44.

8. Philip Zelikow, "American Engagement in Asia," in Robert D. Blackwill and Paul Dibb (eds), *America's Asian Alliances* (Cambridge: MIT Press, 2000), 24.

9. T. R. Fehrenbach, *This Kind of War: The Classic Korean War History* (Washington, D.C.: Brassey's, 2000).

10. Zelikow, "American Engagement in Asia," 25.

11. See the introduction to Michael Green's forthcoming book on the history of US strategy in Asia.

12. Kurt Campbell, Nirav Patel, and Vikram Singh, *The Power of Balance: America in iAsia* (Washington, D.C.: Center for a New American Security, 2008), 60.

Chapter Five: The Pivot and the Asian Future

1. See Kurt Campbell, "Hegemonic Prophecy and Modern Asia: Lessons for Dealing with the Rise of China," in Carolyn W. Pumphrey (ed), *The Rise of China in Asia: Security Implications* (Carlisle: Strategic Studies Institute, 2002).

2. International Monetary Fund, *World Economic Outlook 2015: Uneven Growth: Short-Term and Long-Term Factors* (Washington, D.C.: IMF, 2015).

3. Thomas Christensen, *The China Challenge: Shaping the Choices of a Rising Power* (New York: W.W. Norton, 2015), 112.

4. "Chapter Six: Asia" in *The Military Balance* (London: Routledge, 2015), 210–211.

5. Ash Carter, "IISS Shangri-La Dialogue: 'A Regional Security Architecture Where Everyone Rises,'" US Department of Defense, May 30, 2015. http://www.defense.gov/News/Speeches/Speech-View/Article/606676/iiss-shangri-la-dialogue-a-regional-security-architecture-where-everyone-rises

6. Henry A. Kissinger, *Diplomacy* (New York: Simon and Schuster, 1994), 77.

7. Henry A. Kissinger, *A World Restored: Metternich, Castlereagh and the Problems of Peace, 1812–1822* (Boston: Houghton Mifflin, 1957).

8. Keating is quoted in Peter Hartcher, "Does Australia Really Need the US Alliance?" *Sydney Morning Herald*, May 13, 2014. http://www.smh.com.au/comment/does -australia-really-need-the-us-alliance-20140512-zraey.html

9. For the English-language text of Xi Jinping's remarks, see Xi Jinping, "New Asian Security Concept for New Progress in Security Cooperation," Speech before the Fourth Summit of the Conference on Interaction and Confidence Building Measures in Asia, Shanghai, May 21, 2014. This translates his phrase as "It is for the people of Asia to run the affairs of Asia" rather than the more frequently quoted "Asia for Asians."

10. Minxin Pei, "China's Asia?" *Project Syndicate*, December 3, 2014.

11. Some of these arguments are adapted from Kurt Campbell, "Choreographing the U.S.-China Summit," *Financial Times*, June 7, 2013. http://blogs.ft.com/ the-a-list/2013/06/07/choreographing-the-us-china-summit/

12. John G. Ikenberry, *Liberal Leviathan: The Origins, Crisis, and Transformation of the American World Order* (Princeton: Princeton University Press, 2011).

13. For example, by purchasing power parity, the United States has a per capita income of $54,000, which is roughly four times China's $13,000 and nearly ten times India's $5,800. For these statistics, see International Monetary Fund, *World Economic Outlook 2015: Uneven Growth: Short-Term and Long-Term Factors*.

14. This is a variant on an argument made frequently by Christensen about China's challenges in participating in global governance. See Christensen, *The China Challenge: Shaping the Choices of a Rising Power*, 116.

15. *Trends in Global CO_2 Emissions: 2014 Report* (European Commission Joint Research Center, 2014).

16. Ibid.

17. This logic was first articulated in Hardin Garrett, "The Tragedy of the Commons," *Science* 162 (1968): 1243–48.

18. Scott Moore, "China and America: Raising the Bar on Climate Change," *National Interest*, November 13, 2014. http://nationalinterest.org/blog/the-buzz/china-amer ica-raising-the-bar-climate-change-11667

19. David Schaefer, "The Global Proliferation of Chinese Drones," *Lowy Interpreter*, October 31, 2014.

20. John G. Ikenberry, "The Rise of China and the Future of the West," *Foreign Affairs*, 87(1) (2008).

21. Robert B. Zoellick, "Whither China: From Membership to Responsibility?" (National Committee on U.S.-China Relations, New York City, September 21, 2005).

22. Kissinger, *World Order*, 522.

23. Michael J. Seth, *A History of Korea: From Antiquity to the Present* (Lanham: Rowman and Littlefield Publishing Group, 2010), 17.

24. Jim Garamone, "Harris Says North Korea is PACOM's Biggest Worry, Gives Report on Asia Rebalance," *DoD News*, October 10, 2015.

25. Christensen, *The China Challenge*, 128–130.

26. Alastair Gale, "North Korea and China Tout Ties at Military Parade," *Wall Street Journal*, October 10, 2015.

27. See the Asia Maritime Transparency Initiative for the latest information.

28. U.S. Department of Defense, *Asia-Pacific Maritime Security Strategy*, August 14, 2015. http://www.defense.gov/Portals/1/Documents/pubs/NDAApercent20A-P_Maritime

_SecuritY_Strategy-08142015-1300-FINALFORMAT.PDF, 16; Matthew Rosenberg, "China Deployed Artillery on Disputed Island, U.S. Says," *New York Times*, May 29, 2015. http://www.nytimes.com/2015/05/30/world/asia/chinese-artillery-spotted-on-spratly-island.html

29. "International Energy Statistics," U.S. Energy Information Administration, 2015. http://www.eia.gov/cfapps/ipdbproject/IEDIndex3.cfm

30. "South China Sea" (U.S. Energy Information Administration, February 7, 2013), https://www.eia.gov/beta/international/analysis_includes/regions_of_interest/South_China_Sea/south_china_sea.pdf

31. Robert D. Kaplan, *Asia's Cauldron: The South China Sea and the End of a Stable Pacific* (New York: Random House, 2014).

32. Kate Hodal, "Despite Oil Rig Removal, China and Vietnam Row Still Simmers," *Guardian*, July 17, 2014. http://www.theguardian.com/world/2014/jul/17/oil-rig-china-vietnam-row-south-china-sea

33. Pauline Jelinek, "Chinese Vessels 'Harassed US Navy Ship,'" *Independent*, March 9, 2009. http://www.independent.co.uk/news/world/politics/chinese-vessels-harassed-us-navy-ship-1640814.html

34. Gates, Robert M., *Duty: Memoirs of a Secretary at War* (New York: Alfred A. Knopf, 2014), 414.

35. "Hagel: China Warship Was 'Irresponsible.'" *BBC News*, December 19, 2013. http://www.bbc.com/news/world-asia-25459570

36. Denver Nicks, "U.S. Furious after Chinese Fighter Jet Does Barrel Roll Over American Aircraft," *Time*, August 22, 2014. http://time.com/3161228/china-jet-maneuver

37. Meng Xiangqian quoted in Richard C. Bush, *The Perils of Proximity: China-Japan Security Relations* (Washington, D.C.: Brookings Institution Press, 2010), 65.

38. "Japan, Taiwan Agree on Fishing Rights around Senkakus," *Asahi Shimbun*, April 10, 2013.

39. Andi Arsana, "Indonesia-Malaysia Deal Is Good News for Fishermen," *Jakarta Post*, April 30, 2012.

40. For more on the various claims of ownership of the islands see Sog-u Yi, Shelagh Furness, and Clive H. Schofield, *Territorial Disputes among Japan, China, and Taiwan Concerning the Senkaku Islands* (Durham: International Boundaries Research Unit, 2002).

41. A copy of this interview is contained in "Q&A: Japan's Yomiuri Shimbun Interviews President Obama," *Washington Post*, April 23, 2014.

42. "China-Japan Dispute Takes Rising Toll on Top Asian Economies," *Bloomberg News*, January 9, 2013. http://www.bloomberg.com/news/2013-01-08/china-japan-dispute-takes-rising-toll-of-asia-s-top-economies.html

43. Sheila A. Smith, "A Sino-Japanese Clash in the East China Sea: Contingency Planning Memorandum No. 18," Council on Foreign Relations, April 2013.

44. Tim Kelly and David Brunnstrom, "Japan Jets Scramble at Cold-War Levels as Chinese and Russian Incursions Increase," *Reuters*, April 16, 2015.

45. Sheila A. Smith, "A Sino-Japanese Clash in the East China Sea."

46. US Department of State, *Foreign Relations of the United States (FRUS) 1952–54*, vol. XIV (1), 563–564.

47. Thomas Christensen, *Useful Adversaries*, 194–198.

48. Tseng Wei-chen and Chen Wei-han, "'Taiwanese' Identity Hits Record Level," *Taipei Times*, January 26, 2015.

49. Charles Glaser, "Will China's Rise Lead to War?" *Foreign Affairs* 90, no. 2 (2011). See also Ambassador Chas W. Freeman, "Beijing, Washington, and the Shifting Balance of Prestige," Remarks to the China Maritime Studies Institute, Newport, Rhode Island, May 10, 2011, http://www.mepc.org/articles-commentary/speeches/beijing-washington-and-shifting-balance-prestige

50. Bruce Gilley, "Not So Dire Straits: How the Finlandization of Taiwan Benefits U.S. Security," *Foreign Affairs* 89, no. 1 (January/February 2010): 44–60

51. Nancy Tucker and Bonnie Glaser, "Should the United States Abandon Taiwan?" *Washington Quarterly*, Fall 2011.

52. Kurt Campbell, "Why Taiwan Matters," Testimony Before the House Foreign Affairs Committee, October 4, 2011. www.state.gov/p/eap/rls/rm/2011/10/174980.htm

53. Larry Diamond, "China and East Asia Democracy: The Coming Wave," *Journal of Democracy* 23, no. 1 (2012): 5.

54. Tsakhiagiin Elbegdorj, "Honoring 25 Years of Mongolian Democracy," *Wall Street Journal*, July 28, 2015. www.wsj.com/articles/honoring-25-years-of-mongolian-democracy-1438101908

55. "The Future of Factory Asia: A Tightening Grip," *Economist*, March 14, 2015; "Economic Integration: The Flying Factory," *Economist*, November 14, 2014.

56. An example from "Competing in a Flat World" cited in "Economic Integration: The Flying Factory," *Economist*, November 14, 2014.

57. For these statistics, see the Asia Regional Integration Center's Integration Indicators Database, available at https://aric.adb.org/integrationindicators; see also the World Trade Organization's International Trade Statistics, 2014, at https://www.wto.org/english/res_e/statis_e/its2014_e/its14_world_trade_dev_e.htm

58. Evan Feigenbaum and Robert Manning, "A Tale of Two Asias," *Foreign Policy*, October 31, 2012.

59. "WSJ Interview Transcript: President Obama on TPP, China, Japan, Pope Francis, Cuba," *Wall Street Journal*, April 27, 2015.

60. Peter A. Petri and Ali Abdul-Raheem, "Can RCEP and the TPP Be Pathways to FTAAP?" Social Science Research Network, October 12, 2014. papers.ssrn.com/sol3/papers.cfm?abstract_id=2513893; Joshua P. Meltzer, "Why China Should Join the Trans-Pacific Partnership," Brookings Institution, September 21, 2015.

61. Peter A. Petri, Michael G. Plummer, Fan Zhai, "The Case for Convergence," Social Science Research Network, May 19, 2014.

62. Meltzer, "Why China Should Join the Trans-Pacific Partnership."

Chapter Six: The Plan for the Pivot

1 See Mike Green, Kathleen Hicks, and Mark Cancian, *Asia-Pacific Rebalance 2025: Capabilities, Presence, and Partnerships*, Center for Strategic and International Studies, 2016, xvii.

2. Ibid., p. 195.

3. Guenwook Lee, "Between Multilateralism and Bilateralism," in T. J. Pempel and Chung Min Lee (eds), *Security Cooperation in Northeast Asia: Architecture and Beyond* (New York: Routledge, 2012), 73.

4. For a history of the hub-and-spokes system, see Victor D. Cha, "Powerplay: Origins of the U.S. Alliance System in Asia," *International Security* 34(3) (2010): 158–196.

5. G. John Ikenberry, "American Hegemony and East Asia Order," *Australian Journal of International Affairs* 58(3) (2004): 353.

6. Tim Kelly and Nobuhiro Kubo, "Tokyo, Manila to Agree on Framework for Japanese Military Aid," *Reuters*, November 15, 2016. www.reuters.com/article/us-japan -philippines-military-idUSKCN0T508W20151116

7. Emphasis added. See Michael J. Green, Kathleen H. Hicks, and Zack Cooper, *Federated Defense in Asia*, Center for Strategic and International Studies, 2013, p. 1.

8. Patrick M. Cronin et al., "The Emerging Asia Power Web: The Rise of Bilateral Intra-Asian Security Ties," CNAS, June 2013.

9. See "S. Korea, Japan, U.S. Make Significant Progress in Military Intelligence Sharing," *Shanghai Daily*, December 18, 2014. http://www.shanghaidaily.com/article/ article_xinhua.aspx?id=259447; "US, Japan, South Korea, Boost Data Sharing in Response to North Korean Threat," *Reuters*, February 11, 2015. http://www.reuters .com/article/us-northkorea-satellite-usa-allieslockhe-idUSKCN0VK054

10. "Australia-Japan-United States Trilateral Leaders Meeting Joint Media Release," White House, November 15, 2014. http://www.whitehouse.gov/the-press-office/2014/11/15/ australia-japan-united-states-trilateral-leaders-meeting-joint-media-rel

11. A copy of this interview is contained in the *Washington Post*, https://www.wash ingtonpost.com/world/qanda-japans-yomiuri-shimbun-interviews-president -obama/2014/04/23/d01bb5fc-cae3-11e3-95f7-7ecdde72d2ea_story.html

12. Eric Johnston, "Operation Tomodachi a Huge Success," *Japan Times*, March 3, 2012. www.japantimes.co.jp/news/2012/03/03/news/operation-tomodachi-a-huge-success -but-was-it-a-one-off/

13. "Foreign Trade: Top Trading Partners," US Census Bureau. https://www.census .gov/foreign-trade/statistics/highlights/top/index.html#2015.

14. "Assessment of Member States' advances to the Working Capital Fund for the biennium 2014–2015 and contributions to the United Nations regular budget for 2014," the United Nations, December 27, 2013. http://www.un.org/ga/search/view_doc .asp?symbol=ST/ADM/SER.B/889

15. "Japan's Demography: The Incredible Shrinking Country," *Economist*, March 25, 2014. http://www.economist.com/blogs/banyan/2014/03/japans-demography; Matthew Carney, "Okinawa Base Tensions Remain as Barack Obama Heads to Japan Seeking to Shore Up Asia Pacific Power," *ABC News*, April 24, 2014. http://www.abc.net.au/news/2014-04-23/ an-okinawa-base-tensions-remain-as-barack-obama-seeks-to-shore-/5405838; Jun Hongo, "35,000 Protest U.S. Base Relocation in Okinawa," *Wall Street Journal*, May 18, 2015. http://blogs.wsj.com/japanrealtime/2015/05/18/35000-protest-u-s-base-relocation-in -okinawa/

16. "The Incredible Shrinking Country," *Economist*, March 25, 2014. http://www.econ omist.com/blogs/banyan/2014/03/japans-demography

17. "Japan's Quadruple-Dip as GDP Shrinks .8%," *Financial Times*, November 15, 2015.

18. Jessica Chen Weiss, *Powerful Patriots: Nationalist Protest in China's Foreign Relations* (New York: Oxford University Press, 2014). See also Brad Glosserman and Scott A. Snyder, *Japan-South Korea Identity Clash: East Asian Security and the United States* (New York: Columbia University Press, 2015).

19. Choe Sang-Hun, "Japan and South Korea Settle Dispute Over Wartime 'Comfort Women,'" *New York Times*, December 28, 2015.

20. "China, South Korea Fear Secrets Law Could Lead to Japanese Military State," *Asahi Shimbun*, December 7, 2013. http://ajw.asahi.com/article/behind_news/poli tics/AJ201312070061

21. Ash Carter, "Remarks by Secretary Carter at a Press Gaggle," Yokota Air Base, Japan, April 09, 2015. archive.defense.gov/Transcripts/Transcript.aspx?TranscriptID=5615

22. "Fact Sheet: U.S.-Korea Free Trade Agreement," Office of the United States Trade Representative, March 15, 2014. https://ustr.gov/about-us/policy-offices/press-office/ fact-sheets/2015/march/fact-sheet-us-korea-free-trade-agreement

23. Lee Ka-Young, Kwon Ho, and Sarah Kim, "More Than Half of Public Supports Use of Thaad," *Korea JoongAng Daily*, February 25, 2015. http://koreajoongangdaily .joins.com/news/article/Article.aspx?aid=3001196; See also Bruce Klingner, "South Korea Needs THAAD Missile Defense," Backgrounder 3024, Heritage Foundation, June 12, 2015.

24. Choe Sang-Hun, "Computer Networks in South Korea Are Paralyzed in Cyberattacks," *New York Times*, March 20, 2013. http://www.nytimes.com/2013/03/21/ world/asia/south-korea-computer-network-crashes.html

25. Brad Glosserman and Scott A. Snyder, *Japan-South Korea Identity Clash: East Asian Security and the United States* (New York: Columbia University Press, 2015).

26. John Lee, "The Strategic Cost of South Korea's Japan Bashing," Hudson Institute, November 5, 2014. http://www.hudson.org/research/10775-the-strategic-cost -of-south-korea-s-japan-bashing

27. Park Geun-hye, "Her Excellency President Park Geun-hye: Statesmen's Forum Address at the Center for Strategic and International Studies," speech delivered at the Center for Strategic and International Studies, Washington, D.C., October 15, 2015.

28. Kurt M. Campbell, Lindsey Ford, Nirav Patel, Vikram J. Singh, "Going Global: The Future of the U.S.-South Korea Alliance," Center for a New American Security, February 2009.

29. See "Australia," Office of the United States Trade Representative. https://ustr.gov/ countries-regions/southeast-asia-pacific/australia

30. Tazeem Pasha, *Foreign Direct Investment in the United States: Drivers of US Economic Competitiveness*, December 31, 2013

31. Michael J. Green, et al., "Power and Order in Asia: A Survey of Regional Expectations," Center for Strategic and International Studies, July 2014. http://csis.org/files/ publication/140605_Green_PowerandOrder_WEB.pdf

32. For a useful brief on initiatives that could strengthen the US-Australia alliance, see Michael J. Green, Peter J. Dean, Brandan Taylor, and Zack Cooper, *The ANZUS Alliance in an Ascending Asia*, Center for Strategic and International Studies, July 2015.

33. Jim Thomas, Zack Cooper, Iskander Rehman, "Gateway to the Indo-Pacific: Australian Defense Strategy and the Future of the Australia-U.S. Alliance," Center for Strategic and Budgetary Assessments, 2013, p. 13.

34. Katharine Murphy, "Australia Embraces Missile and Naval Ties as It Cements US Defence Pact," *Guardian*, August 12, 2014.

35. Rory Medcalf, "The Indo-Pacific: What's in a Name?" *American Interest* 9, no. 2 (October 10, 2013).

36. Danielle Rajendram, "Abbott's India Visit: The Agenda," *Lowy Interpreter*, September 4, 2014. http://www.lowyinterpreter.org/post/2014/09/04/Abbott-in-India -agenda.aspx?COLLCC=1190392145&

37. Jenny Hayward-Jones, "Australia's Pacific Aid Budget Spared from Serious Cuts," *Lowy Interpreter*, May 13, 2015.

38. Green et al., "Power and Order in Asia," p. 4.

39. Michael J. Green, Peter J. Dean, Brandan Taylor, and Zack Cooper, *The ANZUS Alliance in an Ascending Asia*, Center for Strategic and International Studies, July 2015, p. 17.

40. Susan B. Glasser, "China's Wrong about American Decline," *Politico Magazine*, June 30, 2014.

41. This paragraph borrows from an overview provided in Murray Hiebert and Hunter Marston, "President Obama Needs to Visit Singapore Next Year," Center for Strategic and International Studies, November 12, 2015. www.csis.org/publication/president-obama-needs-visit-singapore-next-year

42. Hiebert and Marston, "President Obama Needs to Visit Singapore Next Year."

43. P. R. Venkat and Jake Maxwell Watts, "Singapore Election: Polls Close as Ruling Party Braces for Vote Count," *Wall Street Journal*, September 11, 2015.

44. Ernest Z. Bower, "Singapore is Changing and Why That Matters," Center for Strategic and International Studies, October 2, 2014. http://csis.org/publication/singapore-changing-and-why-matters-0

45. Manuel Mogato, "Philippines offers eight bases to U.S. under new military deal," Reuters, October 9, 2014. www.reuters.com/article/us-philippines-usa-bases-idUSKCN0UR17K20160113

46. "Trade in Goods with Philippines," U.S. Census Bureau. January 2016, https://www.census.gov/foreign-trade/balance/c5650.html. See also Murray Hiebert, Phuong Nguyen, Gregory B. Poling, "Building a More Robust U.S.-Philippines Alliance," Center for Strategic and International Studies, August 2015. http://csis.org/publication/building-more-robust-us-philippines-alliance.

47. Murray Hiebert, Phuong Nguyen, Gregory B. Poling, "Building a More Robust U.S.-Philippines Alliance." 10–12.

48. Aaron Meta, "Carter Announces $425 Million in Pacific Partnership Funding," *Defense News*, May 30, 2015. http://www.defensenews.com/story/defense/2015/05/30/carter-announces-425m-in-pacific-partnership-funding/28206541/

49. Murray Hiebert, Phuong Nguyen, Gregory B. Poling, "Building a More Robust U.S.-Philippines Alliance," p. 2.

50. "U.S. Ambassador Helps Open National Coast Watch Center to Enhance Philippines Maritime Domain Awareness," Embassy of the Philippines, April 30, 2015. http://www.pacom.mil/Media/News/tabid/5693/Article/587080/us-ambassador-helps-open-national-coast-watch-center-to-enhance-philippine-mari.aspx

51. Emma Chanlett-Avery, Ben Dolven, and Wil Mackey, "Thailand: Background and U.S. Relations," Congressional Research Service, July 29, 2015. https://www.fas.org/sgp/crs/row/RL32593.pdf

52. See Ernest Z. Bower and Murray Hiebert, "Revisiting U.S. Policy toward Post-Coup Thailand," Center for Strategic and International Studies, February 18, 2016. http://csis.org/publication/revisiting-us-policy-toward-post-coup-thailand.

53. Duncan McCargo, "The Thai Malaise," *Foreign Policy*, February 18, 2014. http://www.foreignpolicy.com/articles/2014/02/18/the_thai_malaise

54. For background on the importance of red and yellow shirts in Thailand see Christopher Shay, "In Thailand, Why Yellow and Red Clash," *Al Jazeera America*, January

24, 2014. http://america.aljazeera.com/articles/2014/1/24/explainer-in-thailandwhy yellowandredclash.html

55. Quoted in Justine Drennan, "Interview: Thai Democracy Is Gone and Won't Return Anytime Soon," *Foreign Policy*, November 25, 2014. http://blog.foreignpolicy.com/posts/2014/11/24/interview_thai_democracy_is_gone_and_won_t_return_any time_soon_coup

56. Assumes the EU trade is not aggregated.

57. "Remarks by President Barack Obama at Suntory Hall, Tokyo, Japan."

58. Clinton, *Hard Choices*, 40–41.

59. Aaron Friedberg, "The Sources of Chinese Conduct: Explaining Beijing's Assertiveness," *The Washington Quarterly*, 37 (4) (2014).

60. For more on the charm offensive, see Evan S. Medeiros and M. Taylor Fravel, "China's New Diplomacy," *Foreign Affairs*, November/December 2003.

61. James Reilly, "China's Unilateral Sanctions," *Washington Quarterly* 35:4 (2012): 121–133.

62. Projections are available using data from the International Monetary Fund, *World Economic Outlook 2015: Uneven Growth: Short-Term and Long-Term Factors* (Washington, D.C.: IMF, 2015).

63. Thomas Christensen, *The China Challenge*, 260.

64. See Robert Blackwill and Kurt Campbell, "Xi Jinping on the Global Stage: Chinese Foreign Policy Under a Powerful but Exposed Leader," Council on Foreign Relations, February 25, 2016.

65. Orville Schell and John Delury, "A Rising China Needs a New National Story," *Wall Street Journal*, July 12, 2013. http://online.wsj.com/articles/SB1000142412788 7324425204578599633633456090

66. "Xi Calls for Patriotism in Achieving Chinese Dream," *Xinhua*, December 30, 2015. news.xinhuanet.com/english/2015-12/30/c_134965704.htm

67. See Robert Blackwill and Kurt Campbell, "Xi Jinping on the Global Stage: Chinese Foreign Policy under a Powerful but Exposed Leader." See also Luke Kawa, "Six Ways to Gauge How Fast China's Economy Is Actually Growing," *Bloomberg*, November 2, 2015. http://www.bloomberg.com/news/articles/2015-11-02/six -ways-to-gauge-how-fast-china-s-economy-is-actually-growing

68. See Blackwill and Campbell, "Xi Jinping on the Global Stage."

69. Brian Bremmer, "Is China Coming Back Down to Earth?" *Bloomberg Business*, January 22, 2015. http://www.bloomberg.com/bw/articles/2015-01-22/china-s-risks -in-shedding-debt-fueled-investment-led-growth#p1

70. Barack Obama, "Remarks by President Obama and President Xi Jinping in Joint Press Conference," Washington, D.C., White Hosue Rose Garden, November 12, 2014. https://www.whitehouse.gov/the-press-office/2014/11/12/remarks-president-obama -and-president-xi-jinping-joint-press-conference

71. This refers to command, control, communications, computers, intelligence, surveillance, and reconnaissance.

72. Ely Ratner, "China Undeterred and Unapologetic," War on the Rocks, June 24, 2014, http://warontherocks.com/2014/06/china-undeterred-and-unapologetic/. Brian Spegele and Vu Trong Khanh, "Vietnam Spat Represents a Chinese Leap," *Wall Street Journal*, May 8, 2014. http://www.wsj.com/articles/SB1000142405270230465530457 9549330994442014.

73. United States Department of Defense, *Asia-Pacific Maritime Security Strategy*, August

14, 2015, p 16. http://www.defense.gov/Portals/1/Documents/pubs/NDAA%20A-. Matthew Rosenberg, "China Deployed Artillery on Disputed Island, U.S. Says," *New York Times*, May 29, 2015. http://www.nytimes.com/2015/05/30/world/asia/chinese-artillery-spotted-on-spratly-island.html

74. Simon Denyer, Craig Whitlock and Steven Mufson, "U.S. Warship Sails Within 12 miles of Chinese-built Island in South China Sea," *Washington Post*, October 26, 2015. https://www.washingtonpost.com/world/us-warship-sails-within-12-miles-of -chinese-built-island-in-south-china-sea/2015/10/26/a178497b-7033-4e4c-a328 -0f3c980cf193_story.html.

75. "Abe backs U.S. operation in South China Sea," *Japan Times*, October 28, 2015. http:// www.japantimes.co.jp/news/2015/10/28/world/politics-diplomacy-world/u-s-warship- passage-contested-south-china-sea-gets-abe-nod-sail-pasts-works/#.Vl0gUHarTIV, "Aus- tralia strongly supports US activity in South China Sea, says Marise Payne," *Guardian*, October 27, 2015. http://www.theguardian.com/world/2015/oct/27/australia-strongly -supports-us-activity-in-south-china-sea-says-marise-payne http://www.wsj.com/articles/ south-korea-calls-for-south-china-sea-rights-1446461006

76. "China Cybercrime Costing US Billions: FBI Chief," AFP, October 5, 2014, http:// www.securityweek.com/china-cybercrime-costing-us-billions-fbi-chief.

77. Adam Segal, "Axiom and the Deepening Divide in U.S.-China Cyber Rela- tions," Council on Foreign Relations: *Net Politics*, October 29, 2014. blogs.cfr.org/ cyber/2014/10/29/axiom-and-the-deepening-divide-in-u-s-china-cyber-relations/

78. Julie Hirschfeld Davis, "Hacking of Government Computers Exposed 21.5 Million People," *New York Times*, July 9, 2015.

79. Ellen Nakashima, "China Still Trying to Hack U.S. Firms Despite Xi's Vow to Refrain, Analysts Say," *Washington Post*, October 19, 2015. Ellen Nakashima, "Following U.S. Indictments, China Shifts Commercial Hacking Away from Mili- tary to Civilian Agency," *Washington Post*, November 30, 2015.

80. Jerome A. Cohen, "Who Gets Punished? Sons and Daughters of Rights Law- yers—Collective Punishment in China," *Jerry's Law Blog*, October 20, 2015. www.jeromecohen.net/jerrys-blog/2015/10/20/who-gets-punished-sons-and-daug hters-of-rights-lawyers-collective-punishment-in-china. See also "China's Long and Punishing Arm," *Washington Post*, October 18, 2015.

81. Nikhil Sonnad, "The Chinese Government Could Use Big Data to Track Individual Students' Political Views," *Quartz*, November 26, 2015.

82. Shannon Tiezzi, "China's Sovereign Internet," *Diplomat*, June 24, 2014.

83. See Wu Winbo, "Chinese Visions of the Future of US-China Relations," in David Shambaugh (ed), *Tangled Titans: the United States and China* (Plymouth: Rowman and Littlefield, 2012), 382.

84. Stanley Lubma, "Document No.9: The Party Attacks Western Democratic Ide- als," *Wall Street Journal: China Realtime*, August 27, 2013. blogs.wsj.com/chinar ealtime/2013/08/27/document-no-9-the-party-attacks-western-democratic-ideals/; Chris Buckley and Andrew Jacobs, "Maoists in China, Given New Life, Attack Dissent," *New York Times*, January 4, 2015.

85. Michael Crowley, "Obama's Asia Problem," *Time*, October 21, 2013.

86. Ibid.

87. Richard C. Bush III, David Dollar, Cheng Li, Jonathan D. Pollack, and Qi Ye, "What You Need to Know about the U.S.-China Strategic and Economic

Dialogue," Brookings Institution, July 7, 2014. http://www.brookings.edu/blogs/up-front/posts/2014/07/07-us-china-strategic-economic-dialogue; "U.S.-China Strategic Security Dialogue," National Committee on United States-China Relations. http://www.ncuscr.org/programs/northeast-asia-security-dialogue

88. Ben Blanchard and Andrea Shalal, "China Naval Chief Says Minor Incident Could Spark War in South China Sea," *Reuters*, October 30, 2015. www.reuters.com/article/us-southchinasea-usa-china-navy-idUSKCN0SO05320151030

89. Some portions of this section are adapted from Kurt Campbell, "How the US and India Can Revitalize Their Partnership," *Financial Times: The A-List*, July 11, 2013.

90. See Strobe Talbott, *Engaging India: Diplomacy, Democracy, and the Bomb* (Washington: Brookings, 2004).

91. Gill Plimmer and Victor Mallet, "India Becomes Biggest Foreign Buyer of US Weapons," *Financial Times*, February 24, 2014. www.ft.com/cms/s/0/ded3be9a-9c81-11e3-b535-00144feab7de.html

92. Tanvi Madan, "Finding a New Normal in U.S.-India Relations," Brookings Institution, June 2014. www.brookings.edu/research/articles/2014/07/08-us-india-relations-normalization

93. "India Looks East: A Strenuous September," *Economist*, August 30, 2014. http://www.economist.com/news/asia/21614184-indias-government-embarking-whirlwind-month-asian-diplomacy-strenuous-september

94. For a discussion of India's infrastructure investments, see chapter 2.

95. Many of these suggestions for intensifying US-India strategic ties can be found in Ashley Tellis, "Back to First Principles: Realizing the Promise of U.S.-Indian Defense Ties," Carnegie Endowment, December 10, 2015. carnegieendowment.org/2015/12/10/back-to-first-principles-realizing-promise-of-u.s.-indian-defense-ties/imz0

96. Parts of this section are drawn from my congressional testimony on US-Taiwan relations. See Kurt Campbell, "Why Taiwan Matters," Testimony before the House Foreign Affairs Committee, October 4, 2011. www.state.gov/p/eap/rls/rm/2011/10/174980.htm

97. The Six Assurances originally proposed that (1) the United States would not set a date for termination of arms sales to Taiwan; (2) the United States would not alter the terms of the Taiwan Relations Act; (3) the United States would not consult with China in advance of or in conjunction with decision making about US arms sales to Taiwan; (4) the United States would not mediate between Taiwan and China; (5) the United States would not alter its position about the sovereignty of Taiwan—that the question was one to be decided peacefully by the Chinese themselves—and would not pressure Taiwan to enter into negotiations with China; and (6) the United States would not formally recognize Chinese sovereignty over Taiwan.

98. Hillary Rodham Clinton, "Remarks with New Zealand Prime Minister John Phillip Key and New Zealand Foreign Minister Murray Stuart McCully," Parliament Theatrette, Wellington, New Zealand, November 4, 2010.

99. See "Fact Sheet: The United States and New Zealand," White House Office of the Press Secretary, June 20, 2014. https://www.whitehouse.gov/the-press-office/2014/06/20/fact-sheet-united-states-and-new-zealand-forward-progress

100. "2011 Earthquake," United States and New Zealand Council, 2014. www.usnzcouncil.org/friends-of-new-zealand-congressional-caucus/2011-earthquake/

101. "The ASEAN Economic Community 2015," June, 2014, KPMG Asia Pacific Tax Center http://www.kpmg.com/SG/en/IssuesAndInsights/ArticlesPublications/Documents/Tax-Itax-The-ASEAN-Economic-Community-2015.pdf, p. 6.

102. Alexander Sullivan, "Strengthening U.S.-Indonesia Defense Ties," Center for a New American Security, October 2014, p. 5.

103. See Murray Hiebert, Phuong Nguyen, and Gregory B. Poling, "A New Era in U.S.-Vietnam Relations: Deepening Ties Two Decades after Normalization," Center for Strategic and International Studies, June 2014.

104. Alexander Sullivan, "Advancing U.S.-Malaysia Security: Cooperation in a Changing Environment." See also Josh Rogin, "Malaysia and U.S. in Talks to Ramp up China Spying," *Bloomberg*, September 3, 2015.

105. Ernest Z. Bower and Prashanth Parameswaran, "U.S. Moves to Strengthen ASEAN by Boosting the Lower Mekong Initiative," Center for Strategic and International Studies, July 24, 2012. http://csis.org/publication/us-moves-strengthen-asean-boosting-lower-mekong-initiative

106. This section draws in part from my testimony, Kurt M. Campbell, "Testimony Before the House Committee on Foreign Affairs Subcommittee on Asia, the Pacific, and the Global Environment: U.S. Policy in the Pacific Islands," September 29, 2010, http://www.state.gov/p/eap/rls/rm/2010/09/148318.htm.

107. Thomas Lum, "The Southwest Pacific: U.S. Interests and China's Growing Influence," Congressional Research Service, July 6, 2007.

108. Annmaree O'Keeffe, "Bilateral Donors in the Pacific: Is It More than Development?" Lowy Institute for International Policy, July 6, 2012. www.lowyinstitute.org/publications/bilateral-donors-pacific-it-more-development

109. Joshua Meltzer, "The Significance of the Trans-Pacific Partnership for the United States," Brookings Institution, May 16, 2012. http://www.brookings.edu/research/testimony/2012/05/16-us-trade-strategy-meltzer

110. C. L. Lim, Deborah K. Elms, and Patrick Low, "What Is a 'High-Quality, Twenty-First Century' Anyway?" in C. L. Lim, Deborah K. Elms, and Patrick Low (eds), *The Trans-Pacific Partnership: A Quest for a Twenty-First Century Trade Agreement* (New York: Cambridge University Press, 2012), 4.

111. Kevin Granville, "The Trans-Pacific Partnership Trade Deal: What It Would Mean," *New York Times*, May 11, 2015. http://www.nytimes.com/2015/05/12/business/unpacking-the-trans-pacific-partnership-trade-deal.html

112. Kurt M. Campbell, "Testimony Before the House Committee on Foreign Affairs Subcommittee on Asia, the Pacific, and the Global Environment: U.S. Policy in the Pacific Islands," September 29, 2010, http://www.state.gov/p/eap/rls/rm/2010/09/148318.htm.

113. Michèle Flournoy and Ely Ratner, "A Trade Deal with a Bonus for National Security," *Wall Street Journal*, March 9, 2015.

114. "China Communist Party Paper Says Country Should Join U.S.-led Trade Pact," Reuters, October 24, 2015. http://www.reuters.com/article/us-china-trade-tpp-idUSKCN0SJ01X20151025

115. Bernard K. Gordon, "Bring China Into the TPP," *National Interest*, April 11, 2014. http://nationalinterest.org/commentary/bring-china-tpp-10227?page=show

116. Tsai Ing-wen, "Taiwan Meeting the Challenges: Crafting a Model for New Asian Value," speech delivered at the Center for Strategic and International Studies, Washington, D.C., June 3, 2015.

117. Park Geun-hye, "Her Excellency President Park Geun-hye: Statesmen's Forum Address at the Center for Strategic and International Studies," speech delivered at Center for Strategic and International Studies, Washington, D.C., October 15, 2015.

118. Doug Palmer, "Crisis at WTO—U.S., Japan Continue Search for TPP Deal—Obama Presses Abe for 'Bold' Action—Conservative Group Fears 'Lame Duck' TPA Vote," *Politico*, October 16, 2014. http://www.politico.com/morningtrade/1014/morningtrade15707.html

119. Stewart Taggart, "A Plan to Save the South China Sea from Disaster," *National Interest*, June 30, 2014. http://nationalinterest.org/blog/the-buzz/plan-save-the-south-china-sea-disaster-10779

120. Kurt Campbell and Brian Andrews, "Explaining the US 'Pivot' to Asia," Chatham House, August 2013, p. 6.

121. Mark E. Manyin, Michael John Garcia, Wayne M. Morrison, "U.S. Accession to ASEAN's Treaty of Amity and Cooperation (TAC)," Congressional Research Service, May 5, 2009, p. 2, http://fpc.state.gov/documents/organization/124064.pdf.

122. Jackie Calmes, "Obama's Trip Emphasizes Role of Pacific Rim," *New York Times*, November 16, 2011. http://www.nytimes.com/2011/11/19/world/asia/obamas-trip-sends-message-to-asian-leaders.html

123. Carl Thayer, "US-ASEAN Defense Ministers Meet in Hawaii," *Diplomat*, April 11, 2014. http://thediplomat.com/2014/04/us-asean-defense-ministers-meet-in-hawaii/

124. Ernest Z. Bower, "John Kerry to Attend ASEAN Regional Forum," Center for Strategic and International Studies, June 26, 2013. http://csis.org/publication/john-kerry-attend-asean-regional-forum

125. For a description of this meeting, see Clinton, *Hard Choices*, 70–71.

126. David Nakamura, "Obama Cancels the Rest of Asia Trip, Citing Difficulties of Travel During Shutdown," *Washington Post*, October 4, 2013. http://www.washingtonpost.com/politics/obama-cancels-the-rest-of-asia-trip-citing-difficulties-of-travel-during-shutdown/2013/10/04/cb1b8f22-2c9c-11e3-b139-029811dbb57f_story.html

127. Ankit Panda, "US Joins Southeast Asia's War on Piracy," *Diplomat*, October 10, 2014. http://thediplomat.com/2014/10/us-joins-southeast-asias-war-on-piracy/

128. Peter Ford, "Philippines Stares Down China in South China Sea Dispute," *Christian Science Monitor*, March 31, 2014. http://www.csmonitor.com/World/Asia-Pacific/2014/0331/Philippines-stares-down-China-in-South-China-Sea-dispute-video

129. Ziad Haider, "US Must Adopt Law of the Sea," *Yale Global*, March 13, 2013. http://yaleglobal.yale.edu/content/us-must-adopt-law-sea

130. Thomas Wright, "Outlaw of the Sea," *Foreign Affairs*, August 7, 2012. http://www.foreignaffairs.com/articles/137815/thomas-wright/outlaw-of-the-sea

131. "Total Military Personnel and Dependent End Strength By Service, Regional Area, and Country" (Defense Manpower Data Center, June 30, 2015).

132. Robert O. Work, "Deputy Secretary of Defense Speech," National Defense University, Washington, D.C., August 5, 2014. http://www.defense.gov/Speeches/Speech.aspx?SpeechID=1873

133. Work, "Deputy Secretary of Defense Speech."

134. Shawn Brimley et al, "Ideas to Action: Suggestions for the 25th Secretary of Defense," CNAS, February 2015, http://www.cnas.org/sites/default/files/publications-pdf/ CNAS_Ash-Carter_Briefing-Book_Feb2015_0.pdf.

135. Ibid.

136. Terry S. Morris et al. "Securing Operational Access: Evolving the Air-Sea Battle Concept," *The National Interest*, February 11, 2015, http://nationalinterest.org/ feature/securing-operational-access-evolving-the-air-sea-battle-12219.
    Terrence K. Kelly, "Employing Land-Based Anti-Ship Missiles in the Western Pacific," RAND Corporation, 2013, http://www.rand.org/content/dam/rand/pubs/ technical_reports/TR1300/TR1321/RAND_TR1321.pdf.

137. Leon E. Panetta, "Shangri-La Security Dialogue," United States Department of Defense, June 2, 2012. http://www.defense.gov/speeches/speech.aspx?speechid=1681; Karen Parrish, "US Following Through on Pacific Rebalance, Hagel Says," United States Department of Defense, June 1, 2013. http://www.defense.gov/news/newsarticle .aspx?id=120186

138. See chapter 2 for deeper discussion of why Asia is particularly susceptible to natural disasters.

139. Zachary M. Hosford, "The U.S. Humanitarian Presence in Southeast Asia," *Diplomat*, December 25, 2013. thediplomat.com/2013/12/u-s-hadr-missions-in-south east-asia/

140. For examples of room for improvement, see Weston S. Konishi and Andrew L. Oros, "Beyond Haiyan: Toward Greater U.S.-Japan Cooperation in HADR," National Bureau of Asian Research, February 2014. http://nbr.org/publications/analysis/pdf/ brief/020614_Kinoshi-Oros_US-Japan_HADR.pdf

141. Fareed Zakaria, "A Conversation with Lee Kuan Yew," *Foreign Affairs*, March/April 1994.

142. Hillary Rodham Clinton, "Remarks on Internet Freedom," Washington, D.C., January 21, 2010, http://www.state.gov/secretary/20092013clinton/rm/2010/01/135519.htm.

143. "China Wants to Tap Big Data to Build a Bigger Brother," *Wall Street Journal*, November 6, 2015. blogs.wsj.com/chinarealtime/2015/11/06/china-wants-to-tap -big-data-to-build-a-bigger-brother/

144. Carola McGiffert, "US Reaches Major Milestone: 100,000 American Students Study in China," *Huffington Post*, July 9, 2014. http://www.huffingtonpost.com/ carola-mcgiffert/us-reaches-major-mileston_b_5571793.html

145. These statistics can be found in "International Students in the United States," *Open Doors Report*, International Institute for Education, 2015. www.iie.org/Services/ Project-Atlas/United-States/International-Students-In-US. See also "Japan: Fact Sheet," *Open Doors Report*, International Institute for Education, 2015.

146. See the report *The Rise of Asian Americans*, Pew Research Center, June 19, 2012. http://www.pewsocialtrends.org/2012/06/19/the-rise-of-asian-americans/

147. Shreeya Sinha, "Indian Leader Narendra Modi, Once Unwelcome in U.S., Gets Rock Star Reception," *New York Times*, September 27, 2014.

148. Zelikow, "American Engagement," 28.

149. Kurt M. Campbell and Wim Geerts, "Preface," in Hans Binnendijk (ed), *A Transatlantic Pivot to Asia: Towards New Trilateral Partnerships* (Washington D.C.: Center for Transatlantic Relations, 2014), vi.

150. "Executive Summary, in Hans Binnendijk (ed), *A Transatlantic Pivot to Asia: Towards New Trilateral Partnerships*, (Washington D.C.: Center for Transatlantic Relations, 2014), xxii.

Chapter Seven: Risks to the Pivot's Promise

1. For more on this oft-repeated quote, see Arthur H. Vandenberg Jr. and Joe Alex Morris (eds), *The Private Papers of Senator Vandenberg* (Riverside Press: New York, 1952).

2. For a full account of the divisions within the Democratic and Republican Parties, see Kurt M. Campbell and Derek Chollet, "The New Tribalism: Cliques and the Making of U.S. Foreign Policy," *Washington Quarterly* 30:1 (2007): 191–203.

3. See Donald R. Kelley, *Divided Power: The Presidency, Congress, and the Formation of American Foreign Policy* (Fayetteville: University of Arkansas Press, 2005), 67–69.

4. For the origins of this split see Ryan Sager, *The Elephant in the Room: Evangelicals, Libertarians, and the Battle to Control the Republican Party* (Hoboken: Wiley, 2006).

5. George Melloan, "Donald Trump, Meet Herbert Hoover," *Wall Street Journal*, November 3, 2015; "Japan-U.S. Security Alliance Not Fair, Donald Trump Says," *Japan Times*, August 27, 2015. See also Jennifer Rubin, "Ted Cruz's Vision Turns Ugly," *Washington Post*, December 16, 2015. https://www.washingtonpost.com/blogs/right-turn/wp/2015/12/16/ted-cruzs-vision-turns-ugly/

6. Josh Kraushaar, "The Most Divided Congress Ever, At Least Until Next Year," *National Journal*, February 6, 2014. http://www.nationaljournal.com/2013-vote-ratings/the-most-divided-congress-ever-at-least-until-next-year-20140206; Michèle Flournoy and Richard Fontaine, "Rebuilding Bipartisan Consensus on National Security," *Defense One*, June 9, 2014. http://www.defenseone.com/ideas/2014/06/rebuilding-bipartisan-consensus-national-security/86116/

7. Johnathan Haidt and Marc J. Hetherington, "Look How Far We've Come Apart," *New York Times*, September 17, 2012. http://campaignstops.blogs.nytimes.com/2012/09/17/look-how-far-weve-come-apart/

8. "Political Polarization in the American Public," Pew Center for the People and the Press, June 12, 2014. http://www.people-press.org/2014/06/12/political-polarization-in-the-american-public/

9. James Q. Wilson, "How Divided Are We?" *Commentary*, February 1, 2006.

10. Hillary Clinton, "Principles for Prosperity in the Asia-Pacific," Remarks to the American Chamber of Commerce, Shangri-La, Hong Kong, July 25, 2011.

11. Demetri Sevastopulo, Shawn Donnan, and Ben Bland, "Obama's Absence Boosts China Trade Deal," *Financial Times*, October 15, 2013. http://www.ft.com/cms/s/0/07d739c2-3556-11e3-952b-00144feab7de.html?siteedition=uk#axzz2hu96cnxy

12. Craig Whitlock, "Hagel Warns of Deep, New Cuts to Defense Budget," *Washington Post*, April 3, 2013. http://www.washingtonpost.com/world/national-security/hagel-warns-of-deep-new-cuts-to-defense-budget/2013/04/03/d2ebdc5e-9c85-11e2-94d6-bf62983d455b_story.html. See "Carter: Sequestration Will Make the U.S. Less Secure," *DoD News*, March 18, 2015. www.defense.gov/News-Article-View/Article/604299/carter-sequestration-will-make-the-us-less-secure

13. Robert Work, "Deputy Secretary of Defense Robert Work on the Asia-Pacific Rebalance," speech before the Council on Foreign Relations, New York, September 30, 2014.

14. "Carter."

15. "Carter."

16. Jeffrey G. Barlow, *Revolt of the Admirals: The Fight for Naval Aviation, 1945–1950*, (Washington, D.C.: Naval Historical Center, 1994).

17. Dean Cheng and Bruce Klinger, "Defense Budget Cuts Will Devastate America's Commitment to the Asia-Pacific," *Backgrounder* 2629 (December 6, 2011).

18. Steinberg and O' Hanlon, *Strategic Reassurance and Resolve*, 77.

19. Chuck Hagel, "Remarks by Secretary of Defense," speech before the IISS Shangri-La Dialogue, Singapore, May 31, 2014.

20. Work, "Deputy Secretary of Defense Robert Work on the Asia-Pacific Rebalance."

21. Andrew Kohut, "Americans: Disengaged, Feeling Less Respected, but Still See US as World's Military Superpower" (Pew Research Center, April 1, 2014). http://www.pewresearch.org/fact-tank/2014/04/01/americans-disengaged-feeling-less-respected-but-still-see-u-s-as-worlds-military-superpower/

22. Barack Obama, "Remarks by the President on the Way Forward in Afghanistan," White House, June 22, 2011. http://www.whitehouse.gov/the-press-office/2011/06/22/remarks-president-way-forward-afghanistan

23. Stephen Sestanovich, *Maximalist: America in the World from Truman to Obama* (New York: Alfred A. Knopf, 2014), 8–9.

24. Robert Kagan, "Superpowers Don't Get to Retire," *New Republic*, May 26, 2015. http://www.newrepublic.com/article/117859/allure-normalcy-what-america-still-owes-world

25. President Bush famously stated in 2001 that "either you are with us, or you are with the terrorists." George W. Bush, "Address to a Joint Session of Congress and the American People," White House, September 20, 2001. http://georgewbush-whitehouse.archives.gov/news/releases/2001/09/20010920-8.html. For more on binary discourse during the Bush presidency see Kevin Coe, David Domke, Erica S. Graham, Sue Lockett John, and Victor W. Pickard, "No Shades of Gray: The Binary Discourse of George W. Bush and an Echoing Press," *Journal of Communication* 54(2) (2006): 234–252.

26. Hillary Clinton, "America's Pacific Century," *Foreign Policy*, November 10, 2011. http://www.foreignpolicy.com/articles/2011/10/11/americas_pacific_century

27. Peter A. Petri and Michael G. Plummer, "The Economic Effects of the Trans-Pacific Partnership," WP 16-2, Peterson Institute for International Economics, January 2016.

28. Richard Fontaine and Michèle Flournoy, "America: Beware the Siren Song of Disengagement," *National Interest*, August 14, 2014. http://nationalinterest.org/feature/america-beware-the-siren-song-disengagement-11078>

29. http://www.thechicagocouncil.org/publication/americans-affirm-ties-allies-asia

30. William Inboden, "The Real Obama 'Pivot': Back to the Middle East," *Foreign Policy*, September 11, 2014. http://shadow.foreignpolicy.com/posts/2014/09/11/the_real_obama_pivot_back_to_the_middle_east

31. Philip Gourevitch, "What Obama Didn't Say," *New Yorker*, September 11, 2014. www.newyorker.com/news/daily-comment/obama-didnt-say

32. Rice, *No Higher Honor*, 485.

33. David Shambaugh, "Assessing the US Pivot to Asia," *Strategic Studies Quarterly* 7(2) (Summer 2013): 13.

34. See Edward Miller, *War Plan Orange: The U.S. Strategy to Defeat Japan, 1897–1945* (Annapolis: Naval Institute Press, 1991).
35. Michèle Flournoy and Shawn Brimley, "Strategic Planning for National Security," *Joint Force Quarterly* 41 (2006): 80.
36. Ibid., 16.
37. Dennis Ross, "Challenges of Long-Term Planning in US Foreign Policy," October 4, 2013, ISSA-ISAC Conference 2013, Elliott School of International Affairs, George Washington University, Washington, D.C.
38. Daniel W. Drezner, *Avoiding Trivia: The Role of Strategic Planning in American Foreign Policy* (Washington: Brookings Institution Press, 2009), 5.
39. Thomas E. Donilon, "Remarks by National Security Advisor Tom Donilon," White House, November 15, 2012. http://www.whitehouse.gov/the-press-office/2012/11/15/remarks-national-security-advisor-tom-donilon-prepared-delivery
40. Brimley and Ratner, "Smart Shift."
41. Carola McGiffert, "US Reaches Major Milestone: 100,000 American Students Study in China," *Huffington Post*, July 9, 2014. http://www.huffingtonpost.com/carola-mcgiffert/us-reaches-major-mileston_b_5571793.html

Chapter Eight: Implementing the Pivot

1. Fareed Zakaria, "Interview with George Shultz," *Fareed Zakaria GPS*, CNN, November 14, 2010. http://transcripts.cnn.com/TRANSCRIPTS/1011/14/fzgps.01.html
2. Robert D. Putnam, "Diplomacy and Domestic Politics: The Logic of Two-level Games," *International Organization* 42, no. 3 (Summer 1988).

Conclusion

1. Clinton, *Hard Choices*, 40–41.

Index

A

Abe, Shinzo, 209, 215
Acheson, Dean, 119
Adams, John Quincy, 98
Afisina, Reza, 79
air pollution, 46, 57–58
Ai Weiwei, 77
Allison, Graham, 243.
    see also Thucydides trap
"America first" policy, 296, 297
arc of ascendance, 1
Armitage, Richard, 3
art market, 75–79
ASEAN (Association of Southeast
    Asian Nations), 14, 19, 146,
    222, 263, 272–274, 291
Asia Infrastructure and Investment
    Bank (AIIB), 163, 167, 233,
    235, 276
Asian Americans, 34, 289–290
Asian Development Bank, 5, 40–41,
    52, 60, 257, 276
Asia-Pacific nations. *see also specific*
    nations
  anxieties about increased
    militarization of China, 68–69
  choices for future, 153–155
  developmental contradictions, 33,
    354n3
  with fledgling democracies,
    189, 286
  globally significant, 23
  importance, 344–345
  investment in, 51

military security, 27
nations as stakeholders in world
    economy, 168
"out of area" pursuits, 22
positive reactions, 16
top world cities, 44
view of US, 6, 321–322, 326–327
Asia's operating system
  at crossroads, 9
  freedom of navigation and, 65,
    237–239
  multilateralism and, 199, 347
  need to become stakeholders in
    global system, 163–166, 168
  overview of, 135, 345–346
  participation of external powers to
    reinforce peace and stability,
    153, 154
  strengthening of, 135, 150–151,
    162–163, 164, 247, 260
  values at heart of, 160, 162
Australia
  China and, 220
  coordinating policies with, 265
  film industry, 72
  importance, 218–219
  military, 67, 217
  strengthen ties with, 217–220

B

Bader, Jeff, 4
balance of power
  economies and, 156–158
  recent shifts, 155–156

balance of power (*cont.*)
US prevention of hegemonic
domination by China
"China first" approach, 23,
147–148
"China threat" approach,
148–149
rapprochement with
China and, 143
bamboo ceiling, 91
Bangladesh
coastal flooding, 59–60
democracy and, 189, 286
economy, 50, 70, 192
Beazley, Kim, 1–2
Beijing consensus, 190
beneficiary imperialism, 139
Blackwill, Robert, 3, 252
Blumenthal, Dan, 17
Brimley, Shawn, 311
Britain
absence of policy of evangelism, 102
annexation of Chinese
territory, 99
opium trade, 96–97
Brunei, 175, 193, 233, 266
strengthen ties with, 262–263
Burma
democracy promotion, 131–132,
190, 285
economy, 50, 158
energy sources, 58
infrastructure, 54
relationship with, reopened, 14,
337–338
Bush, George W., 272
Asian policy, 17–20, 22
Thailand and, 228

C
Cambodia
economy, 50, 52
infrastructure, 54
political turmoil, 189, 263, 286
US bombing of, 332

Cameron, David, 85
Cameron, James, 73–74
Canton system, 96–97, 102
Carington, Lord Peter, 322
Carter, Ash, 157, 213, 300, 301
Carter, Jimmy, 131, 183–184
Castle, William Richards, Jr.,
109–110
Catholic Church, 105
"charm offensive," 121, 145
Chase, Michael, 26
Chen Guangcheng, 31–32
Chen Shui-bian, 186
China. *see also* United States
and China
air pollution, 46, 59, 165, 166
anticorruption campaign, 52
Australia and, 220
"charm offensive," 121, 145
climate change and, 60, 63–64
democracy in, 287
East China Sea and, 27, 66, 68, 162,
180–183
economy, 47–50, 156
art market, 76–77
digital infrastructure, 55, 56
electronics industry, 69–70
film industry, 72–75
infrastructure investments, 53, 54
"middle income trap," 192
Pearl River Delta as engine of, 44
per capita income, 164, 370n13
Singles' Day, 62
slowing, 235–236
US response to assertive foreign
policy, 239–240
energy consumption, 56
energy sources, 57–58, 59
favorability ratings for US, 25–26
governance, 234–235, 236
history
Boxer Rebellion, 107
Communist victory, 118
Four Pests campaign, 36–37
Korean War, 120, 127

military dominance by Japan,
104, 108–111, 139, 208–209,
210–211
missionaries and, 104, 105
increasingly assertive foreign policy,
14–15, 232–235, 236–243, 261,
262
India and, 158, 252–253
military
advances post-September 11
attacks, 121
as most powerful Asian, 156–157,
279, 280–281
need for US-China code of
conduct for encounters,
178–179
relationship with US, 15, 64,
248–250
spending, 65–66, 67, 68–69
nationalism, 235
natural disasters, 61
need to become stakeholder in global
operating system, 168–169,
247–248
North Korea and, 172–174, 247
population, 38
deaths in children under five, 41
demographic dividend, 39
higher education, 42, 43,
103–104
human rights, 241–242
labor conditions, 70
urbanization, 43
poverty, 40
Singapore and, 222–223
South China Sea and, 25, 66, 68,
162, 174–175, 225, 227, 233,
237–239, 275
Taiwan and, 114–115, 183–188, 257
Thailand and, 228
Thucydides trap, 198–199, 231–232,
243–250
trade, 96–99
RCEP, 193, 195, 267
TPP, 268, 269

China Purge, 125–127
Chinese Exclusion Act (1882), 92
Christensen, Thomas, 17,
156–157, 234
climate change, 59–60, 63–64,
165–166
Clinton, Hillary Rodham,
xvi–xviii, 31
ASEAN and, 19, 273
Asian achievements, 337–338
on China, 232, 347
development of Asia experts, 314
on financing foreign policy,
298–299
Internet freedom, 287
number of trips to Asia, 27–28
on Pivot
description of, 12
first use of term, 11
as proper attention to Asia-Pacific
nations, 21
recruitment of Asia team, xvi–xxi, 4
relationship with Obama, 338, 339
staff and, 340
on Wellington Declaration, 258
Clubb, O. Edmund, 126
coal, 57–58
Cohen, Jerome, 241
Cold War, 141–142, 143–144, 207–
208, 295, 310, 311
Compact for Free Association, 265
containment policy, 22, 23–24
Convention of Kanagawa (1854), 98
Cooper, Zack, 206
corruption in Asian nations, 51–52
Cossa, Ralph, 17
Cruz, Ted, 297
cultural stereotypes
Asia as exotic, 87–88
Asian inferiority, 89–90, 140
of Asian males, 89, 90–91, 92
of Asian women, 88–89
consequences, 89–90
Cushing, Caleb, 97
cyberespionage, 239–240

D

danger of misunderstanding,
83, 87–95
Danzig, Richard, xxi
Davies Jr., John Paton, 104, 126,
139–140
democracy
Asian nations with fledging,
189, 286
Beijing consensus as alternative, 190
in Philippines, 107–108,
128–129
promotion, 84, 128–132, 188–191,
200, 247, 284–287, 347
Deng Xiaoping, 233–234
diaspora diplomacy, 289–290
digital infrastructure,
55–56, 287
diplomacy. *see also* foreign policy
alliance management, 205
ASEAN, 14, 19, 146, 222, 263,
272–274, 291
coordination of US-Australian
agendas, 219
diaspora, 289–290
elements of effective, 324–326
lack of appreciation for foreign
service staff, 334–335
national negotiations in
international, 329–330
Open Door Policy, 99
Singapore-US relationship, 221,
222–223
strategic dialogue, 331–334
tactical decision-making control,
318–320
Treaty of Portsmouth, 99
Treaty of Wanghia, 97–98
trilateral ties, 206–207
Washington Treaty System,
100–101, 108–109, 110,
139–140
disease, 42
Donilon, Tom, 4, 12
Dulles, John Foster, 114, 184, 203

E

East Asia, rural population, 43
East Asia Summits (EASs), 14, 215,
273, 299, 338
East China Sea, 27, 66, 68, 162,
180–183
"Economic Asia," 192
economic ties
between China and Taiwan,
186–187, 257
between China and US, 231, 270
enhancing, 347
with Europe, 291
between India and US,
253–254, 270
between Malaysia and US, 262
need for increase in, among Asian
nations, 167
between New Zealand
and US, 259
between Singapore and US, 269
between South Korea and US,
269–270
between Taiwan and US, 255–256
through trade, 191–192
trade agreements, 15, 19–20, 145,
193, 213, 257, 269–270
American public opinion
about, 29
Trans-Pacific Partnership, 15,
19–20, 193–195, 216, 227, 257,
261, 262, 263, 267–268, 269
between Vietnam and US,
261–262
will increase American
prosperity, 306
economies. *see also* trade;
specific nations
Asian nations seen as rivals, 143
Asia-Pacific nations as stakeholders
in world, 168
demographic dividend benefit,
38–40, 51
East Asian development model, 101
effect of corruption, 51–52

effect of US financial crisis, 305
electronics industry, 69–72
employment of college graduates, 43
free trade and, 191
infrastructure, 52–56
middle class, 50–51
Pivot strengthens, 15, 209–210
shipping industry, 62–65
size, 36
Southeast Asia GDP, 260
US investment in, 5
vulnerability to price of oil, 57
world's largest, 47–50
education, 42–43
Eisenhower, Dwight, 114, 118,
      184, 310
electronics industry, 69–72
energy, 56–59, 270
Etzioni, Amitai, 21
European partners, 84–85, 200,
      290–292, 348
evangelism, 83, 102–105, 364n72

F
Fallows, James, 38
federated approaches, 206
Fehrenbach, T. R., 123
Feigenbaum, Evan, 192
Fiji, 264, 265
"Filipinization" policy, 128–129
film industry, 72–75, 330–331
Flournoy, Michèle, 4, 244, 268, 311
Forbes, Randy, 302
foreign policy. *see also* diplomacy; trade,
      agreements
   absence of Asia experts, 313
   absence of bipartisan majority
      consensus, 295–297
   Americans desire for retrenchment
      and focus on domestic issues,
      303–307
   Cold War and US policy planning
      ability, 311
   credibility, 22
   financing, 298–299

increase in aid to Asia-Pacific
      nations, 15
   Middle East factor, 278, 294, 303,
      307–309
   rebalancing of global, 21
   transference of credibility across
      regions, 309
   US State Department China Purge
      and, 125–127
Foreign Policy, 11, 12, 31
Formosa Resolution, 114
Freedom House, 5
Free Trade Area for the Asia-Pacific
      (FTAAP), 193
Friedberg, Aaron, 26
Fukuyama, Francis, 52
Fukuzawa, Yukichi, 108

G
Gailey, Harry, 118
gardening metaphor, 323, 346
Gates, Robert, 178
Germany, 99
Ghattas, Kim, 13
Gilley, Bruce, 188
Glaser, Bonnie, 188
Glaser, Charles, 188
globalization, American public opinion
      about, 29
Global Power City Index, 44
Glosserman, Brad, 17
Gospel for Asia, 104–105
Great White Fleet, 140
Green, Mike
   on federated approaches, 206
   on focus shift to Middle East, 18
   on initial US-Pacific strategy, 139
   Pivot as rejuvenation of US
      strategy, 145
   on resources for Pivot, 26
   twin engagement strategy, 3
Grew, Joseph, 110
Guam, 107
Guam (Nixon) Doctrine, 120,
      143, 205

H
Haass, Richard, 13, 32
Hadley, Steve, 3
HADR (humanitarian assistance and
    disaster relief), 216, 219, 220,
    222, 226, 254, 261, 283–284
Hagel, Chuck, 178, 300, 302
Halberstam, David, 113, 119, 124
Hamaguchi, Osachi, 109
Hard Choices (Clinton, Hillary), 11
Harding, Warren, 100, 109, 139–140
Harris, Harry, 4, 170
Harrison, Selig, 131
Hay, John, 99
Hicks, Kathleen, 206
history of United States-Asian relations
    Cambodia, 332
    Chinese distrust, 244
    Chinese Exclusion Act, 92
    Cold War muscular approach,
        142–144
    costs of being embroiled in regional
        conflicts, 83, 105–116
    cultural differences, 83, 87–95
    democracy promotion, 84, 128–132
    geographic distance, 82–83,
        84–86
    hub-and-spokes system of
        relationships, 203, 271
    India, 251–252
    Japan, 93–94, 109–111, 207–208
    Korean War, 112–114, 120,
        122–124, 127
    lure of commerce, 83, 95–101
    missionaries, 83, 102–105
    New Zealand, 258–259
    Pacific Island States, 264
    prevention of hegemonic domination
        by another power, 136–137,
        139–140
    resource allocation, 122–127
    Roosevelt mission of 1905, 86
    State Department China Purge,
        126–127
    strategic dialogue, 331–332

    surge and retreat, 83–84, 116–122,
        138–145, 197, 310, 345
    Taiwan, 126, 184, 255, 378n97
    Thailand, 228
    US as ultimate guarantor of peace
        and stability, 101
    Vietnam, 115–116, 120, 143, 295
Hong Kong
    art market, 76
    British control, 99
    digital infrastructure, 55–56
Hoover, Herbert, 109, 117
Horinouchi, Kensuke, 110
Ho-sun Chan, Peter, 74
hub-and-spokes system, 203,
    204–205, 271
Hu Jintao, 232–233, 332–333
Hull, Cordell, 110
human rights, 167–168, 241–242, 284
Huntington, Samuel, 132

I
Ikenberry, John, 168, 201, 330
India
    air pollution, 46, 165
    China and, 252–253
    as counterbalance to China, 158
    digital infrastructure, 55
    economy, 49, 50
        automotive industry, 70–71
        film industry, 72, 74, 75
        per capita income, 164,
            370n13
        technology industry, 70, 71
    energy sources, 57–58, 59, 60
    importance of, not reflected in global
        organizations, 165
    infrastructure, 54–55
    military spending, 67, 69
    population
        deaths in children under five, 41
        demographic dividend, 39–40
        density, 38
        higher education, 42, 43
    poverty, 40

sanitation, 45
strengthen ties with, 251–255, 270
Indian Ocean, 274, 280
Indonesia
 art market, 79
 deaths in children under five, 41
 demographic dividend, 39
 digital infrastructure, 55
 economy, 49, 50, 158, 164
 energy sources, 57
 military spending, 67
 regional agreements, 180
 strengthen ties with, 260–261
infrastructure, 52–56, 60
Internet freedom, 287
Islam, 80, 260, 262
isolationism, 296, 297

J
Japan
 automotive industry, 70, 71
 democracy promotion in, 129
 demographic dividend, 39
 determination to be dominant
  regional power, 107–109
 digital infrastructure, 55–56
 dominance of China by, 139
  military, 104, 108–111, 140
  trade, 98–99
 East China Sea and, 180–183
 economy, 49, 101, 209–210
 energy sources, 58, 60
 film industry, 72, 74
 history of trade with West,
  96, 98
 importance of, not reflected in global
  organizations, 165
 infrastructure investments, 53
 military, 67, 208, 211–212
 Nye Initiative, xviii, 144–145, 310
 Okinawa, xviii, 209, 280, 329
 population density, 38
 as predominant military power, 156
 regional agreements, 180
 security treaty with US, 203
 South Korea and, 208–209,
  210–211, 214–215
 strengthen ties with, 207–212
 T. Roosevelt's concerns about power,
  99, 139, 140
 technology industry, 70, 71
 tsunami and nuclear crisis, 14
 War Plan Orange, 140, 310
 war with Russia, 99, 140
 World War II, 208–209, 210–211

K
Kagan, Robert, 21, 305, 330–331
Kalb, Deborah, 115
Kalb, Marvin, 115
Kaplan, Robert, 176
Keating, Paul, 160
"Keating mantra," 160
Kerry, John, 273
Kim Il-sung, 112, 119
Kissinger, Henry, 21, 136, 159, 169,
  331–332
Korean War
 China in, 120, 127
 lack of US China experts, 127
 MacArthur versus Truman,
  112–114
 Task Force Smith, 122–124

L
Laos, economy of, 50
Lee, Mike, 296
Lee Hsien Loong, 16, 221
Lee Kuan Yew, 155, 285
Lee Teng-hui, 185
Lehman, John, 301
life expectancy, 42
Lippert, Mark, 4
Lippmann, Walter, 111
literacy, 42
Lodge, Henry Cabot, 139
Loi, Jim, 4
Lower Mekong Initiative (LMI),
  263–264
Luce, Henry, 94

M

MacArthur, Douglas, 112–113, 122–123, 129–130

Mahan, Alfred T., 139, 140

Malaysia
art market, 77
economy, 50, 158
film industry, 72
higher education, 42
infrastructure investments, 54
military spending, 67
population, 39
regional agreements, 180
strengthen ties with, 262

Malingue, Edouard, 76

Manchukuo, 140

Manchuria, 99, 109

Manning, Robert, 192

Mao Zedong, 36–37, 104, 332

Marshall Islands, 265

Ma Ying-jeou, 186–187

McCain, John, 302

McCarthy, Joseph R., 126–127

McKinley, William, 106

Medeiros, Evan, 4

Meltzer, Joshua, 195

Micronesia, 265

Middle East
as challenge to Pivot implementation, 278, 294, 303, 307–309, 348–349
effect on George W. Bush Asian policy, 18–19
maintenance of attention to, 20–21
"out of area" pursuits of Asia-Pacific nations, 22, 208, 217, 308–309
transference of foreign policy credibility across regions factor and, 309, 313
US resource investment, 26, 301

military
Asian nation modernization, 65–69, 166–167

China
as most powerful Asian, 156–157
need for US code of conduct for encounters with, 178–179
US response to assertiveness, 237–239
federated approach, 206–207
Japanese, 208, 211–212
Korean War, 112–114, 120, 122–124, 127
Pacific Island Forum, 265
Singapore-US relationship, 221, 222
South Korea, 212–213
strengthen ties between US and
Australia, 217–218
India, 254
Philippines, 224, 225–226
South Korea, 213–214, 215–216
ties with Taiwan, 256
trade as cause of US, presence in Asia, 97–98
US in Okinawa, xviii, 209, 280, 329
US in Vietnam, 115–116, 120, 143, 295
US modernization and diversification, 158–159, 199–200, 277–284, 347
US spending, 65–69, 300–303
US strategic presence, 5–6, 15, 27
Washington Treaty System, 108–109, 110

Missile Technology Control Regime (MTCR), 166–167

missionaries, 83, 102–105, 364n72

Mitchell, Derek, 341

Mongolia
as democratic success, 188, 190–191
economy, 50

multilateralism. *see also specific agreements*
Asia's operating system and, 199, 347
benefits, 149–150, 168, 271–272
HADR operations, 284
importance, 31, 347

participation by ASEAN
members, 222
prevention of hegemony and, 149
South China Sea resolution,
273, 275
Southeast Asia Treaty Organization
and, 203
US participation, 206, 275,
323–324, 346

N
Nagano, Osami, 111
Nakanishi, Hiroaki, 71
National Security Council (NSC),
319, 320
NATO, 291–292
natural disasters, 60–62
New Zealand, 14, 258–260, 265
Nine-Power Treaty (1922), 100
Niue, 264
Nixon, Richard, 120, 143, 331–332
Noda, Yoshihiko, 181
Nomura, Kichisaburo, 109
North Korea. *see also* Korean War
China and, 247
nuclear weapons, 121
population, 39
provocations by, 14, 170–174,
212–213, 214
Western cultural stereotypes of, 90
nuclear proliferation, 167
Nye, Gerald, 296
Nye, Joseph, xviii–xix, 3, 144–145,
310, 330
Nye Initiative, xviii, 144–145, 310

O
Obama, Barack
ASEAN and, 273
Burma and, 131–132, 337–338
Chinese cyberespionage and,
239–240
development of Asia experts, 314
East China Sea and, 180–181
as first Pacific president, 338–339
focus on building America, 304
Hu and, 332–333
Indonesia and, 261
need for speeches by, promoting
Pivot, 306
policymaking centralization in
White House, 30, 31
recruitment of state Department Asia
team, xx–xxi
on relationship with China, 23,
231, 236
relationship with Clinton, 338, 339
strategies differences between White
House and State Department,
30–32
on ties between US and Asia, 34
on TPP, 193
on US need to pivot, 3–4
oil imports, 57
Okinawa, xviii, 209, 280, 329
100,000 Strong Initiative, 314
Open Door Notes and Policy, 99,
111, 139
opium trade, 96–97
orchestra conductor metaphor,
206, 323–324, 346. *see also*
multilateralism
Organization for Economic
Cooperation and Development
(OECD), 42

P
Pacific Island Forum (PIF),
264–265, 275
Palau, 265
Panetta, Leon, 15
Papua New Guinea, 264, 265
Parker, Peter, 102, 139–140
Park Geun-hye, 216, 269
Patel, Nirav, 4
Paul, Rand, 296
Pei, Minxin, 162
Perry, Bill, xviii–xix

Perry, Matthew C., 98, 139–140

Philippines
  art market, 77–78
  democracy promotion in, 107–108,
    128–129
  demographic dividend, 39
  economy, 50
  energy sources, 59
  military spending, 67
  natural disasters, 61
  population density, 38
  South China Sea and, 225, 227, 275
  Spanish-American War, 106–107
  strengthen ties with, 224–227

piracy, 64–65, 274

Pivot
  accomplishments, 13–16, 197
  American public opinion about, 29,
    306–307
  Asian hot spots and, 174, 178–179,
    182–183, 188
  build domestic support, 198,
    202–203, 345–346
  challenges, 316–317
    absence of bipartisan majority
      consensus on foreign policy,
      295–297
    absence of clear and present threat
      to American interests, 305–306
    deadlock and dysfunction in US
      government, 297–300
    development of human capital,
      312–314
    inadequate defense spending,
      300–303
    Middle East situation, 278, 294,
      303, 307–309
    public desire for retrenchment
      and focus on domestic issues,
      303–307
    short window of opportunity,
      314–316, 348
    US inability to focus on long-term
      planning, 310–312

China policy
  escape Thucydides trap, 198–199,
    231–232, 243–250
  increase ties with, 22
  manage competition and foster
    greater cooperation, 198–199,
    244, 270
  regional framework for, 199, 232,
    271–277, 347
  responses to increased
    assertiveness, 236–243,
    261, 262
clarify and publicize to partners,
  198, 201–202, 244–245
criticisms
  lack of resources allocated, 26
  provokes China, 22–26
  superpowers do not pivot, 20–22
  term is misleading: US never left
    Asia, 17–20
domestic public diplomacy effort,
  201–203, 315
engage European partners, 200,
  290–292
expand free trade agreements,
  199, 245
federated approach, 206–207
as foreign policy, 20
modernize and diversify US military
  capabilities in Asia, 158–159,
  199–200, 277–284
as modified "bilateral alliances"
  with elements of "transnational
  challenges" and "China first"
  approaches, 151
premise, 1–2, 32
prevent hegemony, 146
promote democratic values, 189–191,
  200, 284–287, 347
as rejuvenation of US strategy,
  145–146
strengthen Asia's operating system,
  135, 150–151, 162–163, 164,
  247, 260

strengthen people-to-people ties,
200, 246, 288–290,
347–348
strengthen ties with Asian
allies, 158–159, 198, 199,
203–207, 347
Australia, 217–220
Brunei, 262–263
India, 251–255, 270
Indonesia, 260–261
Japan, 207–212
Malaysia, 262
New Zealand, 258–260
Pacific Island States, 264–265
Philippines, 224–227
Singapore, 220–224
South Korea, 212–217
Taiwan, 14, 242, 255–258
Thailand, 227–230
Vietnam, 261–262
terminology, 29–30
US economic development aid,
158–159
pollution, 46, 57–58, 59
population, 37–40
deaths in children under five,
41–42
demographic dividend benefit,
38–40, 51, 158
maternal mortality, 42
middle class, 50–51
rural versus urban, 43
poverty, 40–41, 80
Project Solarium, 310
public health, 41–42
Purser, Benjamin, 26
Putnam, Robert, 329

Q
Qi Baishi, 77

R
racism, 89
Ratner, Ely, 268

Reagan, Ronald, 131
Regional Comprehensive Economic
Partnership (RCEP), 193, 195,
267, 299
Regional Cooperation Agreement on
Combating Piracy and Armed
Robbery against Ships in Asia
(ReCAAP), 274
religion
Islam, 260, 262
missionaries, 83, 102–105,
364n72
renewable energy, 58–59
Rhodes, Ben, 4, 340–341
Rice, Condoleezza, 3, 18–19, 272,
307–308
Ridgway, Matthew, 124
RIMPAC (the Rim of the Pacific
Exercise), 15
Roosevelt, Theodore
desire for American dominance
in Pacific, 86, 107,
116–117
Japanese power, 99, 139, 140
Ross, Dennis, 311
Roughead, Gary, 3, 4
Rowell, Milo, 129
Rudd, Kevin, 25, 325
Russel, Daniel, 4, 66
Russia, seizure of Manchuria, 99

S
Said, Edward, 95
sanitation, 45
Scalapino, Robert A., 328
Scudder family, 103
September 11, 2001 attacks, effects on
foreign policy, 18–19
Service, John S., 104, 126
Sestanovich, Stephen, 304
Shambaugh, David, 310
shipping industry, 62–65
Shultz, George, 144, 205, 323
Sigur, Gaston, 131

Singapore
 China and, 222–223
 infrastructure investments, 53–54
 population, 39
 strengthen ties with, 220–224
 trade agreement with US, 269
Sino-Japanese War (1895), 139
Sirota, Beate, 129
Situation Room, 318–319
Six Assurances, 255, 256, 257,
 378n97
Soedjojono, Sindoesoedarsono, 79
soft power, 72, 121, 145
Soon, Simon, 79
South Asia
 literacy, 42
 public health, 41
 rural population, 43
South Asian Association for Regional
 Cooperation (SAARC), 274
South China Sea
 as Chinese lake, 25, 66, 68, 162,
  174–175, 225, 227, 233,
  237–239, 261, 262, 263
 claimants, 175, 176–177
 as trade and energy transport artery,
  65, 175–176
 US and multilateral solution, 273,
  275
 US military exercises, 27
Southeast Asia. *see also* ASEAN
  (Association of Southeast Asian
  Nations)
 energy sources, 58
 literacy, 42
 poverty, 40
 public health, 41
 rural population, 43
 strengthening US military presence,
  279–280
Southeast Asia Treaty Organization,
 142–143, 201, 203
South Korea. *see also* Korean War
 as current Asian hot spot, 170–174
 democracy promotion in, 130–131

digital infrastructure, 55–56
East China Sea claim, 180
economy, 101, 130–131, 213
film industry, 72, 75
higher education, 42
infrastructure investments, 53, 54
Japan and, 214–215
military spending, 67
North Korean provocations and, 14,
 15, 170–171
population, 38, 39
strengthen ties with, 212–217
TPP and, 269
trade agreements, 145, 269–270
World War II, 208–209, 210–211
Soviet Union, managing threats posed
 by, 279–280
Spanish-American War,
 106–107, 139
spheres-of-influence approach,
 160–162
Sri Lanka, 50
Steinberg, Jim, xvii, xxi, 4
Stimson, Henry L., 109, 117
Strategic Security Dialogue, 24
Stuart, John Leighton, 103, 104
Sullivan, Jake, 4, 340
Sunaryo, Arin Dwihartanto, 79
Surin Pitsuwan, 19
Sutter, Robert, 23
Swaine, Michael, 26

T
Taft, Robert A., 296
Taft, William Howard, 128
Taiwan
 China and, 114–115, 121, 183–188,
  242, 257
 democracy promotion, 131
 economy, 257
 film industry, 72
 infrastructure investments, 53
 Japanese control, 108
 regional agreements, 180
 TPP and, 257, 269

US relations with
   and Carter normalization of
     relations with China, 184
   as only Chinese government
     recognized by US, 126
   strengthen ties with, 14, 242,
     255–258
   unofficial, 184, 255–257,
     378n97
Taiwan Relations Act (TRA, 1979),
   184, 255, 382n97
Taiwan Strait, 68, 183–188
Tata Motors, 70–71
technology, 69–72
Tellis, Ashley, 18, 254
Thailand
   China and, 228
   democracy promotion, 285–286
   economic development, 158
   energy sources, 58–59
   higher education, 42
   history, 227–228
   military rule, 228–230
   military spending, 67
   strengthen ties with, 227–230
   trade with West, 96
Thucydides trap, 198–199, 231–232,
   243–250
Toyota, 71
trade. *see also* Trans-Pacific Partnership
   (TPP); *specific nations*
   agreements, 15, 19–20, 29, 145, 193,
     213, 257, 269–270
   create long-term system, 347
   current US-Asian, 5
   with Europe, 291
   history of US-Asian, 83, 85,
     95–101
   issue of free or protected,
     191–195
   shipping, 62–65
Trans-Pacific Partnership (TPP)
   background, 19–20
   diplomatic and military implications,
     267–268

   overview, 15, 261, 262, 263
   Philippines and, 227
   rules and standards, 193–195
   South Korea and, 216, 269
   Taiwan and, 257, 269
   transportation, 52, 53–55, 62–65
Treaty of Amity and Cooperation
   (TAC), 14, 146, 222, 263,
   272–273
Treaty of Portsmouth (1905), 99
Treaty of Wanghia, 97–98
Truman, Harry S., 112–113
Trump, Donald, 297
Tsai Ing-wen, 187, 269
Tucker, Nancy, 188
Twining, Dan, 26
two-level game theory, 329–330
tyranny of distance, 82–83, 84–86

U
UN Convention on the Law of the Sea
   (UNCLOS), 276–277
United States. *see also* history of United
   States-Asian relations; United
   States and China; United States
   Asia strategy
   academia and government,
     328–330
   Asians in, 91–95
   Asia-Pacific nations' view of, 6,
     321–322, 326–327
   China Purge in State Department,
     125–127
   cultural kinship with Europe,
     84–85
   economic ties with Asia-Pacific
     nations, 5
   economy of, compared to Asia's,
     48, 49
   political parties polarization and
     gridlock, 295–300
   public opinion about
     globalization, 29
   reaction to announcement of Pivot,
     11–13

United States and China
   Chinese public opinion about US,
      25–26
   military relationship, 15, 64,
      248–250
   need for US-China code of conduct
      for military encounters,
      178–179
   need for US to establish rules-based
      regional institutional order,
      275–276
   Nixon-Kissinger legacy, 332
   normalization of relations,
      183–184
   Pivot
      escape Thucydides trap, 198–199,
         231–232, 243–250
      increase ties with, 22
      manage competition and foster
         greater cooperation, 198–199,
         244, 270
      provokes China, 22–26
      regional framework for, 199, 232,
         271–277, 347
      responses to increased
         assertiveness, 236–243,
         261, 262
   spheres-of-influence approach,
      161–162
   strategies differences between
      US White House and State
      Department, 30–32
   US prevention of hegemonic
      domination by
      "China first" approach, 23,
         147–148
      "China threat" approach,
         148–149
      rapprochement with
         China and, 143
United States Asia strategy. *see also*
      history of United States-Asian
      relations; Pivot
   as balance of power versus power
      of balance, 321

China's rise in power and, 144–145
Guam Doctrine, 120, 143, 205
maritime to continental domain
   shift, 142–143
mutual anxieties and frustrations,
   314–316
need for consistency, 138, 147, 302,
   345, 346
need for mind-set and culture
   change in Washington, 310
prevention of hegemonic domination
   by other power
   "bilateral alliances" approach, 148
   "China threat" approach,
      148–149
   Cold War muscular approach,
      142–144
   co-option of China approach,
      147–148
   early applications, 136–137,
      139–140
   failures to apply, 140–142, 145
   need for new uses of resources to
      achieve, 147
   rapprochement with China
      and, 143
   "singular issue" approach, 149
   spheres-of-influence approach,
      160–161
   "transnational challenges"
      school, 149
as secondary theater during World
   War II, 141–142
in South China Sea, 175,
   177–180
strengthen of Asia's operating
   system, 150–151
support for liberalization of
   economies, 157
surge and retreat, 83–84, 116–122,
   138–139, 144–145
trade, 85, 95–101, 191–195
urbanization, 43–47
U.S.-China Strategic and Economic
   Dialogue, 24

V
Van Rompuy, Herman, 21
Vanuatu, 264
Ventura, Ronald, 77
Vietnam
   democracy promotion, 286–287
   economic development, 158
   infrastructure, 54
   military spending, 67
   population, 39
   South China Sea claim,
      176–177
   strengthen ties with, 261–262
   US in, 115–116, 120, 143, 295

W
Walsh, Pat, 4
War Plan Orange, 140, 310
wars. *see also specific conflicts*
   current Asian hot spots, 169–170
      East China Sea, 27, 66, 68, 162,
         180–183
      Korea, 170–174
      South China Sea, 25, 66, 68, 162,
         174–180
      Taiwan Strait, 183–188
   embroilment in regional conflicts,
      83, 105–116
Washington Declaration (2014), 258

Washington Post, 13
Washington Treaty System, 100–101,
      108–109, 110, 139–140
Wellington Declaration (2012), 258
Whitney, Courtney, 129
Wilson, James Q., 298
Wilson, Woodrow, 100, 128
Winichakul, Thongchai, 229
Woodward, Bob, 115
Work, Robert, 280–281, 300
World War II, 104, 110–111, 117–118,
      141, 208–209, 210–211
Wu T'ing-fang, 92

X
Xi Jinping
   anticorruption campaign, 52
   assertiveness policy, 162, 179, 231,
      233–236
   cyberespionage and, 239–240
   missionaries and, 105
   North Korea and, 173
   Taiwan and, 186–187

Z
Zelikow, Philip, 119, 141
Zhang Zhao, 74
Zhou Enlai, 127, 332
Zoellick, Robert, 3, 121, 168

About the Author

Kurt M. Campbell is the founder, chairman, and CEO of The Asia Group LLC in Washington, D.C. He served as assistant secretary of state for East Asian and Pacific affairs under Secretary of State Hillary Clinton in the Obama administration. Previously, he co-founded the Center for a New American Security, where he currently serves as chairman of the board. During the Clinton Administration, he served as deputy assistant secretary of defense for Asia and the Pacific. He was also the director of the Aspen Strategy Group, the Henry A. Kissinger Chair in National Security Policy at the Center for Strategic and International Studies, and associate professor of public policy at Harvard's John F. Kennedy School of Government. He was a naval reserve officer serving on the Joints Chief of Staff, a White House Fellow at the Treasury Department and White House, and is currently a member of the Defense Policy Board. Campbell currently serves on the board of Standard Chartered Bank of London and as a Senior Fellow at Harvard's Belfer Center. He received the Secretary's Distinguished Service Award—the nation's highest diplomatic medal—and has been recognized with top national honors across Asia and in Great Britain for his service. Campbell is a graduate of the University of California, San Diego, and received his doctorate from Brasenose College, Oxford, as a Marshall Scholar. He is married to Lael Brainard, former undersecretary of the Treasury and current governor of the Federal Reserve, and together they live with their three daughters in Washington, D.C.